Military Planning
in the
Twentieth Century

Proceedings of the
Eleventh Military History Symposium
10–12 October 1984

Edited by
Lieutenant Colonel Harry R. Borowski, USAF
Department of History
United States Air Force Academy

**OFFICE OF AIR FORCE HISTORY
UNITED STATES AIR FORCE
WASHINGTON, D.C., 1986**

For sale by the Superintendent of Documents, U.S. Government Printing Office
Washington, D.C. 20402

Library of Congress Cataloging-in-Publication Data

Military History Symposium (U.S.) (11th : 1984 :
    United States Air Force Academy)
    Military planning in the twentieth century.

    "Sponsored by the Department of History and the Association of Graduates"–
    Includes index.
    1. Military planning–History–20th century–Congresses. I. Borowski, Harry R.
II. United States Air Force Academy. Dept. of History. III. United States Air Force
Academy. Association of Graduates. IV. Title.
U150.M55   1984   355'.033'004   86-16288
ISBN 0-912799-36-6

The Eleventh Military History Symposium

10–12 October 1984
United States Air Force Academy

Sponsored by

The Department of History
and
The Association of Graduates

* * * * *

Executive Director
Eleventh Military History
Symposium: Major Bernard E. Harvey

Deputy Director
Eleventh Military History
Symposium: Captain Harold G. McKinney

Professor and Head
Department of History: Colonel Carl W. Reddel

President
Association of Graduates: Lt Col Richard M. Coppock,
                              USAF, Retired

Symposium Committee Members:

   Lieutenant Colonel Harry R. Borowski
   Professor Edward M. Coffman
   Captain Thomas E. Angle
   Captain Mark A. Clodfelter
   Captain Mark L. Dues
   Captain Richard J. Mueller
   Captain John L. Poole

Captain Spencer Way, Jr.
Captain Charles H. Wells
Captain Mark K. Wells
Ms. Nellie Dykes
Ms. Jackulene W. Goldston

United States Air Force
Historical Advisory Committee
(As of January 1, 1986)

Mr. DeWitt S. Copp
The National Volunteer Agency

Dr. Philip A. Crowl
Annapolis, Maryland

Dr. Warren B. Hassler, Jr.
Pennsylvania State University

Brig Gen Harris B. Hull,
USAF, Retired
National Aeronautics and Space
Administration

Dr. Alfred F. Hurley,
Brig Gen, USAF, Retired
North Texas State University

Dr. Haskell Monroe
University of Texas at El Paso

Lt Gen Thomas C. Richards,
USAF
Commander, Air University

Gen Thomas M. Ryan, Jr.,
USAF, Retired

Lt Gen Winfield W. Scott, Jr.
Superintendent, USAF Academy

Mr. Eugene R. Sullivan
The General Counsel, USAF

Contents

Military History Symposium Proceedings

1st The proceedings of the first symposium *were not published.*

2nd *Command and Commanders in Modern Warfare* (2nd ed., 1971)
Stock Number 0874–0003.

3rd *Science, Technology, and Warfare* (1971)
Stock Number 0874–0002.

4th *Soldiers and Statesmen* (1973)
Stock Number 0870–00335.

5th *The Military and Society* (1975)
Stock Number 008–070–00367–8.

6th *The Military History of the American Revolution* (1976)
Stock Number 008–070–106109.

7th *The American Military on the Frontier* (1978)
Stock Number 008–070–00432–2.

8th *Air Power and Warfare* (1979)
Stock Number 008–070–00441–1.

9th *The American Military and the Far East* (1980)
Stock Number 008–070–00474–7.

10th *The Home Front and War in the Twentieth Century* (1982)
Stock Number 0870–00511–5.

Note: For information on prices and availability, write to the Superintendent of Documents, U.S. Government Printing Office, Washington, D.C. 20402.

Acknowledgements

The essays, commentaries, and speeches which form this volume were presented at the Eleventh Military History Symposium, held at the United States Air Force Academy on 10–12 October 1984. This conference is a biennial event sponsored jointly by the Department of History and the Association of Graduates of the United States Air Force Academy. Begun in 1967, the series seeks to address problems in military history which have received limited attention and to provide a forum in which scholars may present the results of their research. In this manner we hope to stimulate and encourage interest in military history among civilian and military scholars, members of the armed forces, and the cadets of the United States Air Force Academy.

Conceptualizing and organizing our military history symposium took nearly two years and called on the diverse talents and efforts of many people. As in the past, friends of our symposium have been helpful in sharing ideas, making valuable suggestions, and agreeing to present specific papers for our meetings. In particular, Frank Kierman, Edward "Mac" Coffman, and Dennis Showalter provided the early encouragement for our 1984 conference theme. Professor Kierman first raised the idea of a military planning theme in 1980 as he participated in our Ninth Military History Symposium. When the time came in early 1983 to select a topic, Mac Coffman, then an Air Force Academy Distinguished Visiting Professor, and Lieutenant Colonel Jim Titus, Executive Director for the Tenth Military History Symposium, developed the concept more fully. After Dennis Showalter expanded on their proposal with many fine suggestions, we knew the concept was solid and deserved serious treatment. Colonel Carl W. Reddel, Head of the Department of History, tasked Major Ben Harvey to begin planning our conference on planning. His leadership, diligence, and hard work, along with that of thirty-three department members who shared his burden, account for whatever legacy of success this symposium ultimately enjoys.

Even so, many individuals outside the Academy's Department of History made this event possible; obviously the twenty-two scholars and military officers who delivered papers and speeches, made comments, and chaired each session, head the list. Vital financial support again came from the Association of Graduates of the United States Air Force Academy, the Falcon Foundation, Dr. Donald Backlund, and Major George Monroe. Lieutenant General Winfield W. Scott, Jr., Superintendent of the Air Force Academy, and Brigadier General Ervin J. Rokke, Dean of the Faculty, gave unqualified encouragement and support to our event from the very beginning. As usual, the many Academy support agencies smoothly handled the feeding, housing, and transporting of over 350 symposium guests.

Finally, the proceedings could not have been prepared without the able assistance of Ms. Nellie Dykes and Mrs. Christy Whale who prepared the papers for publication. For designing and putting the manuscripts into volume form, credit is given to Dr. Alfred Beck, Vanessa Allen, David R. Chenowith, and Colonel John F. Shiner at the Office of Air Force History.

As always, it remains for the editor to assume all responsibilities for matters of style and the arrangement of papers and comments presented during the conference.

HRB
USAF Academy
January 1985

Foreword

Harry R. Borowski

Few events traumatize a nation more than losing a war. Defeat can bring down an empire, alter national boundaries, end sovereignty, and dramatically change a society's social structure. Failures are explained in many ways and are seldom of a singular nature. Their roots, however, can be traced to the planning for war. For this reason, no other peacetime activity should command more attention from military leaders and scholars than the study of military planning. In reality, commanders prefer to concentrate on more immediate and understandable concerns—supplying, training, and fighting. Military historians also prefer to study combat and the battlefield where the results of all efforts are starkly evident. Consequently, the Department of History decided to dedicate its 1984 Eleventh Military History Symposium to the too seldom studied topic of military planning, the foundation for successful warfare.

To even define planning invites problems; every scholar and planner views the activity in light of his own special experiences and interest. The 1984 Joint Chiefs of Staff Publication 1, *Dictionary of Military and Associated Terms*, does not define planning but carefully describes planned resupply, planned targets, planning factor, planning force, and planning staff (pp 278–79) and tells us that a strategic plan is, "A plan for the overall conduct of a war" (p 350). Planning for such a broadly defined activity obviously suggests a staggering number of considerations and a high frustration level for military planners.

Because the complexity surrounding military planning is multi-dimensional, students of the subject focus on one, two, or perhaps three principal factors, trying to understand planning by reducing it to its simplest terms. But choosing to observe only certain colors of a brilliant mosaic gives an incomplete and hence distorted view of the entire work; scholars and officers who so restrict themselves in their examination of military planning suffer the same fate. Time, obviously, forced the scholars participating in this conference to limit their focus, and while their works raise numerous key issues that have beset military planners, they by no means encompass all the major elements of this critical and complex activity. Their papers do, however, offer special insights and provide an important basis for further study.

No man has done more to establish a clear foundation for understanding warfare and its planning than Carl von Clausewitz in his 19th century work, *On War*. His most important concept argued that war was an extension and tool of national policy. Because of warfare's grave nature and cost, a government must use it selectively, with great care and thorough planning. Once engaged in conflict, all military actions must work toward the established national goals or else the activity would be, in his own word, "absurd." Although a simple concept, history records multiple examples where state policy and the military action undertaken to achieve those objectives were not congruent. In Clausewitz's time and today, the planning process and its environment usually bear the blame for poor combined effort.

Planners must respect several key elements and avoid numerous pitfalls. Successful military planning within a state cannot be completed in a vacuum. There is no purely military dimension to planning for war—whatever action is taken must be consistent with national goals, resources, and temper. Military planners who ignore public opinion, values, or support in their work court disaster, as history amply shows. As nations expand in population and bureau-cracies grow, particularly in democratic societies, some dimensions of planning increase in importance. For example, the ability to draw up the plans and lobby them through levels of control can be as critical as the soundness of the plan itself. To plan means to predict the future or at least the likelihood of certain events happening. The ability to do so is always threatened by the personal experiences, prejudices and fears of planners, factors which may distort the basic assumptions upon which plans are based. Consequently, choosing planners, training them, and developing guidelines is basic to solid planning. Planners who prefer to feel rather than to know about events and who work with inappropriate doctrine can succeed only with luck. More knowledge and reflection can reduce the chances of planners moving in dangerous directions, but by no means can they ensure correct planning. Invariably in war, plans seldom match reality. A planner may have miscalculated his support requirements, weather, the morale of the fighting troops, that of his adversary, etc.

How well commanders can react and adapt to the unfolding of unforeseen events is itself a dimension of good planning; flexibility rests with clearly knowing the options for handling various eventualities. Obviously the list of considerations is a long one.

Since military historians strive to understand their subject better and military professionals constantly work to expand their knowledge of military art, both struggle with the difficulties surrounding military planning. It is natural, therefore, for them to address the topic jointly in a professional meeting. The best way to accomplish these aims, however, is not clear because the problems inherent in military planning are many and involved. This volume features one approach taken by those participating in the 1984 Eleventh Military History Symposium and makes no pretension to exhaustive treatment. It does, however, strive to provide key insights into recent military planning experiences that will be of value to planners. If it serves to stimulate and inform those entrusted with the difficult burden of planning, it will have succeeded in the real sense.

Introductions

Twenty-Seventh Harmon Memorial Lecture
Brigadier General E. J. Rokke
Dean of the Faculty
USAF Academy

Ladies, gentlemen, and fellow officers. I'm pleased to open this Eleventh Military History Symposium. Indeed we at the Academy consider this symposium to be something truly special. Since 1967 it has made a vital contribution to the military profession by increasing our knowledge and broadening our perspectives of military history. It brings military officers together with civilian and military scholars to share insights about both their interpretations of military history and problems found in their respective careers. These contacts have been invaluable to the continued maturation of the study of military history, military policy, and doctrine. I also am pleased to open the symposium because it gives us all a chance to participate in the camaraderie of a unique event. We are a group bound by a common interest in the military and a common belief that our studies and activities are important both to scholarship and to the military profession. Under such circumstances, it seems only natural that we would also find opportunities for personally exchanging our views and ideas. On behalf of the Superintendent, then, I wish to welcome all of you, particularly our distinguished participants about whom we will be learning more over the next two days. Before I ask Colonel Reddel to introduce Dr. Deutsch, I want to say I personally look forward to hearing from a fellow Minnesotan. Dr. Deutsch, our 1984 Harmon Lecturer, has an extraordinary depth of knowledge about military history, but beyond that he has a love and enthusiasm for his subject that I'm sure will make this evening's lecture exciting, entertaining, and informative. And now, Colonel Reddel.

Colonel Carl W. Reddel
Head, Department of History
USAF Academy

Beginning with World War I, but especially since World War II, the United States has been increasingly drawn into the affairs of a world which was dominated by Europe at the beginning of this century. However, with the suicidal acts of World Wars I and II, Europe lost much of its capability and most of its will to affect the world's future. European military professionals, especially German military men, played a key role in the determination of these events. Their conceptualization of the nature of modern war, the plans they conceived and developed, and their execution of these plans were significant in their effect on the nature and outcome of both World Wars I and II. Given the irrevocable impact of both wars upon our domestic affairs, foreign policy, and the American military profession, an accurate understanding of German military planning holds a special fascination and interest for this particular audience, which has gathered for the specific purpose during the next two days of studying the more general topic of "Military Planning in the Twentieth Century."

Our lecturer tonight is extraordinarily, indeed uniquely, well suited to assist us in understanding German military planners and planning. Prior to World War II he interviewed more of the key German military officers who served in World War I than any other historian, German or American. No one else has interviewed such a large number of the participants in the formulation and execution of the Schlieffen Plan. And we can say emphatically that no other scholar on either side of the Atlantic has had so much direct contact with the German flag officers of World War II. His understanding of the human dynamics between National Socialism and German military professionals is unparalleled. In brief, he possesses extraordinary knowledge and insight concerning the conditions under which military men plan and make decisions.

The path taken by Dr. Harold Deutsch to these unusual credentials and extraordinary experience was not direct, but in retrospect, as with most significant historical contributions, the ways and byways he followed were pertinent to his achievements as a historian.

Hailing from Milwaukee, Dr. Deutsch earned his bachelor's degree from the University of Wisconsin and both his master's and doctor's degrees from Harvard. Before completing his doctorate at Harvard in 1929, Dr. Deutsch began his frequent and numerous travels to Europe, with study and research at the Universities of Paris, Vienna, and Berlin before World War II. Since 1928 he has spent well over a decade in Europe, which provides exceptional first-hand experience and authority for his numerous publications on Europe and American relations with Europe, especially with Germany.

In 1929 Dr. Deutsch joined the faculty of the University of Minnesota, where he taught until his retirement in 1972, serving as Chairman of the Department of History from 1960 to 1966 and also chairing for ten years the University's Program for International Relations and Area Studies.

Subsequently, he was a member of the faculty at the National War College until 1974, and since then he has been on the faculty of the Army War College where he has held a number of positions, currently holding the recently established John McAuley Palmer Chair of Military History. Possibly less well known is Dr. Deutsch's record of extensive government service during World War II, which includes war service with the Board of Economic Warfare from 1942 to 1943, with the Office of Strategic Services in France and Germany, 1944 to 1945, and as a member of the State Department's Special Interrogation Mission in 1945. For his war services Dr. Deutsch received the Medal of Freedom.

His long publications list, in both German and English, begins with his doctoral thesis, *The Genesis of Napoleonic Imperialism*, published by Harvard University Press in 1938 and reprinted in 1975. Of special note to us tonight are his books, *The Conspiracy Against Hitler in the Twilight War* and *Hitler and His Generals: The Hidden Crisis January through June 1938*. He has also had a long-term interest in the Academy's military history symposia, having contributed in 1968 a paper on "The Rise of the Military Opposition in the Nazi Reich" to the symposium on *Command and Commanders in Modern Military History*. Ten years later he provided a commentary on "Ultra and the Air War in Europe and Africa," for the symposium on *Air Power and Warfare*.

This lecture series, "The Harmon Memorial Lectures in Military History," is given in memory of the late Lieutenant General Hubert R. Harmon, the first Superintendent of the Academy. The complete commitment of Dr. Harold Deutsch to history is appropriately commensurate with General Harmon's lifelong interest in military history. Among beginning graduate students, senior scholars and military officers, Dr. Deutsch is known for his generosity of spirit. He recognizes no hierarchy in his selfless willingness to help others. Dr. Deutsch's lecture tonight is entitled, "Military Planning and Foreign Policy: German Overtures to Two World Wars."

The Twenty-Sixth Harmon Memorial Lecture in Military History

Military Planning and National Policy: German Overtures to Two World Wars

Harold C. Deutsch

The celebrated dictum of Carl von Clausewitz that war is the continuation of policy has bred variants which, although not necessarily contradictory, approach the problem of war and peace rather differently. Social revolutionists, notably Lenin, like to switch emphasis by perceiving peace as a moderated form of conflict. Our concern here, the interplay between military planning and preparation for war with the form and conduct of national policy, has less to do with maxims than with actuality in human affairs.

The backgrounds of the two world wars of our century tell us much about this problem. They also indicate how *greatly* accidents of circumstance and personality may play a role in the course of events. This was notably true of Germany whose fate provides the central thread for the epoch of the two world conflicts. At some future time they may yet be known historically as "the German

Wars." This is not to infer that, had Germany not existed as a nation, and, let us say, France and Russia had been geographic neighbors, the first half of our century would have been an era of peace. Some of the factors that led to international stress would have been at work in any event. But the reality of Germany's existence largely determined the nature and sequence of affairs as they appeared to march inexorably toward disaster.

Military Planning and the Coming of World War I

Much is unusual or even unique about the German security and expansion problems during the Hohenzollern Empire. Germany's central position among powers weaker than herself bred among them an inclination to combine against or even encircle her. So central was this anxiety for Otto von Bismarck that he confessed to a sleep troubled by the nightmare of coalitions. German soldiers shared this concern and sense of professional responsibility.

After the 1870 triumph over France, there no longer were fears of any single adversary. To all intents and purposes, the only war one need apprehend would be with two or more opponents, most probably France and Russia. This implied both the hazards and advantages of fighting on geographically opposite fronts. Elementary military logic forbade any equal allocation of forces east and west. The only possible course was to stand defensively on one front and launch an all-out effort on the other. This demanded an early and decisive victory in the initial drive—a matter really of weeks—to make possible a quick shift to the originally defensive front.

We cannot dwell here on the course of development that followed this appreciation. Most vital was recognition that the construction of a massive French fortification system after 1875 made an 1870–type dash toward Paris illusionary. Relying heavily on Austria-Hungary as an ally, the elder Moltke opted without enthusiasm for a first offensive effort against the Russians. He had few illusions about achieving a quick decision in Russia's limitless space but gradually reconciled himself with the idea of occupying Poland and then moving to the negotiating table. But what if the Russians should prefer to stick it out in an endless war of attrition? In a farewell address to the German Reichstag in 1888, Moltke showed how this weighed on his mind when he spoke of a next war lasting as long as seven years—perhaps even thirty!

Moltke's successor one-removed was Count Alfred von Schlieffen, whose legendary figure has dominated German military thought to and beyond Ludendorff's offensive in 1918. His prestige, indeed, lasted into the thirties and World War II. American military thinkers thought so highly of him that his principal literary legacy, *Cannae*, was translated at Leavenworth and distributed at a nominal charge within the U.S. Army and to the academic community. Since the late forties, his reputation has been somewhat dimmed; and among historical critics, he is now something of a controversial figure.

Schlieffen combined extraordinary intellect and persuasive powers with a simplicity and lack of pretension which dominated his principal associates and won him legions of disciples in the younger leadership corps. "Mehr sein als scheinen" (be more than you appear to be) was his principal motto. Single-mindedness that critics have at times labeled obsessiveness characterized his thinking on strategic problems, and the brilliance of his dialectic swept away opposition. He may be counted among the prophets of the indirect approach so much admired by Basil Liddell Hart. Insofar as planning was concerned, he was assuredly its outstanding military practitioner. The most famous product of his mind, of course, was the plan that has been inseparably linked with his name.

In 1938, during the course of interviewing nearly a hundred leading figures of the World War 1 era, the Schlieffen Plan and the eventuating Marne campaign were major topics of discussion. I spoke with five staff officers who had worked on the plan itself or been associated with its execution. The most notable figure among them was Wilhelm Groener who headed the field railways of the prewar army, later succeeded Ludendorff as Supreme Quartermaster General, and ended his career as Minister of Defense under the Weimar Republic. On the political implications of military plans and preparations, I consulted two wartime foreign ministers, Arthur Zimmermann and Richard von Kuehlmann, the secretary and principal man of confidence of Chancellor von Bethmann-Hollweg, Kurt Rietzler, the Bavarian Minister to Berlin, Count Lerchenfeld, and the German Crown Prince. The blocking of my road to the Emperor and Erich Ludendorff, who should have been my principal witnesses, was a great disappointment.[1]

Schlieffen, in contrast to the elder Moltke, lacked all faith in the capacity of modern society to endure the strains of protracted war. He further recognized the special vulnerabilities of Germany in any contest of attrition. Such convictions could only strengthen his resolve to stake all on an early and decisive victory. Given this single and apparently unalterable goal, most of the famous plan on which he commenced work in the mid-nineties undoubtedly conformed with the dictates of logic.[2]

Schlieffen shared fully the fear of many German military leaders of becoming mired in Russian space if the east-first concept should continue to prevail. A switch to the west, however, would only put one back where Moltke had started. Unless, of course, some way around the French fortifications could be discovered. This could only be accomplished by infringing on the territory of small western neighbors. Notably Belgium, once its narrow eastern gateway had been forced, offered flat space in which one could stretch out. Historically it was the favored east-west invasion route. The trouble lay in the tight squeeze of the cramped German-Belgian frontier—a scant fifty miles as the crow flies. Of this a good portion is taken up by the difficult Ardennes. The passage toward Liege in the north features defiles that funnel east-west movement.

Schlieffen could see nothing for it but to include Luxembourg and that extension of the Dutch province of Limburg known as the Maastricht appendix. The railway bridges over the Meuse at Maastricht and Roermond were a particular attraction as they carried most of the traffic from Germany.

As planning proceeded during the 1890s, Schlieffen gave scant attention to the obvious political implications. In 1899 he did inform Foreign Secretary and later Chancellor Bernhard von Buelow who as yet took a complacent view of things. If the Chief of Staff and such a strategic authority as Schlieffen thought this necessary, said Buelow, it was the duty of diplomacy to adjust to it. A year later another army communication on the subject to the Foreign Office elicited a reply in almost the same words from its principal motor, Counsellor Baron von Holstein.

The Emperor also was probably apprised about the same time. Certainly he knew things by 1904 when he sought to intimidate King Leopold II of Belgium and let the cat out of the bag. Buelow himself seems to have had some second thoughts, for in the same year he ventured to argue with Schlieffen about going through Belgium. He recalled Bismarck saying that it went against plain common sense to add an extra enemy to an opposing lineup. Schlieffen insisted that Belgium would confine itself to protesting. In 1912 Foreign Secretary von Jagow did raise doubts about going through Belgium but was fobbed off by a memo from Moltke.

It is noteworthy and leaves one somewhat staggered that no one then or later seems to have urged the convocation of a crown council or lesser gathering of civil and military leaders to deal with a problem of such moment to the German fate. Bismarck, who had scant awe of the military, would assuredly have taken a hand. Yet no council dealing with war plans was convoked by his feebler successors before the ultimate crisis of July 1914.

At least equally strange is the failure of the last two prewar Chancellors, Buelow and Theobald von Bethmann-Hollweg, to attack the problem of armament necessary for a three-front war. For, though the European scene might conceivably produce a future situation in which Britain would accommodate herself to a German march through Belgium, nothing remotely portending such a change was then in evidence.[3]

The second Helmut von Moltke, nephew of the first, owed a position he did not covet to William II's envisaging him as a kind of good luck piece; always mindful of his grandfather, he too wanted to be served by a Moltke. But this modest, rather retiring figure was plagued by lack of self-confidence, particularly in regard to any ability to act decisively at times of crisis. It was only with a heavy heart that he steeled himself to carry on with his predecessor's daring project. Despite somewhat limp efforts in recent years to rehabilitate him as a commander, he remains the chief whipping boy for the disaster of the Marne. Criticisms of Moltke's generalship focus about equally on his alterations in military dispositions in the period 1906–1914 and his conduct of operations in August-early September 1914.

One step for which Moltke is never faulted is elimination of the Netherlands from the sweep westward. In part this derived from Moltke being more sensitive politically than Schlieffen had been. Thus he reckoned the costs of having Britain as an enemy considerably higher. Adding the Netherlands to the list of victims of military necessity doubled the risk of having Britain to deal with. Belgium was enough to give him sleepless hours. "Many hounds are the hare's death," was an old German proverb his dismayed staff would hear him mutter in anxious moments. In fact, Moltke probably put as much thought as anyone in the civil government on how to keep out the British. It was he who first suggested what later became a feeble effort toward that end: a guarantee to Belgium of her sovereignty and boundaries if she permitted the march through.

Aside from hoping to reduce somewhat the certainty of British intervention, Moltke was influenced on the Netherlands by signs that the Dutch were alert to the threat. Extra track and railway sidings on the German side of the frontier screamed danger to them. They announced to all and sundry that they were prepared to protect their neutrality with arms. Perhaps most persuasive was their placement of mine chambers and heavy steel gates on the railway bridges at Maastricht and Roermond.

An additional factor in the decision to give up the dash through Limberg was the rebuilding after 1905 of the British Army into an expeditionary force. With the Netherlands in the war, the possible employment of these troops to threaten the flank and rear of the German rush westward had to be reckoned with. Finally, Moltke's second thought focused on what the Netherlands had to offer as a neutral: a windpipe through the anticipated British blockade by which Germany could draw food and raw materials.

Where Moltke really parted company with Schlieffen before the latter's death in 1913 was on the forces assigned to the east. In a swansong memorandum of 1912 Schlieffen had advocated the virtual denuding of that front, placing there no more than three divisions. In the end, Moltke allocated nine.

Though all of Moltke's eggs were thus no longer in the western basket, its capacity had been shrunk alarmingly by confining the passageway to Belgium and Luxembourg. It was a problem that gained in seriousness and complexity as the German Army grew larger. Though most of the extra troops were stationed farther south, the First and Second Armies, which had to force their way through a bottleneck at Liege were also slightly beefed up. Well over half a million men were to be crowded together at this point.

Liege was one of Brialmont's celebrated fortresses. It was surrounded on a fifty-kilometer perimeter by twelve forts, great masses of concrete and steel, that guarded the vital crossing over the Meuse. The principal problem for the Germans was to get through before the Belgian field army could deploy in the spaces between the forts and erect field fortifications to block these passages.

There is a good deal of irony in that Moltke, who lacked so much of the courage of Schlieffen's convictions on the larger aspects of the campaign, should here be obliged to embark on the greatest adventure of all. For if there was a military gamble in the Schlieffen Plan as it was in 1914, it assuredly lay in the *coup de main* projected

for Liege. Five approaches led from the frontier through the spaces
between the easternmost forts into the city itself. To exploit these,
five brigades were stationed close to the border. Once a state of war
existed, their function was to dash across the border and penetrate
the ring of forts. The project faced stupendous risks: if the major
railway tunnel and/or the bridge over the Meuse were destroyed, the
logistics of the German First and Second Armies would be fatally
affected. Politically the consequences of the enterprise could be
equally serious, for as will be seen, a straightjacket was put on
diplomacy in July 1914.

Both Schlieffen and the younger Moltke considered from time
to time being anticipated by the French in Belgium. Much was
bound to be alluring for them in the thought of the French relieving
them of the onus of violating Belgian neutrality. Both the elder
Moltke and his successor, Count Waldersee, rather liked the idea
militarily. From heavily fortified Alsace-Lorraine they might then
attack the French in flank.

The French had thought much about the Belgian problem since
the 1870s. A book written by Eugene Tenot (1882), at the instigation
of General Sere de Rivieres, stressed that with the building of the
French fortifications, Belgium was "henceforth inseparable from any
rational German offensive plan."[4] For the time being the problem
was considered only from a defensive standpoint. But as the French
Army expanded and the Russian alliance promised to divert large
German forces, speculation about offensive opportunities grew. In
1911, when the replacement of General Michel by General Joffre as
Chief of Staff unleashed a veritable mania for offensive action, the
issue of moving through Belgium and Luxembourg came into the
foreground. Joffre's importunities led to the convocation of the
Superior Council of National Defense on 9 January 1912. The
minutes of this meeting and other documents vital to our problem
were released only in the early 1970s. They show that the only
argument countering Joffre's plea was fear of damaging the military
ties with Britain which just then were in process of being greatly
expanded.[5] Neither legal nor moral scruples concerning a violation
of Belgian territory were mentioned. How little they counted may be
adduced from the fact that Joffre was given the free hand on
Luxembourg denied him on Belgium.

Vital to any discussion of the Schlieffen Plan in relation to the
Empire's security problem is a search for logical alternatives. As Sir
John Hackett has cogently formulated it, the soldier's duty is to
come up with as many options for his government as it is willing to

pay for. Neither Schlieffen nor the younger Moltke ever responded to this challenge. For them, as for all who try to second guess them, the stumbling block is that no one has yet advanced a tenable solution that fits the prescription of a swift and decisive victory. Also, no civilian leader appears ever to have taken issue with this approach of the two generals. Even the far-from-bellicose Bethmann went along with them on a German need for expansion (in his case colonial) as against Bismarck's famous delineation of Germany as a saturated state.

Of course the option which conforms with the wisdom of our current hindsight would have been a defensive posture, in effect a rejection of the total victory formula. Ironically, this might most nearly have met the generals' victory dream through, so to speak, the back door. In view of the superior strength of the defensive and the continually more lethal power of weaponry, not to speak of the compelling French craze for "attack, attack, attack," this assumption is not unreasonable.[6] But in fairness to the generals, it should be noted that neither the civil government nor the nation would have understood such a course, should they have somehow summoned up sufficient spirit of self self-denial to adopt it. It would certainly have been rejected by their military contemporaries in all the powers of Europe who were almost unanimously fostering the offensive spirit and doctrine. It should also be borne in mind that at this period the defensive carried with it the odor of a long war which everyone wanted to avoid.

One is on safer ground in charging Schlieffen and Moltke with never having given the defensive alternative a fair hearing. From the mid-nineties on, alternative options that contemplated defensive or limited war got short shrift. "When such alternatives were evaluated," says a recent study, "they were designed to fail, and they were held to a tougher standard than was the Schlieffen Plan."[7]

In some mitigation of the indictment that frequently is levied against the German military leaders of the period, one should not ignore the calculation that there is not too much to distinguish their approach to the problem from that of soldiers elsewhere. Even those captains who are prepared to recognize the primacy of policy both in peace and war seem instinctively to lean to the assumption that policy is best served by total military victory. There is little difference in their approach both in situations of prewar planning and in the conduct of war.[8]

The seekers of total victory through battles of annihilation tend, of course, to include among themselves the proponents of preventive wars. In the case of Germany, Schlieffen inclined to one during the First Morocco Crisis and Moltke had similar thoughts in the spring of 1914.[9] It follows that military leaders are usually more inclined than their civilian counterparts to doubt in times of crisis the likelihood or possibility of a diplomatic solution. It is natural that this inclination should be the more pronounced when immediate sharp action appears required if war does eventuate.

Despite Schlieffen's one-sided approach to Germany's military problems, his sterner critics go overboard when they picture him as a gambler who staked the fate of Germany on a roll of the dice. It would be grossly unfair, for example, to compare him and his plan to Ludendorff and the sink-or-swim offensive of 1918. It should not be passed over, as is nearly always done, that he was fully determined to cut his losses if things did not turn out as he hoped and expected. In that event, he proposed an immediate peace overture before the grip of the armies was irrevocably set on each other's throats.

Inevitably, indictments drawn against the Schlieffen Plan stress the plain fact that in the end it did fail; in the view of the more severe critics it was *bound* to fail. All of these arguments underline logistics. Undoubtedly Schlieffen was remiss, some say slack, in this area. This is not the place for a full analysis, but it must be pointed out that the issue is not yet settled. The proof of any pudding, to be sure, is in the eating. The failure at the Marne is unquestioned, and the logistic situation undoubtedly played some part. But there is impressive evidence that the latter was by no means catastrophic.

General Groener, who was in charge of railway communication, gave eloquent testimony on the strained but far from desperate state of affairs. As a disinterested party, the General Staff's later strategic specialist, Wilhelm Wetzell, was perhaps more impressive. The proof of the pudding, as he described it, lies not in the failure of the plan itself. He points out how the Schleswig-Holstein Army Corps, in his view the second or third best in the German Army, in recrossing the Marne and lining up against the French on the Ourcq, marched seventy-five miles in three days, and, in fighting with the relatively fresh French troops from Paris, had definitely the best of things. "Bone weary? Yes," said Wetzell in effect; "Exhausted to the point of prostration? Emphatically, no"[10]

German soldiers did not have as much to say as one might have expected during the July crisis of 1914. There was occasional interference as when Moltke, terrified that Conrad von Hoetzendorff would botch the Austro-Hungarian mobilization facing Russia, in effect urged him to ignore the advice Bethmann was giving the Vienna government. But in critical ways prewar military plans and arrangements cut down the diplomats' elbow-room. In this regard statesmen and soldiers equally should note the lesson of how rigidities of military planning may breed fatal political consequences. In question, particularly, is the project of the *coup de main* at Liege.

Although civilian authorities had long been *au courant* about the intended moves through Belgium, Luxembourg, and, initially, the Netherlands, no one seems to have told them of Liege. Groener and more humbly placed officers who worked on the Schlieffen Plan and its implementation knew nothing of such a communication. Zimmermann, then deputy to the Secretary of State for Foreign Affairs, was sure no such information had reached the Foreign Office. Kurt Rietzler, who was privy to most of Bethmann's official secrets, testified to the consternation of his chief when the political implications of the project were brought home to him. The Crown Prince in his turn was sure that his father was unaware of it.

Yet in the crisis that led to war, the Liege *coup de main* may well have wrecked the last faint hope of peace. As the troops could move only after a state of war with someone existed, it had to be brought on as soon as war was virtually, though perhaps not quite, certain. That stage was reached when Tsar Nicholas decreed Russia's general mobilization. The other concerned powers would then follow almost automatically. But the key feature was that while France and Germany had a ten-day mobilization period, that of Russia was about twice as long. Once her own mobilization was completed, Germany would have to go to war. It would be near fatal to lose her time advantage over Russia. But for about ten days the diplomats could have had their final innings. Liege robbed Europe of these last ten days of grace during which by some miracle peace might yet have been preserved. One could hardly move into Belgium without previously being at war with France, and the 1914 situation demanded that this should follow war with Russia.

When was Bethmann apprised of this by Moltke? We do not know exactly, but it must have been sometime after his conversation with the British Ambassador, Sir Edward Goschen, on 29 July. During this exchange Bethmann let the cat out of the bag on the intention to march through Belgium. Pure luck was on his side here, for in their preoccupation with their own problem, the British did not think of immediately warning Belgium. If they had done so, the

Belgian government would certainly not have ordered the commander at Liege, General Leman, not to construct field-works between his forts because of German sensitiveness. The order was dispatched at midnight 31 July and would scarcely have been sent if Brussels had known what the Germans had in store for Belgium.

Moltke, however reluctantly, here called the tune, and the civilian authorities, represented by Bethmann, paid the piper. For many years he had to bear the historical burden of the strange German rush into war; it was declared on Russia at 6 p.m. on 1 August, just *one hour* after the announcement of mobilization.

A further feature of rigidity in the diplomatic scene of July 1914 that was created by military planning concerned Russia. Despite nearly half a century of assumption that only a war on two fronts was possible, Schlieffen and the younger Moltke wished to play it safe and maintained standby plans for Russia and France singly. When Russia was preoccupied with Japan in 1905, Schlieffen would have liked to use the First Morocco Crisis to strike preventively at France. After 1909 Russia made gigantic strides toward military recovery. Her army jumped from 750,000 to twice that in 1914 and was scheduled to reach two million by 1916. Troops were piling up in Poland raising German prospects for a quicker decision in the east. But a war game reviewing the Schlieffen Plan in 1912 showed that by the time one got to Minsk the French would be on the Rhine.[11]

Despite the growing Russian threat Moltke continued to think only in terms of a two-front war. In 1913 he actually cast aside contingency plans for war with Russia alone. This error of committing himself to a single assumption was brought home to him in the July crisis when William II, in a momentary fancy that France might stay neutral, proposed to mobilize against Russia alone. When Moltke in his consternation insisted that military dispositions would not permit so drastic a switch, he got the deeply wounding, "That is not the answer your uncle would have given me."[12]

Not only did the German soldiers in 1914 find themselves in one sense or another the prisoners of their own too-rigid plans. The French discovered the Belgians were putting up a far stiffer resistance than had been expected. On Joffre's staff there arose an impulse to alter dispositions and to strike northward into the flank of the massive German advance. Such inclinations were curbed by Joffre's adamant mental commitment to Plan 17 on which, incidentally, the civilian leadership had never been consulted. The same may be said of British generals who three years before the war promised the French to dispatch immediately an expeditionary corps, this too without consulting civilian authorities.

Since 1897 William II and his closest advisers had geared up German foreign policy to a world-embracing level that was marked by expansionistic coloring. The status quo posture that had characterized Bismarck's policy after unification was left more and more behind. Such aims and moods were bound to be reflected in the military arena, so that some critics voice the claim that Germany's civilian leaders in the end got only what they had bargained for. The military chiefs are occasionally portrayed as having merely adapted themselves to the political aims of the Imperial Government or even as exercising restraint on a venturesome foreign policy. A grain of truth may be found in this: the military was more responsible than any other quarter in Germany for keeping down the size of the Army. Because of anxiety about the social composition of the officer corps, it dragged its feet on expansion and was dragged along by the government, public opinion, and the Reichstag.[13]

Jehuda Wallach, in a volume soon to be published in translation, brilliantly demonstrates how the Schlieffen Plan violated the dictum of Clausewitz, quoted at the start of this discussion, upholding the supremacy of the political imperative over military strategy. Policy and diplomacy became to a large extent the prisoners of military dispositions. But the civilian leadership of Germany in multifarious and, in the end, fatal ways, permitted itself to become the handmaiden of a self-imposed military necessity.

It may appear strange that nothing has been said here about the role of the German Navy in relation to policy and war preparation. It goes without saying that Grand Admiral von Tirpitz did much to exacerbate relations with Britain, and that the growth of the German Navy, so ardently backed by William II, was the principal feature in the estrangement of the two countries. But it is noteworthy that Tirpitz, who perforce had to beat the drums on rivalry with Britain if naval expansion was to continue, straightway sang a different tune whenever war with Britain loomed as a conceivability. In every crisis from 1897 to July 1914 he lay back, protesting that the fleet was not ready. For him, as for the Emperor, it was largely an end in itself. After the war he addressed bitter reproaches to those who had permitted it to come about and destroy his life's work.

As for Buelow and Bethmann, they had little faith in the Navy as a genuine factor in the balance of power. But like the Army leaders who bitterly resented the gigantic slice the Navy cut out of the defense pie, they saw nothing for it but to humor the Emperor.

Dictator and Army in the Coming of World War II

The interwar political and military scenes in Germany (1871–1914; 1918–1939) diverge so diametrically that it is a challenge to discern parallel lines of development. The German Empire founded amidst the victory over France could boast such prestige and power that it stood militarily unrivaled by any single antagonist. Only coalitions could hope to deal with it with any prospect of victory or survival. Its military and external policies were governed by this stark fact.

In bitter contrast, the Germany slowly emerging after 1918 from the ashes of defeat was for a foreseeable time eliminated as a positive factor in European and world affairs. Its armed forces were restricted so severely that they had meaning only for internal order or, conceivably, domestic turnover. The condition and imbalance of the national economy discouraged hope in substantial military recovery even if the Versailles Treaty restrictions should be lifted or dramatically amended. Yet there always loomed in the background an unquestionable prospect for the restoration of Germany as a major power. The obvious potential of population, location, martial tradition, militarily trained manpower, and the conflicting policies of other states had a fixed place in the awareness of all concerned.

The relations of the Army with the political regimes which governed Germany in the twenties and thirties was in large part determined by its social composition. During the Empire, it has been noted, most of its leaders resisted expansion because of hesitation about accepting lower-middle-class officers and working class recruits. The rigorous contraction to a 100,000–man level imposed on Germany by the victorious Allies, though deeply resented, made possible reversing directions, sloughing off border-line elements among the socially suspect. By the time Hitler took office one-fourth of the officers and half the generals were noblemen; the rank-and-file could now be recruited entirely from reliable social strata, mostly country boys.

The Republic for most members of the Reichswehr (armed forces) was the creature of defeat and revolution, and its leading party, the Social Democrats, was a collection of pacifists and internationalists. In effect the political and social horizons of soldiers of all ranks were likely to be limited. As Nazi influence grew in Germany, some split in the officer corps did develop between age groups. The older and higher in rank tended to regard Hitler and his ilk as vulgar upstarts; many also were deeply disturbed by the growing attack on traditional religion. All officers of whatever rank and age found appeal in the national and martial flavor of Nazi ideology, were delighted with the agitation for rearmament, and applauded demands for a vigorous foreign policy aimed at revising the Versailles Treaty.

Younger officers were intrigued by Nazi dynamism, were impressed by Hitler's knack for enlisting national enthusiasm, and found inspiration in the pleas for social solidarity and comradeship. Their generals and colonels were regarded as somewhat stuffy, as too wedded to old ways, and somewhat behind the times. As yet this did not portend any rejection of prestigious leaders, all of them veterans from the First World War and most of them a highly positive selection among the survivors of that conflict. There is little doubt that in 1933 the vast majority of young officers would have obeyed any order from their superiors.

At that time it would have been at least conceivable that the Army could have been thrown into the scale against Hitler's assumption of power. Its Commander in Chief, Kurt von Hammerstein-Equord, was bitterly anti-Nazi;[14] if assured of sufficient support and at least the acquiescence of President von Hindenburg, he might well have acted. His Chief of Staff, the crusty Bavarian Wilhelm Adam, would certainly have gone along. In fact, there was sufficient apprehension among those whose maneuvers and deals made Hitler Chancellor that the new, compliant Defense Minister, Werner von Blomberg, was virtually smuggled into office from his post as disarmament negotiator at Geneva.

Hammerstein and Adam were so suspect to the parties who had brought in Hitler that within a year they were replaced by generals regarded as more amenable to working with the regime. Thus began a process that was to come to a climax only after the attempted coup of 20 July 1944: the systematic though intermittent weeding out of politically suspect or overly independent figures. It is all too often forgotten in looking at the collection of yes-men, careerists, just-soldier types (*nur-Soldaten*), and dyed-in-the-wool Nazis who made up much of the higher *Generalitaet* in the final stage of the regime that they were no longer representative of what it had been in 1933.

There is much irony in the fact that Werner von Fritsch and Ludwig Beck, the men chosen to take the places of Hammerstein and Adam, were later to be counted among the chief military victims of the regime: Fritsch to become the target of the dirtiest of Nazi intrigues, Beck to emerge as the chief of the military conspiracy that grew largely from this episode.

The period 1933–1936 was one of comparative restraint in both domestic and external affairs. Hitler was not yet the uncompromising egomaniac who emerged in the war period. Circumstances also prohibited excessive risk-taking. Though occasionally he dropped the mask sufficiently to hint at more extreme goals than those he publicly professed, the military were not alone in seeing therein flights of fancy that need not be taken too seriously.[15]

Except for a single reckless fling on Austria in July 1934, Hitler's first three years demonstrated tolerable restraint and the enunciation of aims that would be faulted by few Germans. On Poland, the one area where popular feeling would have supported a relatively strong policy, Hitler astonished the world by a non-aggression pact that would have elicited a storm of outrage against anyone who was less a nationalist.

Certainly the Wehrmacht did not object to the clandestine rearmament of these years and down to the repudiation of the Versailles restrictions in the spring of 1935. There was some regret in the Army on the petering out of collaboration with the Red Army by which the Germans had trained Soviet staff officers in return for permission to experiment and train with forbidden weapons on Soviet territory. But as one could now proceed more freely within the Reich itself, this was no lasting setback for the rearmament program. For professionals who for fourteen years had been forced to exercise their craft strictly under wraps, the free hand Hitler gave them must have been felt as a deliverance.

How did Adolf Hitler view the Army and its leadership? At one time he had for them a respect that approached awe. Bridging the psychological gap between the private soldier and an army's chief is no easy task. But in Hitler's case this state of mind in time was translated into an inferiority complex that he seems to have resented. Perhaps his derogation and fault-finding with the generals were meant to compensate for this.

Probably he resented most the lack of commitment of the Army's leaders to the type of armament program and expansionist ideas he was pushing. He could not get over their lack of bellicosity. He once said that he had expected to find them straining at the leash like a butcher's dog. Instead he was continually forced to whip them on. In two 1931 conversations with Richard Breiting, a prominent newspaper editor, he launched into the kind of compulsive self-revelatory perorations that seem the best guideposts to his innermost thoughts. He dwelt bitterly on his lack of confidence in the *Generalitaet* and expressed his intention to fight the big war he expected "with a new Army and a new General Staff."[16]

It is entirely conceivable that even then he had in mind the ideal of an army that was a military branch of the party. The generals would then simply join his other paladins, or conversely, the paladins would be made generals. In principle he can have found little wrong with Ernst Roehm's aspiration to elevate his Brown Shirts into the official defenders of the nation. It might indeed have been after his own heart if he had felt able as yet to dispense with the professionals and the *Sturmabteilung* (SA) had looked more like a manageable instrument. When he later transformed the *Schutzstaffel* (SS) into a branch of the armed forces, with the probable intention of going all the way after the war had been won, it accorded with the desired pattern.

Basically of course, the dictator and the military had irreconcilable positions on rearmament and expansion. It must suffice to enumerate here the more fundamental aspects of his outlook and intentions.

1. Hitler was unalterably wedded to a dream of vast eastern expansion such as was conceivable only on the basis of aggressive war.

2. More nebulous, but only slightly less fundamental, was the concept of a German hegemonial position *vis-a-vis* the Eurasian land mass.

3. Given French and British acquiescence in German eastern expansion, he was prepared to leave them to vegetate, in power-political terms, in the West. At least until 1936 he had at the back of his mind the ideal of a working relationship with the British, for whose empire he had an enduring admiration. Of course if the western powers were obstreperous, he was prepared to shove them aside once and for all.

4. He suffered from the normal ultra-Fascist addiction to the idea that war is the ultimate test of a nation's vitality. Though willing enough to accept what he could get free in response to political or military pressures, to him such gains were only way-stations to what would be in the end a trial of arms.

5. His timetables were vague and depended on circumstance. Though growing more impatient with the years, he was a complete opportunist as to means. He planned and expected to reach top striking power in the period 1943–1945.

6. Getting away with major power plays in the mid-thirties (repudiating the Versailles armaments restrictions and remilitarizing the Rhineland) and profiting hugely from Anglo-French preoccupations in the Mediterranean (Ethiopia and the Spanish Civil War), his growing confidence and impatience spurred his craving to move in bigger ways. They increased his inclination toward risk-taking and made him push harder in armament and aggressive military planning.

7. Arguments on German economic vulnerabilities for a long and even for a short war left him rather cold. He counted on early *blitzkrieg* victories that would give him control of other nations' resources.

The leading figures in the *Generalitaet* saw things differently on almost every point. None of them shared his racial fantasies or dreams of wholesale eastern expansion. They could not but agree with him on detesting the territorial provisions of the Treaty of Versailles but differed greatly, even among themselves, on the urgency and desirability of particular revisions. The composition of Czechoslovakia and Poland looked to them to be both acts of injustice and a serious check to reattainment of the power position to which they aspired for Germany. Probably most of them had little or no objection in principle to war as a justifiable instrument for the attainment of such ends.

Though like general staffs everywhere they perforce had in their files plans for every imaginable contingency, there was little disposition to focus on any of them for the immediate future. The dreary years of crushing military inferiority had bred a tendency to overrate the forces of other countries, notably France. They were keenly aware of their own continuing shortcomings, especially economic gaps and vulnerabilities. These, they figured, would detract seriously from the punch of offensive war and make the long-pull type unthinkable.

In its economic anxieties, the *Generalitaet* was constantly prodded by General Georg Thomas, its economic and armament specialist, as well as by Hjalmar Schacht, Minister of Economics and President of the Reichsbank, almost the only individual who regularly dared to speak up to Hitler.[17] Schacht's alarm about Hitler's growing bellicosity first came to a head about 1936, the year in which he became what may be called a charter member of the anti-Hitler conspiracy. He and Thomas carried on a systematic agitation among Army and business leaders against arguments that a *blitzkrieg* might lead to a quick victory; in their view any next war was more likely to be another competition in exhaustion. Their record as prophets was to prove a somewhat mixed one. Many postwar interpretations of the German prewar economy have held that it coasted too much and could have made Germany far more formidable militarily had it been ready to produce at full steam. Recent studies have raised doubts about this thesis, holding that, except for woman-power, production was much closer to capacity than here assumed.[18]

In some measure, economic considerations did play some sort of role in the Army command's reluctance to force the pace of rearmament—a rare if not unique occurrence in the history of modern states. Quite apart from costs, the Army command, notably Chief of Staff Beck, was uneasy about calling so many men to the colors. Beck was upset when Hitler, in denouncing the Versailles limitations, declared his intention immediately to build the Army up to 550,000 men in thirty-six divisions. His own proposal was to limit growth during the next two or three years to 300,000 men and to reach 500,000 only in the early forties. Here the quality standards of the professional clashed with those of the amateur for whom quantity was most impressive. Hitler, as so often, insisted on the almost limitless power of the human will, holding that the patriotic zeal of a Nazi combat leader was worth as much as training and experience.

The upshot was that both quality and quantity were allowed some innings. Beck had to yield on force goals but, backed by Fritsch and Blomberg, won on officer training. Hitler, needless to say, gave way with ill grace and kept nagging for speed.

There was a further hassle on the sequence in which age groups would be called up for service. Hitler, champing at the bit for maximum early readiness, wanted to start with World War I veterans who, he argued, would only need an intensive refresher course. Beck urged the wisdom of making haste slowly, holding that the soundest policy was to concentrate on basic training for the younger age groups. In largest part he had his way, adding materially to the score which Hitler was tallying up against him and the Army command generally.

Hitler's tone in such disputes became more strident as his domestic and international elbow room widened and he felt the more ready to take chances. Issues were sharpened the more one got away from the first years; then there had been no purpose arguing about maximums when the minimums of a respectable military establishment still seemed far away. As long as there was a large pool of industrial and manpower resources to draw upon, each service had been allowed to launch its own rearmament program. Nothing like a coherent defense policy or systematic planning in the armament field had thus been allowed to develop. The services simply grabbed what they could get away with. Hitler contributed to the confusion by sudden and often inordinate demands. In 1938, for example, he proposed without preliminary warning a fivefold increase in air force front-line strength.

Toward the end of 1937 the Fuehrer's impatience and frustration approached a point where something had to give. He found intolerable a situation in which he felt his style in external affairs cramped. Here lies his basic motivation in calling the historic Hossbach Conference on 5 November.[19] It was the sole occasion that something that looked like the empire's crown council was convoked during the Third Reich. But there was no real discussion. Hitler began a prolonged monologue with the flat statement that his mind was fixed on the matters at issue. This was followed by extensive comment from other participants and that was it! The meeting had been initiated by Blomberg to deal with disarmament problems and, especially, to put a spoke in the wheel of the careening Luftwaffe which grabbed any resource on which it could lay hands. Hitler broadened the subject enormously by relating armament decisions and military planning to broad national policy and by adding the Foreign Minister, Baron von Neurath, to the group.

The course of the meeting has been delineated in scores of studies on the period. It climaxed with Blomberg, Fritsch, and Neurath taking vehement issue with what Hitler had said. The Fuehrer, in effect, had demanded every imaginable speedup in armament and had stated that 1938 might offer fruitful opportunities to do something about Austria and/or Czechoslovakia. He left no doubt about his intentions to wage aggressive war when the appropriate time came, in any event no later than 1943–1945.

To all intents and purposes the fate of the three footdraggers was now determined, and none survived the next three months in office. Surprise is sometimes expressed that Hitler was so ready to part with Blomberg, especially as he now knuckled down and provided the ordered revision of Case Green, the basic plan for war with Czechoslovakia, giving it a flavor of urgency. Blomberg had done much to bring the Wehrmacht closer to the party and had rejected importunities of outraged generals to use his office as a moderating influence on Nazi excesses. On the debit side from Hitler's standpoint, Blomberg had frequently sided with the Army on armament questions or refrained from using his authority to bring it into line with the Fuehrer's wishes. At times of international tension he was always a brake, inducing Hitler to refer to him as an "hysterical old maid."[20]

That had been notably the case in 1936 when diplomats and soldiers had been united in opposing the projected gamble of the remilitarization of the Rhineland. Indeed their unanimous advice might have swayed Hitler if, unknown to them, he had not received a personal message from the French government that it was willing to yield on the basic issue if Germany did not injure French prestige or undermine the European treaty structure.[21] Having learned that the French were ready to give way on substance, Hitler rightly decided that they would not go to war on a matter of form. In the end the dictator was able to make it appear that his intuition outweighed the united judgment of the services and the Foreign and Defense Ministries. It proved a ten-strike in the psychological game of intimidation that Hitler systematically pursued with the generals.

The removal of the three saboteurs in the so-called Blomberg-Fritsch crisis of January-February 1938 was only the central feature of the power play that can appropriately be called a *coup d'etat*. The ongoing crisis had revealed much about how major figures of the *Generalitaet* stood in relation to their own leaders and to the regime generally. Hitler, therefore, determined to make as clean a sweep as possible of those who stood in his way; the consequent purge was the largest and most drastic of the Nazi period. Sixteen generals were retired or transferred, subservient figures like Generals Keitel and von Brauchitsch took over key positions, and, most portentous, Hitler abolished the War Ministry and put in its place an Armed Forces High Command (OKW) of which he was commander in chief. Dozens of other changes were made at critical spots of the Defense and Foreign Ministries and Army high command. The worshipful Colonel Schmundt took the place of the ultra-independent Colonel Hossbach as the Chancellor's Wehrmacht adjutant.

Hitler sailed full speed ahead to take over Austria in March and almost immediately shifted to pile pressures on Czechoslovakia concerning its German-speaking territories, usually called the Sudetenland. Only a summary statement can be made about the September crisis which bears that name and the conspiratorial activity that is associated with it.

The decapitation of the former Wehrmacht and Army leadership gave Hitler control of their command apparatus. But he had not yet seized the final bastion of resistance in the post of Chief of the General Staff occupied by Beck. For no one else had the Blomberg-Fritsch crisis been so much of an eyeopener as for him. Beck was now the key figure among those who joined hands to resist Hitler's drive toward war with Czechoslovakia. Any final doubts where the Fuehrer was heading were removed by himself in a high level meeting in the Reich Chancellery on 23 May.

There was scant prospect of mobilizing the *Generalitaet* against a conflict with that state alone. But the likelihood of attaching thereto a European war featuring French and British intervention was quite another thing.

Though to outward appearances the dictator's mastery of the military sector was now complete, what did not seem to occur to him was that, in slamming the door on protest and persuasion, he left those who were convinced that he was leading Germany to disaster only the resort of conspiracy. No other course is open when a tyrannical regime has reached its nadir by eradicating sources of restraint. In removing Fritsch, whom Beck and many others had regarded as a final refuge against tyranny, the only course left open was to purge the state by toppling the regime itself.

Beck was Germany's most prestigious soldier after the departure of Fritsch; in the summer of 1938 and thereafter to 20 July 1944 he was the center of military opposition. His conviction that the General Staff was "the conscience of the Army" gave him a sense of mission that guided his course at this critical juncture.[22]

What Beck planned in the first instance was a kind of general strike of the generals in which they would address an ultimatum on the war issue to Hitler. The climax of the campaign for the support of the *Generalitaet* came on 4 August when Beck presented the case to the assembled army and army group commanders by reading a memorandum he had prepared for Hitler which argued that an attack on Czechoslovakia meant war with the western powers and disaster for German arms. In the end, with two exceptions (Busch and von Reichanau), the assembled commanders endorsed Beck's position and asked Brauchitsch to convey this to Hitler. But the Army's commander in chief, who was under heavy personal obligation to Hitler, contented himself with merely forwarding the memorandum to the Fuehrer through the army adjutant. This left Beck no choice but to resign, and he left office on 28 August. Unfortunately, he obeyed Hitler's order to keep this quiet, and his departure was not announced until October.

There was, however, another arrow in Beck's quiver—a military coup if Hitler stuck to his war plans. Beck's successor, Franz Halder, was also in the conspiracy, so that the General Staff remained its official, though not its motor center.[23]

Clear proof that Britain and France would actually go to war with Germany in defense of Czechoslovakia was vital to launching a coup with any prospect of success. To assure this a string of messages had been addressed to London and Paris since spring which pleaded for clarification on this issue. They climaxed in the first days of September in meetings between the German *charge d'affaires*, Theo Kordt, and the British Foreign Minister, Lord Halifax, and between Beck himself and a French representative in a Basel hotel.[24]

As is only too well known London and Paris could not be persuaded to act in the desired sense, and the process of appeasement continued on its fatal course. Twice, at what seemed encouraging moments in September, Halder pressed the button that summoned action for the following day, only to have to cancel each call when Britain swept the ground from under the conspirators by Chamberlain's trips to Germany.

Hitler, contrary to world-wide assumption, was more infuriated than enchanted by the Munich agreement. He bitterly resented Anglo-French concessions that took the wind out of his diplomatic sails and forced him to hold his hand militarily with regard to Czechoslovakia. The military leadership in turn was bowled over by what looked like new proof of an uncanny instinct for what foreign opponents could be made to swallow. Thereafter it ceased to struggle against the drift to war.

Hitler savagely struck out at what he labeled the Beck complex: the thesis that the Army could legitimately object to or even exercise a veto on its employment for war.[25] There was no one left in his military entourage to gainsay him; confidence and self-esteem had suffered too severely. A string of generals who had stood closest to Beck but had somehow survived the February purge went the same way. Small wonder that the shrunken Brauchitsch, and more and more Halder, were cowed.

When Hitler summoned army group and army commanders to Berchtesgaden on 22 August 1939 to reveal his coming attack on Poland, he did not permit comment and none dared protest. Though not wholly believing his claim that his deal with Stalin eliminated any chance of the western powers going to war with Germany, there was no getting around his extraordinary past record as a prophet in such matters. It is noteworthy, however, that until the guns began to shoot, the intimidated army leaders remained unconverted to Hitler's policy and continued to drag their feet as much as their cowed spirits would permit.

The relation of military planning and preparation to the development and conduct of national policy in Germany of the two prewar periods offers few parallels and almost inexhaustible contrasts. In fact, in the most basic problem areas, the determination of which was the cart and which the horse terminates in exactly opposite solutions. Before World War I military planning, except perhaps in some aspects of armament, seemed essentially independent of political guidance or decision. At the most critical juncture of all—the crisis of July 1914—plans devised without consultation or advisement of the civilian authorities proved a straightjacket for diplomacy.

In the thirties it was the political leadership which took the bit in its teeth and dragged along a reluctant *Generalitaet*. The latter was always at least one step behind where the dictator wanted it to be, had no sympathy whatever for his larger foreign policy aims, and surrendered to him only after it had been repeatedly chastened and drained by successive purges of its most independent and politically and morally aware constituents.

Why such great contrasts and differences? The answer lies mainly in completely altered military and political realities of the

Third Reich but also in the dawn of a new age in which the role of political leaders assumed forms novel to our century. Notably, totalitarian really means total and permits no exceptions. A dictator with considerably less high flying ambitions of conquest than those of Adolf Hilter was bound to move in sooner or later on the miltiary leadership. The unique situation of Germany with its heavy psychological burdens derived from a disastrous war and catastrophic peace tells much of the rest of the story. Looking at the problem from the standpoint of a democratic society, one can perhaps glean insights from the fate of Wilhelmian Germany. Except in broad human terms there seems little we can gain from that of Adolf Hitler.

Notes

1. The necessary intermediaries confessed to being fearful of the notorious indiscretion of both parties and of the touchy subjects that would have been among the topics of conversation. Especially the former G–2 of the Army High Command, Colonel Walter Nicolai, clearly sought to protect Ludendorff from himself.

2. This is also the view of the most recent and excellent work on the guiding military doctrines of the 1914 belligerents: "Once the necessity of a rapid, decisive victory is accepted, Schlieffen's doctrine follows with inexorable logic." Jack Snyder, *The Ideology of the Offensive: Military Decision Making and the Disasters of 1914* (Ithaca, N.Y., 1984), p 132.

3. The state of British relations with France could be decisive here. In 1887, for example, *The Evening Standard*, the ministerial newspaper, at a time when British dissatisfactions with France ran high, commented that if it came to a Franco-German war Britain might not object to a German march through Belgium. In the meeting of the French Superior Council of National Defense in 1912, the discussion concerned a General Staff request for approval of marching through Belgium. On that occasion one of the ministers, no less a personage than Declasse, argued that the British would not object if they were sufficiently eager to see Germany defeated.

4. Eugene Tenot, *Les Nouvelles-defenses de la France: Les Frontiere 1870–1882* (Paris, 1882), p 313. The importance of Tenot's book is heavily underlined by G. Pedroncini, "L'influence de neutralite belge et luxembourgeoise sur la strategie francaise." Paper presented at The International Colloquium on Military History, Teheran, 6–16 July, 1976, p 1.

5. In 1911 the two General Staffs had agreed on the transfer to France of a British Expeditionary Force in the event of war with Germany. In 1912 a naval convention was to follow. The development of French planning on the basis of newly available French documents is dealt with at length in the Teheran paper of Pedroncini, pp 2–16.

6. The French suffered over 300,000 casualties during a single week (19–25 August), most of them as the result of futile attacks in Lorraine. The result of an overall defensive posture by Germany ought to have been correspondingly more devastating.

7. Snyder, p 122.

8. On the German side during the First World War the sole exceptions that spring to mind are such exceptionally insightful figures as Max Hoffmann and Wilhelm Groener.

9. Bethmann-Hollweg related this to Count Lerchenfeld in May 1914, saying that for Germany the time for preventive wars had passed, and that the Emperor would never agree to one anyway. Lerchenfeld interview, July 1938.

10. Conversations with Groener and Wetzell, July–August 1938.

11. General Dmitri Gourko, G–2 of the Russian Imperial Army, related how he purchased a copy of this war game from a German officer in 1913. This induced the Russians to switch to an offensive strategy against Germany instead of throwing almost everything against Austria-Hungary. The revised plan was ready in April 1914, virtually on the eve of war.

12. Helmut Johannes Ludwig von Moltke, *Erinnerungen, Briefe, Dokumente, 1866–1916* (Stuttgart, 1922), p 19.

13. In 1912 Germany drafted 52 percent of her manpower of military age against 72–82 percent by France (estimates differ sharply on France). In view of the disproportion in the two populations (sixty-five million against thirty-nine million), the size of the two standing armies was about the same after the French had added an extra year of service.

14. Hammerstein stood out among top army figures for wider political and social horizons. He was one of the few generals who did not share in the bitter prejudice against the Republic. In a milieu so ultra conservative or starkly reactionary this looked close to radicalism, and in some quarters he was known as the red general.

15. Five days after he became Chancellor, Hitler told assembled generals that his foreign policy would go far beyond mere revisions of the Versailles Treaty. His aim, he averred, was to destroy the very framework of the treaty itself as well as the existing balance in Central Europe.

16. Edouard Calic, ed., *Ohne Maske: Hitler-Breiting Geheimgespraeche 1931* (Frankfurt, 1968). English edition, *Unmasked: Two Confidential Interviews with Hitler in 1931* (London, 1971), pp 44, 109.

17. Among other pieces of evidence it is so reported in a dispatch of the British Embassy in Berlin.

18. Much light is thrown upon this aspect of the German rearmament problem by two recent studies. R. J. Overy, "Hitler's War and the German Economy: A Reinterpretation," in *The Economic History Review* XXXV No 2 (May 1982), pp 272–91, argues that labor resources were fully employed and that the real brakes on industrial expansion were lack of raw materials, skilled labor, and foreign exchange. A big windfall that came just on time for the war that began in September 1939 was the takeover of rump-Czechoslovakia in March of that year. It yielded the Germans half a billion RM in gold, a huge stock of arms, and nearly two billion RM worth of raw materials. Williamson Murray, in his superb *The Change in the European Balance of Power, 1938–1939* (Princeton, 1984), devotes most of his first chapter (pp 3–49) to a penetrating analysis of the German economic and armament problems that arrives at the same general conclusion.

19. Called thus because the Fuehrer's Wehrmacht adjutant, Colonel Friedrich Hossbach, took notes and later reconstructed the course of the meeting.

20. Interview with General Gerhard Engel, Hitler's army adjutant, 11 March 1970. Also his then still unpublished diary entry of 20 April 1938.

21. As related in 1945 by Richard von Kuehlmann, World War II Foreign Minister and in the thirties confidant of Neurath. Kuehlmann was selected by the French to carry the message to Neurath and through him to Hitler.

22. Quoted by Gerhard Ritter, "Deutsche Widerstand: Betrachtungen zum 10 Jahrestag des 20. Juli 1944," in *Zeitwende—Die Neue Furche*, V25N7 (Jul 1954), no pagination.

23. The motor center lay in the command of of the Abwehr (armed forces intelligence) under its Chief of Staff, Colonel Hans Oster, with the tacit support of the commander, Admiral Canaris.

24. The latter episode has not yet been discussed in print but will be dealt with at length in the writer's forthcoming book on this phase of the military conspiracy.

25. Engel interview, 11 March 1970.

Military Planning
Before and During World War II

Introduction

Clausewitz gives us two perplexing principles in his magisterial work, *On War*. When weak nations face stronger adversaries, when the prospect for war is likely, and when the passage of time promises greater strength for the enemy, he argued, the weaker nation should take some action; to wait only places it in danger of potentially greater loss. While implying an offensive operation in such cases, Clausewitz also argued convincingly that defense was the stronger form of warfare and the hope of the weaker. Offensive operations (the only avenue for decisive outcomes) demanded greater strength for launching and sustaining a successful campaign. Seemingly the paradox was resolved in his mind with a limited offensive operation followed by a consolidation of gains and a defensive posture. While Clausewitz's logic was sound, he gave little guidance as to how a weaker state first determines the inevitability of a war before instigating armed conflict and when success would rest on execution and not superior strength. France, Japan, and the Soviet Union all grappled with these problems in some form after World War I. Clemenceau's prophetic description of the Versailles Treaty after 1919 as a twenty-year armistice suggests that careful planning, planning upon which state security rested, had to be in progress. How that planning developed will serve as a measure to what Clausewitz tells us about undertaking war against a superior adversary.

Treaty guarantees backed by allies provided the foundation for French security after World War I; when its alliances showed declining strength in the 1930s, France had to alter the foundation's structure. Professor Cairns aptly describes a host of contradictions that entered into this process. Although France did not launch an attack, she prepared for aggression. In the end the author notes, "The men who went to war in 1939 were far from clear about what they intended to achieve and how they might achieve it," and when war was about to come, five civilian and military leaders would decide to go to war with confidence, but at the same time, with the acknowledgment that France had no choice. Without good civil-military relationships, planning fell to the military. Still devastated by the Great War, the nation would only permit a defense strategy;

the lessons of that war flowered into the Maginot Line. The advantages inherent in the defense would evaporate through the heat of *blitzkrieg*.

The Japanese dealt with similar problems. During the 1930s, they became convinced that the United States was their greatest adversary and understood, although not completely, the strength of this potential enemy. Professor Coox tells us that they too had a history lesson they could not forget, the decisive victories at Port Arthur (1904) and Tsushima (1905). Feeling that U.S. interests would conflict with their national goals in East Asia and the Pacific, they came to believe that war was inevitable. Unlike the French, they took Clausewitz's advice and elected to strike, hoping for a decisive outcome, but prepared to draw behind a defensive line running through the central Pacific. More than the French, Japanese planning fell to the military, and with no effective counterposition, they came to adopt the notion that Japan had no choice but to go to war in 1941.

Less is known about Soviet prewar planning. Stalin's motives in 1939 for a nonaggression pact were perhaps born out of his feeling of military inferiority at the time. When *blitzkrieg* hit that vast nation, the Soviet military had the space to retreat and eventually established defenses that worked at Leningrad, Moscow, and Stalingrad. The success of their efforts, Mr. Vigor suggests, lay not with excellent planning, but in large measure to grave mistakes by Hitler. When the Wehrmacht offensive wore down, the Soviets concentrated their growing strength and resources and used deep operations and encirclement to win their war.

In these three examples, planning errors became major causes for defeat and victory. The costs of these mistakes to the vanquished should not be lost upon the planner.

Planning For *la guerre des masses*: Constraints and Contradictions in France Before 1940

John C. Cairns

L'offensive seule assure la manifestation de la volonté
Maurice Gamelin[1]

"War plans cover every aspect of a war," Clausewitz observed, "and weave them all into a single operation that must have a single, ultimate objective in which all particular aims are reconciled. No one starts a war—or rather, no one in his senses ought to do so—without first being clear in his mind what he intends to achieve by that war and how he intends to conduct it."[2] A counsel of perfection, of course, from a long time ago when war and much else was a great deal simpler than it seems to be today. Still, Clausewitz's dictum stands as a warning, the repeated flouting of which has littered this century with military disasters. Of these, perhaps none was more electrifying in its day than the defeat of the French Army and Air Force forty-four years ago. It is all but forgotten now, an episode that the expanding war of 1941 swept into limbo. But the defeated leaders, banished to Dante's lower realms, still wait down there to answer our questions. The French of course did not *declare* war in September 1939, but they deliberately went to war (with the British) against Germany. Why did they do so? What did they intend? How did they hope to put it through? No one ever suggested they did this with alacrity, but equally no one ever suggested they stumbled into war.[3] To put it succinctly, the government was divided, parliament was largely silent, the nation was uncertain, even resigned, both fearful and disciplined. In the end, a handful of men made the decision: the prime minister and minister of national defense and of war, Edouard Daladier, and the chiefs of the army and navy general staffs, Maurice Gamelin, and François Darlan. There were others, on stage, off stage, influences, pressures; that is obvious. But at a hurriedly called meeting late in the afternoon of Tuesday, 23 August, the day Hitler and Stalin signed their non-aggression pact, the essential military assurance was given by the general and the admiral (the air force chief, General Joseph Vuillemin was silent)[4] which permitted Daladier to follow the British lead eleven days later.

In the dock at Riom, before his judges and until the end of his life, Gamelin continued to explain his words that afternoon.[5] The handwritten minutes (reproduced many times) may still be read in Daladier's papers.[6] Following the plea by the foreign minister, Georges Bonnet, that the German threat to Danzig not be met by arms and that they should play for time to continue rearming, Gamelin argued against waiting; delay might only worsen the situation for France. "Consequently, France has no choice: the only thinkable solution is to keep our undertakings to Poland, commitments, moreover, that were given prior to the opening of our (failed) negotiations with Russia." A few minutes later, both he and Darlan declared the army and navy were "ready." That was the fatal phrase. Hence the long exegesis of what had been meant: not materially fully outfitted, but "ready to start mobilizing and concentrating."[7] Beyond that, the overall import of Gamelin's statements was a clear recommendation not to abandon Poland because such a course would be harmful to France. Still on 3 September, when he sought unsuccessfully to gain twelve more hours for mobilization before the ultimatum expired, he remained "calm, smiling." "Ah, what a pity," he said to a cabinet minister, "that the Russians betrayed us. We had the Germans by the throat. All we had to do was tighten the noose." Was he confident just the same? He thought for a moment. "Yes. But it will take longer."[8]

Eight months later, on the eve of his dismissal, when the Allied armies were divided and the best part of them was being driven back on the Channel, Gamelin responded to Daladier's request for an explanation of what had gone wrong by both holding his ground on the 23 August recommendation and distributing the blame. First, he singled out "our very conception of war which ruled out of our studies the idea of ourselves precipitating operations (our political outlook permitted only an imposed, hence a defensive, war)," and, last, he blamed "The French soldier, yesterday's citizen, (who) did not believe in war. . . . If for many the old national spirit was rekindled, it was not enough."[9] As these phrases were being readied for dispatch to the minister, Gamelin, fighting to make his case and retain his job, was bluntly disavowed in his optimism by Philippe Pétain. With Daladier and the new prime minister, Paul Reynaud, the old marshal (deputy prime minister) visited the general at his headquarters in the Château de Vincennes. For an hour Gamelin gave them a sparkling map analysis of the situation and of what was being done to rally and regroup the troops who had broken and run.

"Believe me, Gamelin," Pétain cut in, "those men will never fight again." The general fell silent. "All in all," the marshal added, "you have been pitting bodies against machines."[10] On the way out, he shook the general's hand. "I feel sorry for you from the bottom of my heart."[11]

Is it possible to reconcile so much apparent contradiction of thought, to comprehend such cautious but real optimism before the event in light of the disastrous outcome? What could the French have had in mind when they went to war? What were their plans?

One starts with a simple assumption. And though it was the alibi of the defeated generals, it is not less true. Military planning is a function of society, its composition, its dynamics, its goals. Specifically, it reflects the state of society; more accurately, it reflects the perception of that society by the governing elite. Obviously an inquiry into the social foundations of French military planning would take us far afield. At best, we can consider some of the circumstances in the final years. A welter of judgments strew the accounts and commentaries, everything from the verdict that the calamitous outcome was the wrath of God to clever demonstrations that it was the result of technical error. Our purpose is to try to see what existed, how it came about, what was intended.

I

What the French used to call *le problème militaire français* poses the question, Where to begin? Even historians, prone to regress to the point where the question in view fades like the smile of the Cheshire cat, must make a stand, *sans esprit de recul*. Ours, like that of some generals, will be some distance back—in 1871, *l'année terrible*. Then, the French military problem was compounded: two new nation states, Germany and Italy, were henceforth on French borders; the industrialisation of war was becoming a reality: France was demonstrating a comparatively low rate of urbanisation and a marked demographic sluggishness;[12] it was judged necessary to adopt conscription, one of the lessons of the defeat.[13] In short, in addition to ongoing and expanding military commitment in North Africa and the colonies, the new republic assumed the burden of training its youth in the belief (strengthened after 1904, and still more after 1911) that salvation would be found only as a strong partner in an anti-German coalition.[14] Notoriously, prewar planning everywhere failed to foresee the nature of the struggle on the western front. Like other belligerents, France survived her own costly offensives and initial reverses. By the autumn of 1918, she had the largest army in the field. And thereafter she assumed the principal responsibility for policing an imperfect settlement imposed by the threat of force on the German Reich.

All this compounded the problem revealed in 1871. The French had manoeuvred, adapted, found allies, and bled greatly to emerge victorious. The effort was so huge that the question was posed: Could it ever be done again? Demographically, the situation was absolutely worse; it would worsen still more for another twenty years.[15] French industry had been strained to the breaking point when not simply overrun or wrecked by the invader. Socially, the national rift, clear well before 1914, had not been eliminated in the *union sacrée*; bringing the country to the verge of seeking terms in 1917, it was disregarded only by a display of extraordinary military discipline, political will, and as a result of the eruption of the enemy almost to the outskirts of Paris. Militarily, the glaring fact was that, despite mobilisation of almost eight million (out of a total male population of only nineteen million), the French Army had held only as a result of assistance, principally from Great Britain and its empire, and from Imperial Russia, Italy, the United States, and other lesser belligerents.[16] Not surprisingly, the ambassador Jules Cambon had remarked at the end of the Paris Peace Conference, "And now France is going to have to get used to being a second class power."[17] Something like that proved to be the agenda for the next twenty years.

The protective mask of the old Triple Entente had fallen away; with 10.5 percent of the active male population dead or missing, the nation was almost traumatized. What remained, as it seemed to the French, were the guarantees in the treaty. Casting themselves in the role of intended victim of an unrepentant German imperialism, they resisted, but slowly gave way over the fourteen years, seeking to uphold against Germany and some others the clauses on which their security seemed to depend. The record is familiar: a stubborn German refusal to fulfill the terms; a growing British support for revision; an Italian drifting away into fascist adventure; an American refusal of political responsibility while working "to reconstruct and stabilize Western Europe."[18] The result was German defiance and French entry into the Ruhr which deepened the crisis of responsible government in Europe; the loss of control of Germany by 1930; the steady demand in France that the defense burden be reduced.[19] Thus, with the German settlement unraveling, and the public mood at home troubled and restive, the French Army tried to find a solution to the immediate problems.

The solution adopted was: to erect a line of fortresses along the eastern frontier, the immediate manning of which would provide *couverture* against an *attaque brusquée* while the reserves were mobilized; to reduce military service to a period of 12 months, thus making the professional army (scarcely more numerous than Germany's lawful force) a training school, almost a skeleton for a wartime militia;[20] and to seek political and military relations with Belgium, Czechoslovakia, Rumania, Yugoslavia, and Poland (however unfriendly they might be to each other). And while all this was accomplished, the European situation grew less stable. France plunged into a belated depression.

Hitler arrived in office with a program to tear up the treaty and a hidden agenda scarcely to be conceived outside a mental institution.[21] The ground shifted steadily. Germany left the Disarmament Conference and the League of Nations in 1933, proclaimed conscription and the existence of an air force in 1935, remilitarized the Rhineland in 1936, contracted the Axis with Italy, and by early 1937 was on the path to the Anschluss of March 1938, the dismemberment of Czechoslovakia in October 1938, and the final moves into Prague in March 1939, and against Poland on 1 September.[22]

II

French planning in these circumstances was difficult, to say the least. But plans there were, for the army, navy, and air force, the most vital perhaps being those of the land army, variously lettered A, *Abis*, et cetera, down through *Dbis*, E, and a draft F. Put together by the army staff with the collaboration of the Ministry of War (and later National Defense), the military districts (*régions*), the corps of engineers, the Ministry of the Interior and national police, and the railroads, these compendia succeeded one another as perceptions and conditions changed. With a worst-case premise of German and Italian belligerence, they also took account of possible German attack on the Low Countries and/or Switzerland and/or against one or more of France's eastern European clients. They were modified by directives to reflect changing political facts, the availability of new weapons, the anticipated moves of the enemy, the shifting attitudes of vulnerable third parties, and the dubious intentions and capacities of France's allies.[23]

But though they took account of possible assault on France through Belgium or Switzerland and of the possibility of moving forward into Belgium to defend France, essentially they were plans for the mobilization of the French Army and for repelling an invasion of France. Where an offensive into enemy territory was envisaged (as in Plan E, before the Anschluss, providing for the seizure of cities in central Italy while a curiously passive Germany was apparently failing to react), the conception did not survive the brutal facts of Hitler's seizure of territory in 1938. That summer, well before the Czech crisis, the French high command had prescribed preliminary operations on the eastern frontier, to be followed by methodical attacks on the unfinished Siegfried Line, and the ultimate occupation of Trier and Mainz, but *only* in the event of the Germans being solidly engaged on *their* eastern front.

With Czechoslovakia eliminated in March 1939 and the prospect of Poland being attacked, more narrowly circumscribed operations were laid down, along with a vaguely conceived eventual breakthrough.[24] Very largely, then, the military plans amounted to the detailed assembling and disposition of French forces in the initial phase of a war. The rest was very nearly silence. Why was this so? Who made these decisions?

The Constitution of 1875 declared that the president of the republic disposed of the armed forces. In fact, control of them and of their use devolved to the cabinet, with the three service ministers having direct responsibility in a formal way, and with very real authority in the hands of the civil and military functionaries of the ministries and the serving military chiefs and their collaborators. In theory there was close cooperation between the government and the military. From 1906, an interministerial *Conseil Supérieur de la Défense Nationale* (CSDN) grouped president and cabinet with the principal military chiefs as advisors. This clumsy body lost control of strategy to the military, and a new *Haut Comité Militaire* (HCM) in 1935 brought together the service ministers and their principal military advisors. In turn, this body handed over to a *Comité Permanent de la Défense Nationale* (CPDN) in 1936, presided over by the newly created minister of national defense. This CPDN had a still broader authority, encroaching on the old CSDN.[25] But the principal reality of the interwar years was the steady concentration of authority in the military advisors.

Though the 1938 *Loi sur l'Organisation de la Nation en Temps de Guerre* formally instituted overall civil direction of war, the military being consulted, with the mixed civil-military direction of events being assured by the CPDN in the guise of a wartime *Comité de Guerre*, the fact was that the civilian service ministers were not masters of the forces for which they nominally assumed responsibility. This had been clear during the struggles at the disarmament conference, where the French technicians had very much had their way and yielded little of substance. Inevitably, the growing complexity of armed forces worked against the politicians.[26] Though each of the services had a *Conseil Supérieur*, the minister in question did not enjoy an authority in it, though he made appointments to it. Moreover, the chiefs of each service were themselves considerably independent of it. (More important and more limiting to any one of them, from the planning point of view, was the informal meeting of service chiefs together with a high functionary from the Ministry of Foreign Affairs.)[27] In broad terms, then, it may be said that, despite the Constitution and subsequent legislation, a relatively small group of professionals, for whom their ministers took responsibility before parliamentary committees, determined much of the work of the preparation and the strategy of war.

III

They were by no means free agents. The limitations they had to reckon with were immense. These constraints were of a general, a military, a financial and industrial, a foreign policy, and a domestic and personal nature.

Among general limitations one may arbitrarily propose the trauma of 1914–18 and the postwar tides of pacifism and antimilitarism, and the socialism that often embodied aspects of both. The 1914–18 trauma followed from the extremely high loss of life, poignantly reflected in the drastically reduced numbers of the annual contingent during the *années creuses*, beginning in 1935.[28] The army had survived its difficulties with the republic before 1914; it was bitterly assailed for its wartime failures. Joffre had been given enough rope to hang himself; Nivelle committed professional suicide; Pétain and Foch more happily found a powerful master in the partnership with Clemenceau. But the losses and the opprobrium lived on with the glory: the army as hero and villain.[29] A wave of critical literature flowed through the 1920s; it was universal, but in France, with its demographic decline and its ruins, the reception was marked. Geneva was the symbolic home of the new pacifism and a revived antimilitarism.[30] Through the postwar years sounded the terrible expression, "we have been bled white." The implication was that no such effort could be mounted again. The sentiment eventually infused all parts of the political spectrum. "For us, war is the shedding of scarce and precious blood; it's the long martyrdom of French soil; and it's also the futile defense by fire and steel of human values that can be saved only by peace."[31] Politicians and politically sensitive soldiers could not afford to be impatient of such expressions. They were part of the prevailing climate of opinion, manifest everywhere in the village memorials. They sustained a kind of cult of the defensive.

From the first days of the peace, the high command had considered how best to protect the country again. In the debate that opened up, a decision emerged to do so with a line of permanent fortifications on the northeast frontier. The plans and purposes of what eventually became the Maginot Line changed many times, but the basic premise was that the next war would be much like the last, that the whole nation would again be mobilized. The object of the fortified regions was ultimately to permit that *couverture* behind which mobilisation in all its forms could be securely completed.[32] By 1927, the strategic conception squared with the perceived necessity to reduce military service to a period of one year.[33] The financial liability of permanent fortifications, becoming almost an end in itself and draining the professional army, did not square well with the need to train conscripts and modernize a vast aging complement of weapons. This contradiction had the effect of reinforcing the supposed lessons of the 1914–18 war. At best, it permitted the uncertain conception of a mass army sustaining the enemy's blows along the frontier, until, powerfully supported by artillery and armour, it could move out and forward in a methodically prepared battlefield.[34] But clearly, this mass army could not *all* be provided by France and her empire. General Eugène Debeney had laid it down that France should not risk decadence by entrusting her defense to others (he meant the increased use of North African and black troops), and Gamelin after him, refused a contest of effectives with Germany. The proposed solution was to meet quantity with quality.[35] The unspoken assumption was that without powerful allies France could not see it through.

It would be absurd to insist upon the purely defensive thought and capacities of the French Army before 1939. Motorisation and experiments with armour had their prophets and proponents (of whom Colonel de Gaulle was only one).[36] But armoured experiments seemed inconclusive if not discouraging. The lessons of Spain were read ambiguously; many believed that every tank generated a superior antitank weapon, and the preponderance of high command opinion was skeptical.[37] Above all, the psychological and historical burden of the initial defensive period of war, the long preparation following the breaking of some *attaque brusquée,* and the fear of being caught with substantial stocks of obsolete materiel—all deepened the cautious attitude, and reinforced the tendency to defer decisions about what might have to be done thereafter. Those more imaginative spirits, for instance, General Pierre Hering or General Pol Velpry (even, at moments, Gamelin himself) who emphasized the offensive phase, could not or would not prevail against the weight of opinion in the *Conseil Supérieur* and elsewhere.[38] "For us," Gamelin remarked, "it is not a matter of jousting but of well and truly winning the first battle without running risks, and in fighting with all our forces properly grouped."[39] That was in 1936. Over the next three years, no substantial change of outlook took place. Not surprisingly, but perhaps unfairly, the British, when they realized at last that Foch was dead, were taken aback. "The French," General Sir Edmund Ironside noted one month before war broke out, "have their Maginot Line and are absolutely cynical about other countries. . . .They intend to look after their own hides."[40]

A third area of limitations was economic, financial, and industrial. The cost of the line had been high. Though the great fortifications were in place on the northeast frontier, still in the 1930s more credits were requested for additional works and modernisation of the system.[41] France had moved through the 1920s with much outmoded materiel.[42] Whether Foch, Pétain, Debeney, or Weygand, the soldiers had clung to the expensive conscript system for a potential mass army which, in any event, republican ideology demanded. Budgetary deflation, 1931–32 and 1934, affected the forces. But thereafter large increases were voted, especially by the government of Léon Blum. By 1939, the military budget had almost quintupled since 1935 (in constant 1930 francs).[43] Notoriously, though the credits granted were less than the armed forces would have liked (as a consequence of pressure from the Ministry of Finance), still it was not always possible to spend what was provided.[44] Thus was created the apparent paradox of finance crying ruin, the soldiers crying penury, and the flow of materiel not matching the funds available.[45]

In part, this situation was owing to the almost inconceivably complicated procedures for design, testing, and adoption of weapons—the bureaucratic maze, the incessant search for improvement, the endless delays in placing orders.[46] In part, it was also owing to the lack of industrial capacity. French industrialists had not seized the opportunities opened to them by the return of the Lorraine ore fields. If the army was liable to the charge of losing its instinct for the offensive, heavy industry was also. The armaments industry had withered. Lacking domestic orders, it had not sought foreign markets aggressively. Perhaps it felt threatened, as apologists said, "with heavier and heavier taxes, with expropriation and nationalisation," while being "spied on at every turn by a horde of parliamentary carpers and journalists."[47] There was more truth in the fact that rearmament in France (as in Great Britain) began late, that the military were slow, hesitant, unsatisfactory clients, and that the state was a less than prompt paymaster. The result, however accounted for, was a paucity of modern materiel which weighed on everything from the supply of shoes and blankets to the long-delayed decision to create armoured divisions.[48]

If there were space here to turn seriously to the air force, the record would seem no better. The new Air Ministry entered the 1930s with a large obsolete force, espoused (like the British) the misleading obiter dicta of Douhet's true believers, spent little on research, read the news from Spain ambiguously, and only late in the decade began to concentrate on a strong fighter force.[49] The financial credits were there, the industrial potential was not, and much of what was produced was obsolete.[50] Air frames were unduly complicated, engines underpowered. In extremis, funds were expended for foreign purchases rather than invested in French plants, so imminent was the threat from Germany.

For one brief moment (December 1938–January 1939), there were attempts to obtain Daimler-Benz engines for Dewoitine aircraft, as a consequence of the air minister's approach to Charles A. Lindbergh, then ingenuously meddling on the European scene.[51] Like others, United States attachés watched the air force travail, concluding that "graft and crooked politics" were at work, judging "that no American Army officer could comprehend the intricate system of graft which is part of every phase of the industry." French critics confirmed the condition if not the cause. "We have indeed ordered 2000 modern planes," an officer wrote Jean Fabry, former minister of war, "but you would be astonished if you carried out a real inspection to register the number of combat-ready aircraft, that is to say with their cannon, machineguns and other equipment, or if you saw the state of our industrial manufacture," which, he said, was "heart-breaking."[52]

General Vuillemin's desperately gloomy prognoses before and after Munich (losses of 40 percent in the first month of war, 60 percent in the second) were well founded—despite his having been set up by Generals Ernst Udet and Erhard Milch during his inspection of the Luftwaffe in August 1938.[53] Whether all this weighed heavily on the army planners (who, the air force complained, had always treated them as a poor relation) might be hard to say. Years before, even so orthodox a soldier as Debeney had warned that the Maginot carapace was vulnerable from the air. "A time is

46

coming—it's even near at hand," he wrote in 1934, before the Luftwaffe officially existed, "when it will be the right thing to direct the bulk of our national defense efforts to the Air Force." But, he wondered, who would do this, who would say "That's enough concrete! Spread your wings"![54] After 1937, the air force ceased to be the poor relation; in the final years, large credits were available to it. In 1939, the manufacturing takeoff was steep, spoilt temporarily by the mobilisation and subsequent disarray late in the year.[55] Moreover, under Vuillemin and his powerful collaborators, Generals Jean Bergeret and Jean Mendigal, the emphasis shifted to fighters and, to some extent, cooperation with the land army.[56]

Were the soldiers convinced? Yes and no. Some were, some were not. The infantry was especially hard to convince. To Poland, and even beyond, it was believed, as the military attaché had reported late in the Spanish Civil War, that against well-dug-in troops, air attack, though "powerful," was "no longer infallible."[57] Always there was the assumption that on the well-organized battlefield no one ought to be caught out in the open. "What can aviation do against men sheltered in narrow trenches?" Gamelin asked at the CPDN, 24 February 1939. Attacking aircraft would have to fly low. "That," he remembered, "is how our planes in Morocco and the Levant were brought down by rifle fire."[58] The Moroccan and Syrian operations had taken place more than a dozen years before! In all, then, it is not clear that France's air weakness made the high command more defensive minded than it already was, nor, on the other hand, that the prospect of growing air strength encouraged it to contemplate great offensive operations more sanguinely. In this sense, the industrial weaknesses reflected in the state of the air force only underlined defensive attitudes deeply held.

A fourth category of factors weighing on the planners (and "fourth" by no means indicates its significance) was uncertain foreign policy. The intimate relationship of foreign and defense policies was axiomatic. The road away from 1918 was paved with sterile resolutions that France should have the army of its policy, or the policy of its army. Certain objective realities seemed immutable. Whatever the passing relationship with the Weimar Republic or even the Third Reich, Germany was the point of departure, the designated foe. No accommodations or initiatives, whether Locarno or the abortive Four Power Pact, altered the place Germany had in defense plans.

Italy was another case altogether. Its gravitation into the German orbit from 1935 on was a heavy blow, against which the army and the air force planned for the defense of the Southeast, Tunisia, and African colonies, and the navy for securing Mediterranean communications—for which, with the Royal Navy, it justifiably felt prepared. For the army, however, Italian belligerence had daunting strategic consequences, not least for precluding any link with an anti-German second front in eastern or southeastern Europe. After 1935, when the British virtually imposed the sanctions policy at Geneva, Franco-Italian relations were cool. Mussolini took a tough line on Mediterranean and imperial concessions from France, and France stubbornly resisted British pressure to appease. Gamelin was left with his hypotheses. French diplomacy could not, or would not, reduce the potential commitment. The general, however, took some comfort from his acquaintance with Marshal Pietro Badoglio—Gamelin's entourage believed Badoglio had "said he would resign rather than make war on France."[59] It was little enough. The French government and the anti-Fascist Foreign Ministry officials did nothing to diminish the defiant French mood or lessen Mediterranean anxieties.

Nor did French diplomacy have more success, try though it did, with Belgium. In October 1936, King Leopold proclaimed his country's neutrality. The Franco-Belgian military accord of September 1920 had already become a casualty of German resurgence, French weakness, British withdrawal, and the complex nationalities question in Belgium. From 1918 on, it was accepted that France would protect her exposed northern cities and industry, shorten her military frontier with Germany, assist the Belgian Army, and be in position later to advance into Germany by moving forward into Belgium once war came. King Albert was said to have concluded that all this was contrary to Belgian national interest, and Pétain to have declared that, invited in or not, France would nevertheless cross over.[60]

Leopold's actions, and the remilitarisation of the Rhineland in March 1936, compounded the French strategic dilemma and the plight of France's eastern clients.[61] Though secret Franco-Belgian military contacts were maintained, the king never relented and no solution was ever found. Repeatedly the French high command stated its opposition to risking an encounter battle by responding to a late invitation. The Belgian Army was helpless against the grim determination of Leopold and his authoritarian counsellor General Raoul Van Overstraeten to avoid any provocation of the Germans. The French could neither accept the prospect of remaining on their northern frontier while the map of Belgium was rolled up and the enemy approached Lille, nor obtain the military planning and prior access they needed to avoid a ruinous encounter on unprepared ground. A great question mark hung over the North.[62]

As for France's assorted, incompatible eastern allies, after 1934 they slipped steadily away (Rumania and Yugoslavia), or were abandoned (Czechoslovakia), or remained sullenly treaty bound (Poland).[63] Remilitarisation of the Rhineland and the Anschluss effectively doomed the French system. Munich was a catastrophy. Thereafter a powerful sentiment, shared but disavowed publicly by the foreign minister, proposed letting eastern Europe go.[64] The countervailing view, held by Daladier, the foreign ministry high functionaries, and much of the political world, prevailed. Moreover, in the spring of 1939, at precisely the moment when the ruin of the French system was dramatized by Hitler's entry into Prague, the British suddenly lurched forward to try to create a continental coalition. Paper guarantees aside, the situation was grave in eastern Europe, where the Third Reich had progressively established itself by economic means.[65] Neither France nor Great Britain had a solid purchase on Rumanians or Yugoslavs. They now offered credits and a trickle of military supplies. Sent out to see what could be done, General Maxime Weygand remained hopeful, but against the odds. King Carol told him, "I cannot let my country commit itself to a war which in a few weeks will end in the crushing of its army and the occupation of its territory; you see, given the current state of our forces, we cannot even defend ourselves!"[66] The Yugoslavs were as clear; they asked "that France understand (their) situation and not hold it against (them)."[67]

The sole hope for an eastern front to reduce the pressure on France lay with Poland. France's relations with her had deteriorated. Hostile to Czechoslovakia and having taken part of the spoil in 1938, the unpopular Poles were restored to some grace in Paris only by the new German threats and the British efforts to form up a front against Hitler. The final months of the peace were marked by Warsaw's calls for financial and material aid and the graceless cavillings of London and Paris about how much, how soon, and on what terms. In all this, Gamelin had played the diplomatic game, computing and revising what little could be done to supply France's frightened or truculent allies.[68] It is clear, however, that he had virtually written Poland off before the Germans struck. Ironside in London asked himself point blank: *"Is it worth while keeping afloat these weak allies or are we to concentrate on our own affairs and let these people take their chance?"* His conclusion, with which Gamelin might have agreed, was, "Undoubtedly the answer is Russia."[69]

The weeks had passed in a fantasy of western exhortations, hallucinatory Polish bravado, and desperate attempts to urge Poles and Rumanians to accept direct Russian assistance (which it is doubtful the Russians were seriously thinking of offering). To the eve of the Nazi-Soviet Pact, Daladier professed confidence that the USSR would help and that "the Poles would be only too pleased to accept Russian troops to assist them."[70] The Soviets knew better. "They look on us," the Soviet military attaché in Warsaw remarked, "as wild animals."[71] This seemed fair enough to some western observers. "An intelligent rabbit," the British foreign secretary noted, "would hardly be expected to welcome the protection of an animal ten times its own size, whom it credited with the habits of a boa constrictor."[72]

For years the French military had rebuffed Russian approaches for a convention. Unfavourable when not wholly opposed to the Franco-Soviet Mutual Assistance Pact of May 1935,[73] the high command had stalled the overtures while great Britain began to rearm. Successive military missions to the USSR in 1935 and 1936 had reported contradictorily, but it was clear that Gamelin and his collaborators had no great opinion of the Soviet capacity to help out in a European war.[74] Some believed that conflict would leave the Soviets, "in the manner of the United States in 1918, arbiter of the situation in a Europe exhausted by a struggle that Voroshilov contemplates pitilessly."[75]

As late as the spring of 1938, the French military attaché in Moscow was reprimanded for his optimistic estimates of Soviet strength.[76] During the September crisis Daladier mused that the only winners in a new war would be "the Bolsheviks," and that Napoleon's prediction would come true: "Cossacks will rule in Europe."[77] Horrified by the purges, appalled by the "mediocrity" of Soviet military literature, the French military was suddenly anxious in the summer of 1939 to "neutralize" the USSR. They appeared not to remember that it was they, quite as much as the politicians, who had created the situation in which ominous signs of a new Russo-German rapprochement grew clearer. In this way they had complicated the military problem immensely.[78] Some, like Weygand, Victor Schweisguth, and Alphonse Georges, were open in their ideological prejudices; some, like Gamelin, were circumspect and dilatory.[79] Their responsibilities, however, were the same. Like Daladier, they believed that "in the event of war, you could do without Russian help, but not without British...."[80]

Indeed, Great Britain was the essential element in French plans, the indispensable ally without whom no war plan after 1936 at the latest was even thinkable. For France, drifting through the 1930s, embattled but unyielding at the Disarmament Conference, conceiving but not sustaining an encirclement of Germany strategy in 1934, abandoned by the Locarno guarantors in 1936, and herself rebuffing proposals for a military accord with Moscow—France was politically overcommitted and militarily underdeveloped. Then quite suddenly Great Britain, after years of holding the French at arms length, began in the winter of 1938 seriously to contemplate a possible return to the Continent.[81] Not until five months before they led France into war did it become clear that the British were prepared to back the ramshackle coalition they were seeking to put together with a substantial land army. Their imperial responsibilities, their abiding memories of the western front, their pursuit of appeasement, and their fears for home defense had made them elusive. In seeking commitment from them, France had been rebuffed repeatedly. She did not give up because she could not.

Politically and diplomatically sensitive, Gamelin bided his time. But like the Daladier government, he made his wishes known, delicate matter though it was. On the eve of the decision to adopt conscription in Britain, still Sir Maurice Hankey was advising the Paris Embassy, "The French are a little overdoing the pressure about National Service . . . .Service people are beginning to say 'What right had these people to talk? They had spent all their money on funk holes (the Maginot Line) and grossly neglected the main offensive weapon of modern war, the Air Force!'. . .The situation is rather delicate. . .France had better soft-pedal a bit, especially in the press."[82]

It was Hitler, of course, who got serious Anglo-French staff talks going in 1939, despite British fears of French leaks. In light of the enormous military disasters in the offing, these slow and circumspect proceedings have an almost nightmarish quality about them. Even British soldiers registered their impatience.[83] But neither the diplomats nor the military had been able to bring the British fully on side until a profound domestic revolt sustained the changed view at the top that a perhaps mortal continental challenge must be taken up.[84] Not until the summer of 1939, after three rounds of staff talks, could the French military have some sense that their own plans were not (despite the United Kingdom's tiny army) more than hypothetical exercises. In the matter of Great Britain, it is not certain that the French had been derelict. They had had to be patient, even long suffering.[85] But finally they had obtained something like the formal commitments and exchanges they needed to give substance to their plans. "We have built up a strong alliance with France," Ironside noted, albeit with some exaggeration, "and the strategy of Great Britain in the West is, and always must be tied closely to that of France— subservient in fact."[86] By no means did everyone in Great Britain accept this point of view, but many did. At the Bastille Day parade in Paris that year, Winston Churchill, honoured guest but still private member of the House of Commons, remarked, "Thank God we've got conscription or we couldn't look these people in the face."[87]

IV

A fifth order of limitations on the planners lay in the province of personal, intraservice, interservice, and civil-military relations. Differences of character and outlook, as well as rival ambitions, made for inconclusive discussion, unresolved technical problems, and a policy of delay and *laissez-aller*. At the centre of this troubling phenomenon of unexpressed reservations, incomplete communication, uncertain contacts, and vague instructions stood General Gamelin. For there was, to use Colonel Pierre Le Goyet's expression, a *"mystère* Gamelin."[88] Notoriously, Gamelin did not have the army in his hands as Weygand had had before him.

Gamelin had been chosen as chief of the General Staff in 1931 by the politicians to balance the elevation of Weygand as *vice président du Conseil Supérieur*. On Weygand's retirement in January 1935, Gamelin had kept his post and been granted the vice presidency also. It was a reward for his amenability to political and financial realities, a mark of confidence. It did not increase the army's regard for him. His fate was to have as deputy Alphonse Georges, whose following was stronger, whose views on politics were more controversial and more outspoken, and whom he sought subtly to keep at a distance and even to diminish.[89] Intensely sensitive to the political dimensions of military appointment, Gamelin had also to tolerate troublesome political generals of another stamp, notably Victor Bourret, for long solidly lodged as Daladier's *chef du cabinet militaire*, a source of intemperate opinions and calumnies against those soldiers he dismissed as *"un bande de jésuites,"* an unhealthy influence on the minister.[90] Not surprisingly in such an atmosphere, the style of relations within the army was reserved, formal, distant, even embittered. It was mirrored in the proceedings of the *Conseil Supérieur*, in contemporary conversations and diaries, and it infused some part of the Riom trial proceedings after the defeat.

Gamelin was a kind of common denominator, a skilled survivor in the politico-military disputes of the 1930s, asserting himself indirectly, with his ear to the ground, fighting only those battles he had to, more concerned almost to acquire authority than forcefully to use it. He was, for instance, an opponent of Vuillemin's elevation to be head of the air force, he had reservations about his fitness for the post, but he seems to have spoken against him, once the choice was made, only in private.[91] It was not remarkable that Gamelin did not make more of the coordinating powers he was given in January 1938, as *chef d'état-major général de la Défense nationale.* Just as Daladier was the minister of national defense and of war without real control of the air and navy ministers (though his role as prime minister, too, vastly magnified his position), so Gamelin without a real national defense staff was circumscribed in his actions, even if he had had the will. Despite repeated calls for a centralized command (*un commandement unique*), the politicians (the air and navy ministers not least) refused to approve such a concentration of authority.[92] Vuillemin and his entourage not unnaturally resented Gamelin. And Admiral Darlan's prestige and independence were such that he was quite unlikely to permit any meddling in his affairs.[93]

Though Weygand said publicly in 1937 that "the collaboration between our *grands chefs* is perfect,"[94] he well knew it was not. The Conseil Supérieur de la Guerre (CSG) itself met infrequently, charged with technical questions. Stung by his having been isolated there years before when he alone supported the minister (Daladier) against Weygand and the other generals, Gamelin stood stubbornly by the letter of the law which charged him as vice président with the elaboration of plans.[95] He preferred to have as little as possible to do collectively with either the army generals or the commanders of the other two branches.

The vague solution of "coordinating powers" was in a way ideal for such a man, quite apart from the fact that no unified command was politically possible at the time. Foreign observers, such as the Americans, who initially believed that Gamelin's "authority will be greater than that possessed by any general officer in the last hundred years," soon discovered that in the navy, at least, they did not think the situation had changed (and did not intend that it should).[96] Thus it was that plans were prepared to considerable extent separately in the three services. Gamelin, it is true, was in theory privy to all (he appeared, for instance, at the *Conseil Supérieur de l'Air*), but the domains were largely distinct. And in the CSG itself, those generals who would one day exercise command in the field were all but excluded from the planning phase.[97]

The last allusion here must be to the civil-military relationship. Suspicions and grievances in this matter were ancient. Years before Weygand had his clashes with Joseph Paul-Boncour and Daladier over budgetary cuts and proposed reductions of the officer corps, the army exhaled its sense of being let down, disregarded, and then used by the politicians in order to "cover" the assault on national defense. At the 11 November ceremonies, it was said, the politicians shone in the front rows, the victorious generals were ranged unseen in the rear.[98] And the notorious battles in the years of deflation were not the end of it. In the 1936 Rhineland affair while the Foreign Minister Pierre-Etienne Flandin assailed the soldiers for their lack of "spirit," Gamelin found it "intolerable that people are saying that the military did not want to move on March 7," and asked the war minister, General Louis Maurin, to see to it that "in future political and military matters be submitted to the *Haut Comité Militaire* for discussion before being taken up by the Cabinet. . . ."[99] And although the partnership of Daladier and Gamelin lasted from the spring of 1936 to the spring of 1940, their relationship was neither close nor confident.[100]

A series of incidents occasioned lengthy periods when the general and the minister did not see one another. The refusal of special credits requested to meet fresh threats in the spring of 1938, quarrels about "political" appointments to the CSG and other high posts, led Gamelin to threaten resignation, from which course Pétain was said to have dissuaded him.[101] For his part, Daladier seems to have contemplated replacing Gamelin with Georges, despite the fact that Georges' political views were thought to be on the right, and that Gamelin had done nothing to conceal such intelligence from the minister.[102] In the event, no change intervened. Gamelin had his political friends, not least in the Radical Socialist party and on the moderate right. Even if the political will had existed, reform would have been difficult. War found the civil-military relationship still sensitive, unconducive to frank and unbridled exchanges of views. The CPDN was never an effective instrument in this cause. Unlike the British with their Committee of Imperial Defence and the Defence Requirements Committee, or high civil servants such as Hankey or Sir Warren Fisher who played an intermediary role, the French had neither effective forums nor prestigious functionaries to try to bridge the two solitudes of the politicians and the military.[103]

V

Military planning in France before the war was incomplete. It may be judged to have failed the Clausewitzian test—but then so did that of every other belligerent. It certainly did not provide for "every aspect of war"; it perceived dimly the far distant "ultimate objective"; the men who went to war in 1939 were far from clear about what they intended to achieve and how they might achieve it. Planning covered principally the vital first phase of the defense of France. This could perhaps not have been otherwise, for reasons we have suggested. If France's armed forces were to have a larger mission beyond securing the metropolitan area and the empire (something questioned not only by civilians but by Admiral Darlan also), the conditions for it would have to be created in a later phase.[104] And even less did this depend on France alone. France alone had neither the effectives, the materiel, nor the necessary morale. Offensive operations could be undertaken by France and Great Britain only after a great economic, diplomatic, military, and psychological work of preparation had been accomplished; after France herself had fully recovered from the divisions of the depression and Front Populaire years;[105] after the blockade of Germany and perhaps the disposition of Italy one way or another; and after the harnessing of American industry had prepared the ground.

In August 1939, both Gamelin and Daladier thought they saw the elements of all this beginning to come together. But they believed equally that Germany was rapidly growing stronger and that in the short term her relative strength would increase. Thus they hoped to compel her to disperse and to undergo blockade. Their advice was that Hitler had bluffed, that he was still bluffing; but that even if he was not, still he had not attained his full strength. Time in the short term was working against the West.[106] Above all, the indispensable ally, though ill-prepared and almost totally dependent on the French Army to bar the road to the Channel, seemed determined to accept the German challenge and go to war. Taking advantage also of such resistance as might be mounted in the east, France must not let this last opportunity slip. "Consequently," Gamelin said, on 23 August 1939, "*France has no choice*: the only solution to consider is to keep our undertakings vis-a-vis Poland. . . ."[107] The military consequences of all this stretched far over the horizon.[108] Not unreasonably, the planners had only hinted at such a vast new *guerre des masses* and politicians dared not whisper its name.

Notes

1. Capitaine breveté Gamelin, *Etude Philosophique sur l'art de la guerre (essai de synthèse)* (Paris, 1906), p 25.

2. Carl von Clausewitz, *On War*, ed. and trans. by Michael Howard and Peter Paret (Princeton, 1976), p 579.

3. Not even A. J. P. Taylor, *The Origins of the Second World War* (London, 1961).

4. "I spoke up," the Air Minister, Guy La Chambre, explained during the Riom interrogation, "because General Vuillemin did not like speaking in public, but everything I said was agreed with him, since we had just had a long talk about the situation." (21 Dec 1940). Archives Edouard Daladier (hereafter AED), 4 DA 30/Dr 1/sdr b, Fondation Nationale des Sciences Politiques.

5. Darlan, his navy undefeated and himself a member of the marshal's government, was not in the dock. His assassination on Christmas eve, 1942, precluded any role in the later inquiries into the defeat. (On the navy see William Gregory Pereth, "French Naval Policy and Foreign Affairs, 1920–1939," Ann Arbor: University Microfilms, 1977.) Darlan's own judgment of his handiwork was naturally uncritical: "When one considers the naval strength of France at the declaration of war [sic] in 1939, the *perfection* of the Fleet's organisation and its effectiveness, one can say that the credits allotted the Marine (21 percent of the total for national defense, 1929–39) were not only well administered but well used." (Alain Darlan, *L'Admiral Darlan parle* (Paris, 1953), p 42.)

6. Procès-verbal de la réunion tenue au Ministère de la Guerre le 23 août 1939 *à* 18 heures sous la Présidence de Monsieur Edouard Daladier. (This is copy no. 1; AED, 4 DA 3/Dr 5.) See Gamelin's insistent denial of the validity of Decamp's notes as minutes of the meeting (Riom, 28 Sep, 28 Nov 1940; AED, 4 DA 24/Dr 5/ sdr a). Reproduced with his commentary, the "minutes" are in Maurice Gamelin, *Servir*, 3 vols (Paris, 1947), I:29–37. See La Chambre's explanation at Riom, 21 Dec 1940 and his Note sur la Réunion du 23 août (25 Dec 1940), *ibid*, 4 DA 30/Dr 1/ sdr b; and Vuillemin's explanation of his silence and subsequent cautionary letter to the Minister, 27 Jul 1941, *ibid*, 4 DA 23/Dr 3/ sdr b. See also Georges Bonnet's note for Aug 23, as revealed at Riom, Extrait des Notes prises par le Ministre des Affaires Etrangères du 3 juillet au 3 septembre 1939, Fonds Léon Blum, 3 BL2/Dr 5/sdr b, Fondation Nationale des Sciences Politiques. It would seem to have been Bonnet who leaked the Decamp document to *Nouveaux Temps*, which published it 12 Apr 1941. General Jules Decamp, who took the notes as Daladier's chef du cabinet militaire, explained himself and the document at Riom, 5 Oct 1940, 24, 26 May 1941, *ibid*, 4 DA 14/Dr 1. Bonnet's postwar accounts of the meeting constitute a tendentious melange of fact and fancy: *Défense de la paix*, 2 vols. (Geneva, 1946–48), II:299–314, *Quai d'Orsay* (London, 1965), p 253–56, *Dans la tourmente, 1938–1948* (Paris, 1971), p 166–69.

7. Gamelin, *Servir*, I:35.

8. Lucien Lamoureux, Notes de guerre (3 septembre 1939). I owe this reference to the kindness of Mr Lamoureux who communicated his journal to me many years ago.

9. Gamelin to Daladier, 18 mai 1940, 1011 Cab/FT, Service Historique de l'Armée de Terre (hereafter SHAT), 27 N 12, reproduced in Gamelin, *Servir*, III:421–27. The report was in fact drafted by Commandant Jacques Minart, then at Gamelin's headquarters, to whom I am indebted for showing me the original typescript bearing Gamelin's manuscript alterations.

10. Propos recueillis de la bouche du General de corps d'Armée Decamp. . .le 25 avril 1945 au SS Kommando d'Eisenberg (Sudetenland) où il était interné, Fonds Weygand, SHAT, 1 K 130/Dr 25/ sdr 2. There are some errors in this account, but the general outline is correct. Decamp accompanied Daladier to the meeting, 18:20 to 19:30 hrs. See the Notes for that day in Fonds Gamelin, SHAT, 1 K 224, also *Servir*, I:7, III:416–18.

11. *Servir*, I:7, III:418. The irony of course was that as chief of state, Pétain later imprisoned Gamelin, put him on trial, and when the Riom proceedings were shut down at Hitler's direction, kept him incarcerated until the Germans took him away in 1944. He was liberated by the allied armies in 1945.

12. See André Armengaud, *La Population française au XIXe siècle* (Paris, 1971), *La Population française au XXe siècle* (Paris, 1965).

13. See Richard D. Challener, *The French Theory of the Nation in Arms, 1866–1939* (New York, 1955); J. Monteilhet, *Les Institutions militaires de la France 1814–1932: De la paix armée à la paix desarmée* (Paris, 1932), pp 109ff; David B. Ralston, *The Army of the Republic: The Place of the Military in the Political Evolution of France, 1871–1914* (Cambridge, Mass., 1967); Douglas Porch, *The March to the Marne: The French Army 1871–1914* (Cambridge, 1981).

14. See Eugen Weber, *The Nationalist Revival in France, 1905–1914* (Berkeley, 1959); Samuel R. Williamson, Jr., *The Politics of Grand Strategy: France and Britain Prepare for War, 1904–1914* (Cambridge, Mass., 1969); John C. Cairns, "International Politics and the Military Mind: The Case of the French Republic, 1911–1914," *Journal of Modern History*, 25 (1953), 273–85, "Politics and Foreign Policy: The French Parliament, 1911–1914," *Canadian Historical Review*, 34 (1953), 273–85.

15. Armengaud, *Population française au XXe siècle*, pp 15–68, and "La population," in Alfred Sauvy, *Histoire économique de la France entre les deux guerres*, 4 vols (Paris, 1965–75), III:17–46.

16. Armengaud, *Population française au XXe siècle*, p 25. Jean Perré states that of 45,000 officers mobilized, 12,350 were killed (27.45 percent); and of 7,100,000 all other ranks mobilized, 1,375,000 (19.1 percent), "Les officiers de carrière et la nation," *Écrits de Paris*, Feb 1957, p 52.

17. Alfred Fabre-Luce, *Le Secret de la République* (Paris, 1938), p 11.

18. Melvin P. Leffler, *The Elusive Quest: America's Pursuit of European Stability and French Security, 1919–1933* (Chapel Hill, 1979), p 362.

19. See Judith M. Hughes, *To the Maginot Line: The Politics of French Military Preparation in the 1920s* (Cambridge, Mass., 1971), pp 21ff. Of the immense recent literature on the 1920s one may usefully cite Stephen A. Schuker, *The End of French Predominance in Europe: The Financial Crisis of 1924 and the Adoption of the Dawes*

Plan (Chapel Hill, 1976); Jacques Bariéty, *Les Relations franco-allemandes après la première guerre mondiale* (Paris, 1977); Walter A. McDougall, *France's Rhineland Diplomacy, 1914–1924: The Last Bid for a Balance of Power in Europe* (Princeton, 1978); Marc Trachtenberg, *Reparations in World Politics: France and European Economic Diplomacy, 1916–1923* (New York, 1980); Jon Jacobson, *Locarno Diplomacy: Germany and the West, 1925–1929* (Princeton, 1972); Colonel François-André Paoli, *L'Armée française de 1919 à 1939* 4 vols (Vincennes, n.d.), III, *Le Temps des compromis.*

20. Paoli, *L'Armée française*, III:51–119; Robert J. Young, "Preparations for Defeat: French War Doctrine in the Inter-War period," *Journal of European Studies*, 2 (1972), 155–72.

21. See Maurice Vaisse, *Sécurite d'abord: la politique française en matière de désarmament, 9 decembre 1930 –17 avril 1934* (Paris, 1981); Edward W. Bennett, *Germany and the Diplomacy of the Financial Crisis, 1931* (Cambridge, Mass., 1962), and *German Rearmament and the West, 1932–1933* (Princeton, 1979).

22. Gerhard L. Weinberg, *The Foreign Policy of Hitler's Germany*, 2 vols (Chicago, 1970–80); J.B. Duroselle, *La Decadence 1932–1939* (Paris, 1979); Anthony Adamthwaite, *France and the Coming of the Second World War* (London, 1977); Robert J. Young, *In Command of France: French Foreign Policy and Military Planning, 1933–1940* (Cambridge, Mass., 1978).

23. Lieutenant Colonel Henri Dutailly, *Les Problèmes de l'Armée de terre française (1935–1939)* (Paris, 1980), pp 92–114, 303–06.

24. Dutailly, *Problèmes*, pp 100–11.

25. Frederick L. Schuman, *War and Diplomacy in the French Republic* (New York, 1931), pp 341–45; Paoli, *L'Armée française*, III:134–36; Dutailly, *Problèmes*, pp 26–29. See especially, Commandant Jean Vial, "La défense nationale: son organisation entre les deux guerres," *Revue d'histoire de la Deuxième guerre mondiale*, 18 (1955), 11–20.

26. Vaisse, *Sécurite d'abord, passim*; Philip Charles Farwell Bankwitz, *Maxime Weyand and Civil-Military Relations in Modern France* (Cambridge, Mass., 1967), pp 67ff. On the 1938 Law, see Challener, *Theory of the Nation in Arms*, pp 184–214.

27. Dutailly, *Problèmes*, pp 28–29.

28. Paoli, *L'Armée française*, Vol IV: *La Fin* des illusions, 54–60; Dutailly, *Problèmes*, pp 207–26.

29. Jere Clemens King, *Generals and Politicians: Conflict between France's High Command, Parliament and Government, 1914–1918* (Berkeley, 1951), and *Foch versus Clemenceau: France and German Dismemberment, 1918–1919* (Cambridge, Mass., 1960); Jacques Nobécourt, *Une histoire politique de l'armée: de Pétain à Pétain 1919–1942* (Paris, 1967); Paul-Marie de la Gorce, *The French Army: A Military-Political History* (New York, 1963), pp 93ff.

30. Substantial work on French pacifism remains to be done. The memoirs of André Delmas are suggestive, *A gauche de la barricade: chronique syndicale de l'avant guerre* (Paris, 1950); Jean Rabaut, *L'Antimilitarisme en France 1810–1975: faits et documents* (Paris, 1975), pp 135–77 is very light-weight; cf. the interesting passages on veterans' pacifism in Antoine Prost, *Les Anciens combattants français 1914–1939*, 3 vols (Paris, 1977), III:77–119.

31. Fabre-Luce, *Secret de la République*, p 198; Delmas believed that on the eve of war the army was making its influence felt through the reserve officers, *A gauche de la barricade*, pp 198–99.

32. Paul-Emile Tournoux, *Haut commandement, gouvernement et défense des frontières du Nord et de l'Est, 1919–1936* (Paris, 1960), *passim*; Jacques Minart, *Le Drame du désarmement français (1918–1939)* (Paris, 1959); Paoli, *L'Armée française*, III:104–119; Robert Allen Doughty, "The Evolution of French Army Doctrine, 1919–1939" (Ann Arbor: University Microfilms, 1979), pp 111–50.

33. An opponent of the one-year law quoted General Hans von Seeckt as saying, "On the first day of the war, unleash the Reichswehr among the French militia in the process of concentrating, and you will have unleashed a bulldog [sic] in a china shop." General Brindel, "La nouvelle organisation militaire," *Revue des deux mondes*, 1 Jun 1929, p 501.

34. Paoli, *L'Armée française*, Vol IV:32–145; Doughty, "Evolution of French Army Doctrine," pp 151–214.

35. Paoli, *L'Armée française*, Vol IV:78–83; Dutailly, *Problèmes*, pp 215, 221.

36. Ladislas Mysyrowicz, *Autopsie d'une défaite: origines de l'effondrement militaire française de 1940* (Paris, 1973), pp 101–64; Doughty, "Evolution of French Army Doctrine," pp 215–86; Dutailly, *Problèmes*, pp 142–59; Jeffrey Johnstone Clarke, "Military Technology in Republican France: The Evolution of the French Armored Force, 1917–1940," (Ann Arbor: University Microfilms, 1969), pp 107ff; Joseph David Connors, "Paul Reynaud and French National Défense, 1933–1939," (Ann Arbor: University Microfilms, 1977).

37. Mysyrowicz, *Autopsie*, pp 140–43.

38. Dutailly, *Problèmes*, pp 173–4.

39. Extract from Procès-verbal, Séances d'étude du C.S.G. des 14 et 15 octobre 1936, Papiers Paul Reynaud 1927–1942, Ministère des Affaires Etrangères (hereafter MAE).

40. Edmund Ironside Diary, 31 Jul 1939. The late Field Marshal Lord Ironside gave me full access to his diary many years ago.

41. Dutailly, *Problèmes*, pp 166–73; Robert Frankenstein *Le Prix du réarmement français* (Paris, 1982), pp 46, 49, 53–54.

42. General Louis Colson, chef de l'état-major de l'Armée, said that from 1919 to 1930 no serious outlays were made for armaments, save in the matter of fortifications. "Coup d'oeil Retrospectif sur les Armaments Français de 1919 à 1939," Fonds Gamelin, SHAT, 1 K 224, carton 7.

43. Robert Frankenstein, "A propos des aspects financiers du réarmament français (1935–1939)," *Revue d'histoire de la Deuxième guerre mondiale* 102 (1976), pp 1–20, *Le Prix du réarmament*, pp 15–42; Dutailly, *Problèmes*, pp 117–38.

44. Frankenstein, "A propos des aspects financiers," pp 15–18.

45. For example, the discussion between Robert Jacomet, secretary-general of the national defense ministry, and the chiefs of staff on the 1939 figures: the services

ısked for 31,000,000,000 francs; the Prime Minister and the Minister of Finance asked
hat this be reduced to 20,000,000,000. Procès-verbal de la Réunion des Chefs d'Etat-
Major Général du 25 novembre 1938, Service Historique de la Marine, 1 BB2 201.
Four months later, the Minister of Finance, Paul Reynaud, wrote to Daladier to say
ne was worried by extraordinary estimates up from 24,000,000,000 francs to
32,000,000,000, and, if the Air Ministry's recent request for 5,000,000,000 were
added, to 37,000,000,000—a "large, almost monstrous" increase which "threatens to
bring down the whole structure." Reynaud to Daladier, 24 Mar 1939, AED, 2 DA 4/
Dr 4/ sdr d.

46. Dutailly, *Problèmes*, pp 125–31.

47. Robert Darcy, *Oraison funebre pour la vieille armée* (Paris, 1947), p 40; cf.
Frankenstein, *Le Prix du réarmament*, pp 221–69.

48. "If the Germans had attacked in September (1939), a single great battle
would have cleaned us out of munitions," Weygand noted in his *cahiers*, Jacques
Weygand, *Weygand mon père* (Paris, 1970), p 264 fn. "Industrial mobilization has
been completely bungled," Raoul Dautry, the new Minister of Armaments, said 14
Dec 1939. "Nothing had been done although everything has been foreseen. . . ."
Jacques Bardoux, *Journal d'un témoin de la Troisième: Paris-Bordeaux-Vichy, ler
septembre 1939–15 juillet 1940* (Paris, 1957), p 148. For a more formal indictment and
catalogue of deficiencies, see Dautry to Daladier, 1 Jan 1940, AED, 4 DA 13/Dr 5; cf.
Frankenstein, *Le Prix du réarmament*, pp 271–88.

49. Robert W. Krauskopf, "French Air Power Policy, 1919–1939," (Ann
Arbor: University Microfilms, 1965), *passim*; Charles Christienne, et al, *Histoire de
l'aviation militaire française* (Paris, 1980), pp 209–343. As late as March 28, 1939, the
Conseil Supérieur de l'Air approved the creation of a 2–3 seat fighter for the
protection of bombers. Service Historique de l'Armée de l'Air, 2 B 181.

50. Mysyrowicz, *Autopsie*, pp 165–98; Pierre Le Goyet, "Evolution de la
doctrine d'emploi de l'aviation française entre 1919 et 1939," *Revue d'histoire de la
Deuxième guerre mondiale*, 73 (1969), pp 3–41; Patrick Fridenson and Jean Lecuir,
La France et la Grande Bretagne face aux problèmes aériens (1935–mai 1940)
(Vincennes, 1976), pp 10–22, 31–45; Robert J. Young, "The Strategic Dream: Air
Doctrine in the Inter-War Period, 1919–1939, "*Journal of Contemporary History*, 9
(1974):57–76; Jean Truelle, "La production aéronautique militaire française jusqu'en
juin 1940," *Revue d'histoire de la Deuxième guerre mondiale*, 73 (1969): 75–110;
Joseph Roos, "La bataille de la production aerienne," *Icare*, 59 (1971):44–53. It is not
much remembered that the manufacturer who provided high performance aircraft for
the late twentieth century's incessant wars in the Middle East was then responsible for
the Bloch "flying coffins" of the 1930s. Christienne, et al, *Histoire*, p 310.

51. Paul Stehlin, *Témoignage pour l'histoire* (Paris, 1964), pp 128–30; *Berlin
Alert: The Memoirs and Reports of Truman Smith*, ed. Robert Hessen (Stanford,
1984), pp 139–41; Charles A. Lindbergh, *The Wartime Journals of. . .*(New York,
1970), pp 120–48. It was of course at that moment that the first big aircraft orders
were about to be placed in the United States. See extracts from the minutes of the
CPDN, 5 Dec 1938, AED, 4 DA 6/Dr 3/ sdr a, and especially John McVicar Haight,
Jr., *American Aid to France, 1938–1940* (New York, 1970), pp 3–131.

52. Lieutenant Colonel Sumner Waite to Assistant Chief of Staff G–2
Washington, Paris Jan 16, 1939, Report 24,760–W, Modern Military Records
Division, France, 20811492/G, National Archives: Commandant Garsonnin to
Colonel Jean Fabry, 26 Jan 1939, Fonds Fabry, SHAT, 1 K 93. In London, the
secretary of state for air told the cabinet that Guy La Chambre's account of these

things during his visit had been "a depressing affair." 5 Apr 1939, 18(39) Cab 23/98, Public Record Office (hereafter PRO).

53. On Vuillemin's visit, see his report, 2 Sep 1938, *Documents diplomatiques français*, 2e série (hereafter *DDF*), X (Paris, 1976), 537, where he says, somewhat ingenuously, "One may conclude that in the short time available to us, nothing was overlooked in order to show us 'the strength of German aviation'." Indeed. See also Vuillemin to La Chambre, 26 Sep 1938, *DDF*, XI (Paris, 1977), 377; Stehlin, *Témoignage*, pp 86–91; David Irving, *The Rise and Fall of the Luftwaffe: The Life of Luftwaffe Marshal Erhard Milch* (London, 1973), p 63.

54. Eugène Debeney, "Nos fortifications du Nord Est," *Revue des deux Mondes*, 15 Sep 1934, p 261. Four years later, Gamelin seemed to be that man: "Altogether, in the general design of our armaments, we must reserve the preponderant portion for our Air Force and our antiaircraft weapons. . . ." Note sur la situation actuelle, 12 Oct 1938, 853/DN 3, enclosed with Gamelin to Vuillemin, 14 Oct 1938, 864/DN 3, SHAA, 2 B 99.

55. Truelle, "La production aéronautique," pp 75–110; Raymond Danel, "L'Armée de l'Air française à l'entrée en guerre," *Revue d'histoire de la Deuxième guerre mondiale*, 73 (1969), 111–16; Frankenstein, *Le Prix du réarmament français*, pp 264–69.

56. Christienne, et al, *Histoire*, pp 315–26.

57. Bulletin journalier d'information pour le Maréchal Pétain, 23 Aug 1938, sent out by Daladier's military secretariat, based on the military attaché's report of 10 Aug 1938. Archives du Cabinet du Chef de l'Etat, Archives Nationales, AGII 12. In an earlier report Lieutenant Colonel Morel had been clearer on the matter: "The effect of an enormous mass of explosives is very great even on a very level-headed man." Morel to Daladier, Barcelona, 22 Oct 1937, #536/A, SHAA, 2 B. An undated (perhaps 2e Bureau) report was generally optimistic and inclined to see Spain as an exceptional case: "*One must guard against too swiftly generalizing about the air lessons of the Spanish war. Most of them do not seem adaptable without modification to a future war between the great European powers.*" Les enseignements des guerres d'Espagne et de Chine en ce qui concerne l'Aéronautique, n.d., SHAA, 2 B 76.

58. Extracts from the minutes of the CPDN, 24 Feb 1939, AED, 4 DA 4/ sdr d. Lieutenant Colonel Paul de Villelume, a member of the French delegation to the League, remembered being sent back to Paris during the September crisis to sound out Gamelin on the chances if it came to war over Czechoslovakia. The general said that though it would be difficult, he was sure of beating Germany. Villelume spoke of the terrible air inferiority. Gamelin pointed to his office window, streaked by rain: "If we have this kind of weather for the first three weeks, will aviation matter?" MS note, "Gamelin," 6 Feb 1942, Archives Paul Reynaud, Archives Nationales, 74 AP 23. On Gamelin's responsibilities for insufficient air strength, see Le Goyet, *Mystère Gamelin*, pp 93–101.

59. Victor Schweisguth, memento, 9 Nov 1935, Archives Victor-Henri Schweisguth, Archives Nationales, 351 AP 2, 1 Sc/Dr 6. Gamelin had been head of the French military mission when Badoglio was ambassador in Rio de Janeiro; they had maintained "close and confident relations" thereafter. Gamelin, *Servir*, II:162–3. Both the Italian military attaché in Paris and the Marshal were reported by Count Ciano in early 1940 as being impressed with French defenses. *The Ciano Diaries, 1939–1943*, ed. Hugh Gibson (New York, 1946), pp 201, 245.

60. See in general Jean-Marie d'Hoop and Jacques Willequet, "Première période, mars 1936–3 septembre 1939," *Les Relations Franco-Belges de mars 1936 au*

10 mai 1940 (Paris, 1968), pp 17–42; Raoul Van Overstraeten, *Au service de la Belgique. Dans l'étau* (Paris, 1960), pp 25, 38. Pétain had always opposed fortification of the northern frontier. The "true military frontier," he said, was "the Ardennes, the Meuse, and the Albert Canal as far as Antwerp." Paul Claudel to Alexis Léger, Brussels, 23 Mar 1934. *Honneur à Saint-John Perse* (Paris, 1965), pp 711–12.

61. Le Goyet, *Mystère Gamelin*, pp 217–24.

62. See David Owen Kieft, *Belgium's Return to Neutrality* (Oxford, 1972). It was agreed in 1937 that "we can no longer help the Belgians in good time for we should have to enter a priori....," Grand Rapport, 6 Apr 1937, Archives Schweisguth, 351 AP 3, 1 Sc 2/Dr 12. But the hope that the Belgians would change their mind persisted. "Gamelin," Ironside noted on the eve of war, "does not propose to accept battle other than on a prepared position." Ironside Diary, 16 Aug 1939. In the event, of course, he went forward to an encounter battle because he had no choice.

63. See Piotr Wandycz, *France and Her Eastern Allies, 1919–1925: French-Czechoslovak-Polish Relations from the Paris Peace Conference to Locarno* (Minneapolis, 1962); Anthony Tihamer Komjathy, *The Crises of France's East Central European Diplomacy 1933–1938* (Boulder, 1976); Anna M. Cienciala, *Poland and the Western Powers 1938–1939: A Study in the Interdependence of Eastern and Western Europe* (London, 1968).

64. "Persistence of the feeling in influential circles that after all France should abandon central and eastern Europe to Germany, trusting that eventually Germany will come into conflict with the Soviet Union, and that France will remain behind the Maginot Line." Edwin C. Wilson to Cordell Hull, Paris, 24 Jun 1939, *Foreign Relations of the United States. Diplomatic Papers*, 1939, Vol I (Washington, 1956), p 194. Bonnet was to be seen both backing away from and affirming the eastern obligations at the Senate Foreign Affairs Committee, 7 Oct 1938.

65. See David E. Kaiser, *Economic Diplomacy and the Origins of the Second World War: Great Britain, France, and Eastern Europe, 1930–1939* (Princeton, 1980).

66. Adrien Thierry to Bonnet, Bucarest, 6 May 1939, Ministère des Affaires Etrangères (in the papers collected by the committee publishing the Foreign Ministry documents on the origins of the 1939 war); Rapport du Général Weygand sur sa mission à Bucarest, 7 May 1939, *ibid*.

67. Captain de Frégate Pol Lahalle to Ministry of Marine, Athens, 27 Apr 1939, #66, SHM, II BB7 L.5.

68. "For the moment we have the most urgent need of all our production for our land and air forces." Gamelin to Daladier, 12 Apr 1939, *DDF*, XV (Paris, 1981), #416. Faced with requests for aid from Poland, Rumania, Yugoslavia, Greece, and Turkey totalling 2,060,000,000 francs, Gamelin noted, "I am not of opinion to agree right now to give credits in that amount but to proceed by successive instalments." Gamelin to Daladier, 11 Aug 1939, #1657/DN 3 (papers of the committee publishing Foreign Ministry documents).

69. Ironside Diary, 15 Jul 1939 (underlined in red ink).

70. As recorded by the British War Minister, diary, 21 Aug 1939, *The Private Papers of Hore-Belisha*, ed. R. J. Minney (London, 1960), p 216.

71. General Musse to Daladier, Warsaw, 11 Jan 1939, *DDF*, XIII (Paris, 1979), #344.

72. Foreign Policy 1938–1939: An unpublished note. Hickleton Papers, A 4.410.12.1.

73. William E. Scott, *Alliance Against Hitler: The Origins of the Franco-Soviet Pact* (Durham, N.C., 1962); Patrice Buffotot, "The French High Command and the Franco-Soviet Alliance, 1933–1939," *Journal of Strategic Studies*, 5 (1982), 546–59.

74. See General Lucien Loizeau's account of his visit, "Une mission en U.R.S.S.," *Revue des Deux Mondes*, 15 Sep 1955, pp 252–76, and General Schweisguth's report on his, URSS. Manoeuvres de Russie Blanche de Septembre 1936: Rapport du Général Schweisguth, Chef de la Mission Française (5 Oct 1936), Archives Schweisguth, 351 AP 5, 2 Sc 2/Dr 7. Loizeau's report collided with the views of the army chief of staff, General Colson, conservative, defensive-minded, who seems to have prevented it from being read either by Gamelin or the minister of war, Jean Fabry. Dutailly, *Problèmes*, pp 35, 46, 49.

75. Schweisguth, Rapport.

76. See the stinging draft rebukes intended for General Palasse from General Henri Dentz, and the critical notes on Palasse's reports. SHAT, 7 N 3186.

77. Quoted by William C. Bullitt to Hull, Paris, 27 Sep 1938, *Foreign Relations*, 1938, I (Washington, 1955), p 687.

78. Weygand was a case in point: in 1932 he had been favourable to a Franco-Soviet pact; in 1934 he was not consulted about it; in 1936, before it was ratified by parliament, he spoke publicly against it. "In the event of war," he said in private, 28 Mar 1939, "I do not look to Russia for military assistance, but it is essential to neutralize her and to keep her apart from Germany. Communism should be fought on the internal plane, and I favour the suppression of the Communist party in France. On the external plane, ideology must not interfere with strategical needs." Record of Conversations, 28 Mar 1939, in W. H. B. Mack to Department, 11 Apr 1939, Foreign Office Records, FO 371/22969 C 5261/15/18, Public Record Office.

79. Schweisguth noted Georges' opinion that they should "be quit of the Franco-Soviet Pact and its consequences. He is worried about the progress of Communism, and the possibility of a general strike" which "could immediately be exploited by Hitler in a violent move." Memento, 22 Oct 1936, 351 AP 3, 1 Sc 2/Dr 10; Le Goyet, *Mystère Gamelin*, pp 196–216.

80. Schweisguth, memento, 19 Mar 1937, *ibid*, 1 Sc 2/Dr 12. In the summer of 1939, however, the French high command was more pressing than its British opposite number to get the military delegations to Moscow. After the painfully slow voyage on the *City of Exeter* to Leningrad (surer but still slower than the two ancient Handley Page Hannibals proposed as alternative transport), the French were nonetheless equally helpless in the face of Voroshilov's contemptuous dismissal of their empty, procrastinating briefs. (The treasury's later proposal that the French be asked to pay half the chartering costs for the Ellerman Line vessel was dropped as a dismal idea). Admiral Chatfield, Foreign Policy Committee, 1 Aug 1939, Cab 27/625, FP(36)60; Admiral Drax, Mission to Moscow August 1939, Drax Papers 6/5, Churchill College; General Joseph Doumenc, Compte Rendu d'Ensemble 23 août 1939, Souvenirs de la Mission en Russie, and other documents in SHAT, 7 N 3185; S. H. Wright to L. R. Sherwood, 7 Dec 1939, and minutes, FO 371/23074, C 19978/3356/18.

81. Brian Bond, *British Military Police between the Two World Wars* (Oxford, 1980), pp 287ff; Peter Dennis, *Decision by Default: Peacetime Conscription and British Defence, 1919–1939* (London, 1972), pp 127ff; Michael Howard, *The Continental*

Commitment: The Dilemma of British Defence Policy in the Era of the Two World Wars (London, 1972), pp 96ff.

82. Hankey to Phipps, 24 Apr 1939, Phipps Papers 3/3, Churchill College. The reality was that British consular officials, as well as the embassy, were reporting impatience with Neville Chamberlain's hesitation. "Some anti-British posters, saying that the French are being duped to fight for others, were put on the hoardings in Paris yesterday. . . ." Phipps to Halifax, 20 Apr 1939, FO 371/22932, C 5622/282/17. In the staff talks, General Lelong warned that the French populace might lose confidence and turn in fury on Great Britain if the expeditionary force were slow to arrive. London's offers "would not show a happy comparison with the effort which Great Britain made in 1914 and, from the point of view of morale, might have an unfortunate effect on French opinion." 7th Meeting, 3 Apr 1939, Air Ministry Papers, Air 9/104, PRO.

83. For example, Ironside, returning to the War Office from posting abroad: "From what I have seen of it, I now wish that I had been made C.I.G.S. The damned thing is too serious. (Viscount) Gort doesn't begin to realise the danger. He smiles and remains as brave as ever—and optimistic—but-that will not help us. . . .We are a damned lot of amateurs at war." Diary, 15 Jul 1939. "We have practically nothing ready. . . .It will be years before we have anything practical to show. And we still prate of Expeditionary Forces." *Ibid*, 7 Aug 1939.

84. See Sidney Aster, *1939: The Making of the Second World War* (London, 1973); Simon Newman, *The British Guarantee to Poland: A Study in the Continuity of British Foreign Policy* (London, 1976).

85. "In a word, my friend," the French naval attaché in London reported home, "France is going to have to put a little ginger into this English crowd. But we must not be too impatient. You alienate these too chilly people by seeming too excited: 'They are hysterical,' people said about France in September (1938). Doubtless this was an excuse because nothing here was ready at that time. They have certainly been working since. But you don't make good substantial arrears in six months, we ourselves know something about that." Captain de Vaisseau Denis de Rivoyre to Commandant Sanson, 22 Mar 1939, SHM, II BB7 L.5. In general, see François Bédarida, "La 'gouvernante anglaise'," in *Edouard Daladier chef de gouvernement, avril 1938–septembre 1939*, ed. Réne Rémond and Janine Bourdin (Paris, 1977), pp 228–40, and John C. Cairns, "A Nation of Shopkeepers in Search of a Suitable France, 1919–1940," *American Historical Review*, 79 (1974), 710–43.

86. "Strategic Paper Upon my Study of Plans as they exist" (probably July 1939), in Ironside Diary. More reflection brought a change of mood: "*We have no British view of our combined strategy.* We must get this. It is hopeless being overwhelmed by the French volubility of schemes—with their, often, very ineffective execution." *Ibid*, 16 Aug 1939. On the staff talks, see the papers in *Les Relations franco-britanniques de 1935 à 1939* (Paris, 1975).

87. Quoted in *Chief of Staff: The Diaries of Lieutenant-General Sir Henry Pownall*, ed. Brian Bond, 2 vols (London, 1972–73), I:213.

88. Le Goyet, *Mystère Gamelin, passim.*

89. See Pierre Lyet, "L'Organisation de commandement de 1935 au 25 juin 1940," SHAT, 1 N 47/dr 3.

90. Colonel H. H. Fuller reported Bourret as being of "considerable influence," and "more of a politician than a soldier." 14 Jun 1938, Report 24,348W, 2015–1017/42, National Archives.

91. "General Vuillemin," Gamelin is said to have stated, 24 May 1939, "is completely in the hands of his entourage. . . .I have proof of it." Quoted by General Henri Jauneaud, "Note concernant l'activité ministérielle de Monsieur Guy La Chambre," 31 Mar 1941, AED, 4 DA 15/Dr 4. Gamelin had opposed the choice of Vuillemin to head the air force, and had backed his rival General Henri Mouchard. *Servir*, II:319–29.

92. "If I was sure that they would maintain the three Staffs under a single Minister," François Piétri, former minister of the marine, wrote, "I would not say anything . . . But it is too much to be feared that the (Defense) Ministry's formula will lead inevitably to that of a single Staff, which, I tell you, is too dangerous." Letter to André Tardieu, 4 February 1937, Archives André Tardieu, 324 AP 13, Archives Nationales. Of the CPDN meeting, 15 December 1936, where mere "coordination" was accepted, General Georges later noted, "What a meeting. . .you would have to read the minutes to believe it." SHAT, 1 N 47/Dr 3.

93. On Gamelin's position, see Jean Vial, "La Défense nationale: son organisation entre les deux guerres," *Revue d'Histoire de la Deuxième guerre mondiale*, 18 (1955): 11–32.

94. Maxime Weygand, "Sécurite française," *Revue Hebdomadaire*, 6 Feb 1937, p 47.

95. "Don't you think it would be well to consult the Conseil Supérieur de la Guerre?" Daladier asked him during the Czech crisis. "About what, Prime Minister?" Gamelin replied. "Neither the matter of the operational plans, nor that of a declaration of war, has at any time been within its competence," *Servir*, II:344. On the 18 December 1933 CSG meeting, when Gamelin had been isolated, see *ibid*, 98–109 and Maxime Weygand, *Mémoires*, 3 vols (Paris, 1950–57), II:397, 402–05, and Philip Charles Farwell Bankwitz, *Maxime Weygand and Civil-Military Relations in Modern France* (Cambridge, Mass., 1967), pp 103–05.

96. Lieutenant Colonel Sumner Waite, Paris, 25 Jan 1938, Report 23, 991–W, 2015–1049/48; Lieutenant Colonel H. H. Fuller, Paris, 21 Feb 1938, Report 24,054W, 2015–1049/51.

97. Weygand said later that he had "feared" Gamelin's lack of drive," but had thought he would be shored up by the Army General Staff and the CSG. Le Général Weygand (by Jacques Weygand), 29 Dec 1944, SHAT, Fonds Weygand, 1 K 130/Dr 22.

98. See Lieutenant Colonel Frédéric Reboul, "Le malaise de l'Armée," *Revue des Deux Mondes*, 15 Mar 1925, pp 378–95; (Lucien Souchon), *Feue l'Armée Française* (Paris, 1929). "It was in mufti and swallowed up in the crowd," wrote Jacques Weygand, that the general "was present at the November 11, 1938 march past of troops before the Arc de Triomphe at the Etoile." Le Général Weygand, *loc cit*.

99. Schweisguth, Note, n.d. (probably April 1936), memento, 22 Apr 1936, 351 AP 3, 1 Sc 2/Dr 8.

100. On the higher officers' sense of social and intellectual superiority to politicians, Fuller, 21 Feb 1938, *loc cit*.

101. Typed copy of MS Note by Commandant Vautrin, 10–12 May 1938, Fonds Gamelin, 1 K 224; *Servir*, II:312–37; Weygand, *Mémoires*, II:388; General Colson noted that the Minister was unapproachable: "everything labelled 'Etat-Major' seemed to have been placed on the index before-hand. . . .Le drame de 1938–1940 vu du Ministère de la Guerre, SHAT, 1 K 274.

102. Memorandum, Hull to Roosevelt, n.d. (probably March 1939), PSF. I. Diplomatic Correspondence. France: Bullitt, 1936–1940, Franklin Delano Roosevelt Library; Jean Daridan, *Le Chemin de la défaite, 1938–1940* (Paris, 1980), pp 116–17.

103. See the discussion, in need of qualification and correction for France, in Donald Cameron Watt, *Too Serious a Business: European Armed Forces and the Approach to the Second World War* (London, 1975), pp 51–55; Young, *In Command of France*, pp 24–26.

104. "Are we going to pursue a foreign policy that makes us give ground every day and threatens to lead us to the loss of our Empire?. . . German ambitions do not directly threaten any of our interests. Italian ambition, on the other hand, threatens our territories and our vital interests. We must above all hold on to our Empire, the rest is of secondary importance." Note personelle de l'Amiral Darlan, 22 Jan 1939, *DDF*, XIII, #406. (Here may be glimpsed the suggestion of the policy he would support after June 1940).

105. The view that France under Daladier was in fact on the road to economic and political recovery may be found in *Edouard Daladier chef de gouvernement*, previously cited, and the companion *La France et les Français en 1938–1939*, ed. René Rémond and Janine Bourdin (Paris, 1978).

106. Hitler "does not yet have the means to risk a general war,". . .General Henri Didelet, military attaché in Berlin, reported. "The officer corps is not completely committed to the regime." National Socialism, however, was still making progress. "I think therefore that today time still works for Germany. . . ." If war must come in 1939 or 1940, "it would be more advantageous for us if it were in 1939." Didelet to Daladier, Berlin, 11 Apr 1939, *DDF*, XV, #351. It was the judgment of Colonel de Gaulle also that Hitler was bluffing "without wishing to fight, or at least for the moment." De Gaulle to Jean Auburtin, 7 Apr 1939, Charles de Gaulle, *Lettres, notes, et carnets*, 5 vols (Paris, 1980–82), II:484. On the theme of growing German strength 1938–1939, see Williamson Murray, *The Change in the European Balance of Power, 1938–1939: The Path to Ruin* (Princeton, 1984).

107. Procès-verbal, 23 Aug 1939, AED, 4 DA 3/Dr 5; *Servir*, I:33.

108. At the Anglo-French staff talks, General Lelong let slip, "at the end of three months, at a time when the Allies might reasonably be expecting to pass from the defensive to the offensive. . . ." 3rd meeting, 30 Mar 1939, Air 9/104. If he meant it, he was dreaming. The (translated) French paper, "The Strategical Problem Considered as a Whole for the Conduct of the War" (3 Apr 1939), offered no such timetable: three phases were identified: 1) holding and blockading the Axis, 2) knocking Italy out, 3) "The final object of the Allies is still a land offensive against Germany. In view of the magnitude of the resources which would be employed, no date and no possible lines of action can be fixed for this offensive." Air 9/112 AFC(J)27. Gamelin could not have been clearer. In general, see the discussion in Robert J. Young, *"La guerre de longue durée:* Some Reflections on French Strategy and Diplomacy in the 1930s," in *General Staffs and Diplomacy before the Second World War*, ed. Adrian Preston (London, 1978), pp 41–64.

Japanese Military Education
and Planning Before Pearl Harbor

Alvin D. Coox

War Plans and Hypothetical Enemies

For the major powers of the world—none of whom could avoid involvement in the Second World War—the roots of latter-day belligerence can be traced to the era of the Great War of 1914–18 and its aftermath. Insofar as Japan was concerned, the international environment had undergone enormous change.

Tsarist Russia and the House of Romanov had disappeared forever. Russian influence in East Asia was shattered, though geography dictated a continuing Russian presence in Siberia. From the ruins of Russia, a new state and an evangelical ideology had emerged: the Soviet Union and the Bolshevik manifestation of Marxism.

The Germans had been evicted from all their holdings in Asia. French and British global hegemony had been weakened. But American power and influence had soared, and Japan and the United States were at loggerheads over such problems as the disposition of the German possessions, economic and other claims in China, and the extent and objectives of intervention in the Russian Revolution. A costly and potentially dangerous naval race was well under way at the very time that the disturbing Japanese exclusion movement was growing within the United States.

After the Washington Conference of 1921–22, the twenty-year-old Anglo-Japanese military alliance—often called the linchpin of Japanese foreign policy—was sundered. Now, despite the supposed internationalism that was to supplant bilateralism, Japan envisaged the danger of Anglo-American collaboration; strategic thinking consequently underwent marked change in Tokyo.[1]

Armed forces, of course, would lose their credibility, their *raison d'etre*, and their sources of funding, if they lacked hypothetical foes. Before World War I, the Japanese Imperial Defense Policy contemplated that in the event of hostilities against the United States, the fundamental strategy would be defensive, and the Imperial Japanese Navy (IJN) would assume responsibility for commanding the waters of the western Pacific. Enthralled by the dream of winning another battle of Tsushima—the decisive big-gun naval clash of the Russo-Japanese War in 1905—Japanese naval strategists contemplated enticing the main U.S. battle fleet to fight—and be destroyed—in grand fleet maneuvers in the West Pacific.[2]

Against Russia, the Japanese wartime objective was to be accomplished by the Imperial Japanese Army (IJA) which would destroy enemy ground forces in a decisive campaign in Manchuria, while occupying the Russian Maritime Province and Sakhalin Island north of Hokkaido. In case of war against the Chinese, the IJA would occupy key areas in North and Central China. Thus, where the Japanese Army was concerned, Russia was the prime enemy from 1907 until 1918.[3]

With the end of World War I, the Japanese rearranged their roster of hypothetical foes, in terms of emphasis rather than strict numerical order. The most important modification of the national master plan was the prime operational priority now assigned against the United States, over the opposition of the Army, which knew that such a revision would mean a larger share of the defense budget would go to the very expensive Navy. The naval emphasis prevailed, however, although the Army was never as serious as the Navy concerning anti-American operations because hostilities in the near future did not appear to be realistic. Still, Army-Navy seizure of the Philippines, to deny advanced bases to the U.S. fleet, was included in Japanese contingency plans as early as 1918. As the years went by, the Army's peacetime operational planning became less abstract. For example, during the minor revision of the Imperial Defense Policy in 1923, after the Washington Conference, the Hiroshima Infantry Division (which possessed no specific operational mission until then) was assigned to train for a hypothetical campaign in the Philippines, and Guam was added as a target of invasion. But the eyes of the IJA were still mainly fixed on the Continent.[4]

By the late 1920s, the resurgent Soviet Union had proved to the Japanese that it was here to stay and was indeed revealing surprising economic strength and military capability in the Far East, as in the instance of the swift punitive operation launched by the Russians against Chinese forces in Manchuria in 1929. Even if the Japanese had wanted to ignore the Russians—which they did not, in view of their own aspirations on the Asian continent—the IJA now had to take the USSR into serious strategic account. After the Japanese Kwantung Army seized Manchuria in supposed defense of Japanese interests in 1931–32 and parented the satellite state known as Manchukuo, Japan's self-assigned defensive responsibilities now abutted Soviet Siberia and Mongolia. IJA war planners thereupon reverted to the traditional main anti-Russian emphasis.[5]

With respect to the Japanese Army, customarily the Army General Staff (AGS) drew up annual operational plans and submitted them to the Emperor for his *pro forma*, official sanction. In case of actual hostilities, the Army would conduct operations based upon the annual plan then in effect. Ever since the Russo-Japanese War of 1904–05, the Japanese military leaders may have been thinking in terms of strategic self-defense, but the details of their envisaged operations remained inflexibly offensive. In view of the relatively underdeveloped industrial and technological infrastructure, it followed that Japan must plan for a short war stressing opening moves and tactical execution; that is, surprise, provocation of early battle, and quick decision. There was no change in the fundamentals of this philosophy before 1941. Indeed, the security policy of 1936 underwent no further review. Overtaken by events in the next four or five years, it proved unhelpful and obsolete in terms of providing concrete guidelines for Japanese policymakers.[6]

Reflecting the Imperial Defense Policy laid down after World War I, the annual operational plans against hypothetical enemies were coded as follows:[7]

Operation KO (A) vs. the United States;
Operation OTSU (B) vs. the USSR;
Operation HEI (C) vs. China; and
Operation TEI (D) vs. Great Britain, the old friend and, after 1936, new enemy of Japan, to borrow the title of the last book by Arthur Marder.[8]

Thus, contingency plans were drafted against the Philippines under Operation KO and eventually against Singapore under Operation TEI. But there is a marked difference between the progress of Japanese anti-U.S. and anti-U.K. planning. Regarding the United States, the Japanese Navy particularly stressed the growing danger of American containment after the breakdown of the naval accords in 1935. The Japanese drew disquieting signals from the giant building program of the U.S. Navy, the major American maneuvers conducted near Midway, and the espionage reports on the top secret Orange War Plan. By 1936 the IJN had developed new contingency plans based on defense in the north, advance to the south.[9]

The interest of the Japanese Navy in Southeast Asia was bound to bring them into collision with the special interests of the colonial powers already ensconced there, mainly Britain and Holland. But though the IJN began to mention operations against the British starting with the annual operations plan of 1937, almost no concrete studies had been made and little military data had been collected. IJN planning merely laid down broad strategic objectives, such as securing control of the South China Sea and depriving the British of their footholds in Asia by reducing the bases at Hong Kong and Singapore. No detailed operational outline was decided upon, at least before 1939.[10]

Operational planning for a campaign against the Dutch in the East Indies emerged even later, in 1941, when a coordinated scheme of operations against the United States, Britain, and the Netherlands was finally devised.[11]

After the Japanese decision for war against the American, British, and Dutch (ABD) countries was reached in 1941, the Naval General Staff plunged into hostilities with what has been called remarkably little long-term planning. Whereas it is a principle of war to attempt to fight one enemy at a time if possible (which was a feature of the early Japanese Imperial Defense Policy), the Japanese high command defied this time-honored dictum with impunity in 1941. Bogged down in an undeclared but giant war with China since 1937, the Japanese tried to escape from the hole by widening it, as the saying goes. In other words, elimination of China's allies ought to eliminate China itself in due course.[12]

The last-minute nature of Japanese planning for the Pacific War is shown by the fact that, contrary to Allied impressions at the time, the IJA only got around to studying tropical warfare about ten months before the outbreak of the Pacific War and commenced the formulation of specific plans to seize Singapore merely three months beforehand.[13]

As for the Japanese decision to attack the Philippines simultaneously with the raid on Hawaii, Winston Churchill is known to have identified as his "greatest fear. . .the awful danger that Japan would attack British or Dutch possessions in the Far East, and would carefully avoid the United States, and that in consequence Congress would not sanction an American declaration of war." There is evidence that Roosevelt partook of Churchill's worry that the Japanese might choose to detour the Philippines and thereby taunt the Americans with the question of becoming directly involved in the hostilities of other countries in Southeast Asia.[14] After the war, Vice Admiral Ozawa Jisaburo explained the rationale that underlay the thinking of the Japanese high command: "If we tried to carry out an operation only against the Dutch and British, the chance the United States would intervene was too great. From that standpoint, I consider it was better to attack [both of] these major points."[15]

The balance-of-strength factor was very much on the minds of Japanese Army and Navy planners in 1940–41. Classified Japanese studies explicitly identified the country's vulnerability in shipping and natural resources, especially liquid fuel. Japan's outmatched economic and industrial capabilities warranted no confidence beyond two years of the beginning of a war against the West. In the event of initiating such a war, drawing on stocks of fuel available despite the drain of the continuing hostilities in China, the Japanese armed forces could expect to wage air operations for only about a year; at sea, decisive combat could be conducted for approximately a half year.[16]

These direct estimates explain the Japanese military leaders' advocacy of a thesis described as Japan's gradual decline. It was a well-known justification for undertaking war in 1941. The Navy, for example, warned that it was consuming oil at the rate of 400 precious tons per hour. At one of the almost interminable liaison conferences in the autumn of 1941 (the one which took place on 27 October), General Tojo (premier since the 18th) claimed that the IJA could "manage somehow" in 1942 and 1943 but admitted that "we do not know what will happen from 1944."[17]

At the liaison meeting of 28 October, the conferees seriously considered the idea of postponing hostilities until March 1942, but the armed forces' Chiefs of Staff insisted that time was working against Japan, and that the Navy in particular needed to get under-way by the end of November from the standpoint of resources. The study of viable alternatives was finally completed by 30 October. It was concluded, in essence, that although hostilities of course entailed risk, the cost of proceeding without war was prohibitive in terms of Japan's long-term position. Admiral Nagano argued vigorously at the 17–hour marathon session of 1 November that "the time for war will not come later!"[18]

Although each conferee at the climactic liaison meetings nurtured varying degrees of pessimism regarding the prospects of war with the West, the adamant stand of the hawkish elements caused a crystallization of consensus. As the deputy chief of the Army General Staff wrote privately, "One reaches the unavoidable conclusion that we must go to war."[19] The no-war option received short shrift.

On 5 November at an Imperial Conference (the nation's highest level meeting in the presence of the Emperor), the IJA spoke of needing fifty days to subdue the Philippines, one hundred days for Malaya, and fifty days for the Dutch East Indies—a total of five months for the entire campaign. Though Tojo observed that the early stage of hostilities posed no problem for Japan, he confessed that by 1943 there would be no petroleum for military use, and ships would stop moving. There was "no end of difficulties," but Tojo could think of no other method, given the present circumstances. "I fear," he said, "that we would become a third-class nation after two or three years if we merely sat tight."[20]

As for the Americans, they had their share of weaknesses: unpreparedness for operations in two oceans; incomplete strengthening of their domestic structure; shortages of materials for national defense—"they have only enough for one year." But at this Imperial Conference of 5 November, neither Tojo nor the other participants explored the key question of how the war could eventually be ended. Tojo's nearest reference was that if Japan were "fair in governing the occupied areas, attitudes toward us would probably relax. America may be enraged for a while, but later she will come to understand Japan's motivations."[21]

Japan's general war aims are to be found in the wording of the liaison conference's deliberations of 15 November: hasten the fall of the Chiang Kaishek regime; work for the surrender of Great Britain in concert with Germany and Italy; and destroy the will of the United States.

Swift conquest of Southeast Asia and the regions of the western and southwestern Pacific, entailing destruction of the enemy's bases, would ensure a strategically powerful stance with respect to raw materials and routes of transportation, and would lay the ground-work for a protracted period of self-sufficiency. The elimination of the preponderance of the U.S. Pacific Fleet would contribute to an American loss of fighting spirit and a desire to reach a negotiated settlement, leaving Japan in control of the main areas it had sought in the first place.[22]

The rubber-stamp Imperial Conference of 1 December 1941 met to review the failure of the negotiations with the United States and to approve hostilities against the western countries. Starting the war proved to be a relatively easy matter. This time, the only specific mention of the subject of ending hostilities, once begun, was made by Privy Council President Hara, who stated that early settlement of the fighting should be on the leaders' minds. Tojo's reply was cheerfully platitudinous. Though prepared for a long war, the government would seek to bring hostilities to an early conclusion, while striving to preserve public tranquility.[23]

These words obscured the fact that the Japanese had developed no feasible plans for bringing the war to an end, early or otherwise. It is true that the Liaison Conference of 15 November had drafted a "Plan for Accelerating the Termination of War Against the United States, England, and the Netherlands;" but the document was eyewash, "merely summing up Japan's one-sided wishful thinking," as an officer on the Army General Staff put it after the war.[24] Foreign Minister Togo used the word "carefree" to describe the attitude of the high command once the decision had been reached.[25]

The operational details of Admiral Yamamoto's strike plan against Pearl Harbor and of the Japanese Army and Navy campaigns against British, American, and Dutch holdings in Asia are well known, as are the details of Japanese perimeter construction. At this point, one need only mention the larger reasons why the Japanese Imperial General Headquarters (IGHQ) chose the beginning of December 1941 to initiate hostilities: (1) After March 1942, the balance of naval power would veer in favor of the United States. (2) By the spring of 1942, the lion's share of the first-phase southern operations should be completed—for that would be the best time to force the Russians to fight a two-front war. (3) Any postponement of hostilities would give the Western Allies time to step up their own preparations for war against Japan. (4) In January and February, weather conditions in Malaya would not be suitable for the projected landing operations. (5) Lunar tide conditions would be best for amphibious operations in early December, specifically the 8th of the month.[26]

The Japanese planning system was suffused by features that reflected national history and society, and of course military doctrine and training. I have sought to isolate a number of the more illuminating features, though in no particular order of weight or importance, and I have supplied a few illustrations from combat experience where relevant.

1. Prussian/German influence was preponderant in the Army; British, in the Navy. One of the best IJA generals, Ishiwara Kanji, was a great fan of Frederick the Great; Admirals Togo and Yamamoto revered Horatio Nelson.[27]

2. Operations was paramount in Japan's staff work. The other staff elements were theoretically of equal importance, but that was paper equality in practice. In the area of operations, the German influence on the Army was particularly pronounced, in the form of almighty staff officers wearing the braided cord.[28]

3. The role of logistics, considered unglamorous, was secondary. At least until the early Showa era of the 1920s and 1930s, Japanese Military Academy cadets typically opted first for the sabers and the smart uniforms of the horse cavalry, though there were usually three times as many volunteers for this branch as there were openings. I have heard of only one IJA officer who ever volunteered for logistics work as his first career choice. There is a certain connection between planning weaknesses in logistics and the fact that, in the Navy, perhaps the greatest shortcoming was a dearth of fuel and ammunition. It has been suggested that "the (Japanese) Navy's confidence in a quick victory in a decisive fleet encounter contributed to its ultimate lack of an adequate, sustained support force."[29]

The Army, too, was chronically plagued by ammunition shortages, coupled with problems of communication and transportation, apart from inferiority of firepower. This, it is often said, stemmed from the absence of important combat experience in World War I, and even a lack of topnotch reporting of the little that had been observed of that war. An IJA Southern Army staff officer in the Imphal campaign in 1944 reportedly remarked bitterly that the Japanese Army commander in Burma "would fling his troops anywhere if he thought it would bring him publicity. How they are to be supplied he only thinks about afterwards."[30]

4. Intelligence was another area accorded a secondary role. Like logistics officers, intelligence people worried too much. With rare exceptions, only plodders went into intelligence. Collection activities were generally better than analysis and estimation.[31]

5. Much of the reason for the low estate of logistics and intelligence vis-a-vis operations was the tendency to equate prudence with timidity; impetuousness and zeal, with heroism and strength of character. The historian finds it difficult to separate aggressiveness from recklessness. One may recall the heated exchange that took place in Tokyo on 14 October 1941, when War Minister Tojo told Prime Minister Konoe that risktaking was necessary on occasion— that "a man must sometimes dare to leap boldly from the towering stage of the Kiyomizu Temple."[32]

6. There was a failure to appreciate the nature of total war. This tendency was affected again, in part, by a lack of familiarity with the lessons of the First World War. An island people, the Japanese always tended to think small. They also clung to a sympathy for and an identification with the have-not, encircled Germany of World War I. That the Germans defied the world for over four years seems almost to have obscured the fact that they were forced to capitulate as the result of a coalition which could draw upon control of the sea to strangle the homeland.[33]

7. The Japanese were very slow to progress beyond tactics that had won past wars. The Navy, for example, was mesmerized by accounts of the great surface battle of Jutland in 1916. Overlooked was the fact that the engagement had proved tactically indecisive. Warfare, for the Japanese, remained basically one dimensional. The parade of battlewagons seemed to relegate submarines and aircraft to a strictly auxiliary role. As Auer has pointed out, "Routine, less spectacular operations such as convoy and scouting were not emphasized."[34] Like their brethren in other navies of the world, Japanese naval leaders did not diverge from B. H. Liddell Hart's wry observation that "battleships are to admirals what cathedrals are to bishops."

8. The Port Arthur syndrome remained an obsession. It stemmed from the Japanese surprise attack on the Russian Port Arthur flotilla in February 1904, two days before war was declared; and it stressed boldness, early success, and quick decision. But, as Professor S. Toyama has pointed out, both Admiral Togo in 1905 and Admiral Yamamoto in 1941 missed a key point: the incomplete-

ness of the Japanese Navy's first strike; "Togo all but admitted that sea attacks [against Port Arthur] had failed."[35]

9. The IJA and the IJN had different main enemies, and thus were bound to fight different kinds of wars. Naval critics have charged that, like the top German leadership, the Japanese based their larger outlook on continental concepts, and never comprehended—but certainly misapplied—the tool of seapower.[36]

10. There was no independent air force, and no doctrine or capability for strategic bombardment.[37]

11. There was no joint chiefs of staff system in Japan, and no combined chiefs of staff tieup with the European Axis powers.[38]

12. The decisionmaking process generally worked its way from the bottom up, with great importance being accorded to the input of midranking officers. Inevitably, initiative often bordered on insubordination, at least in the eyes of those of us who would rank tight discipline as the hallmark of a fine military organization.[39]

13. Within the upper echelons of the two services, there were often very pronounced differences in outlook and in handling between the general staff and the service ministry. After all, the minister—who headed the administrative elite—was a member of the civilian cabinet although an active-duty general or flag officer; whereas the chief of staff was strictly the head of the command group of his service.[40]

14. The combat experience which the Japanese did acquire between World Wars I and II was derived from the China theater, where conditions were markedly dissimilar from what might be expected against the Russians or the Americans, British, and Dutch. In this sense, much of what the Japanese had learned in China was irrelevant.[41]

15. The Army in particular underestimated or manifested contempt for Japan's enemies ranging from Chinese to Russians to Americans *et al.* As Swinson says, "The amateurishness of other armies—except the German Army—never ceased to astound the Japanese."[42] In Southeast Asia they eventually met only colonial armies manned largely by ill-trained and ill-equipped native forces. The victory disease of the Japanese armed forces at the beginning of the Pacific War is well known.[43]

16. Japanese soldiers, sailors, and airmen relied on cold steel and spiritual strength—often termed the alpha factor—to make up for material deficiencies. The usual Japanese explanation is that theirs is a poor country starved for natural resources. Nevertheless, the famous Banzai charges and the Kamikaze sacred warriors are more evocative of the brave but suicidal feudal knights of Crecy, Poitiers, and Agincourt than the *blitzkrieg* practitioners of World War II. A U.S. Marine Corps report spoke of the IJA's mad charges on Guadalcanal as more "theatrical" than military.[44]

17. Of course the Japanese armed forces possessed a well-developed system of service academies and war colleges. The Naval Academy's curriculum, it has been said, "was considered equal to that of the best national university." To this day, veterans of the old service schools remain proud of their military education. The Naval Academy "sought to impart knowledge rather than skills, which were thought to be the jobs of petty officers." The most negative comment that one IJA officer would make was that "technical education was not deep enough," but he hastened to add that it "was conducted in a broad range of subjects sufficient for my duties." Another IJA officer said of his "disciplined spiritual and technical education" that it was "perfect."[45]

To an outsider, however, the weak points in the Japanese services' educational system can be seen as outweighing the good points. For example, the graduate of the military academy was forever dogged by his class rankings. As Swinson put it, the Japanese martial system not only "produced courage and loyalty, but also stupidity and rigidity. It led to great daring and the acceptance of risks but also to bad staff work and administrative blunders. It led also to a form of 'double-talk'."[46]

Field Marshal Viscount William Joseph Slim, while admitting that fighting the Japanese, at least at the beginning of the war, was "an extremely unpleasant and startling experience," pointed out that "the Japanese were ruthless and bold as ants while their designs went well, but if those plans were disturbed or thrown out—antlike again—they fell into confusion, were slow to readjust themselves, and invariably clung too long to their original schemes."[47]

18. Numerous criticisms have been made of the quality of Japanese generalship. The Japanese commanders, said Slim, had "an unquenchable military optimism, which rarely allowed in their narrow administrative margins for any setback or delay." This was especially dangerous for the Japanese, since

the fundamental fault of [IJA] generalship was a lack of moral, as distinct from physical, courage. They were not prepared to admit that they had made a mistake, that their plans had misfired and needed recasting. . . .Rather than confess that, they passed on to their subordinates, unchanged, the orders they had themselves received, well knowing that with the resources available the tasks demanded were impossible. Time and again this blind passing of responsibility ran down a chain of disaster from the commander in chief to the lowest levels of leadership . . . .The hardest test of generalship is to hold [a] balance between determination and flexibility. In this the Japanese failed. They scored highly by determination; they paid heavily for lack of flexibility.[48]

Marshal Georgii K. Zhukov, who had experience fighting the Japanese on the Mongolian frontier at Nomonhan for about three months in the summer of 1939, was in essential agreement with Slim. Japanese officers, said Zhukov, "especially senior officers. . .lack initiative, and are apt to act according to the crammed rulebook."[49]

19. IJA officers have told me that part of the problem of generalship derived from a lack of training of officers for command at division level and above. Zhukov remarked that Japanese senior officers were "not adequately trained."[50] Still, enrollment in the Japanese war colleges was the route to the stars for the company-grade officers who made up the Japanese peacetime classes. Promotion of a nonwar college graduate proceeded at the speed of a slow local train; for the war college officers, promotions came at express-train speed. It was a very rare graduate of the Army War College who did not make general's rank. Entrance standards were high, examinations were no formality, and the Emperor himself gave special awards to the best performers. But one IJA general was heard to say that Army War College products were unsuited for field command.[51]

As for the Navy, being a much smaller service, it had great difficulty staffing its expanded officer corps prior to the outbreak of the Pacific War, with the result that it could not maintain even one officer student at the Naval War College for a lengthy period before the war. Thus, the Naval War College class of twenty-seven officers that entered in April 1940 left for other assignments in October of the same year. Survivors resumed their studies in December 1942 and did not graduate until June 1943. The last Naval War College class of twenty-five officers (July 1943–March 1944) was made up mostly of commanders and lieutenant commanders, since the eligible officers were piling up. This condition, said one IJN officer, illustrates the Navy's short-war thinking. Incidentally, in one Army War College class of 103 officers which entered in December 1942, sixteen air officers were graduated in May 1944. "Innovation in, or criticism of [accepted] strategy was not tolerated" in the IJN. One admiral told me: "The Naval War College taught traditional, old-style warfare—almost nothing new, such as aviation. The students were highly critical of their instructors. We learned mainly about fighting and commanding, not about war, or at least not about the fighting of a war."[52]

There was some use of the other service's instructors at the respective war colleges, but there was no exchange of students.

20. Promotion to responsible positions in the Army and Navy was done strictly on the basis of seniority. Jump promotions were always posthumous, and the largest jumps eventually went to slain special attack (suicide) personnel during the later stages of the Pacific War. The flexibility of the Russo-Japanese War had been lost, and Admiral Nagumo's assignment to command the Pearl Harbor strike force is often cited as an example of unimaginative personnel assignment; e.g., a torpedo expert being given command of a carrier-centered task force.[53]

21. But no one who met the Japanese soldier in action ever put him down as a fighting man. Zhukov asserted that the Japanese troops he saw in combat were "well trained, especially for fighting at close quarters." They were "well disciplined, dogged in combat, especially in defense. Junior commanding officers are well trained and fanatically persistent in battle."[54] General MacArthur issued a public statement during the climacteric of the Pacific War in September 1944 that presented a balanced approach:

> Japanese ground troops still fight with the greatest tenacity. The military quality of the rank and file remains of the highest. Their officer corps, however, deteriorates as you go up the scale. It is fundamentally based upon a caste and feudal system and does not represent strict professional merit. Therein lies Japan's weakness. Her sons are strong of limb and stout of heart but weak in leadership. Gripped inexorably by a military hierarchy, that hierarchy is now failing the nation. It has had neither the imagination nor the foresighted ability to organize Japanese resources for a total war.[55]

According to another illuminating critique by a wartime enemy, Field Marshal Slim,

> The strength of the Japanese Army lay, not in its higher leadership. . .but in the spirit of the individual Japanese soldier. He fought and marched till he died. If five hundred Japanese were ordered to hold a position, we had to kill four hundred and ninety-five before it was ours—and then the last five killed themselves. It was this combination of obedience and ferocity that made the Japanese Army, whatever its condition, so formidable and which would make any army formidable. It would make a European army invincible.[56]

The no-surrender policy of the Japanese, encountered on every battlefield of the Pacific War, was well known to the Russians too. On the basis of his experience at Nomonhan, Zhukov stated that the Japanese "as a rule do not surrender and do not stop short of 'harakiri.' "[57] General Petro Grigorenko, who served on the Far Eastern front at the same time as Zhukov, adds that "the Japanese never surrendered or moved. . . .they never received orders to retreat from their positions."[58]

Japanese Army and Navy planners knew that their tough forces would always obey any order that was issued to them, without a whimper. Japanese ace Saburo Sakai explains, from the standpoint of the subordinate: "We never dared to question orders, to doubt authority, to do anything but immediately carry out all the commands of our superiors. We were automatons who obeyed without thinking."[59]

The planners also knew that the Japanese armed forces would fight fanatically to the bitter end, and would court or accept death with breathtaking willingness. Their enemies understood this well; in Burma it was remarked that "Everyone talks about fighting to the last man and last round, but only the Japanese actually do it."[60] This should not be surprising, for the Book of the Warrior, *Hagakure*, states at the outset that "the Way of the Samurai is found in death;" and "the greatest calamity for the man of action is that he fail to die. . . ."[61]

22. Lastly—and an appropriate topic for a symposium dealing with military history—I cannot discern the theme of continuity in IJA teaching of military history. The approach seems to have been on an interest basis, to illuminate tactical methods, especially drawn from battles fought in the very modern period. Thus, speaking of the Army, one hears of Port Arthur and Tannenberg and the Marne but not Arbela or Alesia or Lake Trasimene; of small-scale assaults on Japanese medieval castles but not much on Verdun and nothing on the Chemin des Dames or Ypres or Caporetto. Washington and Grant and Lee have name recognition, but it would be difficult to encounter mention of even one of their engagements. "If you were interested in untouched-upon battles," one Army War College graduate told me, "you could go to the library and bone up on your own."[62]

An IJN admiral showed me a breakdown of the curriculum for Naval War College classes in the late 1920s. Of a scheduled total of 2,460 instructional hours, 10 were given to leadership, 30 to fleet

80

commanding, and 265 to history, distributed as follows: 90 for Japanese naval, 45 for U.S. naval, 110 for European including Royal Navy, and 20 for diplomatic.[63]

After the Japanese debacle against Zhukov and the Russians at Nomonhan in 1939, there was some discussion of the *desiderata* of modern battle, but a realistic approach was constrained by the need to avoid excessive praise of an enemy, for reasons of morale.[64] Thus, there was only spasmodic topicality in the IJA and IJN teaching of military history; a pattern of breadth and continuity in warfare is lacking. This seems highly relevant after our examination of the texture of war planning by the Japanese armed forces before Pearl Harbor.

Notes

1. Boeicho Boeikenshusho (BBKS), *Kaigun shinko sakusen: Hito Marei: homen* (Tokyo, 1969), p 12.

2. Masanori Ito with Roger Pineau, *The End of the Imperial Japanese Navy* (New York, 1962), p 17; Sadao Asada, "The Japanese Navy and the United States," in Dorothy Borg and Shumpei Okamoto, eds., *Pearl Harbor as History: Relations, 1931–1941* (New York, 1973), pp 235–36.

3. Saburo Hayashi and Alvin D. Coox, *Kogun: The Japanese Army in the Pacific War* (Quantico, Va., 1959), pp 1, 2, 193.

4. *Ibid*, p 193.

5. BBKS, *Daihon'ei rikugunbu*, Vol 1 (Tokyo, 1979), pp 287–302, 343–50, 466–78; Hayashi and Coox, *Kogun*, p 3.

6. Asada, "Japanese Navy," p 256.

7. Hayashi and Coox, *Kogun*, p 193.

8. Arthur J. Marder, *Old Friends, New Enemies: The Royal Navy and the Imperial Japanese Navy: Strategic Illusions, 1936–1941* (Oxford, 1981). Also see Hayashi and Coox, *Kogun*, p 193.

9. Asada, "Japanese Navy," p 243.

10. BBKS, *Daihon'el kaigunbu: Daitoa senso kaisen keii*, vol 1, (Tokyo, 1979), pp 466–78.

11. *Ibid*, pp 500–08; Takagi Sokichi, *Taiheiyo senso to riku-kaigun no koso* (Tokyo, 1967), pp 191–96; Asada, "Japanese Navy," p 256.

12. Hata Ikuhiko, *Nitchu senso shi* (Tokyo, 1961), pp 161–260, 273–343; Horiba Kazuo, *Shina jihen shido shi* (Tokyo, 1967), pp 8lff.; Akira Fujiwara, "The Role of the Japanese Army," in Borg and Okamoto, *Pearl Harbor as History*, p 195.

13. Masanobu Tsuji, *Singapore: The Japanese Version* (New York, 1960), pp 4–13.

14. Telford Taylor, "Day of Infamy, Decades of Doubt," *Asia Magazine*, 29 Jul 1984, p 8.

15. United States Strategic Bombing Survey (USSBS) interview, Ozawa Jisaburo, #237.

16. See BBKS, *Rikugun gunsenbi* (Tokyo, 1979), pp 339ff.

17. Nobutaka Ike, ed., *Japan's Decision for War: Records of the 1941 Policy Conferences* (Stanford, 1967), pp 190–93.

18. *Ibid*, pp 193–207.

19. *Ibid*, p 207.

20. *Ibid*, pp 208–39.

21. *Ibid*.

22. *Ibid*, pp 244–49.

23. *Ibid*, pp 262–83.

24. Personal interview with Takayama Shinobu.

25. Shigenori Togo, *The Cause of Japan* (New York, 1956), pp 197–98.

26. Hayashi and Coox, *Kogun*, p 34.

27. Personal interviews with Nakamura Teiji and Imaoka Yutaka; Saburo Toyama, "Lessons from the Past," *U.S. Naval Institute Proceedings*, Sep 1982, vol 108, no 9, p 64; BBKS, *Kaigun shinko sakusen*, p 12.

28. Personal interview with Hayashi Saburo.

29. Imaoka interview; James E. Auer, *The Postwar Rearmament of Japanese Maritime Forces, 1945–1971* (New York, 1973), p 22.

30. Arthur Swinson, *Four Samurai: A Quartet of Japanese Army Commanders in the Second World War* (London, 1968), p 123.

31. Personal interviews with Kohtani Etsuo and Imaoka Yutaka.

32. Alvin D. Coox, *Tojo* (New York, 1975), pp 89–90.

33. Imaoka, Hayashi interviews; Asada, "Japanese Navy," p 256.

34. Nakamura interview; Stephen E. Pelz, *Race to Pearl Harbor: The Failure of the Second London Naval Conference and the Onset of World War II* (Cambridge, Mass., 1974), p 30; Auer, *Rearmament*, p 21.

35. Toyama, "Lessons," p 64.

36. USSB interview, Ohmae Toshikazu, #192; Hara Shiro, *Daihon'ei rikugunbu: Daitoa senso kaisen ni kosatsu* (Tokyo, 1976), p 73.

37. Personal interviews with Ikuta Makoto and Kono Shiro. Also see USSBS, *Japanese Air Power* (Washington, 1946), *passim*.

38. Imaoka interview; Hara, *Daihon'ei rikugunbu*, p 73.

39. Alvin D. Coox, *Year of the Tiger* (Tokyo & Philadelphia, 1964), Chap 4.

40. Hayashi and Coox, *Kogun*, p 192.

41. Imaoka, Hayashi interviews.

42. Swinson, *Four Samurai*, p 25.

43. Hayashi and Coox, *Kogun*, pp 44–45.

44. U.S. Marine Corps, "(1st Marine) Division Commander's Final Report on Guadalcanal Operation," May–Jul 1943.

45. Theodore F. Cook, Jr., "Cataclysm and Career Rebirth: The Imperial Military Elite," in David W. Plath, ed., *Work and Lifecourse in Japan* (Albany, N.Y., 1983), pp 150–51; Auer, *Rearmament*, p 21.

46. Swinson, *Samurai*, p 12.

47. Field Marshal the Viscount William Joseph Slim, *Defeat into Victory* (New York, 1961), p 446.

48. *Ibid*.

49. G.K. Zhukov, *The Memoirs of Marshal Zhukov* (New York, 1971), p 169.

50. *Ibid*.

51. Personal interviews with Toga Hiroshi, Hata Ikuhiko, Imaoka, and Ikuta.

52. Personal interviews with Nakamura and Ohmae Toshikazu; Auer, *Rearmament*, p 21.

53. Ikuta, Kono, Hata interviews.

54. Zhukov, *Memoirs*, p 168–69.

55. GHQ, SWPA, Press Release, 15 Sep 44, in General of the Army Douglas MacArthur, *Report of General MacArthur*, vol 1, *The Campaigns of MacArthur in the Pacific* (Washington, 1966), p 178.

56. Slim, *Defeat*, p 447.

57. Zhukov, *Memoirs*, p 169.

58. Petro G. Grigorenko, *Memoirs* (New York, 1982), p 109.

59. Saburo Sakai with Martin Caidin and Fred Saito, *Samurai!* (New York, 1957), p 19.

60. Swinson, *Samurai*, p 17, and Philip Warner, *Japanese Army of World War II* (Reading, England, 1973), pp 13, 29.

61. Tsunetomo Yamamoto, *Hagakure: The Book of the Samurai* (Tokyo, 1979), pp 17–18.

62. Imaoka, Toga interview.

63. Nakamura interview.

64. See Alvin D. Coox, *Nomonhan: Japan Against Russia, 1939*, 2 vols (Stanford, 1985), Chap 42, "The Lessons and Applications of Nomonhan."

Selected Sources

Publications

Japanese-Language Sources

Boeicho Boeikenshusho (BBKS) [National Defense College, Defense Agency]. *Daihon'ei kaigunbu: Daitoa senso kaisen keii (1)* [The IGHQ Navy Department: Details of the Opening of the Greater East Asia War, vol 1]. Tokyo, 1979.

__________. *Daihon'ei rikugunbu (1)* [The IGHQ Army Department, vol 1]. Tokyo, 1967.

__________. *Kaigun shinko sakusen: Hito Marei homen* [Naval Thrust Operations: The Philippines-Malaya Area]. Tokyo, 1969.

__________. *Rikugun gunsenbi* [The Army's Military Preparations]. Tokyo, 1979.

Hara Shiro. *Daihon'ei rikugunbu: Daitoa senso kaisen ni kansuru kosatsu* [The IGHQ Army Department: A Study Concerning the Opening of the Greater East Asia War]. Tokyo, 1976.

Hata Ikuhiko. *Nitchu senso shi* [A History of the Sino-Japanese Conflict]. Tokyo, 1961.

Hayashi Saburo. *Taiheiyo senso rikusen gaishi* [An Outline History of the Ground Battles of the Pacific War]. Tokyo, 1959.

Horiba Kazuo. *Shina jihen shido shi* [The History of War Direction of the China Incident]. Tokyo, 1967.

Takagi Sokichi. *Taiheiyo senso to riku-kaigun no koso* [The Pacific War and the Army-Navy Struggle]. Tokyo, 1967.

Takayama Shinobu. *Sanbo honbu sakusenka* [The Army General Staff's Operations Section]. Tokyo, 1979.

English-Language Sources

Asada, Sadao. "The Japanese Navy and the United States," in Borg and Okamoto, *Pearl Harbor as History,* pp 225–59.

Auer, James E. *The Postwar Rearmament of Japanese Maritime Forces, 1945–71.* New York, 1973.

Barker, A.J. *Japanese Army Handbook, 1939–1945.* New York, 1979.

Borg, Dorothy, and Okamoto, Shumpei, eds. *Pearl Harbor as History Japanese-American Relations, 1931–1941.* New York, 1973.

Buck, James H., ed. *The Modern Japanese Military System.* Beverly Hills, Calif., 1975.

Cook, Theodore F., Jr. "Cataclysm and Career Rebirth: The Imperial Military Elite," in Plath, ed., *Work and Lifecourse in Japan,* pp 135–52.

Coox, Alvin D. *Nomonhan: Japan-Against Russia, 1939,* 2 vols. Stanford, 1985.

__________. "Qualities of Japanese Military Leadership: The Case of Suetaka Kamezo," *Journal of Asian History,* vol 2, no 1 (1968), pp 32–43.

__________. "Sato Kotoku: Maverick General of Imperial Japan," *Army,* Jul 1965, vol 15, no 12, pp 68–75.

__________. *Tojo.* New York, 1975.

__________. *Year of the Tiger.* Tokyo & Philadelphia, 1964.

Dull, Paul S. *A Battle History of the Imperial Japanese Navy (1941–1945).* Annapolis, Md., 1978.

Fujiwara, Akira. "The Role of the Japanese Army," in Borg and Okamoto, *Pearl Harbor as History,* pp 189–95.

Grigorenko, Petro G. *Memoirs,* trans. T.P. Whitney. New York, 1982.

Hayashi, Saburo, in collaboration with Coox, Alvin D. *Kogun: The Japanese Army in the Pacific War.* Quantico Va., 1959.

Humphreys, Leonard A. "The Japanese Military Tradition," in Buck, ed., *The Modern Japanese Military System,* pp 21–40.

Ike, Nobutaka, trans. & ed. *Japan's Decision for War: Records of the 1941 Policy Conferences.* Stanford, 1967.

Ito, Masanori, with Pineau, Roger. *The End of the Imperial Japanese Navy,* transl. A.Y. Kuroda and R. Pineau. New York, 1962.

Kennedy, Captain M.D. *The Military Side of Japanese Life.* London, 1924.

Lory, Hollis. *Japan's Military Masters: The Army in Japanese Life*. New York, 1943.

MacArthur, General of the Army Douglas. *Reports of General MacArthur*, vol 1, *The Campaigns of MacArthur in the Pacific*. Washington DC, 1966.

Marder, Arthur J. *Old Friends, New Enemies: The Royal Navy and the Imperial Japanese Navy: Strategic Illusions, 1936–1941*. Oxford, 1981.

Maxon, Yale Candee. *Control of Japanese Foreign Policy: A Study, of Civil Military Rivalry, 1930–1945*. Berkeley, 1957.

Pelz, Stephen E. *Race to Pearl Harbor: The Failure of the Second London Naval Conference and the Onset of World War II*. Cambridge Mass., 1974.

Plath, David W. ed. *Work and Lifecourse in Japan*. Albany, 1983.

Sakai, Saburo, with Caidin, Martin, and Saito, Fred. *Samurai!* New York, 1957.

Slim, Field Marshal the Viscount William Joseph. *Defeat into Victory*. New York, 1961.

Stephan, John J. *Hawaii Under the Rising Sun*. Honolulu, 1984.

Swinson, Arthur. *Four Samurai: A Quartet of Japanese Army Commanders in the Second World War*. London, 1968.

Taylor, Telford. "Day of Infamy, Decades of Doubt," *Asia Magazine*, 29 Jul 1984, pp 7–10.

Togo, Shigenori. *The Cause of Japan*, trans. Togo, Fumihiko, and Blakeney, Ben B. New York, 1956.

Toyama Saburo. "Lessons from the Past," *U.S. Naval Institute Proceedings*, Sep 1982, vol 108, no 9, pp 62–69.

Tsuji, Masanobu. *Singapore: The Japanese Version*, trans. M.E. Lake. New York, 1960.

U.S. Marine Corps. "(1st Marine) Division Commander's Final Report on Guadalcanal Operation," May–Jul 1943; extract on file, HQ USAF, Office of Air Force History.

U.S. Strategic Bombing Survey (USSBS). *Japanese Air Power*. Washington, 1946.

Warner, Philip. *Japanese Army of World War II*. Reading, England, 1973.

Yamamoto, Tsunetomo. *Hagakure: The Book of the Samurai*, trans. W.S. Wilson. Tokyo, 1979.

Zhukov, G.K. *The Memoirs of Marshal Zhukov*, trans. APN. New York, 1971.

Interviews

By U.S. Strategic Bombing Survey (Tokyo): Fukudome Shigeru, #115, 9–12 Dec 1945; Kawabe Torashiro, #447, 14 Nov 1945; Nomura Kichisaburo, #429, 8 Nov 1945; Ohmae Toshikazu, #192, 30 Oct 1945; Ozawa Jisaburo, #237, 30 Oct 1945; Toyoda Soemu, #378, 13–14 Nov 1945; Yonai Mitsumasa, #379, 17 Nov 1945.

By the author (Tokyo): Hara Takeshi, Hata Ikuhiko, Hayashi Saburo, Ikuta Makoto, Imaoka Yutaka, Itonaga Shin, Kohtani Etsuo, Kono Shiro, Nakamura Teiji, Ohmae Toshikazu, Takayama Shinobu, Toga Hiroshi.

Soviet Planning Successes
in the Great Patriotic War:
The Results of Correct Formulae?

P. H. Vigor

When the subject of this paper was first suggested to me, I willingly accepted it. I had always believed that the Red Army prior to the outbreak of the Second World War had evolved some new operational concepts which, together with their planning infrastructure, could reasonably be described as "correct formulae"; that these were implemented at various times during the Great Patriotic War (GPW); and that, since the Germans were defeated, they must therefore be accounted successes. Consequently, I welcomed the opportunity to put down on paper my views on this matter in the hope of persuading others to agree with me.

Unfortunately, however, when I took up my pen and began the business of writing, I soon discovered that this seemingly simple, infinitely beguiling title was very complex; and that any attempt to write a paper on it would not be at all easy. Only when I had overcome a number of serious difficulties could I proceed to write the sort of paper I had originally envisaged. An examination of those initial difficulties must therefore be the first thing to be tackled.

The chief of these, I discovered, lay in the need to determine the meanings of the words success and failure; because if we do not know what success is, we cannot possibly talk meaningfully about Soviet planning successes. However, while I was trying to work out an acceptable and rigorous definition, my mind strayed to the events in Russia in the summer, autumn, and winter of 1941. It would be reasonable to regard the Soviet retreat to Moscow as a sign of a significant defeat of the Red Army, and hence as a sign of failure; but at the end of the day the German Army was halted, so it was also a Soviet success. The realization of the truth of both these statements did not make things any easier for me.

If we turn from brooding on success and failure, and try to analyze the meaning of planned, we shall find, I think, that we are in similarly deep waters. That same retreat of 1941, for example, was certainly not planned, in the sense that prior to Adolf Hitler's invasion of Russia, Joseph Stalin never intended such a withdrawal; yet the conduct of that withdrawal and also the subsequent operations which led to the Germans being pushed back from Moscow must have had a great deal of planning injected into them. You cannot move troops in large quantities, nor indeed in any but the very smallest quantities, without engaging in detailed planning and lots of it. To try to move them otherwise is to turn a properly conducted expedition into what A. A. Milne's character Eeyore once accurately described as "a confused noise."[1] So, in one sense at least, the Soviet Army's retreat on Moscow and its subsequent counteroffensive was certainly planned, even though in another sense it was not.

We find a similar paradox in the case of the Battle of Stalingrad. We must all agree that the operations around Stalingrad were a major cause of the ultimate defeat of Hitler; yet it cannot truly be said without any qualification that the destruction of the Nazi Sixth Army at Stalingrad was the result of successful planning by the Stavka. It came about as the result of Hitler's errors as a general. It was he, not Stalin, who ordered von Paulus into Stalingrad; and it was he, not Stalin, who forbade him to leave when withdrawal was still possible. Of course, the advantage taken of the situation by Stalin and his generals was the result of successful planning; but is it that kind of planning which this paper is supposed to address?

To take this argument one stage further, let us now turn our attention to the Battle of Kursk. Few would dispute that this battle's outcome was another major cause of Hitler's defeat. Views on the reasons for the Soviet victory will naturally differ widely; but, in my opinion at any rate, the outcome of the battle was decided by the fact that the Russians knew in advance what the Germans were planning. Whether the credit for that advance warning should be given to British, or Soviet, intelligence, is a question hotly debated by the British and Russians. However, it does not matter to us at this symposium which is the correct answer. All that we are concerned with here is to establish that the Stavka was indeed forewarned about the impending Nazi offensive and was therefore able to take countermeasures. The countermeasures were successful; but, in order for them to have been so, they must have involved a lot of successful planning.

At this point in my reflections I had come to the tentative conclusion that successful planning could reasonably be defined as effective reaction to an unexpected development; but then I realized this meant that a planning success could only happen at the tactical or operational levels, and not at the strategic. For, if planning were really and truly successful at the strategic level, there would be none of those awkward unexpected developments, effective reaction to which was to be the hallmark of any planning success. I therefore decided that *really* successful planning would have to consist of successes at all three levels—tactical, operational, *and* strategic. Up to the Battle of Kursk, however, the Red Army did not manage to achieve this.

I have just been using the adjectives strategic, operational, and tactical; and it has suddenly occurred to me that there may be some of my readers who do not know the meaning of the Soviet word *operativny*, which we really have no alternative but to translate into English as operational.

Tactical has the same meaning in Russian as English; *operativny* is the adjectival form of *operatsiya* (operation) which to a Russian means military activities undertaken by an army or an army group. Strategic operations are those conducted by an army group front or a group of army groups (*gruppa frontov*) and intended to achieve sufficiently important results to effect a significant alteration in the way in which the war is going.

The purpose of tactics is to win a battle or series of battles, victory in which will bring success in the operation of which they are a part. A successful operation or series of operations will mean the winning of the campaign of which they are a part or, in some cases, the winning of the war. Admittedly these are rough and ready definitions, but they will be quite sufficient for our present purposes; and those seeking further knowledge are referred to the appropriate entries in *Sovietskaya Voennaya Entsiklopediya* (The Soviet Military Encyclopaedia).

Before that digression I had just been saying that in order to be able to claim any *real* gift for successful planning, the Red Army would have to plan successfully not only at the tactical and operational, but also at the strategic, levels; and it never quite managed to achieve this before the Battle of Kursk. However, I then reflected that at least from January 1944, the Red Army's planning *was* successful at the strategic level as well as at the other two; so presumably my difficulties were over. All I had to do was to concentrate my attention on Soviet planning during 1944–45 and to adjust my thesis accordingly. Unfortunately it very soon transpired that I was not yet out of the woods.

As I probed deeper, I came to the conclusion that the Soviet ability in 1944–45 to plan successfully at the strategic level was due much less to their own brilliance than to Hitler's hideous incompetence as a warlord. In addition to his ridiculous decisions concerning Stalingrad, he was guilty of at least another half dozen major errors; and the cumulative effect of these added to Kursk and Stalingrad was to emasculate the Wehrmacht.

The first of Hitler's major errors was his decision to open another front while the war with Britain was still in progress. To fight a war on two fronts at once has always been regarded, and rightly regarded, as a major military misfortune; to be the one responsible for finding oneself in this grave predicament is sheer military lunacy.

The second of Hitler's major errors was to choose the Soviet Union as the scene for his second front. As Soviet historians are very keen to demonstrate, he grossly underestimated the difficulties of invading Russia, and grossly overestimated Germany's power to do so.

For instance, his successes in 1940 and in the first five months of 1941 had meant that he had to provide garrisons for substantial areas of territory. Norway, Belgium, half of France, Denmark, Holland, Greece, Yugoslavia, Crete—all were hostile to German rule and had to be kept in subjection. In June 1941 fifty-eight divisions were employed in holding down these various countries. This was a serious drain on German manpower, which after all was not so very numerous. In September 1939 there were only 4,250,000 German males of the age groups twenty-one to forty-five who were available for military service. With such comparatively slender resources, to attack a country capable of raising and maintaining an army of over 11,000,000 is bound to be a very risky business and could only possibly be successful if casualties were minimal.[2] Yet casualties could only be kept to a minimum if the *blitzkrieg* worked as brilliantly as it had worked in Western Europe in 1940. As we all know it did not; and the fact that it did not was largely due to a number of Hitler's decisions.

Chief among these was the inadequate number of planes and tanks which Hitler allotted to the Wehrmacht for Barbarossa.

Impressive as they sound when considered merely as totals, they make a very different impression when calculated in relation to the size of the Russian battlefield. Whereas in France the Wehrmacht had had approximately one tank per 29 square kilometres of battlefield, in the USSR it was one tank per 75 square kilometres. The figures for aircraft work out at one per 51, and one per 245, square kilometres respectively.

Furthermore, as we all know, the Wehrmacht was never properly equipped to fight a *blitzkrieg*. It had a large proportion of conventional infantry, and much of its artillery was horse drawn. These were therefore bound to lag behind the armoured elements; and as time went on, the gap between them inevitably would become considerable. In western Europe in 1940 this phenomenon was irrelevant: the distances were short, and the campaign was over quickly. In the USSR, on the other hand, the distances were enormous; and even Hitler did not expect victory till about four months after crossing the Soviet frontier. Hitler, however, ignored these fateful discrepancies, and the Wehrmacht went to its doom.

In my view, it is therefore no coincidence that the real triumphs of Soviet military planning took place in what in Soviet terminology is called the third period of the Great Fatherland War, that is to say, from 1 January 1944 to 9 May 1945, because by the time this period began, the Wehrmacht had been so weakened by its heavy losses in men and equipment that it was in no condition to frustrate anyone's plans. To put the matter bluntly, the Russians had got the Germans on the run.

I do not think that this is a contentious statement. Soviet official histories, for instance, when dealing with this period always show that for any major operation the correlation of forces was heavily in the Russians' favour, and usually by a significant amount. I wish to emphasize that, in saying this, I am not denying the heroic efforts of the Red Army and Navy in the earlier stages of the war, nor am I trying to denigrate their military virtues. What I do say, however, is that if the Wehrmacht, largely as a result of its own and Hitler's blunders, had not been in such a weakened condition in 1944–45, the Russians were not very likely to have found themselves in the position in which they *did* ultimately find themselves, where, as Zhukov (I think) once said, whenever they wanted a victory, they could simply sit down and arrange for one.

Finally, there is the question of what is meant by formulae in the context of the paper. The more one looks at it, the more one feels that it could be made to mean almost anything. This is clearly very undesirable; so I have decided to define it for the purposes of this paper as Soviet concepts for the mounting of offensive operations at the strategic and operational levels formulated before the end of the Second World War.

I have confined it to *offensive* operations, because we are concerned with Soviet *successes*; and success in war, the Russians believe, is not brought about by fighting on the defensive. Whether or not you agree with that view (and it is one, I think, which tells us a lot about the Soviet Union's attitude toward war), it remains a fact that the Soviet successes we shall be talking about were all obtained by conducting *offensive* operations. That being so, I hope that my definition of formulae, as set down at the end of the preceding paragraph, will be acceptable.

My readers must be feeling by now that I am ducking the whole issue. I have been asked to present a paper on Soviet military planning; and all I have done is to edge that subject gradually off stage. Partly, I have done this deliberately. The impressive Soviet victories of 1944–45 continue to exert what, in my opinion, is a deleterious influence on the West's perceptions of the quality of the Soviet armed forces of today. Because they triumphed in battle after battle during that period, the West assumes subconsciously that they would do the same against the North Atlantic Treaty Organization (NATO) in 1984. Perhaps they would! But it is essential that we take into our reckoning the condition of the Wehrmacht during that period. Of course, there have been times during the history of NATO when the latter's capabilities have seemed to be no better than those of the Nazis in 1944–45, and there have even been times when some have thought them worse. If that is so, then on our own heads be it! It is up to us to rectify the matter. Assuming that we have done so, or are in the process of doing so, I then see no reason why we should all assume that the Soviet armed forces will walk over us.

Leaving this consideration to one side, however, I could not in any case have done justice to my subject if I had ignored the point that the German Army of 1944–45 was far from being as militarily effective as it had been four years earlier. As for the Luftwaffe of the period, it no longer exercised the mastery of the air which it had, at least at the strategic level, at the start of Barbarossa. Soviet historians indeed are united in saying that, by 1944 it was the Soviet, not the Nazi, airmen who held command of the skies. Those of us who have fought in a campaign where the other side has had mastery of the air will agree, I think, that under those conditions it can do very much as it likes. I therefore repeat the assertion I made earlier, which was that by the beginning of 1944 the Soviet generals could do very much as they liked. Therefore the next question to confront us is: what did they like to do?

The record of events provides us with a clear answer. They wanted to put into practice the concept of the deep operations (*glubokaya-operatsiya*), which was devised during the late twenties and the late thirties by a group of brilliant military thinkers working under the aegis of Marshal Mikhail N. Tukhachevsky. Associated with this concept was that of the encirclement (*okruzhenie*), derived from Count Alfred von Schlieffen's study of the Battle of Cannae. This work was translated into Russian and went into several editions, the first being by A. A. Svechin in 1923, while the second and third editions were retranslated by L. Feigin and appeared in 1936 and 1938 respectively.[3]

Because the concept of the deep operation had been worked out on paper before the Second World War, it can, I think, be fairly described as a formula in the sense in which that word is used in the title of this paper.

The deep operation was an attempt to provide a solution to several important problems which had confronted the Red Army since the end of the First World War. The experience of that war had shown conclusively that the old methods of attacking an enemy position had ceased to be valid. Infantry could not advance successfully without artillery support. Between 1914 and 1918, that support could easily be given right at the very start of an offensive and for a short period afterwards; but if the offensive was going well, the victorious infantry moved ahead far faster than their supporting artillery could move. Consequently, there came a moment (and usually fairly quickly) when they had to assault enemy positions without supporting fire. When that happened the offensive ground to a halt. This, said Soviet researchers, was the basic reason why the British and French offensives had usually failed.

We have no time now to go into the various reasons why the artillery was unable to keep up with the infantry; we must simply note the fact. The officers of the Red Army who were planning the war of the future decided that the invention of the tank and the parachute offered the hope of a remedy. The tank could advance comparatively quickly even over rough terrain, and therefore its gun could be used as a substitute for that of the artillery and keep the advancing infantry supplied throughout the whole of the offensive with the supporting fire it required. In addition to tanks the air force could be called upon to provide supporting fire.

The armoured forces, however, had more than one role to fulfill. Whereas certain tanks were to accompany the infantry, others were to form a mobile group designed to exploit the breach in the enemy's defences which the infantry attack was to make. The strength of the infantry shock group (which included, of course, artillery and tanks) was to be not less than two-thirds that of the whole of the attacking formation, which was to allot no more than one-ninth of its strength as a reserve.

These two features, the concentration of forces on the sector chosen for the attack and the creation of a mobile group designed to exploit the shock group's success, were highly important features of the concept of the deep operation and were also highly important features of the Soviet Army's plans of attack in 1944–45.

The chief function of the parachute troops was to stop the enemy hurrying reinforcements to the threatened sector of the defence. The ability of the Germans on the Western Front 1914–18 to reinforce a sector under attack was very noteworthy in the opinion of the Soviet researchers in the late twenties; and unless some means could be found of preventing this from happening, the Red Army's dream of an offensive war of movement was most unlikely to be realized. Looking back with hindsight, we can therefore see that it is only natural that the Russians became the first to succeed in dropping an entire formation by parachute.[4]

As so often in the history of the Tsarist/Soviet military, the Red Army in the middle thirties did not possess the technology to give proper effect to their ideas. In particular, they did not possess transport aircraft of a size and range sufficient to allow the successful use of paratroops in the Great Patriotic War on any but a very small scale. Therefore, the job of sealing off the enemy's rear, which the theory of the deep operation envisaged, had to be given to the air force. It was obviously only when the air force had succeeded in winning command of the air that the army was able to do this properly. However, when it did so, the results were very impressive. The isolation of Berlin from the north and west by this method in 1945 is compelling testimony to its efficacy—but once again we have to remember that the Luftwaffe at that time was very weak.

Associated with the concept of the deep operation was that of the encirclement (or, in its perfected form, the double encirclement).

Raymond Garthoff rightly said in his *Soviet Military Doctrine* that this last is undoubtedly a purely Soviet contribution to the art of war.[5] Indeed, for its successful accomplishment it requires such enormous numbers of men that only the USSR or China could possibly hope to tackle it. Even the comparatively simple operation, that of the ordinary (single) encirclement, cannot be undertaken with any but copious forces.

The expressions single and double encirclement are not to be found in modern Russian; but they are, I think, very useful in helping to make clear the distinction between an encirclement battle such as Cannae, where there was no possibility of a relief army coming to succour the Romans, and most of those fought by the Russians, where an attempt at the relief of the surrounded Germans had to be reckoned as probable. In the case of Cannae, every man of the Carthaginian forces was able to face inwards and slaughter his enemy, leaving his back exposed because there were no Romans outside the Carthaginian ring to profit by this circumstance, nor any chance of their being any during the time necessary to destroy their comrades inside.

In 1944–45, however, it was necessary for the Russians to arrange things so that one section of a *front*'s forces faced inward and killed the Germans, while another section faced outwards, ready to repel any attempt at relief by Nazi forces outside. In order to accomplish both these tasks successfully, numbers of men and tanks and guns in excess of those which could normally be provided by an army group were usually found to be necessary; so that as a general rule this type of encirclement, the so-called double encirclement, was deemed to require the employment of more than just one *front*; so that in the end there were groups of army groups *(gruppa frontov)* charged with this operation.

The USSR's attention was directed to the Battle of Cannae as a result of Soviet officers reading the works of the German, Count von Schlieffen. He, it seems, came to be fascinated by this battle, and finally wrote a book on it which was translated into Russian and ran into several editions. Two editions were published during the thirties and seem to have been read by the same sort of Soviet officers who took part in or sympathized with the discussions of the group under Tukhachevsky which was working out the concept of the deep operation. I once worked on a copy of the 1936 Soviet edition which had been heavily annotated in Russian; the impact made on the annotator by Schlieffen's exposition was clearly very considerable. It was his opinion, as it certainly was that of Schlieffen, that the encirclement was unquestionably the most efficient method of destroying the enemy's armies. The only defect of Cannae, it appeared, was that its success was more or less an accident. In other words, it happened, not so much because of Hannibal's genius as a military commander, but because of his foe's incompetence. What was needed, Schlieffen said (and who would say he was wrong?), was to be able oneself to arrange to do a Cannae on the enemy without having to rely on the latter's stupidity or incompetence. Judging by the Russian notes scribbled in the book's margins, the Soviet officer who read it agreed with this sentiment.

These, then, are our formulae. There is no doubt that they were applied in principle during the GPW; so we must now turn to that war's operations and see how far the formulae could be called successful.

In this final section of my paper I shall look at an example of the deep operation of the GPW and also at one of the encirclement. Both examples date from the so-called third period of the war.

The deep operation I have chosen is the Vistula-Oder Operation of 12 January to 3 February 1945.[6] It was designed to deal with seven Nazi defence systems based along the rivers Vistula, Oder, and Varta, of which the most stoutly defended was that based on the Vistula, where the Germans had arranged their defences in four echelons of depths varying between 30 to 70 km. The Soviet formations during this operation advanced on average to a total depth of 300 km, with a maximum depth of advance of 500 km, though one of the tank armies advanced as far as 600 km. The average daily advance was 25 km; but rates of as much as 45 km per day for the rifle formations, and 70 km for the armoured formations, have been recorded.

The enemy consisted of Army Group "A" (called Army Group "Centre" from 26 January 1945); according to Soviet sources it was made up of 560,000 men, 5,000 guns and mortars, more than 1,200 tanks and self-propelled (SP) guns, and over 600 aircraft. Against this force the Russians concentrated 2,200,000 men, more than 34,500 guns and mortars, about 6,500 tanks and SP guns, and about 4,000 planes. This represented almost 35 percent of the men, artillery, and aircraft, and about 50 percent of the tanks and SP guns of the whole of the Red Army engaged in fighting the Germans. The well-known Russian love of masses of everything, and of heavy concentrations of that everything on the important sectors of a front, was thus clearly in evidence here.

The operation was carried out in two stages. The first lasted six days during which the Russians broke through the enemy defences, smashed the Nazi formations opposing them, and created conditions favourable for the development of their offensive into the depths of the enemy's rear. The second stage lasted seventeen days during which the Russians pursued the Germans energetically, destroyed their operational reserves, seized the Silesian industrial region, and took possession of bridgeheads on the west bank of the River Oder. As a result of the operation twenty-five Nazi divisions were shattered (*razgromleno*)[7] and thirty-five totally destroyed (*unichtozheno*), while 147,000 German officers and men were taken prisoner. It was thus one of the biggest operations of the whole war.

The chief participants in the operation were the First Ukrainian *Front* under Marshal Ivan S. Koniev and the First Belorussian *Front* under Marshal Georgii K. Zhukov. In the second stage of the operation these were assisted by parts of the Second Belorussian and of the Fourth Ukrainian *Fronts*.

The First Belorussian *Front* was advancing on an overall width of 230 km; but when it came to attack, the width of the sector of breakthrough was narrowed down to a mere 30 km, while the respective figures for the First Ukrainian *Front* were 250 km and 36 km. This permitted the *front* commanders to mass the following approximate quantities of men and materiel *per kilometre* of sector of breakthrough: one rifle division; 240 guns and mortars; and ninety tanks and SP guns. Consequently, the Soviet forces were able to improve their ratios of superiority over the Germans from roughly 4 to 1 in men, 7 to 1 in guns and mortars, and 5 to 1 in tanks and SP guns to a staggering 9 to 1 in men, 10 to 1 in guns and mortars, and 10 to 1 in tanks and SP guns in the actual sectors of breakthrough.

Within forty-eight hours the First Ukrainian *Front* had effectively pierced the enemy's defences, and its group of exploitation, consisting of two tank armies, had been put into the breach. The original attack had been preceded by a very heavy artillery bombardment of one and three-quarter hours' duration, and the guns then switched to laying down a double box barrage (*dvoiny ognevoi val*) to a depth of about three kilometers inside the enemy's defences. Beyond that point, fire support for the advancing infantry was provided by the guns of the infantry-support tanks and SP guns and from the air, though bad weather reduced the amount of air support which had originally been intended.

The First Belorussian *Front* was similarly successful. The details are a little different, but generally speaking Marshal Zhukov's progress was as triumphant as Marshal Koniev's. There is not time to examine them further here. In any case, enough has been said to demonstrate that the Soviets plan for the Oder-Vistula Operation was remarkably faithful to the prewar concept of the deep operation when to that is coupled the traditional Russian love of enormous numbers. Both Koniev and Zhukov were able to provide fire support over the whole tactical, and subsequently operational, depth of the enemy's defences; they both used mechanised forces as groups of exploitation, and by these methods both of them prevented the enemy from redeploying, reinforcing, or supplying on any but a very small scale. Of course they were helped enormously by their huge numerical superiorities, and by the fact that, as they candidly admit, they had mastery of the air from the outset. As a result of all this, they won.

For my example of the encirclement I have chosen the Jassy-Kishinev Operations (*Yassko-Kishinevskaya Operatsiya*), which lasted from 20 to 29 August 1944. During those ten days the forces of the Second and Third Ukrainian *Fronts* (Army Generals Rodion Y. Malinovsky and F. I. Tolbukhin) annihilated twenty-two Nazi divisions (eighteen by encirclement), and captured more than 208,000 officers and men.[8]

At the start of the operation the correlation of forces in favour of the Soviet Union was 1.4 to 1 in men, more than 2 to 1 in guns and mortars, 4.7 to 1 in tanks and SP guns, and 2.7 to 1 in aircraft. On the actual sectors of breakthrough, however, it was as follows: between 4 and 8 to 1 in men, depending upon the sector, from 6 to 11 to 1 in guns and mortars, 6 to 1 in tanks and SP guns, and 2.5 to 1 in aircraft. Each *front* chose for its sector of breakthrough a narrow strip of sixteen to eighteen kilometres wide. This allowed it to provide *for each kilometre* of that sector a superiority in men which varied from 3.9 to 1 (Second Ukrainian *Front*) to 8 to 1 (Third Ukrainian *Front*), in guns and mortars, 6 to 1 in tanks and SP guns.

The Jassy-Kishinev Operation is a classic in the sense that both army groups delivered converging blows of approximately equal strength. That of the Second Ukrainian *Front* broke through the whole tactical depth of the enemy's defences to a distance of ten kilometres during the first day of the operation, while in that time the Third Ukrainian *Front* had pierced the main, and in places also the second, Nazi defence line. This allowed a mobile group, the 6th Tank Army, to be passed through the gap into the heart of the enemy defences by the end of the very first day, while on the second day more such groups went in. These successes were helped, of course, by the Russians having mastery of the air.

It is not just the speed of the operation which makes Jassy-Kishinev a classic, but also the fact that the double encirclement was used to its best advantage. The inner ring in any double encirclement must face inwards and destroy the surrounded enemy; but the job of the outer ring may be one of two. In many instances (probably in most), the troops comprising the outer ring have got to play a role which is mainly defensive; their job is to prevent the enemy from bringing up reinforcements and relieving his encircled forces. In some instances, however (and Jassy-Kishinev is one of them), the enemy's ability to do this is not considered great; the outer ring of the encircling forces can then be used to continue the advance and thus continue to put pressure on the enemy's strategic reserves. When this happens successfully, the rewards are very great.

If we now take the prewar dream of Tukhachevsky's group of strategists and compare it with the realities of 1944–45, we shall find, I think, that in general the two correspond quite closely. To the extent that there were differences, these were mostly due to the improvements in military technology which came about during the years between the thirties and the final period of the war. The introduction into the Soviet inventory of the SP gun, for instance, was of very great help in solving the problem of how to provide the attacking infantry with artillery support in the later stages of an offensive. The introduction of the Shturmovik airplane is another similar example.

Another difference between the dream and the reality was due to the very high productivity of the Soviet armaments factories. The dream had envisaged a concentration of guns of 35 per km of breakthrough as something so enormous as scarcely to be credible; the reality produced, during the war's third period, a concentration of up to, and over, 250 and produced it regularly.

Furthermore, the actual handling of the artillery was far more sophisticated and far more effective than the prewar dreamers had ever imagined that this could possibly be. The Stavka Directive of 10 January 1942, got things going in the right direction with its concept of the artillery offensive (*artilleriskoe nastuplenie*); but it was not until the introduction, in 1943, of the single box barrage (*ordinarny ognevoi val*) and then, in 1944, of the double box barrage (*dvoiny ognevoi val*) that Soviet artillery really became the god of war, as Stalin, following Napoleon, liked to envisage it.

The huge quantities of guns concentrated on the various sectors of breakthrough, like the huge quantities of tanks and aircraft, were only possible as a result of the introduction of the High Command's Reserve (*Rezerv Glavnogo Komandovania*). This meant that the Stavka had at its immediate and personal disposal a large proportion of the Soviet forces in existence at any one particular time. These it was therefore able to dispense to those sectors of the Eastern Front which it reckoned to be important at that moment. Once these troops had done their job, they were immediately removed and despatched elsewhere where their presence was equally necessary. No such organization was envisaged in the twenties and thirties, at least so far as I am aware.

Naturally, the use of artillery, tanks, and aircraft on this enormous scale required an equally enormous scale of production of ammunition. Soviet figures on ammunition expenditures are relatively hard to come by, but the statement that during the two and one-half months from 19 November 1942 to 2 February 1943, the Soviet artillery fired off five and one-half million shells gives us some idea of the size of the problem facing the munitions factories. Tukhachevsky's dreamers could never have believed it solvable.

In one or two other matters the reality did not live up to the dream. Tukhachevsky had envisaged mass paradrops in the rear of an enemy grouping which, it was hoped, when given effective air support, would prevent the enemy under attack from retreating, and the enemy in the rear from advancing to relieve his encircled colleagues. The triumphant Kiev manoeuvres of 1935 had seemed virtually to guarantee this. As things turned out there were few Soviet paradrops during the GPW, and those that took place were very small-scale affairs. Nor, as a rule, was the Soviet air force, acting alone, capable of doing the paratroops' job and halting enemy reinforcements and supplies. During 1944–45 at least, that job was generally done by the armoured troops, though, of course, in conjunction with the air force and sometimes in conjunction with the infantry.

Where, then, does this leave us? Each of course must decide for himself on the matter. My own view, for what it is worth, is that the formulae were excellent, and consequently correct, so far as they went. However, they did not go very far, because Soviet military technology in the twenties and thirties was often not very good.

Soviet successes in 1944–45 were due, above all, to the exhaustion of the Wehrmacht which by that time, as it seems to me, would have been overwhelmed by numbers, irrespective of the kind of formulae employed to plan their use.

Having said all this, I believe that the Russians have continued to trust those formulae, and that the sorts of new weapons and equipment introduced into the Soviet forces recently have been decided primarily upon their fitness to turn those formulae into account. They still believe in the message of Vladmir K. Triandafillov, and I personally think that they are absolutely right to do so. If Triandafillov's formulae were to be fleshed out with the latest kit of the eighties and then to be launched against us (and assuming, of course, a war that did *not* go nuclear), NATO, I think, would find it had got its hands full.

One final point. The real heroes on the Soviet side of the third period of the war, it seems to me, are those concerned with the rear services, the *Tyl*. How they manufactured, and then delivered to the frontline troops, those enormous quantities of everything which simply smothered the Germans is, in my humble judgement, the real Russian miracle.

Notes

1. A. A. Milne, *Winnie-the-Pooh*, Chapter 8, "In Which Christopher Robin Leads An Expedition to the North Pole."

2. According to Nikita Khrushchev, speaking in January 1960, the strength of the Red Army in 1945 was 11,365,000.

3. An account of the deep operation will be found in the *Soviet Military Encyclopedia*. The 1936 translation of Count Alfred von Schlieffen's *Cannae* was published in Moscow by Gosvoenizdat.

4. The first mass drop was at the Kiev manoeuvers of 1935. For details see *Soviet Military Encyclopedia*. Similar manoeuvers took place in 1936.

5. In the English edition, the title was changed to *How Russia Makes War*.

6. The material in this section is based on *Istoriya Velikoi Otechestvennoi Voiny 1941–1945* (IVOVSS), Vol 5: 58–68.

7. By *razgromleno* the Russians mean that the formations in question had suffered casualties of between 50 to 70 percent.

8. The material for this section is mostly taken from IVOVSS, Vol 4: 254–275.

Commentary

Waldo H. Heinrichs

An easy first impression from these papers would be that military planning in World War II was dismal. In two cases nations went to war without plans for winning; in the third case successful planning occurred when the enemy was on the run. Looking closer, however, the story is more complex. We learn that planning is deeply rooted in history, culture, and national self-perception and therefore is a reflection as well as a source of strength or weakness. Furthermore, the process, based on prediction from fragmentary evidence, is highly dependent on how stable and informative the international environment is. At this deeper level these three papers, drawn from roughly the same historical moment, provide a rich fund of analysis on the nature and problems of military planning.

Professor Cairns' paper offers a good starting point. The extent of his reach into the thought and experience of France between the wars and his carefully executed argument reveal much about the sources and premises of planning. The question he asks is this: how did it come about that France chose war when it was so unclear about how to fight that war beyond its first defensive stage? His answer is the French military elite's obsession with defense, derived from a number of sources: national despair over the cost and slim margin of victory in 1918, expectation that the next war would be like the last, economic weakness and misalignment of national spending, military requirements and industrial capacity, need for and uncertainty about allies, and the lack of candid exchange of views at the top because of communications channels silted up with rivalry and suspicion.

The argument and evidence are very persuasive. As Professor Cairns notes, it is hard to see how planning could have been other than for defense. Paradoxically, if the military was a source of realism about France's plight, it would seem that their inordinate informal influence over high policy was salutary. But in the end, of course, the military opted for war. Certainly Britain's conversion to intervention was a major factor in this abrupt shift. Professor Cairns mentions other factors as well: great preparations, recovery, blockade, and "harnessing of American industry," "elements" which Daladier and Gamelin "thought they saw. . .beginning to come together" in August 1939. It would be so interesting to learn more about these factors and how they contributed to the shift. Especially interesting would be French estimates of American help. But perhaps that is another story.

Professor Coox has given us an authoritative account of Japanese decisions and planning leading to the start of the Pacific War and also a list of features of the planning system, indeed of the whole Japanese military system, which bore, more or less, on any particular enterprise. Chief among these features, it seems to me, are the following: the lack of a decisionmaking structure to reconcile diverse service aims which led Japan to military adventures beyond its means and wars that only widened; impetuosity and misplaced heroism which caused hasty planning with inattention to intelligence, logistics, and routine operations and to emphasis on the first phase to the detriment of ultimate objectives; training, even at the war college level, which only enhanced the narrowness and inflexibility of the Japanese officer caste; the cultural phenomenon of rule from below whereby middle-grade officers exercised undue influence over their seniors in favor of rash decisions. Professor Coox correctly stresses Japan's sense of dwindling potency in the face of the American oil embargo, and, I might add, the American two-ocean navy program of 1940. Time, as in the case of the French, seemed on the side of the enemy. How different the action in anticipation of events of the Japanese, French, Germans, and, in the end, the Americans from the disposition of the Russians to wait out enemies.

Professor Coox is right in his generally negative characterization of Japanese military planning and leadership but he is perhaps too negative. Planning for a decisive fleet encounter with the Americans centered on battleships, it is true, but also included critical roles for air and submarines. Interestingly, American naval planning of the interwar period developed the obverse of the Japanese plan. Indeed, through war gaming and intelligence, the two navies developed roughly the same picture of the same battle in the same place, one of the few instances of precise communication between the two nations in that age. Also on the positive side, Japan, ahead of all other navies, accepted the idea of the carrier as the centerpiece of a long-range striking force, thereby shifting the paradigm of naval warfare, and they employed the idea brilliantly in the six-carrier attack on Pearl Harbor and follow up five-carrier

106

sweep of the Indian Ocean. New thinking could percolate through to the top.

Professor Coox pays due respect to what Field Marshall Slim describes as the "obedience and ferocity" of the Japanese soldier but criticizes the lack of imagination of the generals. Perhaps forces in the Pacific under overall naval command were better led. By 1944 the formidable fighting qualities of the Japanese soldier there were harnessed to superb defensive arrangements on Biak, Peleliu, Iwo Jima, and Okinawa, as the Americans learned to their great cost. The Kamikaze did not fit Blitzkrieg war, but at Okinawa these planes cost the American navy nearly four hundred ships and small craft sunk or damaged. They had a distinct influence, along with stubborn Japanese resistance ashore, on American plans and policies for ending the war. In their own way the Japanese fought not only with tenacity but also with brains.

The paper by Peter Vigor deals with instances of Soviet planning success in World War II at a time when the Red Army had every advantage. Evidence in Soviet history is rare enough and we are fortunate in what Mr. Vigor has found and the insights it provides him. I wish there were more—more about the Tukhachevsky group. How did it stand in comparison with the Soviet military thinking of the interwar period? Was this a brilliant exception to fairly conventional if not shopworn ideas? How did these concepts survive the purge and reenter the mainstream of thinking?

Vigor believes the Wehrmacht was so badly mauled by 1944 that almost any strategy would have worked, but that because these formulae of deep penetration and encirclement succeeded, they became Soviet dogma and may well persist down to this day. This raises an interesting question in the history of ideas: What is the longevity of a strategic or operational concept? How much is timeless abstraction (i.e., double envelopment), how much is history (i.e., textbook battles, Cannae, Jassy-Kishinev), and how much is the current nature and imperative of warfare? How relevant would the battles of World War II seem to a generation of planners now untouched by that war?

According to Peter Vigor, German failure in Russia was due less to Russian success than "Hitler's hideous incompetence as a warlord." If that is so, to whom do we attribute German success before June 1941? Further, was the gross underestimation of Russian capabilities Hitler's fault alone? Was the lag of infantry behind the fast forces as important as the pause resulting from strategic indecision? Was Hitler's determination to complete the envelopments rather than strike for Moscow beyond the bounds of good strategy or was there a real dilemma? Not all German generals were Guderians.

So much for the papers individually. Considered together they may yield further insights. For example, one notes common influences of the war as a whole that affected national planning experience. One of these was the proximity of World War I. Only a little over twenty years separated the two wars, comparable to the period from the beginning of American combat involvement in Vietnam to now. The first war was not only a personal memory of all leaders but a determining professional experience for many officers. In France, as Professor Cairns shows, it bred pessimism. In Japan, which played a marginal role, it fostered the illusion of repeating Jutland, as Professor Coox explains. In the Soviet Union, it encouraged the development of new attack theory, as Peter Vigor shows. Both France and the Soviet Union suffered invasion in World War I, but France learned the lesson of defense while the Soviets learned that of attack. Why? In the event both nations started the war defensively, but the USSR had manpower and space to trade for time to bring about the *guerre des masses* which the French planners only hinted at.

For the Americans World War I was in many ways a helpful preparation for World War II. They fought long enough to gain experience in managing and supplying a distant front, hard enough to gain a sober view of modern war, and yet not so long as to lose the offensive spirit.

A second characteristic of World War II as a whole was the highly volatile state of power arrangements in the world. German and Japanese revisionism devastated the fragile interwar order, leaving the powers jockeying anxiously for position and partners, seeking especially to draw in the great neutrals, the United States, Soviet Union, and Japan. In this situation of great fluidity and unpredictability, planners had to consider bewildering variables. They placed a premium on flexibility, resilience, improvisation, speed, and figuring in the constraints and capabilities of partners or putative partners. The convulsion of world politics encouraged opportunism: Japan, after German victory in Europe in 1940, hastened to join the Axis and advance southward while the time was ripe. France grabbed at the opportunity for an ally in August 1939. At the same time nations tended to lose a sense of control of their destinies and lapse into fatalism. The Japanese Navy manifested this in the circular reasoning with which it justified further southward advance in 1941: expectation of an American embargo necessitated advance to acquire resources which in turn would trigger the embargo and force war.

A third characteristic was an unusual amount of intelligence, especially from decryption of machine cyphers. Temporarily the code breakers prevailed over the code makers, though not all the time nor in every case. Planners had unique knowledge of the enemy. MAGIC did not prevent Pearl Harbor, nor did ULTRA convince the British until June of Hitler's determination unconditionally to attack the Soviet Union. But the take was obviously of historic importance, perhaps at Kursk, certainly at Midway and at several stages of the Battle of the Atlantic, as well as elsewhere. Enigma and its variants almost seemed to serve as a private great power wire service.

These common characteristics by no means limit the insights that can be drawn from these valuable papers. Perhaps more will become evident through comparison of these three planning cases— the French, Japanese, and Russian—with the American. Here it is necessary to distinguish between American planning for a European and for a Pacific War.

American planning for war on Germany and Italy was effective (a more useful word I think than successful). There was no question of inordinate military influence; President Franklin D. Roosevelt was very much in charge. Indeed, with regard to intervention in the Atlantic battle he engaged in planning himself. The service secretaries were actively involved in policy and the service chiefs stayed within bounds. Consultation was extensive and frequent; discussion was frank and at times heated. Secretary of War Henry L. Stimson on occasion bluntly criticized the President for not moving fast enough. None would have accused the head of navy war plans, Rear Admiral Richmond Kelly Turner, of reticence.

For Europe, the Roosevelt administration started late and moved too deliberately, but it planned well. Late in 1940 the Chief of Naval Operations and his planners successfully reoriented naval strategy away from outdated Pacific plans to concentrate on Europe and the ultimate conquest of Germany. Plans of the Rainbow series provided a flexible framework of defense and transition toward intervention. British-American staff talks laid the basis of wartime cooperation which equally served to guide Atlantic Fleet organization and dispositions in the quasi-war circumstances of April through November 1941. The Victory program meshed industrial capacity with anticipated military requirements. Planning provided a plausible and consistent overall purpose and direction as well as considerable leeway for changing operational capabilities, the ebb and flow of battle (the westward drift of U-boat attacks, for example), and the shifting pattern of German threat. Eastwardly the American planning record is impressive.

The opposite was the case with planning and policy toward Japan. Here the President's tendency to compartmentalize his advisers, less evident in the European case, caused trouble. He failed to reconcile the stiff, no-concession policy which he permitted the State Department to pursue with the military's concentration on Europe and need for time and flexibility in Pacific matters. The military leaders were not conversant with diplomatic policy; Secretary Stimson found out Secretary Hull was negotiating with the Japanese by way of MAGIC intercepts. Having wrangled for years over the defense of the Philippines, having reached an impasse with the British on defense of the Malay Barrier, and having turned their attention eastward to the big show, the Army and Navy tended to neglect Pacific problems, at least until July 1941. Fresh and realistic appraisals and new ideas were lacking. Discarded strategic concepts like the Orange Plan grand parade across the Pacific exerted lingering influence. Something like the stagnancy, drift, and ambiguity, which Professor Cairns depicts characterized American Pacific strategy and policy. When Japan moved into southern Indochina the tempo changed. The United States reacted swiftly and dramatically, but not coherently. It set about establishing in the Philippines the largest possible force of long-range bombers as a deterrent to Japan, ultimately to amount to more than two hundred B–17s, nearly all those available.

This force, destroyed 8 December at Clark Field, neither deterred nor inspired Japanese attack. What it did do, however, was to give American policymakers the sense of having solved their frustrating dilemmas of Pacific defense. They leaped at the opportunity for a quick solution. Listen to the words of General George Marshall as transcribed from a telephone conversation on 25 September 1941:

> If we can build up quickly, considering the fact that those planes can operate from Port Darwin [sic] and Australia, from New Britain; from Singapore and the Dutch East Indies; possibly even Vladivostock, [sic]— we can cover that whole area of possible Japanese operations. . . .[This] would exercise a more determining influence on the course of events right now than anything else. . . .Because it practically backs the Japanese off and would certainly stop them on the Malaysian thing. It probably would

make them feel they didn't dare take the Siberian thing and I think it has a better than 50 percent chance of forcing them to practically drop the Axis.[1]

Here was an abrupt change, like France's in August 1939, with similar bounding from strategic despondency to excessive optimism. Quick shifts tend to mesmerize planners.

Parallel to the Philippine reinforcement was application of a full embargo against Japan, which, in spite of recent writings to the contrary, was done with full cognizance of the President. Why Roosevelt chose in this instance to employ not deterrence but coercion remains a mystery. Possibly he believed Asians only expected such firmness; or he was indifferent as to whether the outcome was Japanese submission, a standoff, or a war of long-range blockade and containment; or he hoped to so worry the Japanese to the south that they dare not attack Russia while German armies advanced on Moscow. Perhaps some, one, or all of these motives were at work, or simple negligence. The moment of surprise came, however, late in November when it became apparent the Japanese would not be immobilized. Then came a momentary rush for a diplomatic solution that would finally square with a defensive military posture. This ran on the rocks of coalition maintenance and was quickly abandoned.

American strategy and policy demonstrate that realism and illusion, flexibility and rigidity, coherence and ambiguity can coexist in the complex enterprise of military planning.

Notes

1. Telephone conversation between General Marshall and Lieutenant Commander W.R. Smedberg III, 25 Sep 1941, Op Nav Telephone Records, 1941–1942, U.S. Navy Operational Archives, Navy Yard, Washington, D.C. Smedberg was flag secretary to Admiral Harold R. Stark, Chief of Naval Operations.

Discussion and Comments

Forrest C. Pogue, Moderator

Horst Boog (Federal Republic of Germany): I have a question for Mr. Vigor. You know the United States supplied the Russians with about 427,000 trucks. What was the importance of these trucks in enabling the Soviets to carry out their mobile operations in the later years of the war? In other words, would the Russians have performed as well without these trucks?

Vigor: The allies sent only two items of any value to the Soviet Union: the trucks you have mentioned and food. The trucks played an enormous role in assuring the mobility of the Soviet forces and were used in the typical Soviet fashion. That is to say, they were concentrated in the particular army group conducting important operations at the time. Once that operation was over, they were stripped and sent to the next army group to reuse. Their importance was very great.

Otto Nelson (Texas Tech University): Mr. Vigor, what have the Russians learned from their military experience in Afghanistan over the last five years?

Vigor: Well, one thing you can say they have learned is that it's more difficult to defeat a fairly primitive people, given the right topography for the people to operate in. I don't think Afghanistan is going to be a Soviet Vietnam. The casualties are far too few if you analyze Soviet casualties in terms of casualties per head of population per year. If you compare those with that of the British in Northern Ireland, you will find that actually ours are rather higher, and yet we are still there, and we don't look like we're coming out. I'm quite sure the Russians are not going to come out. There are two things the Soviets have learned by taking part. It always does a unit good to have a battle of some kind; it doesn't matter what. And of course they have learned a very great deal in particular about the use of helicopters.

Unidentified Speaker: I have a question for Mr. Vigor. I was unable to hear precisely how you defined Soviet doctrine, but I understand it features massive fire support at the point of penetration, and after hitting the enemy across the battlefield, sealing off his rear. We've heard much recently about the operational maneuver group which supposedly is a new tactic, a new doctrine. Where do you see that fitting into the Soviet's doctrine, strategy, or planning today?

Vigor: It's not a new doctrine at all. You will find it in the Tukhachevsky school. The thing is, since the Russians are now paying very much more attention to conventional warfare than they did ten years ago, they have started to reintroduce concepts which they already had, and the operational maneuver group is simply the old concept fleshed out with better equipment, that's all. That, if I may say so, is how our little center managed to identify it so easily.

Dennis Showalter (Colorado College): This is really a general question. We heard three papers with matrices in three different systems, democratic, authoritarian, and totalitarian, and yet Dr. Heinrichs pointed out they all seemed to have a common problem developing effective military planning. My question is might there be something inherent in the nature of modern complex plural societies that tends to redo or tends to force military planning, like any other decisionmaking in those societies, into a kind of politics of the diagonal, and might we not perhaps be better off to consider this as opposed to setting up a sort of quasi-Clauswitzian abstract ideal for military planning? I hope the question is reasonable as being opposed to being a statement.

Coox: I think Dennis has given a very good statement rather than a very good question in this case, at least as I saw it. With the Japanese I can say that it was not a matter that transcended services clawing for rare resources. My understanding of the French example, and Professor Cairns can correct this, was to optimize available funds by pouring them into the Maginot Line and into what was necessary to avoid the bleeding of World War I. But the Japanese, the two Japanese services, clawed for finite funding to fight two utterly separate enemies. I was mentioning to one of my colleagues earlier that I don't know about these other services, but the Japanese services actually resorted to violence between themselves in their desperation to maximize the relatively few funds. In our country it's rather cute to talk about Army-Navy football games and to chide each other, but with the Japanese there are instances of violence in staff meetings at very high levels, and of talking back to the war minister. After Tojo became prime minister, if he disagreed with your attitude, you were transferred at 0800 next morning to Okinawa or Iwo or some place else. It was a death sentence actually, so it is taken very very seriously in Japan, and I think it transcends some of the things that were mentioned in the prefatory remarks.

Vigor: As far as the Soviet Union is concerned, I think the difficulties they got into were simply the costs of the coincidence that the war for them started at that particular moment. At first there was the effect of the purchase which was colossal; secondly the radar was only in the process of being built up. In other words it is my impression that if the Soviet Union were to go to war tomorrow against a major enemy, its planning would be in very much better shape than it was in 1941.

Bob Love (U.S. Naval Academy): Japanese intelligence efforts were superb. They seemed to be very good at analyzing their own physical and economic limitations. Professor Coox, how good was their economic intelligence in the United States, given the fact the data were largely open during the New Deal, and how much impact did it have on the staff planning?

Coox: As I indicated Japanese planning was predicated upon some very good staff work, but it was done with preconception. The answers were there and ready for the meetings to discuss. Bulging briefcases were brought in and facts and figures were given, because as you say, they had pretty good access to what was going on over here. But let me say it was entirely colored by the view they had of our willingness to fight—our social constitution. Intelligence was reporting the disunity in the United States. They sent back no positive comments about going to war but stressed intelligence reporting on the isolationist senators, on the racial and ethnic divisiveness in the United States. This was cranked into their decisionmaking process, and thus the intelligence that they brought in might have been technically valid in the collection level, but as I indicated in my talk, the analysis and estimation really stunk.

Frankie Clay (University of New Mexico): Professor Coox, to follow up on that question, to what degree did the 1904–1905 experience, consciously or subconsciously, influence the decisionmaking in Japan.

Coox: Very much to the point. They were going to repeat Port Arthur and Tsushima in one-two fashion in the time frame I mentioned earlier. They had really no stomach, as you can tell, for a very long war. They had no intention of conquering the United

States. They thought that by 1943, certainly and hopefully by 1942, they would get some kind of intermediation by a new Teddy Roosevelt who would appear on the scene from somewhere and would bring a happy ending, from their point of view, to the Russo-German War which they wanted mediated, even if they themselves had to do it, and to their own war with us, believing we'd lose stomach for it. The end would be a spitting image of 1904–1905 with similarly happy results.

Walton Moody (Office of Air Force History): This question is for Dr. Cairns. You spoke about the contradiction between the French adopting a defensive strategy based on the Maginot Line and the quest for allies in eastern Europe, and you suggested the contradiction between these was not as great as might at first appear. I wonder if you could elucidate further on that?

Cairns: Sure. Well, it's not a very elaborate idea but simply this: the line, the fortresses, the famous fortresses, were designed to protect French territory from the kind of invasion and occupation which occurred in 1914. It was never believed at all by the French Army that they would stay behind that line. You know, of course, that when the Rhineland was remilitarized in March 1936, it was said then, and it continues to be said today, that France lost her last opportunity to go to the assistance of her eastern European clients. Here was a remilitarization of the Rhineland, they could never get access to Germany, and so forth and so on. But the point is access was to come not across the Rhine; access was to come through Belgium of course, which took one right into the heart of Germany's industrial area. In this sense I think there is no contradiction, save this: the design depends upon those eastern clients holding out long enough to be saved. But increasingly as the years ran their course, and certainly this was true by 1938—absolutely true by the spring of 1938—there was every realization by the French military that in the event of war, in the event that Czechoslovakia, Poland, whoever it might be, went to war with France and Great Britain, the likelihood was that those states would go down after a certain period of time. But of course they would be resurrected. This was the history of Poland. It has always been resurrected as Layton tells us, never in the same place twice. This basically was what they believed. Now naturally they didn't tell the Poles this, they didn't tell the Czechs this, the Rumanians, the Yugoslavians, and so forth and so on, but the general idea was that in fact the line would provide the time, the time needed to prepare those immense French and British armies which eventually would go, with American assistance of course, to

116

the rescue of eastern Europe. But, as I tried to say, that was projected very far ahead, way over the horizon.

If I may just take one second, Professor Heinrichs asked the question whether this was an illusion; that in 1939 they imagined they were beginning to see the elements of all this coming together. I don't really think so. I think the prospects were grim for the immediate future of course, and nobody could put a date on it. Gamelin variously talked about 1941, and if one goes into the war, one sees that he begins to talk about 1942. So it's perhaps a mirage which disappears as one advances toward it, but that they genuinely believed these conditions were being pulled together I think is absolutely so. It is not extraordinary that they should have done so, because it exactly parallels the situation of 1914. The French went to war in 1914 believing once more that a certain combination of circumstances had come together which they had to grasp. If they failed then, if they didn't move then, the European disposition would be so entirely altered as to leave them entirely alone one day, and although the circumstances are in detail terribly terribly different between the one war and the other, in fact of course there is a quite interesting parallel there.

SESSION II

Technology and USAF Planning

Introduction

Of the many dilemmas facing modern military planners, none is more perplexing than integrating existing and future technology into current war plans. An army can only go to war with weapon systems in being; at the same time, planners, aided by scientific and political advisors, must accurately determine what new weapons are technically possible and the likelihood their governments will provide funds to develop and acquire them. The problem became serious when the internal combustion engine appeared; aviation and nuclear power has made this dimension of military planning even more difficult. For these reasons, the Eleventh Military History Symposium devoted its second session to the United States Air Force and how it grappled with incorporating technology into planning when quantum advances in science appeared frequently and the defense role of America expanded with the cold war.

Proper organization held promise for ameliorating the problem because the primary difficulties revolved around control and coordination among ground commanders, scientists, and fliers. As aviation technology in the 1930s offered greater advances to the Army Air Corps, these difficulties grew more complex. The scientist and civilian manufacturer became increasingly important after World War II, and with the advent of America's new international role, civilian leadership played more of an active role in military planning. The Air Force organizational record proved mixed. As the number of groups necessarily involved with planning grew, coordination became more difficult. Each man involved in planning needed to be knowledgeable about the responsibilities of counterparts in other military divisions and government agencies. Training that knowledgeable planner, however, was too often left to on-the-job experience and chance. In Session II, the authors of our papers carefully outline and describe the many pitfalls and difficulties the Air Force encountered in organizing and incorporating technology into its planning function.

Professor Holley focuses on a single but very important technological innovation slow to develop in the United States—the jet engine—and he asks the simple question, why? He finds no single answer but instead concludes that the failure stemmed from a number of problems in the 1930s Army Air Corps and to some extent, existing purchasing arrangements. The right questions were not asked, structural arrangements within the service's research and development organization stymied progress, and the military itself did not possess officers with adequate technical backgrounds, nor had they the opportunity for truly rigorous professional military development. While the United States won World War II, the same factors which inhibited proper advances in jet engines can exist in today's military, and there is value in remembering these potentially dangerous flaws.

Colonel Gropman's comprehensive paper takes the reader through a maze of problems facing the post-World War II planner. Committed in spirit to the vast potential offered by science and technology to the Air Force, the organization set up to take advantage of those benefits did not always seem appropriate. Planners too often were not philosophically in tune with the nature of planning and remained wedded to operational concepts and day-to-day concerns. Planning shops became the focus of many projects distantly related but inhibitive to good planning. While the introduction of Rand into military planning represented a great step forward in assisting planners, at the same time the commitment to research and development was undercut by lowered budgets and organizational struggles before the Korean War. The author concludes that through the decade following World War II, a nexus for planning between operations, plans, and research was missing as well as appropriate doctrine to guide it. The result was a lack of true strategic planning.

These papers demonstrate the absolute necessity for a nation to organize its planning function with care and to staff it with intelligent men of vision. Only when these criteria are met can complete and appropriate coordination occur—without the proper integration of soldier, scientists, and civilian leadership, planning is incomplete.

Jet Lag in the Army Air Corps

I. B. Holley, Jr.

I. The Threat

By the summer of 1944 the Allied Air Forces were beginning to achieve air superiority over the Luftwaffe above *Festung Europa*. But during the fall they encountered in increasing numbers an extraordinary aircraft, the Me–262, a jet fighter capable of better than 500 mph. By February 1945 these German jets were shooting down bombers with appalling frequency. When sixty Me–262s shot down twenty-five B–17s in a brief action, Allied leaders began to fear they would no longer be able to sustain their program of daylight bombing over Germany. Fortunately for the Allies the multiple pressures already brought to bear on the German nation induced collapse before the Luftwaffe jets could be deployed in sufficient numbers to gain superiority. At the time of surrender, however, the Allies still had no jet fighters over Europe.[1]

The official historians of the Army Air Forces have assessed our lag in perfecting jet fighters as the "most serious inferiority" in weaponry experienced by the United States in World War II.[2] How can we explain this technological failure? During the interwar era Air Corps leaders had repeatedly assured the people of the United States that our military aircraft were at least equal and often superior to any in the world.[3] Nevertheless, the Germans put substantial numbers of jet fighters in European skies, and we did not. Even the jets we eventually did produce, though not in time for combat, were based on the Whittle engine developed by the British before the war. In short, we were taken unawares; we suffered a technological surprise.

I am indebted to my colleague Professor Alex Roland for very helpful, constructive comments on early drafts of this paper and to the staff members of the Office of Air Force History, the Air University Library, and the USAF Historical Research Center, Maxwell AFB, for assistance in tracking down elusive sources.

Surprise is a cardinal principle of war; technological surprise has long been a major factor in victory. Therefore technological planning and decisionmaking must aim at avoiding such breakthroughs by the enemy while striving for them to our own advantage; this involves continuous effort on two fronts: incremental improvement in existing weaponry on the one hand, and on the other the search for novel weapons, new principles, or new possibilities for creating hitherto unknown means for achieving a decided advantage over the enemy.

Our concern here is with the Air Corps planners in the pre-World War II years. How did they go about making their decisions on weaponry, for to plan is to decide? How were they organized and funded? How were they educated? And how effectively did they integrate their resources to plan for the nation's aerial defense?

If the United States led the world in aeronautical development for most of the between-war years, why did we fail to lead the pack in perfecting jet fighters? Robert Schlaifer, the author of the immensely valuable study on *The Development of Aircraft Engines*, dismisses this failure as simply "the result of a historical accident," attributing "no particular significance" to the fact.[4] In my view this too easy dismissal won't do. In a field where failing to back the right technological prospect may literally endanger national survival, it behooves us to learn all we can about the process by which such decisions are made. And as military historians we know that even the seemingly distant past may divulge insights to inform the present.

II. The Evolution of Jet Propulsion

The principle of reaction propulsion was by no means unknown in the United States during the years between the wars. Reports of French and British experimental work with jets appeared in the scientific and engineering journals in the early twenties.[5] In the United States the staff at McCook Field, the Air Services engineering center at Dayton, Ohio, asked the Bureau of Standards in 1922 to investigate the reaction principle as a means of aircraft propulsion. The findings of Edgar Buckingham, the bureau investigator, were published in 1924. His conclusions were decidedly negative.

Even at the highest flying speed then in sight, which Buckingham set at 250 mph, he found that fuel consumption for a jet would be four times that of a piston engine with a propeller. This was undoubtedly true—at the speed indicated—but then he went on to

124

assert, quite erroneously, that a reaction engine would be "far more complicated than a piston engine." Finally, he concluded, there was no prospect that jet propulsion would *ever* be of practical value, "even for military purposes."[6]

Here was the classic example of a careful investigator who compiled evidence with meticulous accuracy, and then proceeded to make an inferential leap which carried him far beyond what the evidence warranted. The practical effect of Buckingham's report was to taint the concept of jet propulsion. If a competent investigator found the principle impractical, why pursue the idea any further? But the concept of a reaction engine refused to go away.

Scarcely a year passed without someone in the United States surfacing anew the notion of jet propulsion. Responses to such proposals tended to take two different forms. There were those who saw *possibilities* and those who saw only *difficulties*. One is reminded of the old saw that defines the optimist as one who says the whiskey bottle is half full and the pessimist as one who says it's half empty. It would be unfair to categorize these two groups as the scientists and the engineers, but it was men who *thought* like scientists, whatever their formal titles, men such as Robert Goddard and Alexander Klemin, the professor of aerodynamics at New York University, who articulated the promise of jet propulsion though well aware that many difficult problems remained to be solved.[7] The nay-sayers are typified by the Bureau of Standards investigator whose studies led him to conclude that developing a jet aircraft would be a "difficult if not impossible task."[8]

The persistent reappearance of proposals for jet aircraft led to further investigations of the reaction principle. Some of these were performed at the Bureau of Standards; others were conducted by staff members in the laboratories of the National Advisory Committee for Aeronautics (NACA) at Langley Field, the research arm of the agency created in 1915 to coordinate aeronautical research and disseminate the latest findings in the field. These studies tended to confirm Buckingham's conclusions: at currently available speeds, the concept of jet propulsion was unacceptable, because it was hopelessly inefficient in comparison with piston engines.[9]

In the 1930s, however, aircraft speeds were advancing rapidly. The British won the Schneider cup races in 1931 with a top speed of 407 mph which the Italians topped soon afterward with 440, giving a strong indication of the quantum jumps in speed that were just over the horizon.[10] In 1934 John Stack, one of the leading NACA

investigators, reported that as an aircraft approached the speed of
sound it encountered a marked increase in drag and a sharp decline
in propeller efficiency. This clearly indicated that there was a
practical limit on the speeds to be achieved by propeller-driven
aircraft.[11]

John Stack's findings made no discernible splash in those Air
Corps circles most concerned with developing faster fighter aircraft.
It would, however, be exceedingly difficult for Air Corps officials to
be unaware of the famous Volta conference on high-speed aircraft
sponsored by the Italian Academy of Sciences in 1935. This
international congress attracted leading aerodynamicists from all the
major nations, men such as Prandtl, von Karman, Buseman, Taylor,
and Jacobs. Most of the practical or developmental studies cited in
the papers presented there referred to work done in the United
States, largely at the NACA Langley center. By contrast, in the
realm of theoretical studies, the Germans were way out ahead of
everybody else. And two of these theoretical papers dealt with the
principle of reaction propulsion.[12]

Among those attending the Volta conference was Theodore von
Karman, the Hungarian-born scientist who studied under Prandtl at
Göttingen and later took up a professorship at the California
Institute of Technology. He returned from Italy immensely impressed with what he had seen there. At Guidonia, the Italian
research center, for example, he had observed a 2,500–mph wind
tunnel where investigations of supersonic phenomena were well
advanced. When he attempted to communicate to Air Corps officials
his excitement and sense of urgency on the need to start immediately
to secure supersonic wind tunnels, he met with but little response:
too expensive; where would the money come from?

When von Karman approached the NACA to urge construction
of a supersonic tunnel, the response he received from George W.
Lewis, the executive director, was even more discouraging. Why,
Lewis asked, would anyone want a wind tunnel operating at speeds
much greater than the existing 650-mph NACA tunnel, since
propellers lose their efficiency rapidly in the regions above 600 mph?
Manifestly Mr. Lewis was the victim of his unexamined assumption
that airplanes had to rely on propellers. This assumption is all the
more curious in light of the almost continual discussion of reaction
propulsion in the aeronautical press and in the studies made in his
own laboratories.[13]

If the top Air Corps officials failed to respond with enthusiasm to von Karman's plea for facilities to investigate the supersonic region, at least somebody in the Office of the Chief of Air Corps was sensitive to the important implications of the Volta conference. The *Air Corps Newsletter* for 15 January 1937 reprinted in translation an article from the Italian aeronautical journal *Ala d'Italia* by one Arturo Crocco of the Italian Academy.[14] I regard this article as a most important piece of evidence in our investigation of the Air Corps approach to jet propulsion. In the first place, someone at Air Corps headquarters had to be sufficiently impressed by the article to have it translated from the Italian. Moreover, the editor of the newsletter had to be impressed enough with its significance to grant it the space required. Given the lack of funds which marked all Air Corps activities, the newsletter was then a crudely mimeographed affair appearing twice a month with a very limited number of pages.

Crocco's article described three regions of speed: subsonic, transonic, and supersonic, which he called ballistic since artillery shells already reached such speeds. For aircraft to reach supersonic speeds, he observed, the Volta conference had shown that streamlining akin to that of an artillery shell would be required. But then he went on to add:

> Not only the aerodynamical basis but also the principles of propulsion and power will have to change if we want to reach ballistic flight. New technical principles will have to be realized for propulsive apparatus and for engines. This change will not be a gradual evolution but a revolution.

A more obvious roadmap would be hard to imagine. And it was circulated to every Air Corps installation in the nation. But no evidence has been turned up to indicate that the idea took root anywhere in the service. Meanwhile, as we know, a similar path of reasoning had sparked the mind of a young RAF cadet at Cranwell by the name of Frank Whittle.

The story of how Whittle developed his jet engine is so well known we need only touch on the highlights. In a cadet term paper on the future of aircraft design, he assumed that aircraft speeds beyond 500 mph would be achieved only in the upper atmosphere where the density would be less than a quarter of what it is at sea level. Inevitably, he reasoned, propellers and piston engines would have to give way to some other form of propulsion. This led him to conceive of a turbojet engine, an idea he patented in 1930. Although the Air Ministry regarded his idea as impractical, he went ahead with it, publishing an article in the Royal Aeronautical Society *Journal* in 1931.

The Air Ministry apparently thought enough of Whittle's potential to send him to Cambridge for two years of advanced study under the leading British aerodynamicist, B. M. Jones. The following year, while still a serving officer, Whittle rounded up financial backers and opened a tiny shop, Power Jets, Ltd., to develop a turbojet engine. A year later, in 1937, he had a bench model of his engine running. It was still a crude affair with many bugs to iron out, but there was progress enough to demonstrate the feasibility of the concept in terms of the thrust-to-weight ratio, fuel consumption, and the like.[15]

Always short of funds, Whittle again approached the Air Ministry for support. When referred to the engineers at the Royal Aircraft Establishment at Farnborough, the British equivalent of Wright Field, he received no encouragement. However, in Sir Henry Tizard, who chaired the engine subcommittee of the Aeronautical Research Council at the Air Ministry, he found an adherent who eventually persuaded the ministry to assist Power Jets, Ltd., with a modest contract. Tizard, it is worth noting, was a distinguished scientist in his own right and rector of the Imperial College of Science and Technology. Once again there seems to have been a difference in the way the developmental engineers approached the problem compared to the scientist.[16]

Another contrast worth noting was the difference between the British and American organizations for the development of weapons. Unlike its Air Corps counterpart in the United States, which had no real internal scientific office, the Air Ministry during most of the between-war years had two major entities, a Directorate of Scientific Research and a Directorate of Technical Development. The former was specifically enjoined to link the latest advances in the realm of science with the ongoing work of developing aircraft.[17]

The story of German jet development also offers some revealing contrasts to what happened in the United States. In 1933, Hans von Ohain, a Göttingen student, began toying with the idea of jet propulsion. Shrewdly surmising that the leading engine manufacturers would not be enthusiastic about a radical departure in engine design which threatened to undercut their stock-in-trade, he approached instead, Heinkel, the aircraft manufacturer, who was known to be much interested in high speed airplanes. In 1935 he secured a patent for his turbojet design and in August 1939, just three days before the coming of war, the von Ohain-Heinkel jet made its first flight. Of course, it was far from ready to be put into production, but it did serve to demonstrate the feasibility of the turbojet principle.[18]

German aircraft designers, with their close ties to the scientific community, with Prandtl at Göttingen and others, needed no practical demonstration in flight to convince them that the turbojet was the wave of the future. Even before the von Ohain jet first flew, every major German airframe concern had initiated a jet design project. While many months and even years would be required to push these designs to the point of practical hardware, the conceptual revolution had already taken place—in Britain and in Germany, but not in the United States.[19]

To put the problem in perspective, it is worth noting that the Whittle jet first flew in May of 1941. The first production item didn't appear until early 1943, and initial flight tests proved disappointing. In another year, however, Whittle jets were making an impressive 500 mph. Nevertheless, even though a few British jets were used successfully against V–1 buzz bombs in England, none saw service against German fighters over Europe.[20]

In Germany, meanwhile, at least one of the several turbojet development projects showed sufficient progress to justify production in quantity. This was the Junkers Jumo 004 engine. Installed in a Messerschmidt jet fighter airframe, the Me–262, this combination subsequently achieved a top speed of 541 mph in its production version. Its progress toward mass production was, to say the least, erratic. After his quick victories of 1940, Hitler ordered a stop on all research and development projects which would not produce weapons in eighteen months. His decision seriously delayed work on the jets.[21] After Technical Director Udet's suicide in 1941, General Erhard Milch, who was Deputy Air Minister under Goering, had to make a decision on whether or not to divert skilled labor from current production on the Me–109 fighter to work on the Me–262. Apparently fearing Hitler's wrath if production totals declined, Milch opted for the piston-driven Me–109, so it was July of 1942 before the Me–262 jet first flew. Rave reports from experienced fighter pilots who tested it finally led to an order for mass production to begin. The tradeoff was not a bad one, for the Junkers Jumo engine required only 700 manhours to build, in contrast to the 3,000 to 5,000 hours needed to build a conventional piston engine.[22]

At this juncture Hitler's intuition intruded. Just as production of the 262 began to gather momentum in the spring of 1944, he abruptly ordered Messerschmitt to reconfigure the jet as a fighter-bomber, which is to say, as a close air support, low-altitude airplane for use as an anti-invasion weapon, rather than a high-altitude, air superiority fighter and interceptor. He seemed not to have realized that such reconfiguring was more than a simple matter of attaching pylons for armament stations. Bombsights had to be installed, and the landing gear beefed up to bear the added weight of the bomb load. These modifications injected further delays. Finally, in December 1944, Hitler reversed himself and ordered all-out production of the Me–262 as an air superiority fighter. By then, of course, it was too late; the German economy was already staggering, and her badly battered fuel supply could no longer meet Luftwaffe demands.[23]

If the German high command had not made so many mistakes, one shudders to think what the consequences might have been for the Allied cause. If the Me–262 had been produced in volume even a year sooner, would the Allies have achieved air superiority? Would Overlord have succeeded? Admittedly, the Rolls Royce Welland, the production version of the Whittle engine, was in many respects superior to its German counterpart. It was soundly engineered, highly reliable, and would go a hundred hours before overhaul. By contrast, the Junkers Jumo was unreliable, suffered seriously from Germany's lack of high temperature alloys, and would run scarcely twenty-five hours before overhaul. But even conceding these defects, the potential for disaster to the Allies seems obvious.[24]

In the United States, the Air Corps technological planners and decisionmakers seriously jeopardized the nation by failing to anticipate the need for jet propulsion and to initiate an aggressive development program in the late 1930s. [25] And once again this brings us back to our initial question; why? The Air Corps officers principally involved in this failure were honorable and able men. They were unquestionably sincere, dedicated to their calling, and hardworking.

Various excuses have been offered, most commonly the scarcity of funds. This explanation scarcely holds water when one realizes that Whittle's firm, Power Jets, Ltd., was a seriously undercapitalized, ill-equipped organization using a makeshift machine shop in borrowed quarters, which until 1939 had received no more than about $5,000 from the Air Ministry. Whittle was able to demonstrate the feasibility of the turbojet principle at a total cost of about $35,000. Nor can blame be readily assigned to faulty technological intelligence. Beginning with the Volta conference in 1935 there were unmistakable signs of the coming revolution in propulsion, even if

130

one looked no further than the *Air Corps Newsletter*, published in the Office of the Chief of Air Corps![26]

The major engine manufacturers in the United States were certainly not unaware of the pending revolution in propulsion which so clearly posed a potential threat to their conventional markets. Both Wright Aero and Pratt and Whitney initiated turbine studies at their own expense. So too did two airframe firms, Northrop and Lockheed, but none of these projects attracted Air Corps support or even provoked much interest. In the absence of strong Air Corps leadership, it is scarcely surprising that these firms were reluctant to invest scarce capital in radical innovations at the very time when the war scare in Europe was loosening congressional purse strings and providing ever larger orders for conventional equipment.[27]

Not until February 1941 did the Air Corps ask the NACA to establish a Special Committee on Jet Propulsion to study rockets and jets. Shortly after this, General Arnold visited England where a General Electric representative had learned of the Whittle engine and alerted an Air Corps technical liaison officer in London of this remarkable development. General Arnold secured permission to visit the Power Jets, Ltd. plant where he not only saw the turbojet engine but "to his great astonishment" learned that it was about to be flight tested. To his great credit, he immediately grasped the startling implications of what he had seen and arranged for the shipment of a Whittle jet to the United States. There the General Electric Company, because of its long experience in building superchargers, was selected to build an American production version of the British engine.[28] At long last the turbojet revolution had reached the United States. But why did it take so long?

There were, broadly speaking, three major factors shaping the development of aircraft engines in the interwar years: these were the Air corps decisionmakers, the National Advisory Committee for Aeronautics, on which the Chief of the Air Corps sat as one of the service representatives, and the engine manufacturing firms who actually produced the engines used by the military services. All three areas deserve close study, but in this analysis we shall concentrate our attention on the Air Corps planners and decisionmakers.[29] To do this, it will be helpful first to look briefly at the Air Corps organization for research and development as it evolved over the years.

III. The Air Arm Organization for Research and Development

During World War I the Signal Corps, as the aviation branch of the Army, established an experimental laboratory at McCook Field in Dayton, Ohio, in order to be near the major aircraft manufacturing plants of that era. When the U.S. Army created the Air Service as a separate entity after the Armistice, McCook Field was designated the Engineering Division of the new service. Under the able leadership of an imaginative young lieutenant colonel, Thurman H. Bane, McCook soon became noted both for its scientific investigations and for its developmental engineering work. The McCook site, was, however, unsatisfactory. It was too small, the flying field was inadequate, and the wartime buildings of makeshift temporary construction. The Air Corps Act of 1926, which converted the air arm from its ancillary status as a service into a combat arm along with the infantry and artillery, led to a major institutional realignment in which the old McCook Engineering Division gave way to a new organization, the Materiel Division, which moved several miles from Dayton to Wright Field, a magnificent 4,500–acre site presented to the government by the city. It was equipped with extensive laboratories, wind tunnels, and test facilities of permanent construction.[30]

Our account of what the Air Corps did or did not do in the development of jets is centered at Wright Field in the Power Plant Branch of the Engineering Section of the Materiel Division.[31] The officers of the Power Plant Branch, mostly captains and lieutenants, had their goals rather clearly laid out for them: they were to strive for better engines, meaning more horsepower at less weight. They were to minimize fuel consumption, to reduce frontal area in order to reduce drag, and to achieve maximum reliability and durability or sturdiness for operation under field conditions. All this, of course, was to be accomplished at the least possible cost, at both initial purchase and in annual maintenance charges.[32]

To understand the psychology of those engineering officers, one must recall that in the 1920s and early 1930s the death rate among aircrew members averaged more than one every other week. The *Air Corps Newsletter* seldom appeared without at least one obituary.[33] Flying pay in those days went largely for excess insurance premiums. Engine reliability was therefore an objective urgently sought at Wright Field. But engine development costs money, and Congress was reluctant to provide funds to perfect aircraft engines so long as a large inventory of World War I Liberty engines remained on hand. Unfortunately, the Liberty, while powerful, was unreliable. When Assistant Secretary of War for Air F. Trubee Davison and Chief of Staff Major General J. E. Fechet flew to Panama in 1928 in an Air

Corps plane still using an unreliable and inefficient Liberty engine, they experienced not one but several harrowing forced landings along the way.[34] There were more than 8,000 Liberty engines still on hand a decade after the war; these continued to inhibit engine development until 1934 when the colorful ex-World War I pilot, Congressman Fiorello LaGuardia, finally managed to slip a rider in the appropriations bill "to protect the lives" of Air Corps pilots by forbidding further use of Liberty engines.[35]

Lacking funds to underwrite the heavy costs inevitably incurred in any effort to develop radically new high-powered engines for combat use, the Materiel Division officers in the Power Plant Section directed their efforts toward drawing up ever more demanding specifications and then testing the successively larger and more powerful engines developed by industry. Probably the most impressive achievement in the aircraft propulsion field between the wars was the emergence of the air-cooled radial engine. Since the radiator and associated plumbing on a water-cooled in-line, such as the Liberty twelve-cylinder, 400-horsepower engine of the World War I era, accounted for about 25 percent of the engine weight and a substantial increase in drag, there was a powerful incentive to seek alternative approaches to the central problem of cylinder cooling.[36]

Two firms dominated the air-cooled engine field, Wright Aeronautical in New Jersey and Pratt and Whitney in Connecticut. From the point of view of the military services this offered an ideal situation: two well-capitalized firms, each with an outstanding design staff, provided lively competition but at the same time concentrated the small volume of military business in a way to make the competition worthwhile to the manufacturers. By 1928 the Pratt and Whitney Hornet was turning out 525–horsepower engines for Air Corps bombers. A decade later the Wright twin-row fourteen-cylinder Whirlwind was producing 830–takeoff horsepower. By the eve of World War II, Pratt and Whitney and Wright Aero were both turning out eighteen-cylinder, twin-row radials giving 2,000 horsepower or more with a weight to power ratio of 1.1 to 1.[37]

The Air Corps Materiel Division played an important role in the impressive achievements of industry. As each of the two major firms turned out more powerful and more reliable engines, they were brought to Wright Field for testing to see if they met the rigorous standards required for combat aircraft. By the mid–1930s the Materiel Division was insisting upon a gruelling 150-hour torque stand endurance test along with before and after waterbrake or electric dynamometer tests to measure power output. These were followed by disassembly and microscopic scrutiny for signs of undue wear. The superb test facilities, the best in the nation, and the exacting procedures employed by the laboratory staff won a national reputation for the Materiel Division.[38]

Step by step the manufacturers' designers, working against the demands of the Materiel Division, eliminated one problem after another to produce ever better aircraft engines. Difficulties with cooling, crankshaft vibration, bearings, and carburetion, succumbed one by one to the patient incremental approach of the engineers.[39] Because they *were* incremental, small but significant improvements, they seldom attracted much attention. The engineers and designers involved were inclined to see themselves in the position of Paul Revere's horse—essential but unheralded![40]

The achievements of the engine builders and their Wright Field monitors were indeed impressive. But the obvious success of their incremental advance seems to have concealed a number of underlying problems, blinding those in positions of authority to the wider implications of some serious weaknesses in the Materiel Division at Wright Field. Many of these problems relating to technological planning and decisionmaking extended to the Air Corps command structure as a whole. A clue to the central difficulty may be symbolically present in the ultimate piston engine, the largest one ever built, probably the culminating example of its type, a 5,000-horsepower, thirty-six cylinder, four-row radial behemoth developed by Lycoming at the end of World War II.[41]

But did we want a 5,000–horsepower piston engine in 1945? Did we need one? Does bigger and bigger necessarily mean better and better? The obvious answer in light of the turbojet engine is that an entirely different solution was called for, in Thomas Kuhn's terms, a paradigm change. So our concern here is to understand just why this different solution was so delayed in coming. With that in mind, it behooves us to take a closer look at the Wright Field Materiel Division organization for research and development to see how it actually functioned.

Official statements about the Materiel Division generally described Wright Field as the principal research and development center of the Air Corps. Regrettably, the phrase "research and development" has become a cliche, glibly repeated as R&D, rather too readily concealing the range of activities actually involved. In the period from 1919 to 1926, the technical staff at McCook Field had been heavily committed to scientific investigation and fundamental research; the procurement function was largely performed in Washington. With the move to Wright Field in 1927, however, the situation changed drastically. The procurement staff, the contracting officers, negotiators, and clerks who formerly had been located in the Office of the Chief of Air Service in Washington, were now moved to the newly established Materiel Division to improve coordination between those engaged in the work of contracting on the one hand and those involved in technical development on the other. While the desired coordination was decidedly improved, the move had a number of unintended side effects. Most notably, the demands imposed by the procurement side of the house absorbed an ever larger portion of the available technical manpower, both military and civilian, in carrying out routine testing of items submitted by manufacturers under current procurement contracts to determine whether or not they lived up to specifications. The practical consequence of this was that purely experimental research tended to suffer.[42]

The procurement side of the house influenced aircraft engine development in yet another way. Because funds for experimentation were sharply limited, Air Corps policy was to award only infrequently contracts which reimbursed the manufacturer for all his development costs. Instead, contractors were encouraged to absorb such costs themselves as they were incurred. This policy had several advantages. The engine builders liked it, because it left them entirely free from bureaucratic supervision during the design and development stage. They were free to consult with the engine specialists at Wright Field without being constrained by them. To offset this heavy investment by the engine companies, Air Corps contracting officers permitted these firms to include their development costs when computing allowable overhead on subsequent production contracts entered to secure engines in quantity. The advantage of this procedure lay in the fact that the engine firms sold the same type of engine to commercial customers and even to foreign military buyers, and such sales helped absorb costs which the Air Corps would have had to pay entirely if it had undertaken a full reimbursement development contract.[43]

Unfortunately, there was an offsetting disadvantage to this accounting arrangement. It had been contrived to stretch scarce development funds, but it resulted in an entirely unanticipated by-product. The practice of reimbursing development costs in subsequent production contracts tended to discourage radical innovations in the way of engine design on the part of the manufacturers. Since a radical innovation would almost inevitably require years of trial and error development work before an item suitable for mass production could be perfected, the manufacturer had little incentive to follow this course. If he stuck with less spectacular incremental improvements in existing designs he could move quickly—and more certainly—to a production contract and thus to prompt recovery of his earlier development costs.

Since the engine builders normally derived a substantially greater margin of profit from their commercial sales than from those made to the military services, this operated as a further disincentive to radical innovations in design. Why bother to go back to liquid-cooled in-line engines or some other alternative when more certain earnings were to be had from air-cooled radials which seemed to offer promising opportunities for incremental improvement and quicker profits?[44]

By opting for incremental improvements rather than radical innovations, the engine firms were able to present modified models to Wright Field for testing much more frequently, so the dynamometers and test cells there were almost continuously busy. This heavy load of testing absorbed a great many engineering manhours, further aggravating the prevailing scarcity of technically competent individuals.

The scarcity of technically qualified staff at Wright Field had long been a problem. During most of the between war years there were never more than 1,300 or 1,400 officers in the entire Air Corps.[45] Not until the outbreak of World War II in Europe did the Wright Field complement rise above 100. This austere staffing had to be spread woefully thin. For example, as late as 1939 there was only one project officer assigned to bombardment, and one to pursuit, each with a single civil service engineer as an assistant, and one typist, even though each of the project officers was expected to ride herd on as many as two or three separate airplane projects.[46]

While the civil service engineers helped to provide continuity in contrast to the continual rotation of officers, the Air Corps experienced great difficulty in retaining the ablest and most experienced civilians. Civil service regulations which fostered promotion by seniority offered little incentive to the most gifted younger men who were repeatedly lured away by industry.[47] Although congressmen occasionally complained of the excessive number of highly paid civilians at Wright Field, the facts scarcely warranted the charge. Most of the engineers drew salaries in the $3,300 to $3,400 range with a mere half dozen above that. The highest paid civilian, the chief aeronautical engineer, received $7,500 a year, substantially more than his commanding officer, the Chief of the Materiel Division, even when including the latter's allowances.[48]

If congressional parsimony held the research staff to the slenderest proportions, the situation with regard to funding experimental development projects was even worse. In no year prior to 1940 did the entire research and development budget at Wright Field reach three million dollars. And this, mind you, had to cover everything, all aircraft projects, power plants, propellers, and the full range of accessories. At least 20 percent of this slender total was absorbed in overhead within the Materiel Division and therefore not available for development contracts.[49] From the perspective of the present day, the wonder is that the Wright Field staff and the manufacturers accomplished as much as they did with so little.

As if the paucity of research money wasn't bad enough, of and by itself, Congress repeatedly imposed restrictions which whittled away at what little money was available. For example, as an economy measure during the depression a seventeen-day furlough was imposed on all civil service employees. This produced a $96,000 saving in payroll but resulted in the loss of 114,000 manhours not available for developmental work. Again, in an effort to increase benefits without incurring costs, leave for civil servants was increased from fifteen to twenty-six days per year. This meant, of course, that there were eleven fewer days devoted to experimental engineering, let alone research of a more fundamental character.[50]

Thus far we have considered some of the institutional, organizational, and procedural factors which appear to have inhibited timely recognition of the turbojet revolution. It remains for us to consider what may be the most important factors of all, the attitudes or mind set and thought processes of those officers chiefly responsible for making the crucial decisions on research and development and the selection of weapons for the Air Corps. What were their qualifications and what professional education did they receive?

IV. The Technical Qualifications and Thought Processes of Air Corps Leaders

My findings here startled me. Not one of the officers who served as chief of the air arm between the wars had any scientific or engineering education above the undergraduate level. Four of the six attended the U.S. Military Academy, but in their day the Academy faculty members normally lacked advanced preparation, and the generalized engineering course offered there did little to prepare an officer for decisionmaking in aeronautical engineering. Yet these were the men who sat on the National Advisory Committee for Aeronautics and helped to decide on the fundamental research to be undertaken. Similarly, the officers who headed the Materiel Division throughout its prewar existence were also devoid of any specialized scientific or engineering qualification. Not even all the branch chiefs within the engineering sections had engineering backgrounds.[51]

One officer, who served with distinction and subsequently retired as a four-star general after World War II, recalled with some asperity how difficult it was to communicate effectively on technical issues with the top commanders such as General Foulois who, though Chief of the Air Corps, didn't know how to use a slide rule or read a log table. He found General Arnold equally lacking and therefore unreasonably impatient with his subordinates as they labored over complex computations he didn't understand.[52]

The technical limitations of the officers in key positions at Wright Field was in some measure mitigated by civil service engineers who, unlike the officers, did not rotate every four years. These men could thus accumulate a considerable expertise from extended experience. But they were always subordinates, reporting to military chiefs who made the final decisions. Little wonder that the abler civilians tended to move off to industrial positions.[53]

The Howell Commission appointed by President Roosevelt urged the military services to seek remedial legislation to secure technically qualified individuals for key positions:

> We are convinced that aeronautical progress. . .will be in direct proportion to the engineering ability and sound judgment of the technical personnel charged with its development. . . .There is at the present no system for recruiting or training officers to carry on this important work. . . .A decision has indeed to be taken on whether primary dependence is to be placed on officers or civilian employees for technical work.[54]

No change in policy with regard to greater use of civilians in positions of authority resulted from the recommendations of the Howell Commission. However, the Air Corps did continue to send a few officers to do graduate work in aeronautical engineering at such centers as MIT, Cal Tech, and the University of Michigan. For the most part these were junior officers, and it would be some years before their influence would be evident in the upper reaches of the research and development organization.[55]

In an effort to rectify the all too common lack of technical competence within the officers corps, the Air Corps had for many years conducted a one-year engineering school at Wright Field.[56] This in no way compared with a four- or five-year university course in aeronautical engineering, but it did offer a most useful introduction to such subjects as aerodynamics, stress analysis, propeller theory, and the like, which substantially enhanced an officer's ability to cope with the challenges of a research and development organization. Unfortunately, because many of the officers entering the school lacked an adequate grounding in mathematics, a considerable fraction of the school year had to be devoted to refresher courses to remedy this shortcoming. Moreover, not all of the ten or so yearly graduates received assignments in research and development duties. One exceedingly able officer was annoyed to find himself, upon finishing the course, assigned to duty as a club officer.[57] Many graduates joined operational units where they doubtlessly provided a beneficial leaven in the maintenance echelons.

While relatively few officers were fortunate enough to be selected to attend the engineering school or go off for graduate work in a university, virtually all who attained positions of authority in materiel matters attended one or more of the Army professional schools. These included, in ascending order of status, the Air Corps Tactical School, The Army Industrial College, the Command and General Staff School, and the Army War College. But whatever merits these schools may have had as centers of study in strategy and tactics or in the procedures of staff work, none, not even the Army Industrial College, offered instruction on the art, problems, and practices of technological planning and decisionmaking. As General Eisenhower's chief of staff, Walter Bedell Smith, wrote to General Lucian Truscott in the middle of World War II, "the fact is. . .our service schools simply did not know how to tell us to do real planning."[58]

That the schools were not, in the main, intellectually demanding, is suggested by no little evidence from the period. After going through the Air Corps Tactical School, Major Ira Eaker reported that high marks were definitely not deified there, so there was little indication of serious boning by students officers to lead the class. Instruction ran from 0900 to 1200 each weekday morning with afternoons reserved for flying, except for Wednesday afternoon which, with Saturday and Sunday, was set aside for recreation. Despite this relaxed academic schedule, Eaker reported that students "found little time" for library reading.[59]

Major Eaker's reaction to the Command and General Staff School, which he attended the following year, is even more revealing. "Don't fight the course," he advised his fellow aviators. "If you don't agree with the school on a particular solution or doctrine, just make a mental note of it; keep your opinion to yourself. The school authorities don't seem to relish it when some student explodes with a contrary opinion. . . ." All of which suggests that indoctrination, rather than the cultivation of a capacity for critical thinking, was the dominant objective at the staff school.[60]

Not only did the Army professional schools suffer from a lack of rigor in their courses and from neglect of technical decisionmaking, they also appear not to have communicated to their students any substantial appreciation of the relationship between science on the one hand and the development of weapons on the other. When Vannevar Bush, then a vice president of MIT, came to Washington as a member of the National Advisory Committee for Aeronautics, he learned "with dismay" that the military officers with whom he dealt "had little idea of what science could provide" in the way of helping to develop superior weaponry.[61]

A telling example of the disconnect between the Air Corps and the scientific community cropped up when a bright young captain returned from a year of study at MIT to duty with the Engineering School at Wright Field. There he pointed out that the Air Corps was taking almost no advantage of the excellent aeronautical research being undertaken in the universities. Academic investigators, he observed, were anxious to cultivate direct relationships with the Air Corps rather than work exclusively through the NACA. When General Arnold, who was by then Chief of the Air Corps, received this report, he simply forwarded it to the NACA without attempting to explore, let alone implement, the suggestion on its merits.[62]

That General Arnold was not receptive to the notion of greater cooperation with the universities on Air Corps research, is scarcely surprising. Earlier, when testifying before the appropriations subcommittee on Capitol Hill, he displayed only the vaguest notion of what kinds of investigation were actually carried out by the universities, erroneously asserting that they were primarily involved in applied rather than fundamental research. When asked to explain the difference between fundamental and applied research, his embarrassingly garbled answer suggested that he wasn't very clear in his own mind just what the distinction was. In any event, he opposed federal funding of aeronautical research in the universities on the dubious grounds that this would scatter the research activities all

140

over the country and the Air Corps would then "lose control of it."[63] From this it would seem that in the general's mind, fundamental research was something best left to the NACA as it long had been.

The difficulty the Chief of the Air Corps experienced in trying to explain the difference between fundamental and applied research appears to have been symptomatic of a pervasive weakness in the education and training of Air Corps leaders during the between-war years. Their schooling apparently not only gave insufficient attention to the interrelationship of science and technology, but, more seriously, failed to develop adequate skills in objective analysis, in critical thinking, in separating fact from opinion, or in reaching conclusions only when warranted by verifiable evidence founded upon clearly recognized assumptions.

A single example involving two successive Chiefs of the Air Corps, General Westover and General Arnold, will serve to illustrate my contention, though the same point could be made with most of the other interwar-year chiefs. In 1936 the Materiel Division at Wright Field held a design competition for an interceptor aircraft. Lockheed submitted a design which later evolved into the P–38. Bell came in with a highly original design which it called the XFM–1, *X* for experimental, *F* for fighter, *M* for multiplace. This twin-engine aircraft had 37-mm forward-firing cannon mounted in the engine nacelles but no rear-firing armament. It was expected to be so fast it could overtake bombers, destroy them with its cannon from a safe distance, and then rely upon its speed to elude hostile pursuit. The Lockheed design was evaluated at Wright Field as better engineered, but the Bell submission won the competition, largely because of the impressive potential of those twin cannon. By the end of 1937 the paper design submitted by Bell had been reduced to practice as a flyable aircraft, the experimental XFM–1. The plane showed sufficient promise to warrant procurement of a service test order of thirteen items, but these were to be rather extensively modified to include rear-firing guns and a number of other features substantially changing the design.[64]

Early in 1938, before the service test model had yet come off the assembly line, General Westover was boasting about the aircraft to Congress. "The XFM–1," he said, was "probably the most formidable fighting weapon of its type yet developed." A year later, with the service test models still not yet received from the contractor, his successor, General Arnold told a congressional committee that this airplane was "the most striking example of development" in the past year "anywhere in the world." This hyperbole may seem innocent enough, but it prompts us to ask just what the Chief of the Air Corps knew or did *not* know at this time about the Mitsubishi Zero or the Messerschmitt 109.[65]

Without waiting for service tests to verify his expectations, General Arnold continued to assure the U.S. public that with the XFM–1, the Air Corps had "jumped to an early lead." To substantiate his claim, he quoted a British magazine as saying that "the new Bell fighter is the coming thing. The technical department of every air force in the world would give a lot to have 48 hours alone with this machine." More curious than this reliance on journalistic puffery, was Arnold's assertion that the XFM–1 would have sufficient range "to accompany and defend our bombardment formations on long raids."[66] Aside from the fact that no solid evidence of the actual, as opposed to the design, range of the FM–1 was yet available, this reference to bomber escorts contradicted the contentions of the Air Corps officials over the past several years that bombers were so fast and so well defended, they no longer required fighter escorts.[67]

What makes General Arnold's rhetoric so disturbing is the simple fact that the FM–1 *Airacuda*, as it was called, never remotely lived up to the Chief's careless and, indeed, unjustified assertions. Even when one discounts the inevitable bugs which plague all new model aircraft, the FM–1 never came close to its intended 300–mph top performance and thus lacked the speed differential so essential for an interceptor. Moreover, it lacked maneuverability, not to mention an inferior rate of climb and ceiling. Even Larry Bell's laudatory biographer had to admit that the FM–1 was stillborn.[68]

Still more curious was General Arnold's assertion that because of the high efficiency attainable from airplanes equipped with controllable pitch propellers, "it will be many years before any other means of propulsion, such as rocket or jet. . .can be expected." In this one sentence the general managed to leap from an unexamined assumption, through a logical non sequitor, to an unwarranted conclusion. Nor was this just a chance unguarded expression, a momentary lapse or aberration; not infrequently Arnold would slip into dubious reasoning, shooting from the hip. Somewhat earlier, for example, when serving in the GHQ Air Force, he had pitted an already obsolescent P–26 (remember those wire-braced wings, the open cockpit, and the fixed landing gear with boots!) against a late model B–10 and then solemnly generalized from this utterly inadequate test that pursuit aircraft would rarely be able to intercept bombers, except accidentally.[69]

142

Don't mistake my purpose here. This is no Monday morning quarterback attack, wise after the event, taking iconoclastic cheapshots at a long-dead charismatic leader. The function of the historian is neither to praise nor to blame but to understand. I speak not to censor but to illuminate a problem. I use General Arnold to illustrate not *his* individual idiosyncracies but to underscore a pattern of reasoning all too common among Air Corps leaders of the period. These men were simply products of the prevailing system, whether one speaks of their professional education, their training, or their experience.

In fairness to General Arnold, let me point out that while he may have been slow to appreciate the significance of reaction propulsion, once he had seen the Whittle engine he moved briskly to secure it for production in the United States. No less significantly, he eventually came, however belatedly, to recognize the critical role of scientific research in pushing forward the cutting edge of weaponry. Late in 1944, he assembled a distinguished advisory panel of scientists headed by Dr. Theodore von Karman, which not only advised him during the war but contributed a virtual blueprint for research and development in the postwar Air Force. That Arnold's conversion, when it finally came, was total is indicated by his instructions to von Karman that no idea, however impractical it might seem at the moment, was to be ignored by the advisory group so long as it did not violate the laws of nature.[70]

The Scientific Advisory Group's postwar report, *Toward New Horizons*, by implication at least, pinpointed the major weaknesses of the prewar Air Corps in technological planning and decisionmaking. In a chapter entitled, "Science, the Key to Air Supremacy," the report observed that:

> The Air Force must have the means of recruiting and training personnel who will have a full understanding of the scientific facts necessary to procure and use equipment which is more advanced than that used by any other nation. . .; scientific results cannot be used efficiently by soldiers who do not understand them.[71]

The report further declared that it was imperative for the Air Force to maintain connections "spiritual and contractual" with the universities, with outside research laboratories, and with individual scientists. And with no hedging to spare feelings, it went on to point out that many of the shortcomings of research and development in the prewar Air Corps originated "from a lack of appreciation at higher levels of the qualifications necessary for successful direction of a lab or proving ground." The theory that any intelligent line officer, whatever his lack of scientific or technical preparation, could fill such billets competently, was, said the report, no longer acceptable.[72]

The principle fix, as seen by the scientific advisors, was compressed into a single sentence: the Air Force must be "permeated" by officers so educated as to be capable of evaluating scientific facts with good technical judgment and with vision. *Training the mind*, the report concluded, was more important than specialized knowledge.[73]

Now then, what are we to conclude from the evidence presented here? What insights emerge from this rather sorry tale of technological planning and decisionmaking? The Germans launched imperfect but nonetheless effective jet fighters into combat and we didn't. This failure on our part might have proved disastrous for the Allied cause had not Hitler's persistent meddling in technical matters he didn't understand deprived the Luftwaffe of its last best hope. Why did this happen?

There were, as we have seen, a number of institutional and organizational factors: because procurement dominated research, scarce engineering talent was diverted from experimental work to testing. The financial aspects of procurement policy favored incremental development which, for all its substantial benefits, came at the expense of radical innovation. The very success of the air-cooled engine, a monument to incremental development, tended to create a false sense of security; just build more of the same, only better.

More subtle was the failure of those who shaped the Air Corps to comprehend fully the vital interaction of fundamental and applied research. The institutional arrangement, the tacit division of labor between the National Advisory Committee for Aeronautics and the Materiel Division at Wright Field only served to aggravate this problem. To apprehend the full potential of the turbojet revolution called for a sensitivity to the convergence of thermodynamic with aerodynamic principles. Few if any of the officers in the upper echelons had enjoyed educational opportunities fitting them to perceive and appreciate this convergence. A surprisingly large fraction of the officers in key positions throughout the research and development organization came to their duties with no background in aeronautical engineering and even no general scientific or engineering work beyond their often sketchy undergraduate studies, if that.

Because the National Advisory Committee for Aeronautics rather jealously guarded its virtual monopoly on fundamental research in aeronautics, that agency must accept part of the responsibility for the Air Corps failure to develop a jet engine in time to play a saving role in World War II. The NACA seriously scanted engine research until after the outbreak of war in Europe. Worse yet, NACA officials compounded this neglect when they failed to move more decisively into theoretical studies of supersonic flight after the Volta congress had pointed the way so emphatically. With no little justice Air Corps apologists could argue that radical innovation is fostered by fundamental research, and fundamental research was the province of the NACA, so much of the responsibility for lag in developing jets should rest there.

But whatever may have been the shortcomings of the NACA, we are primarily concerned with the performance of the Air Corps and its leaders in successive echelons. Certainly those responsible for planning research and development were remiss in their lack of appreciation for and reluctance to draw upon the academic community for aeronautical research. This brings us to the matter of money. While lack of adequate appropriations was indeed a serious handicap, we only deceive ourselves if we think this excuses all failures and neglects. When funds are short, sheer brainpower must strive to take up the slack.[74]

We have seen how the top leadership of the Air Corps in the between-war years was substantially unprepared, educationally, to cope with the mounting complexity of aviation technology, especially where it involved the interaction of science and technology. The more regrettable, because it was probably the more remediable within existing institutional and financial constraints, was the apparent inability of the several service professional schools to develop adequately the analytical and critical skills of the officers attending.

Courses in the military professional schools emphasized training rather than education. School curricula reveal slight evidence of instruction in objective analysis or the derivation of disciplined conclusions, certainly not with regard to technological issues. On the other hand, one encounters, all too often in Air Corps officers holding leadership positions, examples of decidedly defective reasoning. Too often they built their arguments upon unconscious or unexamined assumptions; they made unsupported assertions and employed opinion as if it were fact, and from this shaky substructure they tended to leap to unwarranted inferences.

If history is to be useful in shaping the future, let our present day leaders reflect upon our findings from the past. Let them ask themselves how far our professional schools, our research and development organizations and our people—in and out of uniform—have advanced beyond the stage our studies here depict.

146

Notes

1. L. E. Neville and N. F. Silsbee, *Jet Propulsion Progress* (New York, 1948), pp v-vi; E. M. Emme, *Hitler's Blitzbomber* (Maxwell AFB, Ala., Air Univ., 1954), p 1; W. F. Craven and J. L. Cate, *The Army Air Forces in World War II* (Chicago, 1951), III, pp 715–19; Carl Spaatz, "Strategic Air Power," 24 *Foreign Affairs* (Apr 1946), p 394, and USAF Oral History No 755, May 1965, p 24; Adolf Galland, *The First and the Last* (New York, 1954), p 324; L. Thomas and E. Jablonski, *Doolittle* (Garden City, 1976), pp 298–99.

2. Craven and Cate, VI, p 246.

3. See, for example, *Air Corps Newsletter*, (15 Dec 1937), p 1, and Aeronautical Chamber of Commerce (ACC) *Yearbook* (New York, 1938), p 56.

4. Robert Schlaifer, *The Development of Aircraft Engines* (Cambridge, Mass., 1950), pp 293, 489. Edward Constant, *The Turbojet Revolution* (Baltimore, 1980), offers a more penetrating interpretation of the reasons for the lag in U.S. jet development, which he attributes to a combination of cultural factors in which the United States differed from other nations. The present paper, which examines only one aspect of those cultural factors—the military, is but a modest footnote to Constant's brilliant monograph.

5. Vol 42 *Mech. Engnrg.* (Apr 1920), 234; 133 *Sci. Am.* (Jul 1925), 57–58; 134 *Sci. Am.* (Apr 1926), 266; Schlaifer, p 754; J. L. Naylor and E. Owen, *Aviation: Its Technical Development* (London, 1965), p 160.

6. Neville and Silsbee, p 99; E. Buckingham, "Jet Propulsion for Airplanes," NACA Report 159, 1924.

7. See, for example, R. H. Goddard, 146 *Sci. Am.* (Mar 1932), 148; A. Klemin, 139 *Sci. Am.* (Sep 1928), 260, and 148 *Sci. Am.* (Apr 1933), 232–33; M. Walter, *Annals. of Am. Acad.* (May 1927), 11; G. B. Warren, 55 *General Electric Rev.* (May 1952), 34–36, reporting on his jet calculations in 1929; Schlaifer, p 450.

8. Vol 215 *Jour. Franklin Inst.* (Feb 1933), 200.

9. Constant, pp 141–2; M. Roy, NACA Tech. Memo 571 (Jan 1930), and G. B. Schubauer, Tech. Memo 442 (Jan 1933).

10. *The New York Times* (14 Sep 1931), 1.7 and (20 Sep 1931), IX, 7.6; Constant, pp 169–72.

11. J. C. Hunsaker, *Some Lessons of History* (New York, 1966), p 22. See also, H. A. Ricardo, FRS, "Development and Progress of Aero Engines," 34 *Royal Aeronautical Society Journal* (Dec 1930), 1001.

12. Constant, pp 143, 154; Schlaifer, p 451.

13. Theodore von Karman, *The Wind and Beyond* (Boston, 1967), pp 223–24; Constant, p 159. By way of contrast, when U.S. teams investigated Nazi aeronautical centers in 1945 they found Mach 3 wind tunnels (3,400 mph), 12 *Smithsonian* (Jan 1982) 83.

14. For further details on General Crocco's advocacy of jet propulsion, see 148 *Sci. Am.* (Apr 1933), 233.

15. Frank Whittle, *Jet: The Story of a Pioneer* (London, 1953), pp 20–29; R. L. Perry, *Innovation and Military Requirements* RAND Memo RM–5182–PR (Aug 1967), pp 15–19; Constant, pp 182–86; 35 *Journal of the Royal Aeronautical Society* (1931), 1047.

16. M. M. Postan, D. Hay, and J. D. Scott, *Design and Development of Weapons* (London, HMSO, 1964), p 179; Constant, pp 185–93.

17. Postan, *et al*, pp 47–48.

18. Constant, pp 194–98; Neville and Silsbee, chronology, pp 203–11.

19. Constant, p 206.

20. Neville and Silsbee, p 33.

21. Schlaifer, pp 424, 436; Galland, p 331; E. L. Homze, *Arming the Luftwaffe* (Lincoln, Nebr., 1976), p 142ff.

22. Schlaifer, pp 399–400; Galland, p 336; David Irving, *The Rise and Fall of the Luftwaffe* (London, 1973), p 219.

23. Schlaifer, p 400; Galland, p 232; Irving, pp 258, 265; Emme, p 31; Neville and Silsbee, p 16. Some 1,400 Me–262 jet aircraft were ultimately produced.

24. Schlaifer, pp 429–31; Neville and Silsbee, pp 13–16; V. C. Finch, *Jet Propulsion Turbojets* (Palo Alto, Calif., 1955), pp 7–8. Operational Me–262 were achieving about 490 mph as opposed to about 390 mph for the P–51. See also W. J. Boyne and D. S. Lopez, eds., *The Jet Age* (Washington, Smithsonian Institution, National Air and Space Museum, 1979), p 17.

25. *Aircraft* (Production, Development, Research) Additional Report of Special Committee Investigating the National Defense Program, Sen. Report 110, part 6, 79th Cong. 2nd sess (Washington, 1946).

26. Irvin Steward, *Organizing Scientific Research for War* (Boston, 1940), p 3; Schlaifer, pp 483–84; Whittle, p 135; Perry, p 16; Sen. Report 110, 79th Cong, 2nd sess cited above. For an illustration of the ramshackle Power Jets, Ltd. shop, see 31 *Fortune* (Jun 1945), 132. See also Frank Whittle, USAF Oral History No 931, Mar 1975, *passim*.

27. Pratt and Whitney Aircraft Division, United Aircraft Corporation, *The Pratt & Whitney Aircraft Story* (Hartford, 1950), p 154; Schlaifer, pp 447–49, pp 451–53.

28. Neville and Silsbee, p 145; Schlaifer, pp 458–61. The NACA Special Committee on Jet Propulsion (Durand Committee) reported in July 1941, two months

after the Whittle jet first flew, that it seemed advisable "to pursue investigation of the jet propulsion power plant." Some writers credit the Air Corps with initiating jet studies as early as 1938, but these efforts appear to have been turboprop projects, not turbojets. Before 1941, the term *jet* was sometimes also used in reference to rockets. In a rocket the oxygen for combustion is contained in the fuel; in a turbojet, the oxygen is drawn from the atmosphere. Craven and Cate, VI:246 refers to "jet engines" but Louis Johnson, Acting Sec'y War to Sec'y Nat'l Research Council, Nat'l Academy of Sciences, 2 Apr 1938 and Preliminary Report of Conference, NAS and A.C., 27–28 Dec 1938, both in NAS Archives, Adm. Org. NAS, Govt. Relations, clearly indicate the jets concerned only auxiliary power units. Schlaifer, pp 457–58 also gives a different interpretation. For an illustrated account of the turbojet principle, see "Thrust," 34 *Fortune* (Sep 1946), 128ff.

29. Although the aircraft engine industry, as such, has only been imperfectly studied by scholars, both Schlaifer and Constant, despite their broader focus, offer many insights on the engine industry. See also R. Miller and D. Sawers, *The Technological Development of Modern Aviation* (New York, 1970); J. Rae, *Climb to Greatness: The American Aircraft Industry, 1920–1960* (Cambridge, Mass., 1968); and I. B. Holley, Jr., *Buying Aircraft: Materiel Procurement for the Army Air Forces* (Washington, 1964). For the NACA, the definitive study is A. Roland, *Model Research: The National Advisory Committee for Aeronautics, 1915–1958*, NASA SP–4103, 2 vols, (Washington, 1984).

30. A brief history of McCook and Wright Fields can be found in *Air Corps Newsletter* (1 Aug 1939), p 17.

31. For a description of the Materiel Division in its mature state, see *Air Corps Newsletter* (18 Jan 1938), p 10.

32. G. F. McLaughlin, "The Story of the Airplane Engine," 131 *Annals of the American Academy* (May 1927), 36, and C. L. Lawrence, "Modern American Aircraft Engine Development," 30 *Royal Aeronautical Society Journal* (Jul 1926) 405–33.

33. ACC *Yearbook* (New York, 1932), p 82; Hearings before a subcommittee of the Committee on Appropriations, House of Representatives, War Department Appropriation, FY 1937, 74th Cong, 2nd sess (Washington, 1936) pp 300–34; FY 1929, 70th Cong, 1st sess (Washington, 1918) p 420. Hereinafter, all references to appropriations hearings are cited in abbreviated form as in note 35, below.

34. P. S. Dickey, *The Liberty Engine: 1918–1942* (Washington, Smithsonian Institution, 1968), p 105.

35. HR Hearings, War Dept. Appropriation, FY 1935, 73rd Cong, 2nd sess, p 567.

36. ACC *Yearbook* (New York, 1924), p 251. Prestone coolant, in lieu of water, which came in about 1930, permitted a substantial reduction in radiator size, but by then the radial air-cooled engine had largely replaced in-line engines for military use. See HR Hearings, War Dept. Appropriation, FY 1932, 71st Cong, 3rd sess, p 761. For an excellent discussion of the advantages and disadvantages of in-line and radial engines, see "The Engine and the Propeller," 23 *Fortune* (Mar 1941), 114ff.

37. ACC *Yearbook* (New York, 1929), p 86 and (1930), p 95; 50 *Mech. Engnr.* (Nov 1928), 840 and (Feb 1941), 103.

38. Vol 50 *Mech. Engnr.* (Nov 1928), 839–45; *Air Corps Newsletter* (15 Jan 1936), p 17; (1 May 1936), p 13; (1 Nov 1939), p 2.

39. The best general account of the incremental approach to engine development is in Robert Schlaifer's *Development of Aircraft Engines*. For bearings, see Schlaifer, p 53; for cooling, see *Air Corps Newsletter* (15 Dec 1937), p 3 and (1 Jan 1939), pp 14–15 and HR Hearings, War Dept. Appropriations, FY 1932, 71st Cong, 3rd sess, p 761; for carburetion see Schlaifer, pp 101–02; for vibration see *Air Corps Newsletter* (15 Jan 1936), p 17.

40. ACC *Yearbook* (New York, 1930), p 95.

41. Boyne and Lopez, p 36. This giant engine can be seen on display at the Silver Hill aircraft facility of the National Air and Space Museum.

42. For an illustration of this phenomenon, see HR Hearings, War Dept. Appropriations, FY 1936, 74 Cong, 1 sess, pp 537–8. R. F. Futrell, *Ideas, Concepts, Doctrine* (Maxwell AFB, Ala., Air University Study No 19, 1974), p 137 quotes von Karman's retrospective view that air arm practice "made research and development subservient to the procurement of materiel." For insights on the differentiation of "research" and "development," see J. A. Bright, ed., *Research, Development and Technological Innovation* (Homewood, Ill., 1964), pp. 3–4, 21–31.

43. Schlaifer, p 9; ACC *Yearbook* (New York, 1931), p 146. For more on the inclusion of deferred development costs in overhead, see Holley, pp 34–36.

44. Miller and Sawers, p 87; Schlaifer, pp 9, 12–13, 41, 45; J. C. Hunsaker, *Forty Years of Aeronautical Research* (Washington, Smithsonian Report No 4237, 1956), p 263. For a statement of the responsibilities of the Materiel Division, Experimental Engineering Section, for engine development, see Special Text #182, Extension Text of the Air Corps Schools, *Air Corps Engineering System*, 1941, pp 9, 26, 55, 66, and 73; Air University Historical Research Center, 248.1011–182 Army Extension Courses. Materiel Division responsibilities included keeping informed of trends and progress of aeronautical development "at home and abroad" and recommending to the Chief of the Air Corps new and experimental types of materiel. Materiel Division G.O. #6, 9 Dec 1936, Air University Historical Research Center, 145.91–391 (1936–1941) Mat. Div.

45. *Air Corps Newsletter* (15 Mar 1937), p 1 and (15 Jan 1940), p 1.

46. M. Claussen, "Materiel Research and Development in the Army Air Arm, 1914–1945" (Washington, AAF Historical Study No 50, 1946), p 45; ACC *Yearbook* (New York, 1931), p 80.

47. John F. Whiteley, *Early Army Aviation* (Manahattan, Kan., Aerospace Historian, 1974), p 74; HR Hearings, War Dept. Appropriation, FY 1926, 68th Cong, 2nd sess, p 344; FY 1931, 71st Cong, 2nd sess, p 732; fy 1936, 74th Cong, 1st sess, pp 608–9; FY 1940, 76th Cong, 1st sess, p 323; Colonel E. E. Aldrin, Sr., USAF Oral History No 573, 1967, pp 9, 13; Lieutenant General D. L. Putt, USAF Oral History No 724, pp 22–24, 48, 74, 243.

48. I. B. Holley, Jr., *Development of Aircraft Gun Turrets in the AAF, 1917–1944* (Maxwell AFB, Ala., Historical Monograph B–69, 1945); *Air Corps Newsletter* (1 Jan 1937), p 8.

49. For an illustrative account of a single year, see HR Hearings, War Dept. Appropriation, FY 1932, 71st Cong, 3rd sess, pp 778–79.

50. HR Hearings, War Dept. Appropriation, FY 1936, 74th Cong, 1st sess, pp 537–38 and FY 1939, 75 Cong, 3rd sess, p 476.

51. These observations and the following paragraphs are based on an extensive study undertaken by the author on the careers of more than thirty officers who played leading roles in the technological decision arena. For a similar situation in the Luftwaffe, see H. H. Boog, "The Luftwaffe and Technology," 30 *Aerospace Historian* (Sep 1983), 200-06, which suggests that the habit of putting line officers rather than qualified engineers in key technical positions "in the long run proved fatal." See also Chief, Materiel Division to Chief of Air Corps, 28 May 1937, Air University Historical Research Center, 145.93–391 (1939–1941) Mat. Div.

52. General Orval Cook, USAF Oral History No 740, Jun 1974, pp 58–63. For an example of a senior officer who resolved to remedy his lack of technical competence, see account of Colonel W. G. Kilner who attended the Air Corps Engineering School as a colonel so he could keep up with his young engineers who always pulled out a slide rule when he asked them a question: *Air Corps Newsletter* (15 Jul 1937), pp 1–2. See also Major General Don Wilson, USAF Oral History No 878, Dec 1975, p 162, for comments on Arnold's technical qualifications. For the same on Foulois and his hostility to schooling, see Brigadier General H. Peabody, USAF Oral History No 867, Sep 1975, p 240.

53. Miller and Sawers, p 250; Whiteley, p 74; A. Goldberg, *A History of the United States Air Force, 1907–1957* (Princeton, 1957), p 37; Craven and Cate, VI, p 730, footnote 91, gives an indirect clue to the relative status of civil service engineers at Wright Field. When the war came, Ezra Kotcher, who had for some years been the principal instructor in the engineering school, received a commission but only as a first lieutenant. Civil service engineers at Wright Field and in the Air Corps in general have never received adequate historical recognition. They are almost invisible in the official accounts of the Materiel Division and they have been largely neglected by Air Force historians, Goldberg, cited above, being a rare exception.

54. *Report of the Federal Aviation Commission* (Howell Commission) Sen. Document 15, 74th Cong, 1st sess, 22 Jan 1935, (Washington, 1935) recommendation 58, pp 154–5. By way of contrast, in the British Air Ministry, the Director of Technical Development was an RAF officer, but all his subordinate technical staff members were civilians. See Schlaifer, p 71.

55. *Air Corps Newsletter* (15 Jan 1938), p 2; B. S. Kelsey, *The Dragon's Teeth: The Creation of U.S. Airpower for World War II* (Washington, Smithsonian Institution Press, 1982), p 93. For the then current status of aeronautical engineering, see R. Bilstein, *Flight Patterns* (Athens, Ga., 1903), pp 110–15.

56. For brief insights on the Air Corps Engineering School in the period under discussion, see *Air Corps Newsletter* (1 Sep 1953), p 3; (1 Jan 1937), pp 32–33; (15 Aug 1937), p 5; (1 Feb 1938) p 9; and (1 Dec 1940), p 13, as well as Whiteley, pp 46–50, and Cook, pp 26–28 for recollections of former students. For attendance, see Air University, Historical Research Center, K110.7027–7 (22 Jul 1952).

57. J. W. Sessums, Jr., USAF History Interview, No 951, Historical Research Center, Maxwell AFB, Ala., 1977–78, pp 86, 97, 496.

58. W. P. Snyder, "Walter Bedell Smith: Eisenhower's Chief of Staff," 48 *Military Affairs* (Jan 1984), 8. For interwar school curricula, see R. T. Finney, *History of the Air Corps Tactical School, 1920–1940*, USAF Historical Study 100, (Maxwell AFB, Ala., 1955); George S. Pappas, *Prudens Futuri: the U.S. Army War College, 1901–1967* (Carlisle Barracks, Pa., Alumni Assn. of the U.S. Army War College, 1967). Although ACTS offered a seventy-six-hour course on aeronautical engineering and administration, 1921–24, this was dropped after 1924 to give more time to tactics. Until 1923, there was a twenty-five-hour course in stable management! Finney, pp 8–12: Joseph M. Scammell, "A History of the Army Industrial College," 1947,

Manuscript draft in Scammell papers, Duke University Library Manuscript Department.

59. *Air Corps Newsletter* (15 Apr 1936), pp 1–11. See there also the views of an infantry officer attending ACTS. For retrospective views of participants on the character and quality of ACTS, see General E. E. Partridge, Oral History No 729, Apr 1974, pp 217–18, 222, 228–9, 258; Major General H. C. Davidson, Oral History No 817, pp 363–4; Lieutenant General Joseph Smith, Oral History No 906, Jul 1976, pp 110–13; Major General Don Wilson, Oral History No 878, Dec 1975, pp 117–130.

60. *Air Corps Newsletter* (15 Jan 1937), p 3. Futrell, p 47, observes that Captain L. S. Kuter, when a member of the ACTS faculty, encouraged students to question existing doctrine freely in class. Ironically, he himself was subjected to official reprimand by the Secretary of the Navy for voicing supposedly hereticai views from the lecture platform. See General L. S. Kuter, USAF Oral History No 810, Sep 1974, p 517. For retrospective views of participants on the character and quality of C & GSS, see Brigadier General H. Peabody, USAF Oral History No 867, Sep 1975, pp 295–304; Major General A.F. Hegenberger, USAF Oral History No 854, p 49; Major General A.W. Vannaman, USAF Oral History No 655, pp 134, 143. For further insights on the C & GSS curriculum, see Annual Reports of C & GSS in Command and General Staff College Library, Fort Leavenworth, Kans., and Dastrup, B. L., *The U.S. Army Command and General Staff College* (Manhattan, Kans., 1982) pp 60–77 and no author, "A Military History of the U.S. Army Command and General Staff College, Fort Leavenworth, Kansas, 1881–1962," Chapter 3, in Command and General Staff College Library.

61. I. Stewart, *Organizing Scientific Research for War* (Boston, 1948), pp 3–4; R. C. Cochrane, *The National Academy of Sciences* (Washington, 1978), pp 387–88. For a retrospective view of the Army Industrial College, see Vannaman, pp 150–53. On the Army War College, see Peabody, pp 357–60.

62. M. Claussen, "Materiel Research and Development in the Army Air Arm, 1914–1945," Historical Monograph B–57, Historical Research Center, Maxwell AFB, Ala., 1946, pp 84–6, 92. See also Putt, p 23. "It really wasn't until after World War II that the Air Force started paying attention to its technical and scientific capabilities," and p 74, "There used to be a lot of attitudes within the military . . ." that "those long-haired scientists, we can do without," and p 243 for slighting of R&D staff by operational officers.

63. HR Hearings, War Dept. Supplemental Appropriation, FY 1940, 76th Cong, 1st sess, pp 30–35; and FY 1941, 76th Cong, 3rd sess, p 494. By way of contrast, in Germany the close association of designers and university research led to impressive results. On this point see Miller and Sawers, pp 23–24, 247.

64. D. J. Norton, *Larry: A Biography of Lawrence D. Bell* (Chicago, 1981), pp 60–68. For Air Corps efforts to conceptualize an interceptor, see Air Corps Board studies and related papers in Air University Historical Research Center, 167.5–11 (1936–37).

65. HR Hearings, War Dept. Appropriation, FY 1939, 75th Cong, 3rd sess, pp 422–3 and FY 1940, 76th Cong, 1st sess, p 284. For the U.S. tendency to disparage Japanese aircraft and ignorance of the performance of their latest models, see A. D. Coox, "Rise and Fall of the Imperial Japanese Air Forces," 27 *Aerospace Historian* (Jun 1980), 75. In midsummer 1938, when the U.S. still had not developed a thoroughly reliable in-line engine for fighter aircraft and the British were still struggling to turn out the first half-dozen Spitfires, the Germans were producing five ME–109 fighters a day in a single factory of which there were several. See Norton, pp 73–75.

66. Arnold address to Society of Automotive Engineers, Detroit, 11 Jan 1939, quoted in *Air Corps Newsletter* (15 Jan 1939), p 5.

67. HR Hearings, War Dept. Appropriation, FY 1938, 75th Cong, 1st sess, pp 521–22.

68. Norton, p 67; R. Wagner, *American Combat Planes* (Garden City, 1968), pp 202–04.

69. Futrell, p 42. The bomber was a B–12 which was a modified B–10. Although I use Arnold to illustrate faulty reasoning, other examples abound in the upper echelons of the Air Corps. See, for example, his predecessor, Oscar Westover, who argued that since pursuit aircraft lacked the range to accompany heavily armed bombers, the latter could take care of themselves. In HR Hearings, War Dept. Appropriation, FY 38, 75th Cong, 1st sess, pp 521–2, and ACC *Yearbook* (New York, 1938), p 56. For similarly defective reasoning at subordinate echelons at Wright Field, see Holley, "Development of Aircraft Gun Turrets for the AAF, 1917–1944" (Maxwell AFB, Ala., Historical Monograph B–69, 1947), pp 42–43. For a rather extreme example of careless reasoning, see Report of Air Corps Board, 9 Feb 1940, which concluded that it would be virtually impossible for pursuits to shoot down a B–17C; F. L. Howe, "Bomber Invincibility and Fighter Escorts: Doctrine and Dogma at the Air Corps Tactical School," Air War College strategy course reading, 1982, pp 8–10.

70. Craven and Cate, VI, p 234.

71. T. von Karman, *Toward New Horizons* Report to General of the Army, H. H. Arnold, submitted on behalf of the AAF Scientific Advisory Group, 15 Dec 1945 (Washington, 1945), pp 81–82. For the continuing impact of this report in the Air Force, see attachment to the report, Lieutenant Colonel Howard to Defense Documentation Center, 23 Dec 1966.

72. *Ibid*, pp 85, 103.

73. *Ibid*, p 107. Emphasis added.

74. On this point it may be useful to hark back to the insights of a World War I leader, General Johnson Hagood, "our unpreparedness did not come from lack of money. . . .It came from lack of brains. . . ." *The Services of Supply* (New York, 1927), p 23.

Air Force Planning and the Technology Development Planning Process in the Post-World War II Air Force—the First Decade (1945–1955)

Colonel Alan L. Gropman, USAF

I. INTRODUCTION

A. Scope of the Effort

This paper will examine the evolution of the Headquarters United States Air Force planning directorate and its interactions (or lack of them) with those responsible for technology development planning. The period explored extends from August 1945 to the middle of the the 1950s. We found that before the end of World War II, the Air Force had acknowledged that advanced technology had become a key to victory, but we also discovered (through reading official histories) that there were difficulties in establishing the processes for developing technology, and, more to the point, there was no formal nexus between the Headquarters Directorate of Plans and other Pentagon or field technology development organizations. We believe two devices—doctrine and long-range or strategic planning—might have unified the headquarters efforts, had they been in existence during the decade under review.

B. Definitions

We need to spend a moment at the outset defining what we mean by technology and planning. Technology is the science of applying knowledge to practical purposes (or, put another way, "the purposeful manipulation of the material world").[1] The mission of Air Force research and development is to provide the service with the capability to produce the weapons needed to support national security goals.[2] The unit histories cited in the bibliography indicate that the process for furthering and exploiting technology for the Air Force (and it is process—not specific technological developments—in which we are interested) has been the shared province of the headquarters deputate responsible for research and development and a major command. The headquarters organization has been responsible for articulating research and development policy and constructing and defending the research and development budget within the larger Air Force and defense budgets. The major command, on the other hand, has been responsible for managing the actual research and development efforts (there has been, of course, overlap here). We will focus on the headquarters while not totally ignoring the field.

Planning does not yield as readily to an agreed definition. The Pentagon planning we are dealing with is neither operation nor contingency planning, but it is force structure planning—a term not defined in military dictionaries (in fact, planning itself as an activity is also not defined). For our purposes, force structure planning means directing the building and putting in place the forces (and their support) necessary to achieve national security objectives in the future (which may be relatively near or distant but is never the present). Whereas operation or contingency planning is largely a science (strategically allocating known forces to meet an expected or probable situation), force structure planning is an art because it deals with unlimited unknowns. Some operation planning has been done by the Air Force Directorate of Plans in the Pentagon, but the majority of the Air Force Pentagon planning has always been force structure planning. Given the length of the development cycle, all force structure planning has long-range implications, but that is certainly not to say that force structure planning in the era we are addressing was coherent, long-range planning.

The cited official histories reveal that Headquarters Air Force Directorate of Plans has rarely written plans but has always been involved in a prodigious amount of planning (and other) activity. A dictionary defines planning as the establishment of goals, policies, and procedures for a unit, but this is inadequately simple. The Air Force (and the other services) has never defined military force structure planning, probably because of its complexity. It is actually a process whereby decisionmakers or their planning assistants have engaged in some form of logical foresight before committing themselves to action. Planners involved themselves in establishing objectives, forecasting the nature of the future (or the nature of a range of futures) in which they or their successors would be required to carry out their organization's goals, designing alternative solutions (that is, strategies) to meet those goals, and then monitoring progress along the strategy paths.[3] These procedures can be collapsed into the following definition: planning is the systematic process of formulating objectives for the future and developing strategy and resource allocation alternatives for reaching those goals. Intrinsic to this process is a system for monitoring the implications, in an uncertain future, of the chosen decision alternatives.[4] We do not assert by our definition that the various directors of plans or their subordinates since the end of World War II either used it or understood it.

II. PLANNING PROBLEMS

Planning beyond the immediate future has always been difficult because there are numerous barriers to effecting change. Vannevar Bush, with a keen eye and superb vantage point as chief science and technology adviser to two Presidents and counselor to five others, looked carefully at defense planning in the late 1940s and did not like what he saw. He asserted:

> We have done military planning of actual campaigns in time of war well, and we have done military planning of a broad nature in time of peace exceedingly badly. Yet both have been done largely by the same individuals. How have we determined such vital questions as the fraction of our effort to be placed in strategic air facilities, or whether an outsize aircraft carrier is not worth its great cost? By careful judgment in which expert opinions are balanced, supplemented and vitalized by cool headed public discussion? No. Rather, by arguments of these highly technical subjects, in public, in the press, in magazine articles, some of them vitriolic and most of them superficial. By statements of high-ranking generals and admirals attacking one another's veracity. By presidential and Congressional commissions paralleling almost entirely the organization for planning purposes established by law. By the action of committees of Congress, based on superficial examination of the facts and analyses, attempting to pick out from the chaos something that corresponds to reason. By the personality and appeal of enthusiasts for this or that, wherever placed. This is not planning; it is a grab bag. It will lead us to waste our substance. It will lead to strife between services of a nature that can destroy public confidence. It will render us vulnerable to a hostile world. . . . Why the striking contrast? First, peacetime planning deals with facilities and techniques of the future rather than the present. Second, the bond that holds men in unison under stress of war becomes largely dissolved when peace returns. Third, peacetime planning is done in a political atmosphere.

(Bush, after describing the complexity of the planning problem, outlined a simplified solution to one aspect of it.)

> It is. . .easier to grasp the performance and usefulness of a novel device already at hand than to understand the trends of science and the potential influence upon warfare of their future applications. Military men. . .can grasp the value of a device before them; they. . .by no means. . .can visualize intelligently the devices of the future. Yet military planning for the future that ignores or misinterprets scientific trends is planning in a

vacuum. Military men are therefore in a quandary; there is a new and essential element in their planning that they do not understand. To leave it out is obviously absurd. To master it is absolutely impossible.

Bush (who we recognize was unduly pessimistic and also hyperbolic) called for a close partnership of scientists and military planners to solve the planning problem. He defined planning as "bringing the light of reason to bear on the future as a basis for logical action."[5]

A. Trying to Innovate in Large Bureaucracies

Bush thereby identified one key problem with defense planning but certainly not all that was difficult about it. In addition to the ineffective marriage between warriors and scientists, we would note that the difficulties were, among other things, often structurally bureaucratic. Technological or organizational innovation in any large, multifaceted bureaucracy is difficult, whether or not its members are in uniform.

A business scholar studied International Business Machines, General Electric, Xerox, the Bell Labs, and other industrial giants for twenty-five years and concluded, "not a single major product has come from the formal product planning process."[6] It would seem large bureaucracies are generally killers rather than producers of new ideas, and innovation comes either (a) from an independent or small group of people not affiliated with any company, or (b) from a very small company, or (c) from an individual in an outgroup in a large company, or (d) from a large company in a different industry; some examples:

> Kodachrome was invented by two musicians; a watchmaker fooling around with brass castings came up with the process for continuous casting of steel; outside chemists developed synthetic detergents, while the industry's chemists turned down this development as uninteresting; reciprocating aircraft engine people thought the jet engine was useless (those who developed the jet engine were finally able to peddle it not to engine makers but to airframe makers). . . .Bloomingdale's invented faded jeans for Levi Strauss. Levi's picked up the original riveted jean patent for about $70 from an itinerant Nevada peddler to silver miners.[7]

In the late 1940s the total market for mainframe computer sales was projected to be a half dozen—a couple each for the Census Bureau, Bell Labs, and Lawrence Livermore Labs. Studies in the 1960s suggested that a thousand machines, at maximum, might be placed, but twenty years later the orders could not be filled fast enough. Simultaneously, but only after the personal computer emerged from its garage development facility into the house down the street, International Business Machines lumbered into action to address the mass market for home computers.

Even more interestingly for our purposes, other researchers in this field cite the tendency in large industry to limit investment in new technology in order to "pour even more money into buffering the old." Not only "does the leadership not embrace the new, but they actually—in absolute and relative dollar terms—reduce their investment in the new in order to hold on to the old."[8] (Air Force investment in long-range cruise missiles instead of intercontinental rockets in the 1940s and early 1950s is a parallel example.)

Closer yet to the military, Thomas Peters investigated Lockheed Corporation, concentrating on the development of the U–2 by Kelley Johnson and his off-line "Skunkworks," and asserted that so revolutionary an aircraft could not have come from the regular Lockheed product line. Similarly, he argues, was General Electric forced into the jet engine business. He writes that everywhere in industry he sees what General Electric calls bootlegging to bring fresh ideas to the top. Whatever innovation there is in large organizations, according to his evidence, is clearly a "skunkworks" tale—a small group competing against a stronger technological group in-house." He puts both the Polaris submarine and the air-launched cruise missile in this category,[9] the rapid and relatively inexpensive building of the Thor missile and the revolutionary development of the nuclear submarine may be better examples yet.

B. The Special Nature of Military Bureaucracy

The Air Force, however, is not only a larger organization and bureaucracy than any of those previously mentioned, it has within it semiautonomous units competing for limited funds. These organizations, moreover, do not always share compatible views of the world, similar objectives, or (most important) congruent needs. The Air Force, therefore, has industry's planning problem compounded.[10]

Air Force planners join the headquarters from the semiautonomous agencies (commands) in the field, each with differing agendas, and try to turn their planning into an effective program or budget within the complex bureaucracy. The planning/programming/budgeting interface poses yet more problems.

Military planners, doing their job properly, think in terms of a relatively distant future. Programmers and budgeteers faced with a limited number of dollars and charged with achieving objectives in the face of palpable short-range but vague long-range threats, almost always concentrate on the former. How then can the planner with his eye on the future and distant technology cope with the programmer whose eye is inevitably fixed on the present? This appears to be an eternal conundrum.

C. Coping with Uncertainty

Complicating the planners' mission of influencing the programmers and budgeteers is the enormous uncertainty in which they must operate.[11] Planners themselves, uncomfortable with attempts to see through the dense fog, find it easier to make assumptions about the future than to live with ambiguity.[12] Programmers and budgeteers deal with a threat they see, and they are uncomfortable with planners' assumptions in the face of uncertainty. One scholar of the military, Arthur J. Alexander, expressed it this way: "military bureaucracies. . .often plan as though the world were certain, although that is far from reality."[13] Alexander acknowledges that the planners' task is both "dangerous and difficult,"—hazardous because of the consequences of incorrect decisions, and difficult because of the "informational ambiguities, organizational rigidities, and un- cooperative technologies."[14]

In general three types of uncertainty plague planners. There is, first of all, uncertainty about the "relevant planning environment."[15] The American military planner deals with an adversary who operates from a closed society, who is extremely stingy about providing information, and who, most disconcertingly, reacts to planning initiatives. American military planners rely on intelligence to tell them about the relevant future of the Soviet Union; thereafter, actions proposed by the American military planner to achieve national objectives change the future with which planners thought they were dealing because Soviet actions are responsive to American initiatives.[16]

There is also enormous uncertainty within another aspect of the planner's relevant planning environment: namely, American techno- logical development. (Technology, while not everything with which force structure planners must deal, is at the heart of their work.) Over the years, attempts either to force or forecast the pace of advanced technology have had two customary outcomes: the system rarely comes in on time and it seldom comes in anywhere near the original estimated cost. Consider the systems that were ordered in the early 1950s. The F–102 was produced at more than four times the manufacturer's original estimate. In fact, after the cost of this system had gone through a series of seven estimates, it still cost 130 percent of the final guess. The B–58 had a similar record. The F–94 came in at more than two and a half times its original estimate (and it was a derivative system with relatively few technological unknowns); the F–89 at more than twice its first guess, the F–84F at more than twice; the B–52, at more than two and a half times; and the C–133, at more than one and a half times. The Bomarc missile cost more than seven times as much as its first estimate. Granted, some systems were built for not much more than their original estimated cost (F–86A, F–86D, KC–135, the Thor missile), but they were rare. Estimating improved in the 1960s: the C–5A was undeservedly notorious, exceeding its initial estimated cost by only 36 percent.[17]

It takes no imagination to see what runaway costs do to planners. To meet an objective in the face of a threat they think they understand, planners believe that a number of a specified system is required, but the system is then produced at four times the original estimate, the budget cannot expand, and the planner either sees an inadequate one quarter of the aircraft on the ramp or gives up something else which is also necessary to achieve objectives in the face of the threat. And programmers and budgeteers are more uncomfortable than planners with such uncertainty because it is their responsibility to allocate inexpandable dollars to compelling needs.[18]

Civilian enterprises, of course, are not exempt from such overruns. The Sydney Opera House was begun in January 1957 for completion in January 1963 at a cost of 7.2 million Australian dollars. It was completed ten years late at a cost of 102 million deflated Australian dollars. The British and French governments began to work on the Concorde expecting to spend from 150 to 170 million pounds for research and development, but the research and development bill exceeded 2 billion pounds.[19]

In addition to uncertainty about the relevant environment (such as the state and reactions of the Soviet Union and equipment costs), there is also uncertainty about decisions in related decision areas with the American system itself. Compounding the planners' problem of dealing with decisionmakers within the Air Force hierarchy who may disagree, there are other decisionmakers within the defense community (say in the Department of Defense or the National Security Council) who may differ. Moreover, decisionmakers in the executive structure but outside the Defense community (in the

Cabinet or in the Office of Management and Budget for instance) can object and, if all of these decision participants are brought into harmony, there are 535 decisionmakers on Capitol Hill (fewer in 1947) who can argue decisively with the planner because they control the money.

There is finally, uncertainty about value judgments that come into play when the final decision turns upon values (which is almost always). Here planners can call for technologies and techniques that take into account the values of all the decisionmakers previously mentioned, and their excursions can be overturned because they may offend the values of the American public or sometimes even the world community, forcing planners to change directions.[20] (Poison gas and the neutron bomb are examples.)

D. The Operator as Planner

Although frustrating, planning had to be done and the Air Force appointed operators who were highly qualified career officers with the perceived highest potential to perform this task. Nearly all Air Force planners in the decade under review were operators in from the field who fully expected to return to operations. This, however, created additional problems. Then as now, operators' success was based almost entirely on how well they handled immediate problems with existing material. They seldom planned, programmed, or budgeted; they executed.

This point of view was not readily turned off in their several years' Pentagon service. Nonetheless, while in the Pentagon, they were to be advocates for the future. In fact, General H. H. Arnold and General Carl A. Spaatz established the postwar Air Force headquarters on the basis that it would be divorced from the daily operating duties and concerns of the combat commands. The Air Staff, and particularly the Directorate of Plans, was to be involved in planning and policy development. Arnold went so far as to force changes in the regulations which previously had barred nonflyers from the Air Staff.[21] Regardless of Arnold's intentions, however, the Directorate of Plans was largely manned and was always run by officers whose reputations and skills derived from their successes as operators in the field.

While in the Pentagon, the weight of the planners' responsibilities (although not their sole emphasis) lay in planning for the future. Planners were expected to concern themselves with developing an

Air Force so far beyond the present that the senior officers in the directorate would probably see the plans in action only as retirees, yet they were also to accommodate considerations of readiness for war today (or at least tomorrow). But readiness for war was the primary (although not the sole) concern of the unified, specified, and major operational commands (which were created in 1946, before Air Force independence). The official histories show that Pentagon planners, who expected to return to these commands, found it difficult to focus on long-range planning. The unit histories of the era suggest that officers in the Directorate of Plans were involved in constant and furious activity, nearly all of it dealing with the present. They must have found it difficult to do detached thinking about the future.

Another difficulty that Pentagon planners probably faced was dealing with the four-star commanders of the major commands. These individuals were at the top of the hierarchy, and they got there because of decades of outstanding and intelligent service to the country and its defense institutions. On that basis alone they got a rapt audience when they spoke. These top leaders probably saw the world differently from the planners in the Pentagon because they faced the adversary directly. While not neglecting the future, these generals necessarily emphasized readiness. There is possibly also a mundane reason for planners paying attention to the senior field commanders: planners hoped to return to the commands with the blessings or at least the acquiescence of these commanders. Of course, the major commanders also influenced programmers and budgeteers who, in the final analysis, controlled the money.

Readiness, therefore, preoccupied planners partly because of their own inclinations, and also because of the natural pressures they faced in a military hierarchy.[22] Even if they could have overcome their own biases and could ignore the readiness theme of the senior field generals, world events could have made them painfully aware of the dangerous reality of the present.

Consider the Korean War. The United States military was unprepared for a conventional war in a remote theater in 1950. Demobilization and stringent defense budgets had weakened the armed forces. That did not prevent President Harry S Truman from going to war half the globe away with ill-trained troops and inadequate weapons. If a planner in May 1950 could not count on an unadventuresome United States military policy given the weak state of the armed forces, then could a headquarters planner ever focus on

162

the future and let others concentrate on being ready to fight today's enemy today?

Readiness and modernization (by which we mean fostering technology to develop future weapons or requisite improvements in current ones) are elements in a zero-sum game, and the Air Staff planner, then and now, was responsible for seeing to it that the future was not held hostage to the present. This was demanding. It is not that Air Force leaders were uninterested in technology or the future; it was that looking beyond the present danger has always been extremely difficult.

III. AIR FORCE INTEREST IN TECHNOLOGY BEFORE INDEPENDENCE

Unquestionably, American military leaders recognized the extraordinary results of sponsoring technological innovation during World War II. Spending on research and development (especially the latter) during and after World War II dwarfed spending in previous wartime and peacetime periods.[23] Electronics, atomic energy, and reaction propulsion did not determine the outcome of World War II, but they transformed the mental context of the military leadership. Thereafter, what seemed to matter most was ensuring for one's forces a superior scientific and technological capability, while maintaining the ability to fight today if called upon to do so.[24]

A. General Arnold's Deep Interest in Technology

Before the end of World War II in September 1944, General Arnold was expressing himself on the long-range technological future of the postwar Air Force. That month he talked with the Army Air Force's leading scientific advisor, Theodore von Karman, who had known Arnold since the 1930s when the scientist was Director of the California Institute of Technology's Guggenheim Aeronautical Laboratory and Chief of the California Institute of Technology's Rocket Research Project (the forerunner of the Jet Propulsion Laboratory). They met privately in Arnold's car at LaGuardia Airport. The Hungarian-American scientist had just left a sanitarium at Lake George after intestinal cancer surgery. Von Karman remembered Arnold's comments this way:

> We have won this war....I do not think we should spend time debating whether we obtained the victory by sheer power or by some qualitative superiority. Only one thing should concern us—what is the future of air

power in aerial warfare: What is the bearing of the new inventions such as jet propulsion, rockets, radar, and other electronic devices?[25]

With the war in the Pacific still raging and with nine months of war in Europe yet to come, Arnold was looking toward the future. The commanding general of the Army Air Forces invited von Karman "to come to the Pentagon and gather a group of scientists who will work out a blueprint for air research for the next 20, 30, perhaps 50 years."[26] In December 1944, von Karman gathered his people from academe, from laboratories, from industry, and from the services. Arnold addressed this group nonparochially telling them:

> I see a manless Air Force. I see no excuse for men in fighter planes to shoot down bombers....For 20 years the Air Force was built around pilots, pilots, and more pilots....The next Air Force is going to be built around scientists—around mechanically minded fellows.

Arnold charged the Scientific Advisory Group to search into every science, to squeeze out basic developments that could make the United States "invincible in the air."[27]

In his formal letter to the group, Arnold wrote:

> I believe the security of the United States of America will continue to rest in part in developments instituted by our educational and professional scientists. I am anxious that Air Force's postwar and next-war research and development programs be placed on a sound and continuing basis. In addition, I am desirous that these programs be in such form and contain such well thought out, long range thinking that, in addition to guaranteeing the security of our nation and serving as a guide for the next 10–20 year period, that the recommended programs can be used as a basis for adequate Congressional appropriations.[28]

Arnold then outlined a series of assumptions and assertions that might guide the scientists:

> Global war must be contemplated, [but the Army Air Force's] portion of the budget is likely to decline....Our prewar research and development has often been inferior to our enemies'....It is a fundamental principle of American democracy that personal casualties are distasteful. We will continue to fight mechanical rather than manpower wars....Offensive, not defensive, weapons win wars. Countermeasures are of secondary importance....Our country will not support a large standing army....More potent explosives, supersonic speed, greater mass offensive efficiency and increased weapon flexibility and control are requirements.

Arnold then asked a series of questions:

> Is it now now possible to determine if another totally different weapon will replace the airplane? Are manless remote control radar or television-assisted precision military rockets or multiple seekers a possibility? Is atomic propulsion a thought for consideration in future warfare?

164

Arnold asked von Karman and his team to "divorce" themselves from the "present war in order to investigate all the possibilities and disabilities for postwar and future wars' development as respects the Army Air Forces." Arnold asked for a report on the "recommended future" of the Army Air Forces' research and development programs. He then asked several final questions:

> What assistance should we give or ask from our educational and commercial scientific organizations during peacetime? Is the time approaching when all our scientists and their organizations must give a small portion of their time and resources to assist in avoiding future national peril and winning the next war? ...What proportion of available money should be allocated to research and development?[29]

Would such an effort have begun but for Arnold? Probably not; no one else in the Air Force top leadership structure was as concerned about the future. In his report to the Secretary of War in November 1945, Arnold emphasized the future:

> National safety would be endangered by an Air Force whose doctrines and techniques are tied solely to the equipment and processes of the moment. Present equipment is but a step in progress, and any Air Force which does not keep its doctrines ahead of its equipment, and its vision far into the future, can only delude the nation into a false sense of security.... The basic planning, development, organization and training of the Air Force must be well rounded, covering every modern means of waging air war, and the techniques of employing such means must be continuously developed and kept up to date.[30]

B. Theodore von Karman's Toward New Horizons

It took about a year for the von Karman group to finish the project. About half way through the study process, it issued a report after visiting German research establishments. The report, "Where We Stand," is considered a volume of the *Toward New Horizons* study. In the report von Karman's Scientific Advisory Group outlined the main fields in which significant advances had been made. It tried to show where we stood, with some indications as to where we should go. For future planning of research and development the following new aspects of aerial warfare would have to be considered as fundamental realities:

1. Aircraft, manned or pilotless, will move with speeds far beyond the velocity of sound.

2. Due to improvement in aerodynamics, propulsion and electronic control, unmanned devices will transport means of

destruction to targets at distances up to several thousands of miles.

3. Small amounts of explosive materials will cause destruction over areas of several square miles.

4. Defense against present-day aircraft will be perfected by target-seeking missiles.

5. Only aircraft or missiles moving at extreme speeds will be able to penetrate enemy territory protected by such devices.

6. A perfected communications system between fighter command and each individual aircraft will be established.

7. Location and observation of targets, takeoff, navigation and landing of aircraft, and communication will be independent of visibility and weather.

8. Fully equipped airborne task forces will be enabled to strike at far distant points and will be supplied by air.[31]

This author finds von Karman's group's prescience breathtaking (even if all of its predictions have not fully blossomed), but even geniuses, one supposes, get some things wrong. Von Karman's group wrote also about atomic propulsion and air power, probably setting the Air Force down a fifteen-year fruitless path that cost about a billion dollars.[32]

> ...the progress in the utilization of nuclear energy will strengthen and accelerate the trends of aeronautical developments advocated in this report.... The Air Forces should, as soon as possible, take the lead in investigating the possibilities of using nuclear energy for jet propulsion."[33]

Von Karman and his group did their best in "Where We Stand" (and also in their final, multivolume report) to encourage the Air Force to launch into serious research on what we would call today, intercontinental ballistic missiles. For example:

> The Scientific Advisory Group agrees that the German results of wind-tunnel tests, ballistic computation, and experience with the V–2 justify the conclusion that a transoceanic rocket can be developed....A part, if not all, of the functions of the manned strategic bomber in destroying the key industries, the communication and transportation systems, and military installations at ranges of from 1,000 to 10,000 miles will be taken over by the pilotless aircraft of extreme velocity. The use of supersonic speeds greatly reduces errors due to wind drift and other atmospheric conditions and the tremendous zone of damage of the atomic bomb diminishes the required precision.[34]

Von Karman's group foresaw both long-distance cruise missiles and also long-distance rockets. It suggested that developing the concept of staging would yield rockets with a 17,000–mile-per-hour speed and ranges of several thousand miles.[35]

In mid-December 1945 von Karman published, *Toward New Horizons*, in thirty-three volumes. He introduced his study to Arnold with a covering letter:

> The discovery of atomic means of destruction makes powerful air forces even more imperative than before. The scientific discovery in aerodynamics, propulsion, electronics and nuclear physics opens new horizons for the use of air power. The next 10 years should be a period of systematic, vigorous development devoted to the realization of the potentialities of scientific progress, with the following principal goals: supersonic flight, pilotless aircraft, all-weather flying, perfected navigation and communication, remote controlled and automatic fighter and bomber forces for aerial transportation of entire armies. The research problems should be considered in their relation to the functions of the air forces, rather than as isolated scientific problems. . . . Development centers should be established for new types of equipment and for making novel methods suggested by scientific discoveries practical. . . . Development centers for definite tasks are more efficient than separate laboratories for certain branches of science. The use of scientific means and equipment requires the infiltration of scientific thought and knowledge throughout the Air Force. . . . A global strategy for the application of novel equipment and methods, especially pilotless aircraft, should be studied and worked out. The full application of air power requires a properly distributed network of bases within and beyond the limits of the continental United States.[36]

Regarding how much to invest in science and technology, von Karman wrote:

> The money to be allocated for research and development should be related to one year's aerial warfare. It appears that spending for research in peacetime five percent of one war year's expenditures, in order to be prepared for or avoid future war, is not an exaggerated drain on the national pocketbook. . . . If in peacetime 15 to 20 percent of the sum spent in a war year were allowed for total expenditure of the air forces, the amount required for research and development should constitute 25–33 percent of the total Air Force budget.[37]

The study group attacked the technology problem by asking the right questions properly; in other words, they approached the problems generically so as not to bias the answer. The questions and the answers to those questions make up the thirty-three volumes of the study. For example: How to move swiftly and transport loads through the air? How to locate targets and recognize them? How to hit targets accurately? How to cause destruction? How to defeat enemy interference? How to perfect communications from ground to air and from air to air? How to defend the home territory?[38]

The report, then, outlined a rational research and development structure and suggested fruitful avenues to pursue. For example, von Karman's group was more than forty years ahead of its time with the suggestion that "every item of equipment in the Army (naturally, with the exception of railway guns, heavy seacoast guns, and the like) must be air transportable."[39]

Von Karman's group also articulated the most fruitful areas for research regarding Air Force missions. For example, it wrote:

> the Air Forces must not only be able to move swiftly and transport loads through the air, but the movement must be directed to bring the aircraft or missile and its means of destruction from a base to the vicinity of a military target which may be anywhere on the globe. The target must then be recognized. The technical problem is one of locating two objects, the aircraft or missile, and the target, with respect to some frame of reference, and of bringing the two locations in coincidence by guiding the aircraft or missile.[40]

Regarding the organization for research and development, von Karman's group recommended:

> a permanent Scientific Advisory Group should be available to the Commanding General to advise him on questions of long range scientific planning. . . . the office in charge of research and development should establish research panels for coordination of Air Force research with that of government agencies and other scientific organizations. Scientific intelligence at home and abroad should be strengthened by including scientific personnel in the Intelligence Service, appointing scientific attaches abroad, and frequently sending scientific-trained officers or civilians to meetings and for study in foreign countries. . . . Operational analyses and target studies should be continued in peacetime with adequate scientific personnel. . . . Officers in charge of laboratories should be kept in such positions long enough to be really useful, without being handicapped in promotion by long tenure of such assignments. . . . Appointments and compensation of civilian scientific personnel should be freed from Civil Service regulations, to enable the Air Forces to employ first-class scientists and employees.[41]

Arnold endorsed the basic principles of *Toward New Horizions* and, although the report has been termed by some the "loadstone and touchstone for Air Force research and development, a final arbitrator of argument, a main source for inspiration and motivation,"[42] one cannot be sure of the report's ultimate influence.

The report undoubtedly impressed Arnold, but he left active service before his enthusiasm for *Toward New Horizons* could be translated into entirely effective action. The report did lead directly to the establishment of the Scientific Advisory Board with von Karman as its chairman, but it did little else, at least for the time being. Arnold circulated *Toward New Horizons* in January 1946 and directed Lieutenant General Nathan F. Twining to evaluate it. Arnold retired soon thereafter, and his immediate successor did not bring to the Chief's position the same sense of urgency for future or scientific matters. There was, moreover, what one historian has termed "formidable resistance" within the Air Staff to carrying out the *Toward New Horizons* program.[43] Most important, however, there were terrific distractions—rapid demobilization, declining budgets because President Truman feared galloping inflation, and an Air Staff that focused nearly all of its energies on service unification and Air Force independence, to list just a few of the barriers to effecting a scientific apparatus based upon *Toward New Horizons*.

Von Karman himself wrote: "There has been no implementation of our suggestions." He credits first Air Force Secretary Stuart Symington with striving hard to "bring into reality some of my proposals," but he lamented that there was great resistance from manufacturers who were opposed to the Air Force establishing research facilities. He was most pleased, as one might expect given his background in aerodynamics, with the founding of the Arnold Engineering Development Center with its supersonic wind tunnels in Tullahoma, Tennessee, based on the Scientific Advisory Group's recommendation. He also was proud of the establishment of the Scientific Advisory Board which was also a *Toward New Horizons* initiative. Von Karman believed the board encouraged Arnold and his successors to create and nourish the Rand Corporation, and he was happy with that development. He was generally disappointed, however, and he believed that his most constant problem in the early years after World War II was with operators who wanted scientists to stay out of their business.[44]

C. The Creation of Rand and the Scientific Advisory Board

The establishment of Rand is another example of Army Air Forces interest in research. That organization, then unique, has become a prototype for a proliferation of companies devoted to thinking and helping operators to escape the tyranny of their in-baskets. Rand was the first of what became by 1970 more than 350 outside corporations (most nonprofit) engaged in research. In contrast, before World War II, practically all the specialized research of the government was done by government laboratories.[45]

Project Rand, founded on 1 March 1946, was originally part of the Douglas Aircraft Company. General Arnold sent $10 million to Douglas to found a research center.[46] F. R. Colbohm, Assistant to the Vice President of Engineering, was chosen to direct the project and serve as its chief executive, which he did for nearly two decades. Colbohm was chosen because he had been actively involved in formulating the idea for development of a research entity with guaranteed independence in carrying out its work, which was to be long-range in nature. The 1946 charter read: "Project RAND is a continuing program of scientific study and research on the broad subject of air warfare with the object of recommending to the Air Force preferred methods, techniques, and instrumentalities for this purpose."[47] Rand, furthermore, was to have a large measure of freedom in controlling its own research program. It was to receive Air Force intelligence and planning information and, when Rand saw fit, make reports and recommendations. The idea was to provide continuing, unbiased, thoughtful research to Air Force planners.[48]

On 14 May 1948 Rand became an independent, nonprofit corporation although all of its funding still came from the Air Force. Rand and the Air Force had found it necessary to sever the relationship with the Douglas Company, and the new think tank received sufficient foundation financing to do so. Rand secured initial working capital of $100,000 and bank lines of credit of $900,000 from the nascent Ford Foundation. The Ford Foundation later increased its loan to $1,000,000 and in 1952 converted the loan to a grant for research.[49] By the fall of 1947, the employees at Rand numbered 150, rising to around 800 by the end of the decade; and this group was producing hundreds of studies a year.[50]

Rand's first formal report was released in May of 1946 on a topic suggested by the Air Force, which wanted Rand to study the feasibility and military usefulness of an artificial earth satellite, an object at that time of interest primarily to science fiction writers. The report was called *Preliminary Design of an Experimental World-Circling Space Ship*. Rand concluded that a primitive satellite could be launched by 1952. In its cover letter on the report Rand concluded that the problems associated with instrumentation and guidance were more difficult to solve than those of building the vehicle itself. "The scientific data which a satellite can secure and transmit to earth are extremely valuable and the vehicle has important military uses in connection with mapping and reconnaissance, as a communications relay station and in association with long-range missiles." Inside the report Rand forecast the following:

> Since mastery of the elements is a reliable index of material progress, the nation which first makes significant achievements in space travel will be acknowledged as the world leader in both military and scientific techniques. To visualize the impact on the world, one can imagine the

consternation and admiration that would be felt here if the U.S. were to discover suddenly that some other nation had already put up a successful satellite.[51]

(Rand's forecast became painfully true in the autumn of 1957.)

In the late 1940s Rand studied a wide variety of subjects including ramjets and rocket engines for strategic weapons, boron and other high-energy fuels, the statistical theory of radar detection, atmospheric physics, the theory of games, econometrics, nuclear propulsion, metal fatigue, optimal design of structures for military aircraft, bomber and fighter design, air traffic control, and high-energy radiation. Rand was also active among the advocates demonstrating to the Air Force in this early period the gains in operational flexibility that could be realized by in-flight refueling of aircraft.[52]

Although Rand's early work was technologically oriented, it recognized early that the physical sciences themselves were necessary but not sufficient to provide effective solutions to major problems of national security. Olaf Helmer of the Rand Mathematics Division, an individual with doctorates both in mathematics and logic who worked for the Office of Scientific Research and Development during World War II, believed Rand might be too limited in its outlook. He argued that military problems were not just engineering, mathematical, or physics problems, but that they involved questions that often were better investigated by historians, political scientists, or economists. So in 1947 a nucleus of humanists and social science scholars was brought to Rand.[53]

In its first fifteen years Rand distributed more than a million copies of about 7,000 Rand publications and 150,000 copies of about 2,700 technical papers prepared for presentation at scientific meetings or for publication in professional journals. Rand also published seventy scholarly books of which more than 300,000 copies were sold by commercial publishers and university presses.[54]

A small sample of Rand's early achievements will give the reader an idea why the Air Force nurtured this institution. Rand developed a system for training Air Defense ground controllers in the Air Defense Command in 1953 and then provided the initial training and the computer programs for the Semiautomatic Ground Environment System (SAGE). Rand created a separate organization—the System Development Division—for that purpose. That unit became, in time, twice the size of the rest of Rand and spun off in 1957 as the System Development Corporation, another independent, nonprofit (initially) corporate entity. In the early 1950s Rand also performed a massive and extremely important study on overseas bases which, with other studies, led to the Air Force revising its strategic air base structure. According to an Air Staff estimate, that advice saved a billion dollars in proposed installation costs while maintaining the same strategic capabilities (Rand has not cost the Air Force a billion dollars since it was founded). Rand was the pioneer in game theory and one of the earliest users and improvers of systems analysis.[55]

A small sample of some of the Rand books provides an indication of the breadth of Rand's work. Probably the most notable book, one still in print twenty-five years after publication, was Bernard Brodie's *Strategy in the Missile Age* (Princeton: Princeton University Press, 1959). Another Rand classic is Raymond L. Garthoff's, *Soviet Military Doctrine* (Glencoe, Ill.: The Free Press, 1953). Another notable publication was W. Phillip Davidson's *The Berlin Blockade: A Study in Cold War Politics* (Princeton: Princeton University Press, 1958). There was also H. S. Dinerstein's *War in the Soviet Union: Nuclear Weapons and the Revolution in Soviet Military and Political Thinking* (New York: Praeger, 1959). Another important work was Charles J. Hitch's and Roland McKean's *The Economics of Defense in the Nuclear Age* (Cambridge, Mass.: Harvard University Press, 1960).

Over the years Rand has received praise from people who have observed its work. In 1962 Director of the Bureau of the Budget David Bell cited Rand for its "detached quality" and the "objectivity of its work." In 1963 Secretary of Defense Robert S. McNamara cited Rand as the most notable of the nonprofit organizations which contributed to the Defense Department. Speaking later of annual dollar costs of the Rand contract to the Air Force, McNamara said that the Air Force received "ten times the value of the money the Air Force invested in it."[56]

Rand became, in the first decade after World War II, a part of the Air Force and yet was praised for its objectivity and creativity. It was in effect an intellectual inspector general for Air Force thinking. Because Rand recognized that publishing reports, essential for documentation, was a comparatively poor way to influence thinking, its researchers spent a great deal of time in the Pentagon and in the field advising, inquiring, conversing, lecturing, briefing, convincing, arguing, hectoring and haggling, stimulating and improving Air Force thought.

Like the Rand Corporation, the Scientific Advisory Board was formally organized in 1946, and like it, the board still exists. Its mission, moreover, was not altogether unlike Rand's: to provide the Air Force with "guidance in the planning and programming of research and development activities." There were initially thirty people on the board, of whom more than two-thirds had worked on the wartime Scientific Advisory Group that produced *Toward New Horizons*. Initially the board was organized into five panels ranging across the Air Force activities from medicine to missiles. The board initially suffered growing pains and had more difficulty than Rand in establishing itself within the Air Force. Not until more than two years after its founding were its members paid anything and then just a token. And while over the years the board studied many subjects at the formal request of the Chief of Staff, its greatest early contribution was its recommendation on removing research and development from the control of logistics, allowing the former to flower. The Scientific Advisory Board (like Rand) worked to nudge the Air Force to do more intense work on intercontinental ballistic missiles in the 1940s and 1950s.[57]

These two organizations worked hard to move the Air Force into the future, and we now turn to the way the Air Force organized for the future, examining its bureaucratic planning and technological development processes.

IV. POST-WORLD WAR II AIR FORCE, PENTAGON, AND TECHNOLOGY DEVELOPMENT ORGANIZATIONS

A. Organizing the Air Staff in the Postwar Era

As noted, before the war ended the Army Air Forces started to draw a blueprint for a research and development organization and to specify fruitful technologies worth pursuing—it also began to plan for its postwar future, one in which it aimed to be independent. World War II and the lessons the leadership thought it learned from that war determined the character of the postwar service. By the time the war ended in the summer of 1945, the Air Force had already drawn up and tabled several plans for a postwar military establishment that included a strong and independent Air Force. In fact, Air Force planning for the postwar era began two years before the victory, and this activity was performed by such powerful and astute planners as Laurence Kuter, Jacob Smart, Fred Dean, Emmett O'Donnell, Jr., Charles Cabell, Lauris Norstad, and Orvil

Anderson. A problem, however, was that not all planners worked in the same organization, and there was duplication, redundancy, and rivalry among the numerous offices within the Army Air Forces and War Department staffs assigned responsibility for parts of the postwar plan.[58]

From the time the war ended in 1945 until independence, however, the Air Force was immersed in a turmoil caused by implosive demobilization: from a peak in March 1944 of 2,411,294 men and women to less than 900,000 at the end of December 1945, then to approximately half a million in March 1945, and finally to about 300,000 in May of 1947. The chaos this produced hampered work on creating an effective staff organization.[59]

The Air Force's leadership, moreover, faced other critical issues. Among the most serious were redeploying the rapidly shrinking force and determining a valid postwar force structure. Planners, moreover, had to assess the impact of the atomic bomb on the armed forces and their organization (which was by no means as clear to those going through it then, as it is to those who do such planning now, because of the great physical weight of the devices, their scarcity, and the supposed global paucity of nuclear raw materials). Finally, the Air Staff was determined to help reorganize the defense establishment and create their own independent postwar organization.[60]

Complicating all of these problems was President Truman's concern with postwar inflation and his fear of gigantic budget deficits which led him to withhold the money needed to build what Army Air Forces leaders thought was an adequate force structure. Late in the month the war ended, the Army Air Forces insisted (erroneously as events turned out, given the fact that we had many fewer groups and successfully deterred the Soviet Union) that seventy groups of aircraft concentrating on heavy bombers were necessary to defend the country's interests. This structure had the support of both the Army Air Forces' military and civilian leadership and also that of Army Chief of Staff Dwight D. Eisenhower,[61] but budget stringency prevented its realization.

Under War Department pressure, Generals Norstad and Ira Eaker came to this seventy-group figure assuming that the Army Air Forces would have a one-year warning of war to flesh out further that force. (Norstad and Eaker wanted a significantly larger number of groups.) Even when the Army Air Forces took an additional manpower cut of 150,000 men in 1945, they stayed with the seventy-group figure.[62]

In late 1947, faced with what was to him severely restricted funding, General Spaatz, who shared Arnold's views about the role of the headquarters as a policy and planning institution, organized his independent headquarters around a three-deputy-chief-of-staff system. He appointed a Deputy Chief of Staff for Personnel and Administration, one for Materiel (which had within it a Director of Research and Development) (figure 1), and a Deputy Chief of Staff for Operations (which had within it a Director of Plans and Operations) (figure 2).[63]

B. The Directorate of Plans and Operations

The formal responsibility of this directorate was to formulate, develop, direct, supervise, and coordinate both current and future strategic, mobilization, special and operational plans. In addition to being responsible for all psychological warfare activities of the Air Force, the Director of Plans and Operations served as the senior Air Force planner in the supervision and coordination of the planning activities of the Air Staff and major commands. The directorate was broken down into five divisions, four of which were connected to planning and one to operations.[64]

Among many things that can be said of the Directorate of Plans and Operations, these three seem to be the most crucial: people came and went rapidly, the organization was reorganized continually, and the people were busy. By mid–1949 the two divisions most germane for the purposes of our paper were the War Plans Division (figure 3) and the Policy Division. The War Plans Division was responsible for:

> developing strategic plans and broad operational concepts for the deployment and employment of the Air Force either unilaterally or in participation with joint or the combined agencies; for maintaining close liaison with such agencies and furnishing strategic guidance to the Air Force member thereof, as well as the Air Staff; and for reviewing and recommending action on all strategic planning matters affecting the Air Force.[65]

One can see that the emphasis was on strategic guidance and planning for the Air Staff and others, and in this case, strategic meant overarching as opposed to describing a method of bombing.

The division was organized first into five, and then later seven, planning teams: Red, White, Blue, Rainbow, Black, Air Defense,

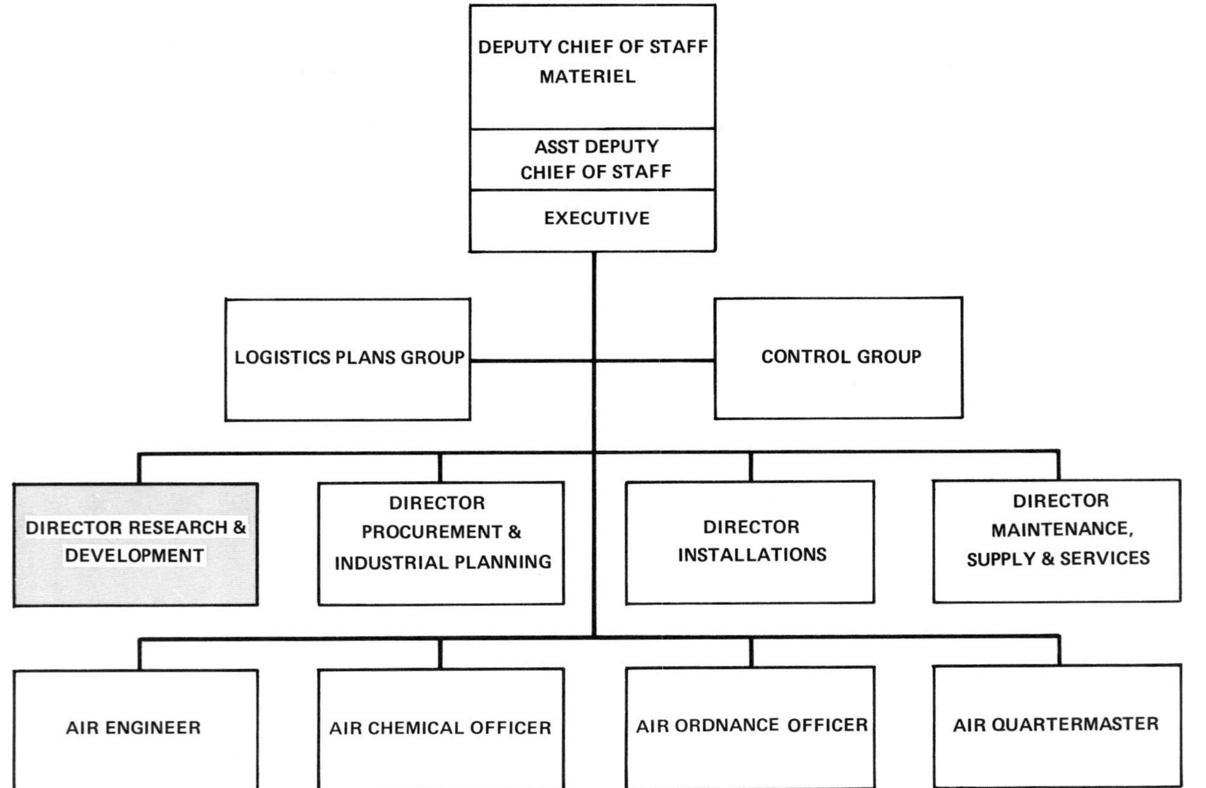

Figure 1. Deputy Chief of Staff, Materiel (1947).

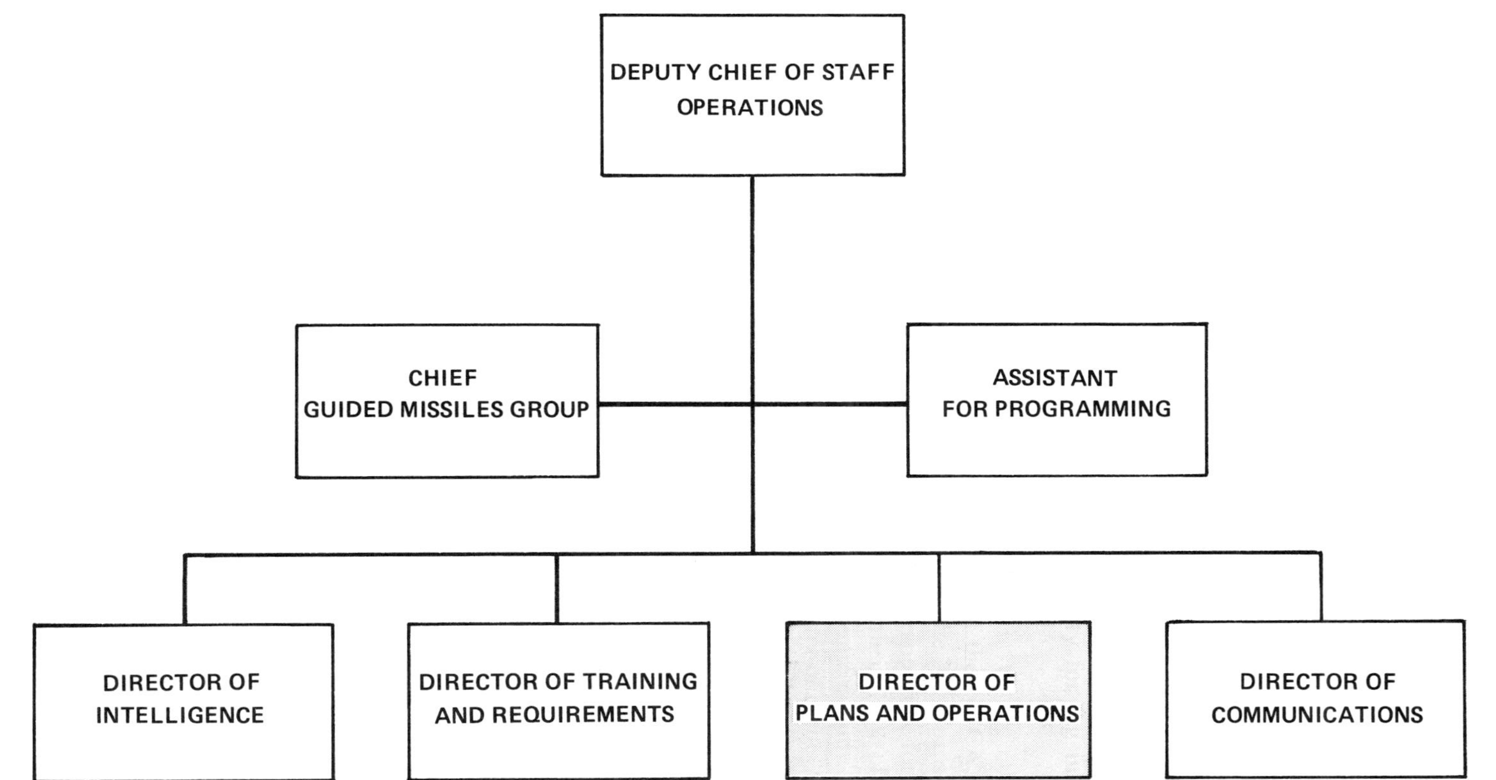

Figure 2. Deputy Chief of Staff, Operations (1947).

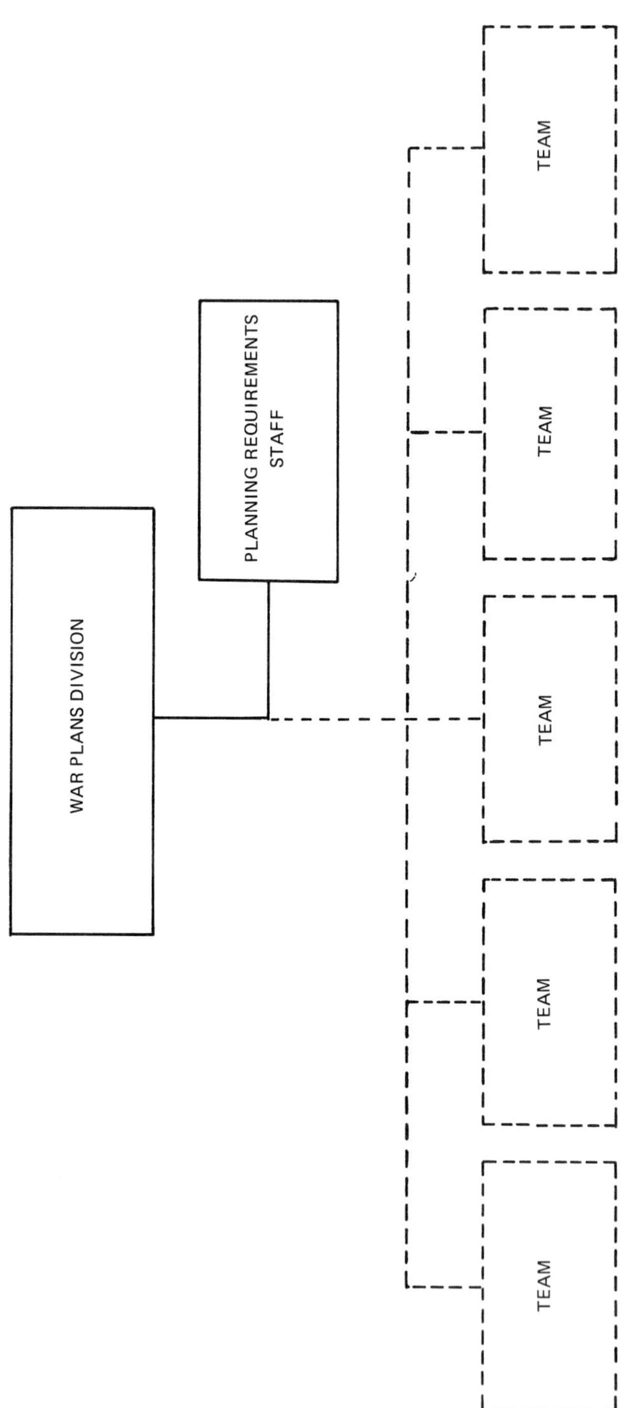

Figure 3. DCS/Operations, Director of Plans & Operations, War Plans Division (1 February 1949).

178

and Special Weapons. It was so organized to provide maximum flexibility for dealing with the divisions' many and diverse action papers. The division chief wanted to avoid a rigid delineation of functions to preserve flexibility. Consequently, although each team had a normal sphere of interest and activities, it was possible during blitz periods for the Chief to assign Air Staff actions at his "discretion to almost any team." The goal here was to keep workloads equitably balanced.[66]

The Red Team was primarily concerned with short-range or emergency war plans. The White Team was the intermediate-range planning agency and the Blue Team was responsible for long-range planning activities. During 1950 the Blue Team worked the long-range war plan for 1957 and the long-range facilities plan for the Far East for 1955. Given the nature of the development cycle, one sees that working issues five or so years into the future should not be considered long-range. The Air Defense Team was involved in developing force structure for the defense of the continental United States and Alaska. The Special Weapons Team worked issues involving the uses of atomic weapons and guided missiles.[67]

The Policy Division was responsible for "the Politico-Military Aspects of Air Force Planning," maintaining liaison with and furnishing staff members for the National Security Council and other joint, combined, interdepartmental, and international agencies concerned with politico-military plans and with civil aviation matters, furnishing guidance on politico-military matters to the Air Force members of such agencies and to the Air Staff.[68]

There was a major organizational break in mid–1950 because of the Korean War. On 6 July of that year the Directorate of Plans was separated from the Directorate of Operations. The Directorate of Plans charter was reworded, and it became responsible for the

> Politico-military, strategic, and operational war planning for the Air Force; for initiation, coordination of preparation, and review of war plans of Major Subordinate Commands, including Reserve Forces; for review of plans submitted by JCS Commands; for Air Force participation in joint and combined planning, including military aid programs; for initiating action in the Air Staff to related Air Force policies and strategic planning responsibilities of the North Atlantic Treaty Organization, and for furnishing guidance to the Air Force representatives thereof.[69]

The War Plans Division continued to be divided into a number of teams. After the war began in the summer the organization's activity increased markedly, and the division was working more than twice as many major actions at the end of 1950 than at the beginning. More than half of the division's officers left between the first of July and 31 December 1950, dropping the experience level to a low state and vastly increasing the individual workload. The division was authorized sixty-one officers, but it never reached that figure. The forty-eight officers in the division on New Year's Eve 1950 were responsible for reviewing seventy-five information items daily, in addition to the important action items that occupied their major attention. The leadership of the division, moreover, moved on as rapidly as the subordinates.

The Red Team continued to be responsible for worldwide short-range emergency war planning, the White Team was still responsible for Air Staff planning for the intermediate-range period, but their primary duty was to support the budget. The Blue Team began 1950 as the sole organization responsible for long-range war plans but, with the outbreak of the Korean War, diverted its attention to near-term problems of a more urgent nature. The history says:

> most of the Team's energy was consumed in processing papers which could be categorized mainly under the heading of "miscellaneous" or possibly "strategic studies." The majority of the Team's work was independently produced rather than team produced, the latter usually being impossible because of time limitations.

This team was well wrapped up in the Korean War as well as short-term actions for basing Air Force people around the world.[70]

The Policy Division continued to study National Security Council issues, but a reading of the history indicates that they were heavily engaged in day-to-day activities of Air Force units overseas and took action on such issues as lifting the restriction on the time intervals between gunnery exercises in Libya, air rights in Pakistan, military assistance to Saudi Arabia, proposed stockpiling of bombs in Libya, storage of conventional bombs in Saudi Arabia, proposed B–50 overflights of Germany from United Kingdom bases, United States Air Forces, Europe, maneuvers with the French Army, display of two B–50 aircraft at Collinstown, Ireland, etc. The division also took part in the preparation and coordination of numerous policy papers for the National Security Council. Some of interest were "Appraisal of U.S. National Interest in South Asia;" "Assessment and Appraisal of U.S. Objectives;" "Commitments and Risks in Relation to Military Power;" "Provision of Armed Forces for the United Nations;" "U.S. Objectives and Programs for National Security (NSC 68);" "Future U.S. Policy with Respect to North Korea;" "The Position of the United States with Respect to Iran," "The Rearmament of Western Germany;" "U.S. Policy towards Spain;" "Position of the United States with Respect to Indochina;" Provision of a Police Force for Jerusalem;" etc.[71] Our list contains only about a quarter of the NSC papers which this division helped to shape. One sees that they were busy people.

Into 1951 the Directorate of Plans remained especially busy, and personnel changes continued to be rapid.[72] The War Planning Division was still organized by teams, with the Red Team continuing to be responsible for day-to-day planning and the White Team responsible for Air Staff planning for the intermediate-range period, but a reading of the papers produced by the organization indicate that this team was more active on short-range planning issues. The Blue Team continued to be responsible for the "promulgation of long-range war plans and the preparation of Staff studies in connection therewith." But the history records that "urgent matters" necessitated that the main efforts of the team be concentrated on near-term geographic issues in the Far East, Africa, and the Balkan nations.[73] During this historical period the Air Defense Team changed its name to the Planning Requirements Team but it continued to study mainly "worldwide air defense systems and their components."[74]

The Policy Division continued to take action on a variety of international security issues as they had done in the previous history. The great majority of these were short-range matters, really not planning issues at all. For example: "Protest from Prefect of Police, Paris, Concerning Low-Flying American Planes;" "Violation by USAFE Aircraft of the Czechoslovakian Border;" "Civil Air Patrol Cadet Exchange Program for 1951;" "Request for an Air Attache to Ethiopia;" "USAF use of Danish Aviation Gas;" "Offer of Twelve Dutch Jet Pilots for Service in Korea;" "Yugoslavia Border Violation." Again, this division was thoroughly immersed in day-to-day activities throughout this historical period, hampering its efforts to focus on policy.[75]

In the last half of 1951 the Directorate of Plans continued to concentrate on the issues that they worked the previous six months, and the rate of personnel changes was still stunning. The organization changed directors on 2 July 1951 with Major General Thomas D. White leaving to be succeeded by Major General Joseph Smith, and General White had not been in the position for a year. Major General Smith moved in November to be replaced by Major General R. M. Lee.[76]

During this period all pretense that the Blue Team of the War Planning Division was focusing on long-range issues was dropped. The organization concentrated on current activities in the Far East; on air bases in Africa, Spain, the Middle East, and the Balkans; and on strategic oil problems, as well as on aerial refueling![77]

The Planning Requirements Team was again reorganized and given different responsibilities. No longer were they to work air defense issues, but now took up interservice matters.[78] The White Team, which was supposedly responsible for planning for the intermediate-range time period, apparently spent a great deal of time struggling with Army/Air Force interservice controversies. A good part of the history is devoted to such problems, despite the fact that these matters were also handled by another team within the division.[79] The Policy Division continued to deal with immediate issues in the geographic regions of the world.[80]

Not until April of 1952 did Plans drop the team organization, which was designed to balance work loads, and begin to specialize into branches.[81] In that month, the War Plans Division was divided into branches that handled areas within their expertise. For example, the Rainbow Team became the Combined Plans Branch which worked issues with United States alliances.[82] The Red Team became the Joint Plans Branch which dealt with issues that involved the Army and the Navy.[83]

The White Team became the Air Force Plans Branch and that organization, while supposedly responsible for intermediate-range plans, spent "a great portion of its efforts in assisting other Air Staff agencies in tasks not the primary responsibility of the team." A reading of the Plans Branch history finds that no unit dealt with a more diverse range of issues than this one. Geographic, doctrinal, conceptual, exercise, strategic, congressional, air base issues—all fell within the responsibility of this branch.[84]

The Black Team of the War Plans Division was reorganized and renamed the Western Hemisphere Branch, concentrating on issues dealing with Canada, and Central and South America. This branch also worked matters dealing with Iceland.[85]

The Blue Team and the Planning Requirements Team were joined into the Strategic Studies Branch. This organization focused on geographic issues, but also explored the preparation of a long-range war plan which was to have guided long-range research and development.[86]

182

The Policy Division became larger in this time period but continued to act on issues similar to those they had worked in the past. That is, current international security issues, interface with the National Security Council, etc.[87]

C. Ineffective Attempts to Establish Long-Range Planning

In the last half of 1952 the Strategic Studies Branch continued activity on long-range war planning. Both a plan dealing with the years 1960–1965 and a staff study on "Warfare in the Future, after 1965," were completed.[88] These studies and reports were polished over the next six months, and the main branch activities were "largely confined to providing Staff guidance primarily from a long-range point of view to the Air Planners, the Chief of Staff, and the Secretary of the Air Force."[89]

In addition to the two documents previously mentioned, the branch also produced an Air Force long-range strategic estimate to provide guidance to research and development agencies. The history reported that all "these documents project air strategy into the future and, in so doing, attempt to stress the impact of technology on strategy and the decisiveness of air weapons." In June 1953 the Air Force Council approved the use of these documents as the basis for strategic guidance to Air Force research and development activities.[90]

However, a review of the histories of the Deputy Chief of Staff, Development, and the Air Research and Development Command from the same period and for the next several years indicates that the documents were either never received or were ignored despite the fact that the highest policymaking entity in the United States Air Force directed their use.[91]

Through 1954 the Strategic Studies Branch of the War Plans Division of the Directorate of Plans continued to deal with long-range issues. They produced during the first six months of 1954 a first draft of the "Air Force Long Range Strategic Estimate for 1959–1964." This document was designed to "provide long-range strategic guidance for Air Force research and development activities and other long-range programs by translating the national strategy of the United States into long-range supporting military strategy and objectives." The first draft was submitted for comment in early 1954. However, because of a shortage of personnel in the Strategic Studies Branch and the assignment of higher priority projects, progress on the study did not proceed beyond securing comments on the initial draft. In other long-term activities an action officer from the branch represented the directorate on a committee established in 1954 to provide the Department of Defense with an estimate of the Air Force requirement for aircraft engines and major component equipment for the next ten years.[92]

In June of 1954 a Long Range Objectives and Programs Group was established within the Directorate of Plans with the purpose of conducting continuing study of Air Force objectives and concepts. They launched immediately into a study of Air Force structure, including the types of equipment and deployment which, in conjunction with the other United States forces and forces of our allies, would be capable of:

a. Affecting a decision within the first thirty (30) days of a general war with the Soviet bloc;

b. Bringing this war to a successful conclusion within twelve (12) months; and

c. Affecting a decision in limited wars while maintaining the capability to meet general war requirements.

This study, completed for the Director of Plans himself, was not formally coordinated within the Air Staff. It included, furthermore, a strategic appraisal influenced by the fact that in this time period both the United States and the USSR would enter into an era of nuclear plenty. Force requirements were also developed by considering the tasks which had to be performed by "defensive, offensive and support forces, and deriving numerical requirements from these." The group paid great attention to intercontinental ballistic missiles and asserted that "strategic forces should undergo a trend toward an intercontinental force capable of launching a decisive attack regardless of who delivers the first blow." The total number of aircraft in the strategic force, the group argued, could be reduced because of the increased destructive capability of nuclear and thermonuclear weapons. The group also believed the numbers of aircraft in the tactical forces could be reduced for the same reason. The group asserted that in the latter part of the period overseas bases would become vulnerable, necessitating reliance on United States bases and a large airlift capability. Finally, the planners wrote with prescience that missiles would comprise an increasingly significant portion of all categories of forces during the period 1957–1965.[93]

The Long Range Objectives and Programs Group, however, was not the sole owner of the nascent long-range planning effort in plans. The Strategic Studies Branch was still in existence, and it published "A Strategic Concept for the Basis of U.S. Military Strategy, 1957–1965." This large effort drew in members from the rest of the Air Staff and advanced the thesis that the development of nuclear weapons, coupled with the progress in weapons delivery systems, "are of such significance that the strategy and tactics of warfare should be fundamentally reoriented: all efforts must be peaked toward the all-important initial phase of the war in which each side will attempt to deliver massive nuclear firepower on the other." As with the objectives group, the Strategic Studies Branch worked many other studies and issues (many short-range) and developed papers to influence the program and budget.[94]

On into 1955 the Long Range Objectives and Programs Group continued to focus on Air Force objectives and concepts ten years ahead. The efforts of the office during the first six months of 1955 were primarily focused on revising the "USAF Force Structure and Program Objectives, 1957–1965" which had originally been published as an Air Force Council position in December 1954. In February of 1955 the Chief of Staff transmitted the document to the major commands in the United States for comment indicating that, after the document had undergone final revision and obtained his final approval, it would be used to provide "guidance to those activities responsible for the planning, programming, and development of the Air Force." Each of the major commands had significant comments and the document was revised and sent again to the Air Force Council and the Chief of Staff, and in May 1955, the Chief and the Under Secretary of the Air Force approved the document. In so doing, the leadership stated that the document would be reviewed and revised annually with each revision projecting the program for the following ten years.[95] Meanwhile, the Strategic Studies Branch continued to concentrate on long-range issues that also were to provide guidance for those responsible for developing and programming the future Air Force.[96]

In the first half of 1955 the Long Range Objectives and Programs Group, given the fact that the "USAF Force Structure and Program Objectives, 1957–1965" had been approved in May as official guidance for the Air Force, "devoted considerable attention for several months to establishing the relationship of this guidance to development, programming, planning, and procurement activities." The group's activities were considerably hampered by the fact that the Chief of Staff had ordered that the document's contents were to be tightly held with extremely "strict limitations imposed upon access to the document." The history does not explain why a document that was designed to guide Air Force programming and development was held so closely, and the history indicates that this restriction hamstrung the plans office in getting its message out.[97]

In summary, the reader can see that despite the fact that Generals Arnold and Spaatz directed that the headquarters be concerned with the future, the headquarters was obviously embroiled in day-to-day activities. Not until the end of the Korean War was the Directorate of Plans able to establish any organization devoted to long-term planning, and even then it was a part-time effort. There is no question that in that time period the Air Force developed advanced systems and began initiatives that had consequences far into the future (consider, for example, just the B–52). But this author would question, after reading the histories and comparing them with the histories of the Deputy Chief of Staff for Development and the Air Research and Development Command, the relevance of the activities of the Directorate of Plans in terms of advancing its concept of the future and watching it guide the Air Force. Significantly, the "USAF Force Structure and Program Objectives" does not appear in the relevant histories of the Air Research and Development Command; if it was not ignored, it certainly did not make a major impression as a Chief of Staff-directed road map.[98]

It was apparently not until 1956 that the Deputy Chief of Staff, Development, formally commented on this Directorate of Plans long-range planning and programming effort, admitting that this was a "first effort" on their part.[99] Long-range planning was, therefore, a sometime effort, and when a strategic plan was written, those for whom it was largely written generally ignored it because there was no institutionalized long-range planning process and no formal connection between the Directorate of Plans on the one hand and the Deputy Chief of Staff, Development, and the Air Research and Development Command on the other hand.

D. Establishing an Independent Research and Development Entity

In 1949 Major General R. C. Lindsay, lecturing at the Air War College, told the assembled lieutenant colonels and colonels:

> To synchronize planning with those technical and scientific advances that may influence the character and techniques of war 8, 10, 15 or more years in the future is a difficult piece of business, and. . .you may discard any

tendency to conclude that the processes are well established, systematic and clearly defined.[100]

Certainly the situation described by General Lindsay in 1949 was symptomatic of the period between the end of the war and that date and, in fact, characterized the situation for some time to come. We just observed how the Directorate of Plans "Warfare in the Future" study, the "Long Range Strategic Estimate," and the "Force Structure and Program Objectives" were apparently ignored by the development community despite their support by the Air Force Council and the Chief of Staff. We would note further that, at least in 1950, when the Deputy Chief of Staff, Development, was founded, the organization recognized the primacy of the Directorate of Plans in outlining the strategic direction for research and development. The initial Deputy Chief of Staff, Development, history reveals:

> The Air Staff now consisted of one deputy charged with operating the present Air Force and with planning for the operation of the future Air Force; one deputy charged with providing that future Air Force; and three deputies responsible for the support, in men, money, and materials, of both the present and future force.[101]

Yet as we have seen, long-range planning documents such as the "USAF Force Structure and Program Objectives, 1957–1965" had slight if any impact because there was no regular mechanism or process for connecting the output of the Directorate of Plans with the research and development community.

A major part of the problem was that an independent organization for research and development policy and technical advance had difficulty finding its identity in the post-World War II period, despite the interest that the military leadership and their civilian superiors had in technology. During World War II, research and development was performed by numerous agencies on the staff and in the field; and in December of 1945, General Arnold directed the establishment of a Deputy Chief of Air Staff for Research and Development, raising it to a much higher level than it had been during the war. Arnold, moreover, assigned to it one of the most operationally oriented and bluntly direct major generals in the Air Force, Curtis E. LeMay. His new Air Staff office was charged to prepare the overall research and development program for the Air Force and to concern itself with policy matters affecting the research and development program. But in the field, the Air Materiel Command, primarily oriented toward logistics, continued as the field agency responsible for research and development programs. (The Air

Materiel Command was the new name in March 1946 of the Air Technical Service Command.)[102]

General LeMay's newly organized Deputy Chief of Air Staff for Research and Development did not last two years. When the Air Staff was organized in the fall of 1947 research and development was placed in the Deputy Chief of Staff, Materiel, office as a directorate among many. The Director of Research and Development would also serve as the military director of Dr. von Karman's Scientific Advisory Board, but otherwise he would be subordinated to the Deputy Chief of Staff, Materiel.[103]

One might expect that placing research and development under materiel could have some shortcomings, and it did. During the war years, Air Materiel Command, or its predecessors under different titles, had been much more concerned with production, logistics, and maintenance than with research and development. In the postwar period the Air Force continued to subordinate research and development to maintenance and support of those things produced.[104]

The Scientific Advisory Board under von Karman was dissatisfied with the arrangement of having research and development beneath production, logistical, and maintenance considerations. But moves to break out research and development from under materiel, both on the Air Staff and in the field, were opposed strongly by the people responsible for the materiel function. Probably most vociferous in his objection was Lieutenant General Benjamin W. Chidlaw who was the commander of Air Materiel Command in the mid- to late–1940s. He wanted research and development subordinated to his function, and he wanted it kept nearby to keep his eye on the potential rival for resources. Chidlaw's view prevailed with research and development remaining subordinate until the end of the decade within Air Materiel Command.[105]

The Scientific Advisory Board believed research and development could not flourish in this atmosphere and continued to fight this arrangement. In 1949 Chief of Staff General Hoyt Vandenberg commissioned a study by the Scientific Advisory Board to be led by Dr. Louis N. Ridenour to review the state of Air Force research and development and make recommendations. On 21 September 1949 Ridenour reported his findings and recommended the establishment of a research and development organization to be called the Research and Development Command, which would function as an operational entity separate and independent of the Air Materiel Command. Ridenour believed that the new organizational and functional revision would "make it easier to introduce the necessary improvement in personnel, program and budget policies" needed to assist in the development of complete weapon systems. Simultaneously, a study was conducted at the Air University under its commandant, Major General Orvil A. Anderson. The Air University study, which is also known as the Anderson Report, reached the Air Staff in November 1949, and it proposed an independent Pentagon Deputy Chief of Staff for Research and Development and, like the Ridenour Report, the removal of those activities from the organizational control of the Air Materiel Command. The Anderson Committee report said: "We can hardly bury the responsibility for the Air Force of the future under the logistic responsibility for the Air Force of the present."[106]

Anderson's report asserted that the Air Force was "dangerously deficient in its capacity to insure the long-term development and superiority of American power." The report argued that the Air Force was not "providing an adequate foundation for the productive operation and healthy growth of the Research and Development structure," and also that there was no system to ensure the "interaction between strategy and technology." Anderson's report concluded that "current emphasis upon day-to-day operational and material problems has been so great as to radically and adversely affect the long-term development of the Air Force," and as a final grabber, the report asserted that the Army and Navy might "take over responsibilities abdicated by the USAF" if the Air Force continued to neglect its technological responsibilities.[107]

The recommendations of both the Ridenour and Anderson reports struck a responsive chord. The vast, sprawling, heterogeneous Air Materiel Command, because of its diverse responsibilities, focused on the immediate—such as supply, procurement, production, and testing—as well as research and exploratory development. But activities such as the improvement of a product and its procurement and support weighed most heavily on the command. Major General F. O. Carroll, who was the command's Director of Research and Development, noted in the late 1940s that "we in the Command in Research and Development are continually faced with the responsibility of figuring out a way to get this or fix that."[108]

The whole operational context of the Air Materiel Command was channeled into the quick payoff end of the spectrum, giving priority to the short-term and short shrift to long-term projects. But that was really only part of the story. In the final analysis, all research and development, whether long- or short-term, was undervalued, being overwhelmed in an environment dominated by such quantitative functions as procurement, maintenance and supply.

Because of the findings of the Ridenour and Anderson Committees, the Research and Development Command was born on 23 January 1950, but initially not nourished. The Air Force leadership, unfortunately, called for the new command to gradually assume responsibility for research and development activities from Air Materiel Command, and the emphasis was on the adverb gradually. Air Materiel Command had three principal divisions of which one was the Research and Development Directorate. This directorate with its major segment, the Engineering Division, became the foundation of the Research and Development Command, but removing it from Air Materiel Command "proved more difficult than envisioned." The commander of the Air Materiel Command wanted a gradual move; the Research and Development Commander naturally wanted full assumption of his responsibilities on a one-time, one-date basis, and quickly. Chief of Staff Vandenberg decided in mid-October 1950 (things not moving quickly enough for him) that the move would be completed by 15 May 1951, and not until then would Research and Development Command be able to perform its mission independently. In time this date was moved forward to 2 April 1951, and on that date the Research and Development Command became fully independent and received in its domain Edwards Air Force Base, Holloman Air Force Base, the Air Force Cambridge Research Laboratories, Griffis Air Force Base, Watson Laboratories, Climatic Projects Laboratory, Upper Air Research Station, and the research and development activities at Wright-Patterson Air Force Base, which included the Office of Air Research, Flight Test Division, All-Weather Flying Division, and the Engineering Division, all of which had been former components of Research and Development at Air Materiel Command.[110]

Simultaneously with the creation of the Research and Development Command on 23 January 1950, a Deputy Chief of Staff for Development (figure 4) was created within the headquarters, moving the Directorate of Research and Development out from under the Deputy Chief of Staff for Materiel to an independent status. The first Deputy Chief of Staff for Development was Major General Gordon P. Saville, taking his position in January 1950, while Major General D. M. Schlatter became the Commanding General of the Research and Development Command.

The reorganization of both commands and the Air Staff did not go smoothly. Neither the Deputy Chief of Staff for Materiel nor the

190

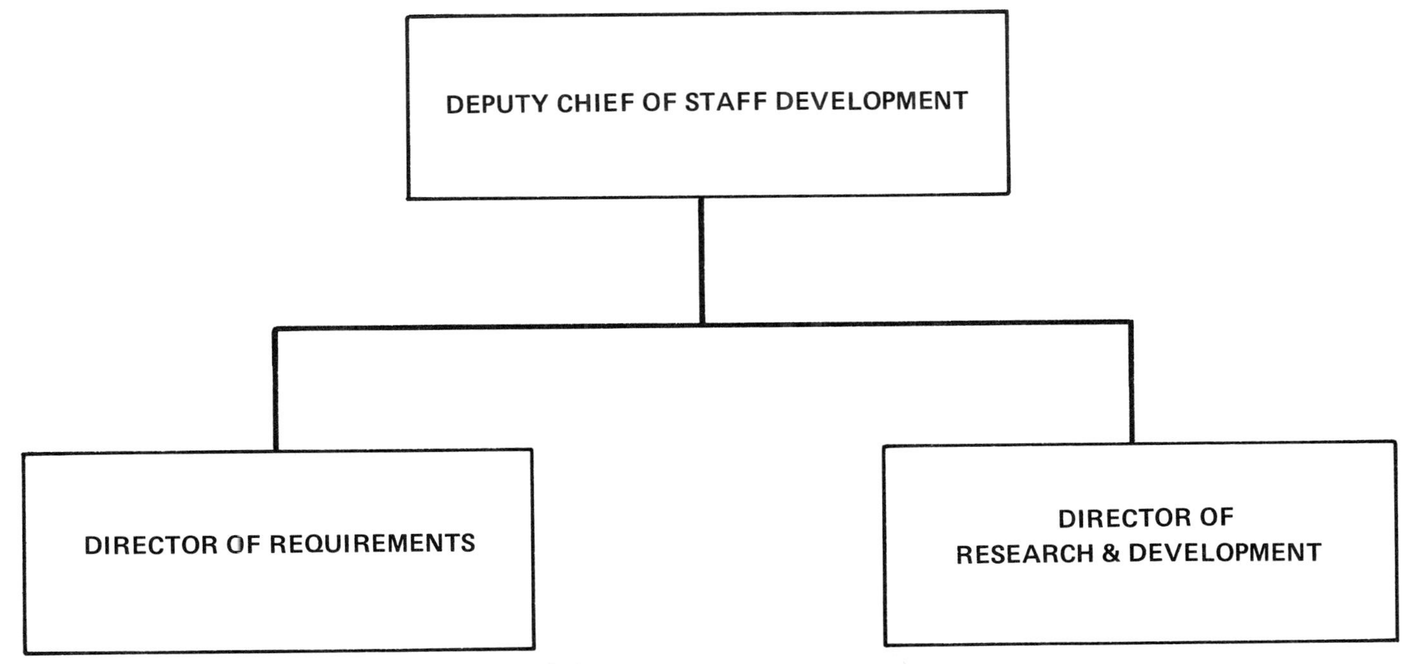

Figure 4. Deputy Chief of Staff, Development, as of January 1950 (1 February 1950).

Air Materiel Command commander believed that the move needed to be made and actually obstructed a smooth transition; that was especially true of the command in the field.[111]

The reorganization was supposed to be controlled by the Vice Chief of Staff, General Muir S. Fairchild, but he died soon after the decision to separate the organizations was made, and the exchange was not controlled from the headquarters as specified. Moreover, the beginning of the Korean War in June of 1950 turned everyone's focus to that war and the possibility of a larger one. And so it happens that in times when operational concerns become supreme, readiness has the highest priority, and research and development for the distant future always suffers.[112]

There were bitter charges of bad faith between the two commands in 1950 and 1951. Finally, General Vandenberg appointed retired Lieutenant General James Doolittle to oversee the change and to eliminate the friction. It was Doolittle who recommended a rapid separation and Vandenberg followed his advice.[113]

E. Inadequate Research and Development Funding

In addition to the bureaucratics that plagued research and development after World War II, science and technology was badly underfunded from the end of World War II until the Korean War began to loosen the purse strings.[114] Although it is true that in fiscal year 1946 the research and development budget was large by comparison to previous peacetime eras, the world had moved into a new epoch where technology might decide wars, and the Air Force recognized this. Air Force commanders and subordinates generally shared General Arnold's point of view:

> The first essential of air power necessary for peace and security is...preeminence in research. . . . We must remember at all times that the degree of national security rapidly declines when reliance is placed on the quantity of existing equipment instead of its quality. . . .We must count on scientific advances requiring us to replace about one-fifth of existing Air Force's equipment each year, and we must make sure that these additions are the most advanced in the whole world.[115]

But saying that and doing that are two different things. Unquestionably, the officers who were in command of the Air Force recognized the importance of research and development, but they and their civilian superiors better understood the predatory nature of the Soviet Union characterized by the dropping of the Iron Curtain around eastern Europe, the 1948 rape of Czechoslovakia, the land blockade of Berlin, and, of course, (soon after the move on the Air Staff and in the field to create independent research and development organizations) the outbreak of the war in Korea. General James H. Doolittle summed it up in a neat epigram. He said of these years, "everyone is for research and development. . .just as everyone is against sin; however, very few people will sacrifice for it."[116]

Because of the relatively parsimonious funding of research and development and, worse, because of the irregular nature of that funding—there having been no steady financing of research and development—a several-year project begun one year may not have received money the next because of cuts. Financing was irregular until the Korean War. For these reasons, coordinated development within the Air Force did not really begin until after the Korean War when the Air Force settled down to preparing for future wars instead of fighting the war in which it was currently involved. There were serious research and development cuts each year in 1947, 1948, 1949, and 1950, and promising programs which had been started had to be cut.[117] One example is the intercontinental ballistic missile which was cut out of the program in the late 1940s, while the Air Force pressed on with long-range cruise missiles. The Air Force had to make a choice between the two and the Air Force chose to cut the rocket and continue with the subsonic, jet-powered cruise missile for some time to come.[118] When in 1954 the Air Force finally turned to what soon became a crash development of rockets for the intercontinental strategic mission, it was a skunkworks effort because the senior defense leadership believed intercontinental ballistic missiles could not be developed rapidly in any other fashion.[119]

Similarly underfunded for a good deal of its early history, and just as much snarled in internal bureaucratics, was the Air Force's organization for basic research. In October 1951, the year the Air Research and Development Command gained its independence, that organization established, as a small staff section in the headquarters, an office to write basic research policy and to monitor its development for the Air Force. The office changed names many times, becoming the Office of Scientific Research in 1955, a name retained to this day. The fact that the organization was established in the first place is a tribute to the determination of Theodore von Karman, who valued basic research. Doctor von Karman covered the September 1949 Ridenour Report with a letter that called on the Air Force for "full use of the technical talent and facilities possessed by the industries and the universities of the country." Von Karman asked for "a small recurring investment in the support of fundamental scientific investigations." He believed the Air Force was "clearly faced by problems requiring fundamental scientific investigations."[120] The office, from the time of its establishment through the end of the period under review, had to fight continuously for an adequate and stable budget and for the ear of the major command commander. The history of the organization reveals that it was continuously reorganized in this time period and whipsawed by changes in philosophy with each new director. One historian characterized the early period this way:

> how guided should the research be; that is, was the Air Force properly in the business of pure science or should it be guiding the research efforts of the laboratories with which they contracted? During this period, in other words, the office was pulled back and forth in an eternal tug of war between what could be properly called science and what could be reasonably titled technology.[121]

F. Deputy Chief of Staff for Development

Whipsawing research and development was the mode of operation through the mid–1950s. The Deputy Chief of Staff, Development was established on 23 January 1950, and it had difficulties separating itself from the clutches of the Deputy Chief of Staff, Materiel. In fact, several of the directors of the new organizations were required to attend staff meetings of their old organizations and were required "to perform all services required by those Deputies in the same manner as they would have performed prior to the recent reorganization."[122]

During 1950 the organization was revised three times and, by the end of the year, was organized into two directorates and two assistant deputy chiefs of staff organizations, namely, an Assistant for Development Programming, an Assistant for Evaluation, a Director of Requirements, and a Director of Research and Development. The mission of the Deputy Chief of Staff of Development was (according to the official "Organizations and Functions of the Headquarters USAF, the so-called "Chart Book") to represent the Chief of Staff "in all matters pertaining to the technical development or qualitative improvement of the Air Force." The Deputy Chief of Staff, Development, was also to provide the "integration of scientific planning and technical development into the strategic and operational activities of the Air Force," and also to provide the Air Staff with "recommendations relative to the scheduling of quantitative data concerning materiel or systems under development, and relative to application of newly developed materiel or weapons systems."[123]

The Assistant for Evaluation had beneath it a Strategic Plans Division whose responsibility it was to establish:

> close working relationships with Air Force operational planning and intelligence staff agencies and other Air Staff agencies to insure an integration of strategy and technology, and to insure that strategic guidance is properly reflected in Air Force development programs.[124]

We have seen, however, that "close working relationships" were never established. In fact, the official history does not even include the Chart Book mission, and the mechanism by which the division might implement such a connection is unmentioned.[125]

The Assistant for Development Programming had responsibilities not unlike the Strategic Plans Division. This office was responsible for:

> the establishment and implementation of administrative policies, controls, and procedures affecting Air Force qualitative development programming. Collects and collates Air Force development policies and insures that all interested agencies and personnel are aware of such policies. Insures that research and development projects have received proper staff coordination; provides final certification of overall Air Force programs and of Headquarters USAF-directed projects affecting the development of the Air Force.[126]

In 1951 the Assistant for Evaluation changed its title to Assistant for Development Planning. The intent of the change was to emphasize the primary function of this office, which was "to develop and publish the long-range objectives and plans of our research and development effort."[127] The unit history recorded that the programming and the conduct of research and development was to be linked "to the operational plans of the Air Force." In the summer of 1950 Colonel Bernard A. Schriever was made chief of the organization.[128]

The mechanism, however, for linking the strategic objectives and plans for research and development with operational planning in the Air Force was not outlined in the history, and we have noted previously that a perusal of the Air Force Directorate of Plans histories for the same period indicates also the lack of an interfacing mechanism. In fact, the next volume of the unit history complains that:

> In the past there has been little organized effort made to relate specific projects to each other and to a governing requirement, and to integrate these projects with organizational plans and missions. There had been a tendency to regard any research and development effort as somewhat isolated from the main problem of operating an Air Force. . . . In the past, . . . this Headquarters had spent more time worrying about the conduct of

specific projects than about the correlation of projects and programs to objectives and plans.[129]

There were also, as one might expect, frictions between the Deputy Chief of Staff, Development, apparatus and the field command. A memorandum to the Deputy Chief of Staff, Development, argued that the Air Staff "must not only let Air Research and Development Command run the program," but must also be content "that the field command knew best how to manage what the Pentagon directed." The headquarters, indeed, by late 1951, had to give the field command some autonomy because, by November of that year, there were 3,000 individual projects in the Air Force Technology Program.[130]

The memorandum that highlighted the marital difficulties between the Pentagon and the field also cited three essential elements in the mission of the Deputy Chief of Staff, Development. These were to define the "existing and clearly foreseen requirements of the operating Air Force, planning the development of the future Air Force," and designing broadly the research and development program "necessary to meet the often conflicting demands of both the present and the future." The author admitted, though, that "among the elements of the DCS/D mission, development planning has most successfully eluded adequate definition."[131]

The Assistant for Development Planning was the key organization for dealing with the rest of the Air Staff and the Air Force at large on structuring a valid technology program to advance the Air Force. There were two divisions within the organization—the Operational Systems Division and the Technical Analysis Division. The former dealt with "long-range problems within the conventional U.S. Air Force mission areas consisting of strategic and tactical operations, air defense, air logistics and reconnaissance." The division was divided into teams with a team captain assigned for each of these major mission areas, and this individual was made responsible for directing the planning efforts of "flexible teams composed of appropriate Air Staff and other representatives." The history records that the division chief believed that the composition of the teams was sufficiently broad to include participation by, or contributions from, all agencies and institutions having data or advice bearing on the mission problem. For example, the reconnaissance team had representatives from six Air Staff agencies, including Air Force Plans, three major air commands, including Air Research and Development, as well as civilian representatives from three universities and the Rand Corporation.[132]

The Technical Analysis Division (the other organization within the Deputy Chief of Staff, Development) was concerned with long-range problems within technical areas such as aeronautics, sensing, atomic energy, and armament. The history records that there was "maximum interrelation" between the two divisions to ensure coordinated results.[133]

The Deputy Chief of Staff, Development, took the view that "organized long-range planning which delineates the general goals of qualitative development for future years," was a "fundamental necessity for the success of the U.S. Air Force in the accomplishment of its mission." This general officer believed the Air Force continually needed to introduce "qualitatively superior weapons systems and improved techniques," in order to accomplish its mission. He believed, however, that he was responsible for long-range planning, not the Director of Plans, with whom he had no formal connection. Consistent with that view, in the last six months of 1952, the Assistant for Development Planning devoted his primary effort to developing, in an apparently uncoordinated fashion, planning objectives for air operations out to 1960,[134] a task that belonged rightly in the Directorate of Plans.

In 1952 the Deputy Chief of Staff, Development, published a journal titled *USAF Development Reports*. Volume I was titled "Development Organization in the USAF: How a Piece of Equipment Evolves." Nowhere in this article (that describes the evolution of equipment) is there shown any contact between the Deputy Chief of Staff, Development, and the Deputy Chief of Staff, Operations, or the Directorate of Plans.[135] One would ask: for whom is equipment being developed, if not operations?

Not only was there no organized connection between the Directorate of Plans and the Assistant for Development Planning, but in the autumn of 1952 the Deputy Chief of Staff, Development, lost its independence making a link even more difficult to effect. For the next three years the Deputy Chief of Staff, Development, existed in some form of limbo because the Secretary of the Air Force, Harold Talbott, decided to subordinate development to materiel again. Official histories are always muted on such subjects, but the hurt comes off the pages clearly. We read that "some elements of the aircraft industry have been unsympathetic to the Air Research and Development Command since its inception." Apparently this attitude was "shared by many people within the Air Force who disagreed with the philosophy which led to the establishment of the Command and a new Deputy Chief of Staff for Development." The history recorded that it was evident "that the Air Materiel Command and the Air Research and Development Command were not always in harmony." Mr. Talbott apparently was concerned that the technology and materiel (especially procurement) efforts were not integrated and decided to subordinate the Deputy Chief of Staff, Development, to the Deputy Chief of Staff, Materiel (figure 5). Although the Air Research and Development Command was not affected by this shift in responsibility, the Deputy Chief of Staff, Development, in the Pentagon was now required to report to the Deputy Chief of Staff, Materiel. The history wrote candidly that these announcements had a "demoralizing effect" on people in the Pentagon and in the field. People believed that these changes marked a significant loss of emphasis and stature of research and development in the Air Force.[136] The arrangement downgrading research and development and placing it under the Deputy Chief of Staff, Materiel, remained in effect through the spring of 1955.[137] In the summer of that year, and ever since, apparently because technology could not flower under such an arrangement, research and development was broken out again as an independent deputy chief of staff (figure 6). For three years, however, the future was subordinated to the present.

It would appear that formal coordination other than ad hoc commentary by the Deputy Chief of Staff, Development, on Air Force long-range planning products did not emerge until the mid–1950s when the Assistant for Development Planning was elevated to a directorate. The official history records that his office went through "more than the normal growing pains." General Bernard Shriever stayed with this office for a number of years, in fact, until he departed to take over the control of the ballistic missile program. In July 1954 the new Assistant for Development Planning forwarded a study which advocated "the interaction of strategy and technology through the process of participation, in conjunction with appropriate Air Staff agencies and Major Air Commands, in the preparation of long-range strategic estimates, United States Air Force strategy and operational concepts." His organization was, furthermore, to provide long-range research and exploratory development guides to operating research and development agencies and the Air Staff. The assistant was also to sponsor from the Air Staff level long-range research objectives recommended by the Air Research and Development Command. Finally, the assistant would provide long-range guidance for the development of systems and techniques to accomplish most effectively Air Force operational missions under future war conditions. "This function was to be

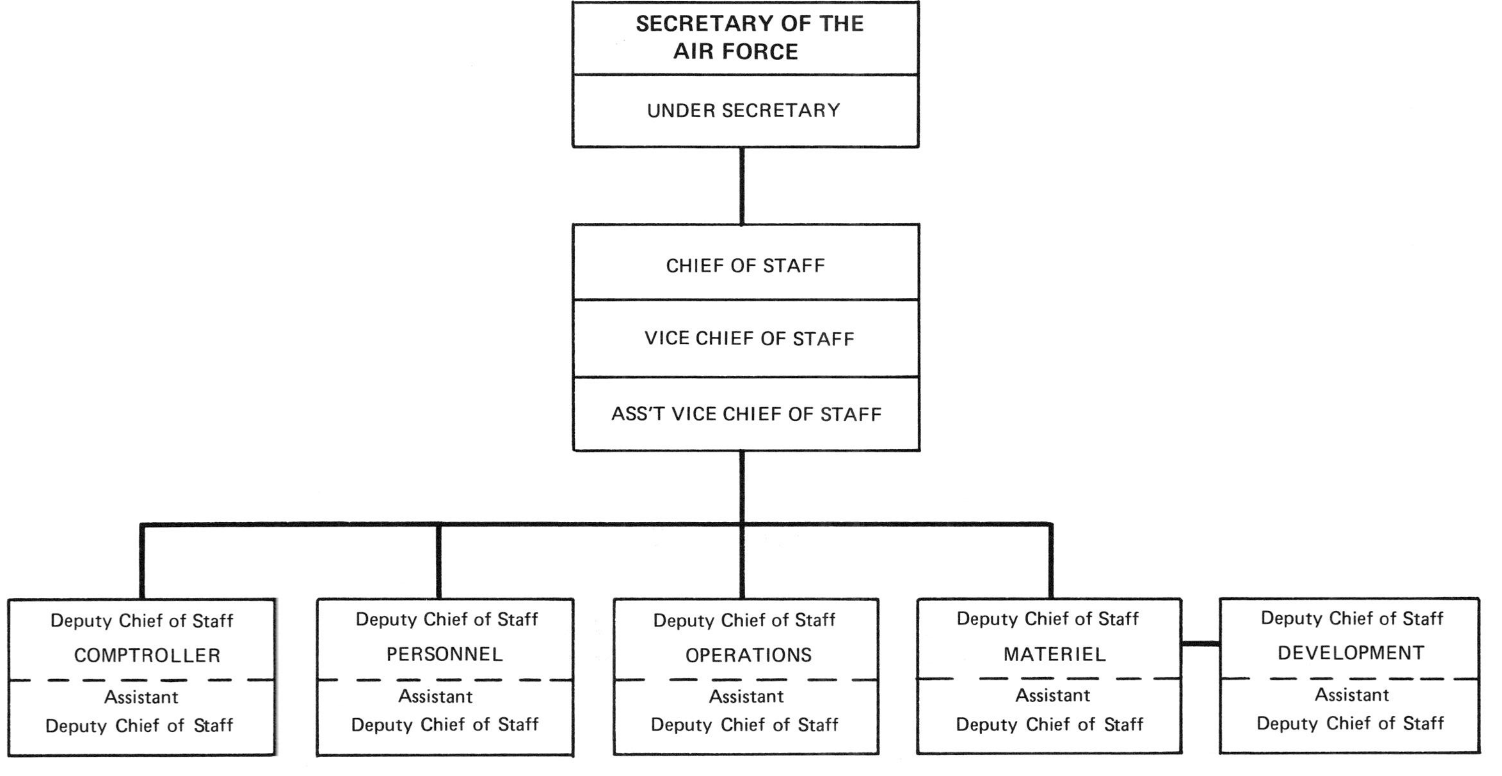

Figure 5. Air Staff Alignment from Mid–1952 to Mid–1955 (May 1955).

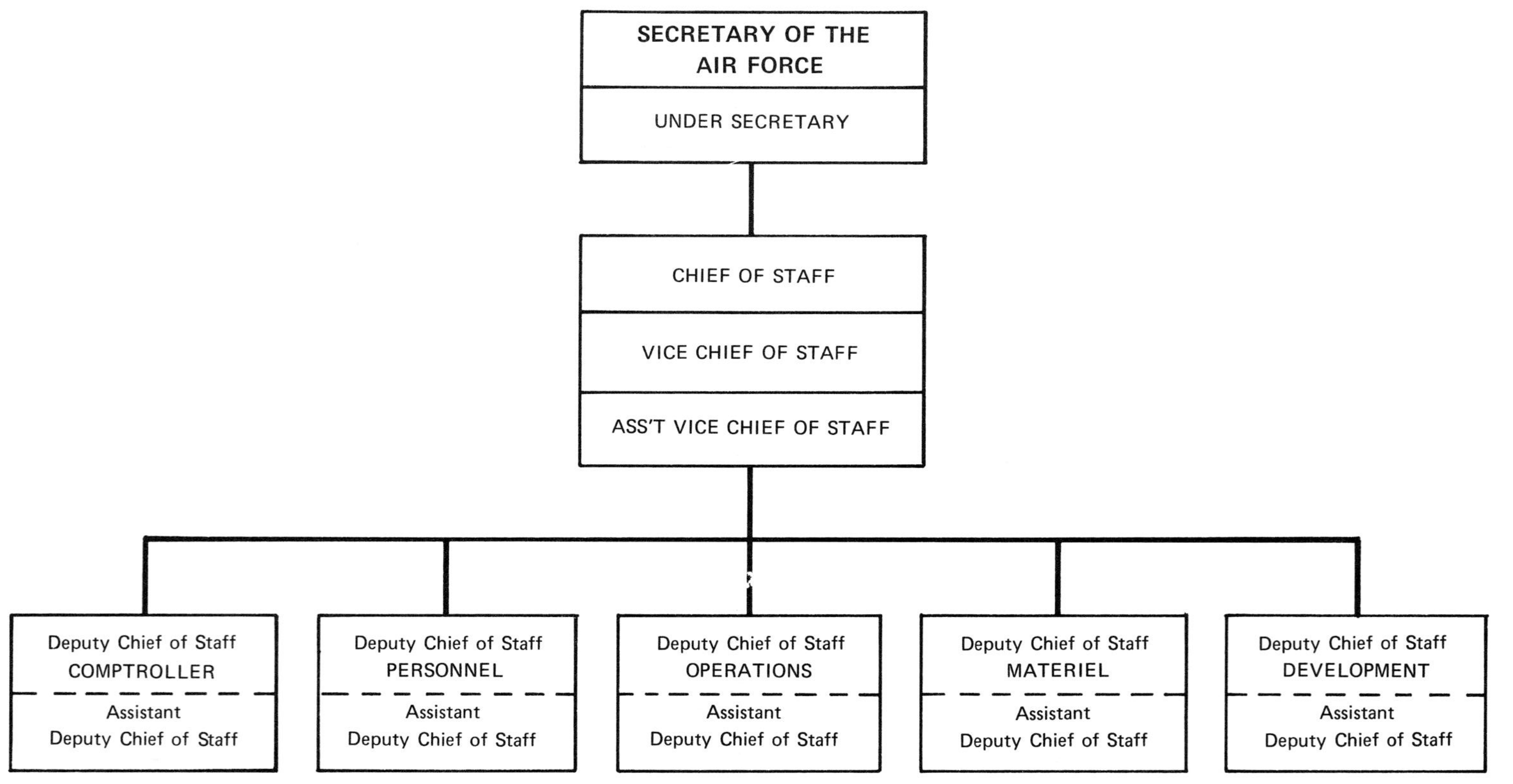

Figure 6. Air Staff Alignment after Mid—1955 (August 1955).

performed primarily through the preparation and promulgation of Development Planning Objectives."[138]

In February 1956 the now Directorate of Development Planning published an appendix for the "U.S. Long-Range Wartime Objectives Plan, 1958–1971" on research and development considerations and trends. (This document, the reader will recall, was produced in the Directorate of Plans.) This annex provided the headquarters planners at the early stages of planning an appreciation of the current projected capabilities of weapons, technology, and techniques for application and employment. Additionally, the directorate provided comments on the overall plan. Similarly in May 1956, the directorate provided a research and development section for the "Force Structure and Programming Objectives, 1958–1971" document from Air Force plans. This document was (according to the official history) to be sent to the appropriate operating research and development agencies,[139] but a review of Air Research and Development command histories for 1956 and 1957 indicates that it could not have made much of an impact, because the document is never mentioned.[140]

Despite the fact that the Directorate of Development Planning was finally formally commenting on Directorate of Plans products, an appendix to the history titled "Development Planning for Future U.S. Air Forces" that was intended to show how the headquarters integrated the processes of scientific development with strategic plans, operations concepts, and programs, indicates that the development directorate saw systems advances as being technology driven as opposed to operations plans driven. The appendix argues: "with the passage of time, the research and development program will, undoubtedly, assert an ever-increasing influence on the strategic plan, possibly becoming the major determination in the formulation of strategy." The remainder of the document is taken up with the writing of development planning objectives, a responsibility the authors firmly placed within the Deputy Chief of Staff, Development, and specifically within the Assistant for Development Planning. There is no link in the document with the Deputy Chief of Staff for Operations or the Directorate of Plans.[141] One sees then that by the mid–1950s, only a potential and imperfect nexus had been formed between the two organizations in the Air Staff that could coherently move the United States Air Force into the future.

V. UNIFYING THE PENTAGON BUREAUCRACY

What emerges from a reading of the histories of the various Deputy Chiefs of Staff in the Pentagon is the lack of a unifying force that required the organizations to pull together to move the Air Force into the future. There was in the Air Force during the first ten years after World War II no coherent strategic or long-range planning performed as we have defined it in this paper. Had there been genuine strategic planning there probably would have been more unity of effort. Despite the fact the Air Staff was defined as the policymaking entity in the Air Force, even a cursory reading of the Directorate of Plans' histories indicates that the Directorate of Plans immersed itself in near-term, current activities. This probably was not a choice made freely, but in any case, it is a fact. We noted that one of the teams in the War Plans Division was supposed to be involved in long-range planning, but it never quite got off the ground. We also noted later that such organizations as the Long Range Objectives Group and the Strategic Planning Branch produced products that were not used consistently by other Air Staff organizations or probably at all by the Air Research and Development Command. Not until 1963 did the Directorate of Plans create a Long-Range Plans Division (figure 7) responsible for relating scientific and academic development to Air Force objectives, among other responsibilities (see the appropriate Air Force chart books). This division was the basis for the creation in 1966 of the Director of Doctrine, Concepts, and Objectives (figure 8). When that new organization was created in 1966 (figure 9), however, Air Force Plans ceased to engage in all long-range planning, leaving the formulation of strategic objectives to the newly formed directorate which had the responsibility to "formulate and evaluate basic long-range concepts, objectives, and strategy for Air Force-wide guidance." (figure 10)[142]

There is, however, more to long-range planning than just formulating objectives and strategy. The Air Staff continued with the Directorate of Plans, on the one hand, dealing with policy for war planning and force structuring, and the Directorate of Doctrine, Concepts and Objectives, on the other hand, a parallel organization, weaving long-range objectives with no connection between the two. In the summer of 1978 the Director of Doctrine, Concepts, and Objectives was eliminated and no formal organization was assigned any part of the long-range planning task in its place. (See the 1978 Chart Book.)

Another element that could have provided a unifying force for the Air Staff in its first decade was doctrine, but this was as absent as

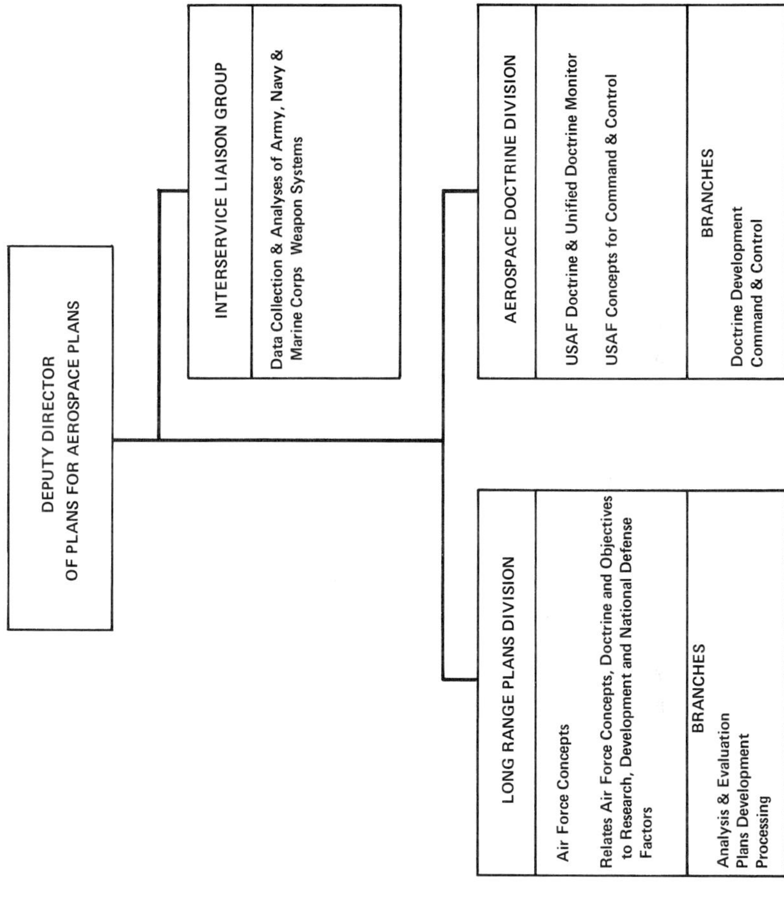

Figure 7. Deputy Director of Plans for Aerospace Plans (1 July 1963).

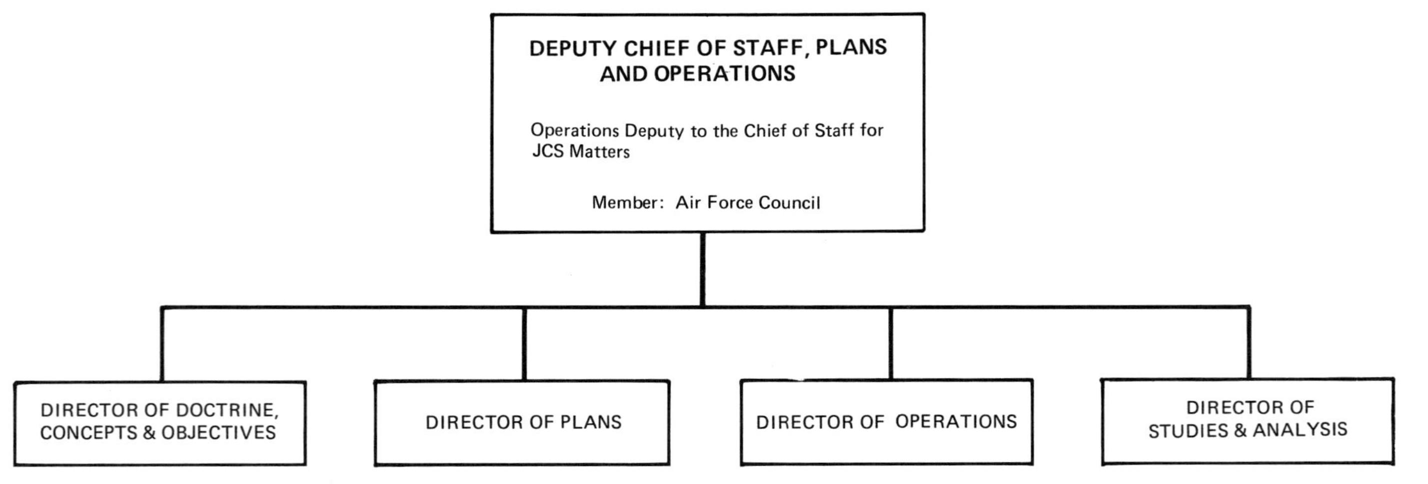

Figure 8. Deputy Chief of Staff, Plans and Operations (September 1966).

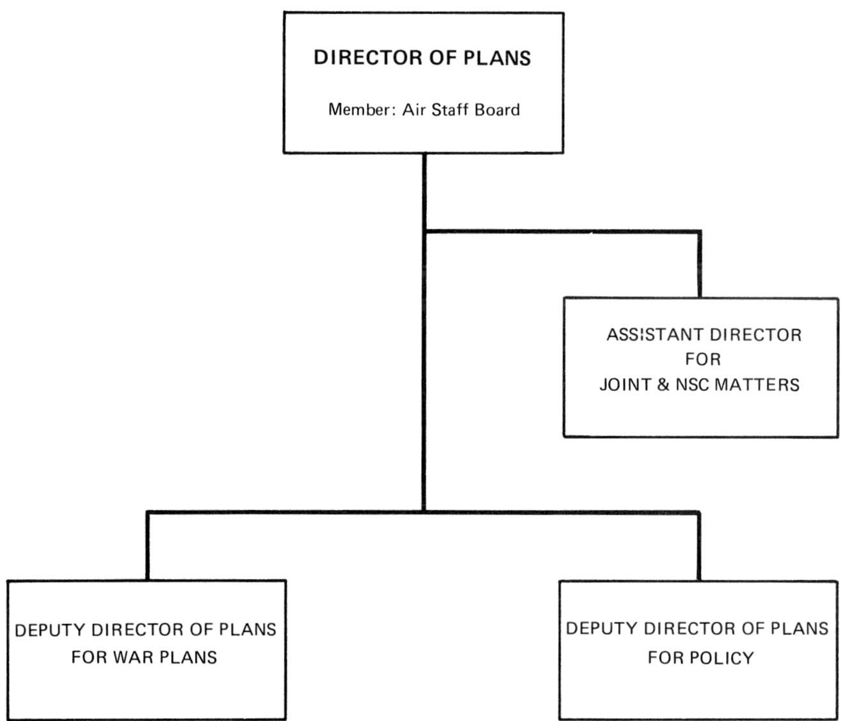

Figure 9. Director of Plans (September 1966).

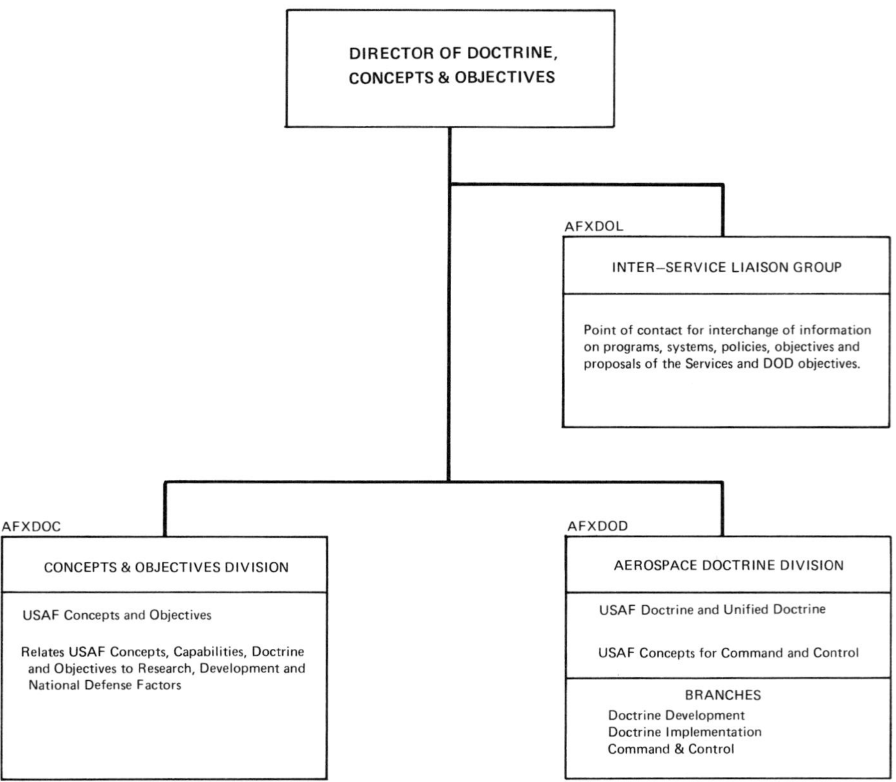

Figure 10. Director of Doctrine, Concepts, & Objectives (September 1966).

was strategic planning. The contemporary doctrine during the entire period of Air Force and Air Staff reorganization through the early 1950s was Field Manual 100–20, *Command and Employment of Air Power*, which had been published in July 1943. That document, often called the Magna Carta of the Air Force, was made obsolete by the atomic bombs exploded over Alamogordo, Hiroshima, and Nagasaki. Leaders in the Air Force recognized immediately after the war that the doctrine had to be reevaluated and rewritten, but deciding who was to do the writing and who was to review the product of the writing tied the Air Force in a knot for eight years.[143] The Air University was originally charged to review, revise, and prepare Air Force "Basic Doctrine," but the Air Staff did not permit Air University carte blanche in this arena.[144] Despite the fact that Brigadier General Francis H. Griswold, Deputy Chief of Air Staff for Operations, declared Field Manual 100–20 "obsolete and entirely inadequate" and despite the fact this view was shared by senior officers on the Air Staff and at the Air University, the Air Force could not collectively pull together sufficiently to write a new doctrine.[145]

The Joint Chiefs of Staff in September 1951 published the first *Joint Action Armed Forces* which included doctrinal statements for all four services, and this joint document was published in the Air Force as Manual 1–1. But the entire manual was only four pages long, and the mission statements were in no cases longer than a sentence, leaving too much open for interpretation.[146]

Finally, in March 1953, under Chief of Staff Vandenberg's signature, the Air Force published Air Force Manual 1–2, *United States Air Force Basic Doctrine*. The doctrine was thin, seventeen short pages, and though fairly roundly criticized by senior uniformed leaders, when the major commanders were given the opportunity to review and comment on the manual as requested by the Chief of Staff, they suggested very few changes, which demonstrates to this author that basic doctrine was not taken seriously.[147] This led to the publication of another Air Force Manual 1–2, *Basic Doctrine* a year later, but the changes were cosmetic and the two manuals looked alike. This led to yet another Air Force Manual 1–2 another year later that was more solid than the two previous editions. This manual struck a responsive chord in the Air Force, which must have been embarrassed at the fact it took them three publications in three years to get it right.[148]

Of the two lacks—strategic planning and doctrine—the former was the more significant, and the responsibility for establishing a valid long-range planning apparatus rested with the Deputy Chief of Staff for Operations and the Directorate of Plans. During the first decade, research and development planning, programming, and budgeting were separated from other corporate planning, programming, and budgeting activities. There was, furthermore, no entity within the Air Staff that dealt directly with the Air Force chief executive to formulate a strategic plan or, for that matter, even to outline the Air Force's long-range goals. During the first decade, the views of the Chief of Staff and the Secretary of the Air Force, and the rest of the top management about the relative importance of different capability alternatives and planning directions were not communicated regularly to the Air Force at large. This comes through clearly in both the Air Force Plans histories and the Deputy Chief of Staff, Development, histories.

Corporately endorsed strategic goals and policies are necessary so that all of the staff agencies that interact in the extremely complex research and development planning process can act from the common recognition of where the Air Force thinks it should be heading over the long term. As the process operated then, it was possible for each office to follow, more or less, its own perceptions of what the future direction should be.

What was needed was a systematic strategic planning effort by a corporate planning staff that could assist the Chief of Staff in concert with others at the highest levels in articulating their long-range goals. In other words, what was needed was a planning effort similar to the one defined in the opening pages of this paper, one that identified the organization's long-range goals in an uncertain future world. That process was lacking, and the Air Staff effort was disunified because of it. Today, the Air Staff has a strategic planning entity, but relating its structure, methodology and activities would be the subject of another paper of equal length.[149]

Acknowledgements

I am a most fortunate historian. Numerous people generously helped me with this manuscript, and I am eternally in their debt. First of all, without the approval of the Director of Plans, Major General John A. Shaud, I could not have embarked on this enterprise. He kindly and generously permitted me to distract myself from my duties as supervisor of five planning divisions while working on this project and, more than that, he read and commented on my manuscript. I received extraordinary assistance from the Office of Air Force History. Dr. Richard H. Kohn's people were generous with their resources and time. Especially helpful were Lieutenant Colonel Elliott V. Converse, III; Mr. William C. Heimdahl; and Master Sergeant Roger A. Jernigan. Mr. Jacob Neufeld and Mr. Herman S. Wolk, from the same office, read and edited the entire manuscript. I was similarly fortunate in the help I received from the Office of History at Air Force Systems Command. Especially generous were the Chief of the Office, Mr. Walter L. Kraus; Dr. Michael H. Gorn; and Mrs. Thelma Smith. Without the assistance of the professional historians at Bolling and Andrews Air Force Bases, this paper could never have been written. Mr. Robert L. Perry, a senior analyst at the Rand Corporation, supplied me with dozens of documents and read the entire manuscript several times helping me avoid serious errors.

I was also blessed with the good wishes and hard work of the officers, enlisted people, and civilians in my organization, the Deputy Directorate of Air Force Plans for Planning Integration. Numerous people pitched in to advise, edit, and type. They were the soldiers in the army that made the whole process work. Three individuals helped me conceive the project Cadet First Class Lawrence M. Martin, Jr., who worked for us in the summer of 1984, Lieutenant Colonel James E. Klusman, and Lieutenant Colonel Richard L. Perry. Colonel Perry, in addition to his initial work on the project, was a full-time research assistant who helped me dig out material all over the Washington area and who read source documents to help me direct the study. He also was the wizard of the word processor who kept the revisions flowing smoothly and rapidly. Colonel John D. Sullivan provided me with advice and criticism in laying out the intellectual parameters of the paper. I also received research assistance from Staff Sergeant John D. Simpson who provided me with numerous useful insights into the intracacies of the early history of the Air Research and Development Command. Staff Sergeant Wendi C. Becker typed note cards and also performed as a research assistant finding material in the offices of history in the Defense Department, Organization of the Joint Chiefs of Staff, Air Force Systems Command, and the Air Force. Sergeant Becker also performed as an editor. Similarly, Master Sergeant William P. Hughes supervised the activities of the other enlisted people and helped me with working out the tables of organization so that I could first learn and then demonstrate how the Air Staff was organized (and malorganized). Sergeant Hughes also edited the manuscript. Final editing was provided by Major C.L. Rufus Hutchinson and Colonel Frank A. Black. Finally, I owe an enormous debt to Miss Gail M. Johnson to whom I dictated the entire manuscript, including the footnotes, who imbibed *Turabian*, formatted the paper properly, typed the manuscript into the word processor, and retyped the numerous revisions. All of the assistance from all of the others would have gone for nothing without the diligence, patience, good will, and good humor of Miss Johnson. I, of course, bear full responsibility for any errors of fact, omission, or lapses of style.

Notes

1. This is a standard dictionary definition with which the Air Force would probably agree. The Rand Corporation probably understands the nuances of the distinctions between the various categories in research and development better than others in this field. One of their long-time staff, Thomas K. Glennan, Jr., defines research done under military auspices as "all effort directed toward increased knowledge of natural phenomena and environment toward solutions to problems in physical, behavioral, and social sciences having no clear, direct military application." He also defines the various categories of development from exploratory development to advanced development to engineering development each of which moves a potential system closer to, but not into, actual production for the Air Force. He believes that research combined with exploratory development provides the technological base for future systems as well as much of the information required for defense planners. Engineering development, on the other hand, includes the efforts to meet immediate and near future equipment needs of the service. See his *Policies for Military R&D* (Santa Monica, The Rand Corporation, 1965), pp 1–6. The definition inside the parentheses came to me from Professor I.B. Holley, who attributes it to his Duke University colleague, Alex Roland.

2. Glennan, *Policies for Military R&D*, p 3.

3. This definition is a condensation (and adaptation) of one offered in Peter Hall, *Great Planning Disasters* (London, 1980), pp 1–2.

4. This definition is currently used in the Deputy Directorate of Air Force Plans for Planning Integration which is the organization responsible for Air Force long-range planning among other responsibilities. It can be found in slightly modified form in Alan Gropman, "Long Range Planning—A New Beginning," *Air University Review*, Nov-Dec 1979, p 50.

5. Vannevar Bush, *Modern Arms and Free Men, A Discussion of the Role of Science in Preserving Democracy* (New York, 1949), pp 250–61. Bush has been called by his *New York Times* biographer, Robert Reinhold, the "engineer who marshaled American technology for World War II and ushered in the atomic age." During World War II he directed the work of 30,000 engineers and scientists throughout the country who were largely responsible for such sophisticated devices as the proximity fuze, improvements to radar, fire control mechanisms, and even the atomic bomb. It was Bush who convinced Franklin D. Roosevelt of the need to harness technology for war, and it was he who explained the technical details and outlined the powers of the atomic bomb to Harry S Truman. Bush, furthermore, conceived the National Science Foundation after the war. During the war he had direct access to both Presidents and the Secretary of War. In 1941 Roosevelt appointed Bush Chief of the Office of Scientific Research and Development, and after the war Bush remained a valued adviser to President Truman. (Robert Reinhold, "Dr. Vannevar Bush is Dead at 84," *The New York Times Biographical Edition*," Jun 1974, pp 802, 803.)

6. Thomas Peters, "The Mythology of Innovation, or a Skunkworks Tale, Part I and II" from *Stanford Magazine*, Summer and Fall, 1983, pp 12–21, 11–19. The authority cited in this assertion was Brian Quinn of Dartmouth's Amos Tuck School

of Business Administration, who the author believes to be the premier student of American industrial innovation.

7. Peters, "Mythology of Innovation."

8. Peters, "Mythology of Innovation." Peters here cites James Utterback of the Massachusetts Institute of Technology.

9. *Ibid.*

10. Graham Allison and Morton Halperin argue that the "maker of government policy is not one calculating decision-maker but rather a conglomerate of large organizations and political actors who differ substantially" about what should be done on any particular issue, and "who compete in attempting to affect both decisions and actions." See their "Bureaucratic Politics: A Paradigm and Some Policy Implications," *World Politics*, 24 (1971), 42, cited in Edmund Beard *Developing the ICBM: A Study in Bureaucratic Politics.* (New York, 1976), p 10.

11. Merton J. Peck and Frederick M. Scherer, *Weapons Acquisition Process: An Economic Analysis* (Boston, 1962), pp 17–54, 581–82. The authors write: There are "substantial uncertainties permeating the weapons acquisition process." The major uncertainties are "internal uncertainties, which originate largely in the strategic environment." Also: "the extended duration of major weapons programs mean that the risks involved in each program are great." See also Peter DeLeon, *The Evolution of Technology and R&D: A Continuing Dilemma* (Santa Monica, The Rand Corporation, 1981), pp 10–23. DeLeon argues that "uncertainties exist throughout the process." See also Glennan, *Politics for Military R&D*, pp 14, 15.

12. An assumption is a "presupposition on the future course of events. . .assumed to be true in the absence of positive proof. . . .to enable the commander in the process of planning to. . . .make a decision on the course of action." *Department of Defense Dictionary of Military and Associated Terms* (Washington, The Joint Chiefs of Staff, 1 Apr 1984), p 39.

13. Arthur J. Alexander, *The Linkage Between Technology, Doctrine, and Weapons Innovation: Experimentation for Use* (Santa Monica, The Rand Corporation, 1981), pp 5, 12.

14. *Ibid*, p 9.

15. Hall, *Great Planning Disasters*, pp 1–7.

16. See A. A. Alchian, *The Chef, Gourmet and Gourmand* (Santa Monica, The Rand Corporation, 1952), p 7, for a similar point of view.

17. R. L. Perry, Giles K. Smith, Alvin J. Harman, and Susan Henrichsen, *System Acquisition Strategies* (Santa Monica, The Rand Corporation, 1971), pp 11, 6; and Perry, *et al, System Acquisition Experience* (Santa Monica, The Rand Corporation, 1969), p 16. See also Burton H. Klein, *Policy Issues Involved in the Conduct of Military Development Programs*, (Santa Monica, The Rand Corporation, 1962), pp 5–25. Klein argues taking the Air Force "Century Series" fighters as examples that none of these six aircraft turned out in the end anywhere close to the initial design ideas. Four of the six were manufactured with different engines (F–102/F–106, F–104, F–105, F–107), three with different electronic systems (F–102/F–106, F–105, F–104), five had to have airframes extensively modified once built to make them "satisfactory flying machines" (F–102/F–106, F–101, F–105, F–107), and three ended

up having quite different operational roles from what was originally planned (F–101, F–100, F–104).

18. Melvin Kranzberg in "Science-Technology and Warfare; Action, Reaction, and Interaction in the Post-World War II Era," in *Science, Technology, and Warfare* (Washington, Office of Air Force History/United States Air Force Academy, 1969), p 158, describes the uncertainty affecting planners, programmers and budgeteers this way: "There is uncertainty about the future detailed objectives of our military forces, about the future effectiveness of these forces, and about the alternative means available for achieving these objectives. . . .There are many internal uncertainties also. Will a particular technological approach work as predicted? Will the components integrate together without serious interference? Will the system be sufficiently reliable to permit the achievement of mission objectives?" Kranzberg, however, unfortunately omits the disagreement factor. A planner may be convinced and certain, but he may well have to compete with other planners who disagree and even if all the planners are lined up in certainty (impossibly unlikely), planners can almost count on programmers and others disagreeing.

19. Hall, *Great Planning Disasters*, pp 7, 8, 142, 188.

20. *Ibid*, pp 4–5. Hall supplied the concepts of the types of uncertainty.

21. Herman S. Wolk, *Planning and Organizing the Postwar Air Force, 1943–1947* (Washington, Office of Air Force History, 1984), pp 138–140.

22. Navy Captain Gerald G. O'Rourke wrote half in jest and wholly in earnest a piece called "Great Operators, Good Administrators, Lousy Planners" in the August 1984, *U.S. Naval Institute Proceedings*, pp 75–78. O'Rourke argues that the Navy is run by operators, and young officers learn that fact early on and plan accordingly. Those who become great operators become senior planners, and they are no good at it at all. "Great Operators who become Great Planners come along once or twice a generation." Further: "there have been so few Great Naval Planners and so many rotten ones over the past three or four decades that the talent itself seems to have atrophied to extinction." Finally: "The real planning—that affecting long-term needs, types and quantities of forces and providing foresight into the future—is done by upper echelon leaders on a personal, *ad hoc* basis. It is rarely recorded and of very short longevity. It changes with the tides of Congress, budgets, current events, and assignments of individuals. It is reactive, not creative. It provides good solutions to short-term problems and ignores long-term effects. It is the type of planning to be expected from Great Operator leadership—wonderfully effective for today but ignorant of tomorrow. It is in fact, Lousy Planning."

23. William H. McNeill, *The Pursuit of Power: Technology, Armed Force and Society Since AD 1000* (Chicago, 1982), p 370. See also Glennan, Jr., *Policies for Military R&D*, p 1.

24. Kranzberg, *Science, Technology and Warfare*, pp 128–31. Kranzberg writes that the military benefited greatly from the scientific technological revolutions of the time—power sources deriving from the exploitation of nuclear energy; materials deriving from lighter elements and alloys, communications, etc. Consider the change in mental attitude brought about by the war by looking back at one example of slow technological growth: in 1939 when the Army Air Corps had almost completely converted to enclosed cockpit, metal, retractable landing gear fighters, every shipboard fighter in the United States Navy was a wire-braced, fabric-skinned biplane. (Germany at this moment was testing its first turbojet-powered aircraft). See Robert Perry, *The Interaction of Technology and Doctrine in the USAF* (Santa Monica, The Rand Corporation, 1979), p 5; and also see Alexander, *Linkage between Technology, Doctrine, and Weapons Innovation*, pp 12, 13.

25. Theodore von Karman and Lee Edson, *The Wind and Beyond, Theodore von Karman, Pioneer in Aviation and Pathfinder in Space* (Boston, 1967), pp 267–80.

26. *Ibid.*

27. *Ibid.*

28. Theodore von Karman, *Toward New Horizons*, "Science the Key to Air Supremacy," 1945, pp iii–vii. The *Toward New Horizons* study can be found through the Defense Technical Information Center.

29. *Ibid.*

30. This quote was taken from Frank Futrell, *Ideas, Concepts, Doctrine, a History of Basic Thinking in the United States Air Force, 1907–1964* (Maxwell AFB Ala., 1971), p 94.

31. Theodore von Karman, "Where We Stand, A Report of the AAF Scientific Advisory Group," 1945, p iv. This report is considered part of the *Toward New Horizons* study and can be found through the Defense Technical Information Center.

32. Kranzberg, *Science, Technology, and Warfare*, p 130.

33. Von Karman, *Where We Stand*, pp iv, 37.

34. *Ibid*, pp 13–14.

35. *Ibid*, p 16.

36. Von Karman, *Science, the Key to Air Supremacy*, pp ix–xiii.

37. *Ibid.*

38. *Ibid*, p 6.

39. *Ibid*, p 13.

40. *Ibid*, p 31.

41. *Ibid*, p 104.

42. Thomas A. Sturm, *The United States Air Force Scientific Advisory Board: Its First 20 Years,* (Washington, USAF Historical Division Liaison Office, 1967), pp 8, 9, 11.

43. Nick A. Komons, *Science and the Air Force, a History of the Air Force Office of Scientific Research* (Arlington Va., Historical Division, Office of Information, Office of Aerospace Research, 1966), pp 6–7.

44. Von Karman, *The Wind and Beyond*, pp 198–207.

45. Kranzberg, *Science, Technology, and Warfare*, p 135.

46. Fred Kaplan, *The Wizards of Armageddon* (New York, 1983), p 59.

47. *Ibid.*

48. *The Rand Corporation, The First Fifteen Years* (Santa Monica, The Rand Corporation, 1963), pp 6–7. This report can be obtained from the Rand Corporation.

49. *Ibid*, pp 1–3, and Fred Kaplan, *The Wizards of Armageddon*, pp 61–62.

50. I. B. Holley, "The Political and Institutional Setting, 1946–1958," in *Science, Technology, and Warfare*, pp 94–95, and Kaplan, *The Wizards of Armageddon*, pp 61–62.

51. Kaplan, *The Wizards of Armageddon*, p 60; *The Rand Corporation, The First Fifteen Years*, pp 8–9.

52. *The Rand Corporation, The First Fifteen Years*, pp 9–10.

53. Kaplan, *The Wizards of Armageddon*, p 62; *The Rand Corporation, The First Fifteen Years*, pp 10–11.

54. *The Rand Corporation, The First Fifteen Years*, p 32.

55. *Ibid*, pp 14–22.

56. *Ibid*, pp 38–39. (Both the Bell and McNamara quotes come from this source.)

57. Sturm, *The United States Air Force Scientific Advisory Board*, pp 15–54, 166–77. (This entire paragraph comes from this source.)

58. Wolk, *Planning and Organizing*, pp 1–2, 46–47, 107, 124–31, 234–41.

59. *Ibid*, p 117.

60. *Ibid*, p 113.

61. *Ibid*, p 75.

62. *Ibid*, pp 61–63.

63. Futrell, *Ideas, Concepts, and Doctrine*, p 108.

64. "Organization and Functions of the Headquarters, USAF (The Chart Book)," 1948, pp 7.D through 7.D.5. These chart books can be found, in one form or another, at the USAF Office of History at Bolling Air Force Base.

65. "History of the Directorate of Plans and Operations," 1 Jul 1949 to 30 Jun 1950, p 6.

66. *Ibid*.

67. *Ibid*, pp 7–12.

68. *Ibid*, p 21.

69. "Organization and Functions of the Headquarters, USAF, (The Chart Book)," 1950, p 7.D.

70. "History of the Directorate of Plans," 1 Jul 1950–31 Dec 1950, pp 10–34.

71. *Ibid*, pp 51–64.

72. "History of the Directorate of Plans," 1 Jan 1951–30 Jun 1951, pp 1–7.

73. *Ibid*, pp 9–29.

74. *Ibid*, pp 41–45.

75. *Ibid*, pp 55–112.

76. "History of the Directorate of Plans," 1 Jul 1951–31 Dec 1951, p 2.

77. *Ibid*, p 9.

78. *Ibid*, p 72.

79. *Ibid*, pp 85–99.

80. *Ibid*, pp 114–188.

81. "History of the Directorate of Plans," 1 Jan 1952–30 Jun 1952, pp 2–4.

82. *Ibid*, pp 13–30.

83. *Ibid*, pp 54–89.

84. *Ibid*, pp 92–108.

85. *Ibid*, pp 110–116.

86. *Ibid*, pp 117–124.

87. *Ibid*, pp 128–185.

88. "History of the Directorate of Plans," 1 Jul 1952–31 Dec 1952, p 75.

89. "History of the Directorate of Plans," 1 Jan 1953–30 Jun 1953, p 24.

90. *Ibid*, p 25.

91. "Semi-Annual Historical Report of the Deputy Chief of Staff, Development," 1 Jul 1953 to 31 Dec 1953, pp 1–34. See also: "Semi-Annual Historical Report of the Deputy Chief of Staff, Development," 1 Jan 1954 to 30 Jun 1954, pp 1–17, and "Semi-Annual Historical Report of the Deputy Chief of Staff, Development, 1 Jul 1954 to 31 Dec 1954, pp 1–12, and "History of the Air Research and Development Command," 1 Jan 1953–31 Dec 1953, pp xiv–xviii, 313–327, and "History of the Air

Research and Development Command," 1 Jan 1954–30 Jun 1954, pp xii–xvii. The staff of Air Force Systems Command Office of History checked the documents for the author while the author read the supporting documents and the indexes for relevant material.

92. "History of the Directorate of Plans," 1 Jan 1954 through 30 Jun 1954, pp 46–48, 53–58.

93. *Ibid*, pp 1–3. (This source covers the entire paragraph.)

94. *Ibid*, pp 97–110.

95. "History of the Directorate of Plans," 1 Jan 1955–30 Jun 1955, pp 3–6.

96. *Ibid*, pp 47–58.

97. "History of the Directorate of Plans," 1 Jul 1955–31 Dec 1955, pp 3–6.

98. See "Air Research and Development Command History," 1 Jan 1955–30 Jun 1955, pp v–ix, 363–83; and "Air Research and Development Command History," 1 Jul 1955–31 Dec 1955, pp v–ix, 472–89; and "Air Research and Development Command History," 1 Jan 1956–30 Jun 1956, pp vii–x, 335–58. A check of the supporting documents filed in these histories does not indicate that these long-range planning documents were used in writing the command histories.

99. "History, Directorate of Development," 1 Jul 1955–30 Jun 1956, pp 19–21.

100. Lecture, "Trends in Air Force Planning" by Major General R. C. Lindsey, 15 Jun 1949. This lecture may be obtained through the Air University Library. Major General Sam Anderson was the Director of Plans in June 1949.

101. "History of Deputy Chief of Staff, Development," 1 Jul 1950–31 Dec 1950, p 2.

102. Futrell, *Ideas, Concepts, and Doctrine*, p 105.

103. *Ibid*, pp 107–08.

104. *Ibid*, p 103.

105. Nick A. Komons, *Science and the Air Force, a History of the Air Force Office of Scientific Research* (Arlington, Va., Historical Division, Office of Information, Office of Aerospace Research 1966), pp 10–11.

106. Dennis J. Stanley and John J. Weaver, *The Air Force Command for R&D, 1949–1976, The History of ARDC/AFSC* (Washington, Office of History, Headquarters Air Force Systems Command, 1977), pp 9–11; and Edmund Beard, *Developing the ICBM: A Study in Bureaucratic Politics* (New York, 1976), pp 108–12.

107. Beard, *Developing the ICBM*, pp 112–14.

108. Komons, *A History of the Air Force Office of Scientific Research*, p 13.

109. *Ibid*, pp 13–14.

110. Stanley and Weaver, *An Air Force Command for Research and Development*, pp 9–11 and 12–16. (This source covers all the material in this paragraph.)

111. Beard, *Developing the ICBM*, pp 112–15, 116.

112. *Ibid.*

113. *Ibid.*

114. Futrell, *Ideas, Concepts and Doctrine*, p 112; and Harry R. Borowski, *A Hollow Threat: Strategic Air Power and Containment before Korea* (Westport, Conn., 1982), pp 18, 23–28, 54, 96.

115. This statement comes from General Arnold's testimony on 18 Oct 1945 before the Congress, and it is cited in Futrell, *Ideas, Concepts and Doctrine*, p 103.

116. The quote can be found in numerous places, for example, Stanley and Weaver, *An Air Force Command for Research and Development*, p 8.

117. Regarding the stability of stable-funding, Robert Perry of the Rand Corporation estimates that in the United States only about 25 percent of the money expended on research and development in all categories comes from stable-fund sources, where in contrast, in the Soviet Union the proportion is nearly 75 percent. What Perry means by stable-funding is that the Air Force supports continued operations of the research and development establishment at relatively constant levels over a relatively extended period. Perry notes that in the United States three-fourths of the research and development funding is provided from annual appropriations. All of it is usually correlated with production programs. Fluctuation in procurement budgets or in funding for major systems can, therefore, have an immediate and potentially devastating effect on the level of research and development funding. "Such fluctuations introduced serious inefficiencies. They probably increased the relative costs of United States research and development as compared with those in the Soviet Union. During periods of budget contraction in the United States, any Soviet research and development enterprise able to obtain stable-funding would acquire a relative advantage over its erratically funded United States counterpart." Perry also notes another striking difference between the United States and the Soviet Union. More than two-thirds of all U.S. research and development, he argues, "is performed by industrial enterprises that both compete with one another for funds and manufacture the product that incorporates the research and development." Where in the Soviet Union, on the other hand, specialized autonomous organizations independent of producing plans (and funded almost ritually) do the bulk of the Soviet research and development. Defense-oriented research and development in the United States is principally supported by industry from overheads, profits arising in federal contracts or subsidies of some sort. Such support tends to shrink proportionately as demand for the product lessens. Robert Perry, *Comparisons of Soviet and United States Technology* (Santa Monica, The Rand Corporation, 1973), pp 5–6. Robert Perry is one of a long line of Rand Corporation researchers who have focused on research and development within the Air Force. Since the Rand Corporation was designed primarily for developing long-range issues in the Air Force, research and development would be one of the keys, perhaps the greatest key. In 1952 A. A. Alchian argued, and Rand has never really fallen from this point in general, that the function of research and development decisionmakers are those of the "chef, who concocts new dishes and plans a menu of available alternate dishes from which the gourmet, at a later time, has the privilege of choosing in light of his tastes, companions, and income. A good chef provides a broad menu—thereby assuring the gourmet the opportunity to make the best selection. The difference between the task of the chef and the gourmet must be kept strictly distinct. To confound the two is as disastrous in the military as in the restaurant business." Finally, Alchian would argue that research and development not

only advances the United States technically, but it also provides the flexibility and wide range of choice for the future. This point of view, that technology is intrinsically worthwhile, is a common Rand point of view, one that can be found in Alvin J. Harmon, *Analysis of Aircraft Development* (Santa Monica, The Rand Corporation, March 1973), *passim,* and A. A. Alchian, *The Chef, Gourmet, and Gourmand* (Santa Monica, The Rand Corporation, March 1952), pp 7, 8. See also, Robert Perry, *American Styles of Military Research and Development* (Santa Monica, The Rand Corporation, 1979), p 4, and by the same author, *The Mythography of Military Research and Development*, pp 1–16. Perry argues that the central purpose of research and development is to "exorcise uncertainty." Mythography, incidentally, Perry defines as a situation in which an "unreal representation of events and the causation becomes widely acceptable and is eventually transcribed into a procedural ritual. (Rand is not sure that the Air Force understands research and development.)

118. Beard, *Developing the ICBM*, pp 75–76. See also, Futrell, *Ideas, Concepts and Doctrine*, pp 124–126, and Borowski, *A Hollow Threat*, p 54.

119. See for example Alexander, *The Linkage Between Technology, Doctrine and Weapons Innovation*, p 15. He argues that "it took powerful outsiders (allied with a few enthusiastic insiders) to force ballistic missiles on a reluctant Air Force." Also Robert Perry, *The Interaction of Technology and Doctrine in the USAF* (Santa Monica, The Rand Corporation, 1979), pp 8–18. Perry argues the Air Force misread where technology would lead them and bet on an evolutionary advance to long-range cruise missiles, an approach they thought they understood because of their experience with airplanes, rather than focusing on rockets, which they considered the more radical or revolutionary methodology. Although Edmund Beard in the previously cited *Developing the ICBM*, believes the Air Force deliberately underfunded the long-range rockets for purely parochial reasons (in his breathtaking now-it-can-be-told style) so that bomber pilots could protect the bomber, Perry and others offer evidence that the Air Force leadership had some solid—at the time—support for its decision to not focus on rockets. Perry cites Vannevar Bush's testimony before Congress in December 1945 (p 10 in Perry's *Interaction of Technology and Doctrine*) in which Bush argued that long-range ballistic rockets were well off into the distant future because nobody in the world knew how to make one. Four years later in Bush's previously cited *Modern Arms and Free Men*, he argued that pilotless airplanes as cruise missiles would be too expensive and vulnerable to produce, and he had much less faith in the capabilities to produce intercontinental rockets. He argued that the short-range German V–2 rocket was not cost effective, and that a rocket of vastly longer ranges might be able to hit a target within one or two miles, but at an "astronomical" price, one that would make us "economically exhausted long before the enemy." (pp 71–89). With advice like that and following their own bent, the Air Force developed cruise missiles, simultaneously the Snark and the Navaho with the former becoming lamely operational for a few months in 1960 and 1961 and the latter falling farther and farther behind each year until it was finally cancelled in 1957. (See Robert L. Perry, *System Development Strategies: A Comparative Study of Doctrine, Technology and Organization in the USAF Ballistic Missile and Cruise Missile Program, 1950–1960* (Santa Monica, The Rand Corporation, 1966), pp 12, 30, 31, 35, 37, 38. See also E. Michael Del Papa from *Snark to SRAM: A Pictorial History of Strategic Air Command Missiles* (Offut Air Force Base, Nebr., 1976), pp 1–6. In 1953, a number of streams—economic, political, intelligence, technological—converged, and the Air Force began to rush development in long-range strategic rockets. When the Air Force did so, the decision was made largely outside of the Air Force to produce the weapons outside the normal framework of development. An advocate of missiles and an Air Force superstar, Major General Bernard A. Schriever became the effective czar of this development in 1954. He performed his mission in California with a civilian engineering firm for support and a direct line to the commander of the Air Research and Development Command, the Chief of Staff of the Air Force, and the Secretary of the Air Force. It worked. See Beard, *Developing the ICBM*, pp 171–215, and Perry, *System Development Strategies*, pp 61–80. Incidentally, another truly revolutionary weapon, the laser-guided bomb, was also developed out of the

mainstream as a skunkworks effort in the 1960s. See Peter DeLeon, *The Laser-Guided Bomb: Case History of a Development* (Santa Monica, The Rand Corporation, 1974), pp 1–46.

120. Komons, *A History of the Air Force Office of Scientific Research*, pp iii and 1; The Office of Scientific Research, Office of Aerospace Research, *AFOSR Research; The Current Research Program, and a Summary of Research Accomplishments*, undated, pp 12–13.

121. Komons, *A History of the Air Force Office of Scientific Research*, pp 2–142. The author wrote that, until the early 1960s, the Office of Scientific Research was the "fitful, aggressive, and turbulent stepchild of the Air Research and Development Command."

122. "History of the Directorate of Research and Development for Fiscal Year 1950," p 11.

123. "Organization and Functions of the Headquarters, USAF (Chart Book)," 1950, p 9.

124. *Ibid*, p 9A.

125. "History of the Directorate of Research and Development for Fiscal Year 1940," pp 1–59.

126. "Organization and Functions of the Headquarters USAF, (Chart Book)," 1950, p 9C.

127. "History of the Deputy Chief of Staff, Development," 1 Jan–1 Jul 1951, p 3.

128. *Ibid*.

129. "History of the Deputy Chief of Staff, Development," Jul 1951–Jun 1952, pp 1, 6.

130. Memorandum for General Putt, "Report on Air Force Research and Development Organization, with Particular Reference to DCS/D-ARDC Relationships," 26 Nov 1951, pp 3–6, 19–20. The report was signed by Brigadier General James McCormack, Jr.

131. *Ibid*, pp 8–9.

132. "Semi-Annual Historical Report for the Deputy Chief of Staff, Development," 1 Jul 1952–31 Dec 1952, pp 6–7.

133. *Ibid*, p 7.

134. *Ibid*, pp 6, 7–9.

135. *USAF Development Reports*, Volume I, "Development Organization in the USAF: How a Piece of Equipment Evolves," May 1952, pp 1–12.

136. "Semi-Annual Historical Report for the Deputy Chief of Staff/Development," 1 Jul 1953–31 Dec 1953, pp 1–3.

137. "Organizational Functions of the Headquarters USAF (Chart Book)," 1955, see unpaged line diagrams for Feb 1955, Mar 1955, May 1955, which all show Development subordinated to Materiel, and Aug and Oct 1955 which show an independent Deputy Chief of Staff/Development.

138. "History, Directorate of Development Planning, 1 Jul 1955–30 Jun 1956," pp 1–6.

139. *Ibid*, pp 18–20.

140. See "History of Air Research and Development Command," 1 Jul 1956–31 Dec 1956, pp vii–xi, 590–618; "History of Air Research and Development Command," 1 Jan 1957–30 Jun 1957, pp v–vii, 312–328; and "History of the Air Research and Development Command," 1 Jul 1957–31 Dec 1957, pp vii–x, 397–413. The volumes of these histories which contain supporting documents also do not include relevant planning documents.

141. See "History, Directorate of Development Planning," 1 Jul 1955–30 Jun 1956, Appendix 3.

142. "Department of the Air Force Organization and Functions Chart Book," 1966, pp 17A–1 to 17B–1.

143. Futrell, *Ideas, Concepts and Doctrine*, pp 182–87.

144. *Ibid*, p 182.

145. *Ibid*, p 183.

146. "Air Force Manual 1–1," 19 Sep 1951, pp 17–20.

147. Futrell, *Ideas, Concepts and Doctrine*, pp 201–02.

148. *Ibid*, pp 202–203, and "Air Force Manual 1–2, Mar 1953;" "Air Force Manual 1–2, USAF Basic Doctrine, 1 Apr 1954;" and "Air Force Manual 1–2, USAF Basic Doctrine, Apr 1955." This author would note that when there is no agreed-to doctrine, as there was none between 1945 and 1953, there are, in fact, as many basic doctrines as there are people involved in planning and budgeting. Perry McCoy Smith in *The Air Force Plans for Peace, 1943–1945* (Baltimore, 1970), pp 27–31, makes the argument that when the Air Force was planning for independence, it was hidebound by the strategic bombing doctrine. Smith argues that the Army Air Corps leadership in 1945 "firmly believed that superior arms favored victory; they recognized the relationship between doctrine and weaponry; and they understood the need for effective techniques for recognizing and evaluating potential weapons." Smith argues, though, that the focus before, during, and shortly after the war, was "narrow, so that only ideas and weaponry which favored the offensive role of evaluation were given consideration" and, thus, systems other than strategic bombardment weapons were underdeveloped. Smith argues that the postwar planners made similar errors to the prewar planners, and neglected tactical aviation. He asserts that the "quest for autonomy led to the advocacy of strategic bombardment which led, in turn, to the deprecation of not only defensive aircraft but of pursuit aircraft. Bombardment and autonomy were so inextricably bound together that the questioning of bombardment by an Air Corps officer was not only impolitic but unwise. One can accept Smith's argument that the prewar, during the war, and shortly after the war thinking was indeed stunted by the strategic bombing doctrine and the quest for autonomy, and still argue that what Smith would call the gyroscopic nature of doctrine was absent in the period from the end of the war to the mid–1950s. We have in this section of the paper

also ignored the cogent statements regarding the relationship between doctrine and effective employment of weapons expressed by I. B. Holley, Jr.: the concept that while technological advances might lead to better weapons, such innovations can be exploited effectively only insofar as suitable doctrines are devised to govern their employment. See his *Ideas and Weapons; Exploitation of Aerial Weapons by the United States During World War I; A Study in the Relationship of Technological Advance, Military Doctrine, and the Development of Weapons* (Washington, Office of Air Force History (New Imprint), 1983), pp 1–178.

149. This interpretation relied very heavily on the author's personal experience as a long-range planner and William Simon's, *et al, Long-Range Development Planning in the Air Force* (Santa Monica, The Rand Corporation, 1976), pp iii–132.

<h1 style="text-align:center">Selected Bibliography</h1>

Published Works

Articles:

Gropman, Alan L. "Long Range Planning—A New Beginning." *Air University Review*, Nov-Dec 1979, pp 49–54.

O'Rourke, Gerald G., Captain. "Great Operators, Good Administrators, Lousy Planners." *U.S. Naval Institute Proceedings*, Aug 1970, pp 75–78.

Peters, Thomas. "The Mythology of Innovation, or a Skunkworks Tale, Parts I and II." *Stanford Magazine*, Summer and Fall, 1983, pp 11–21.

Reinhold, Robert. "Dr. Vannevar Bush is Dead at 84." *The New York Times Biographical Edition*, Jun 1974.

Books:

Armacost, Michael H. *The Politics of Weapons Innovation: The Thor Jupiter Controversy.* New York: Columbia University Press, 1969.

Bush, Vannevar. *Modern Arms and Free Men, A Discussion of the Role of Science in Preserving Democracy.* New York: Simon and Schuster, 1949.

Beard, Edmund. *Developing the ICBM: A Study in Bureaucratic Politics.* New York: Columbia University Press, 1976.

Borowski, Harry R. *A Hollow Threat: Strategic Air Power and Containment Before Korea.* Westport, Conn.: Greenwood Press, 1982.

Hall, Peter. *Great Planning Disasters.* London: Weidenfield & Nicholson, 1980.

Holley, I. B. *Ideas and Weapons.* Washington: Office of Air Force History, 1983.

Kaplan, Fred. *The Wizards of Armageddon.* New York: Simon and Schuster, 1983.

Komons, Nick A. *Science and the Air Force, a History of the Air Force Office of Scientific Research.* Arlington, Va.: Historical Division, Office of Information, Office of Aerospace Research, 1966.

McNeill, William H. *The Pursuit of Power: Technology, Armed Force and Society Since AD 1000.* Chicago: The University of Chicago Press, 1982.

Peck, Merton J. and Scherer, Frederick M. *Weapons Acquisition Process: An Economic Analysis.* Boston: Harvard University Press, 1962.

Scherer, Frederick M. *The Weapons Acquisition Process: Economic Incentives.* Boston: Harvard University, 1964.

Sherry, Michael S. *Preparing for the Next War: American Plans for Postwar Defense, 1941–45.* New Haven: Yale University Press, 1977.

Smith, Perry McCoy. *The Air Force Plans for Peace, 1943–45.* Baltimore: The Johns Hopkins Press, 1970.

The Joint Chiefs of Staff. *Department of Defense Dictionary of Military and Associated Terms.* Washington: 1 Apr 1984.

Von Karman, Theodore, and Edson, Lee. *The Wind and Beyond, Theodore von Karman, Pioneer in Aviation and Pathfinder in Space.* Boston: Little, Brown & Co., 1967.

Wolk, Herman S. *Planning and Organizing the Postwar Air Force, 1943–1947.* Washington: Office of Air Force History, 1984.

Wright, Monte D. and Paszek, Lawrence J., eds. *Science, Technology and Warfare.* Proceedings of the Third Military History Symposium. Washington, 1971.

Reports:

Alchian, A. A. *The Chef, Gourmet and Gourmand.* Santa Monica, Calif.: The Rand Corporation, 24 Mar 1952.

Alexander, Arthur J. *The Linkage Between Technology, Doctrine, and Weapons Innovation: Experimentation for Use.* Santa Monica, Calif.: The Rand Corporation, May 1981.

DeLeon, Peter. *The Evaluation of Technology R&D: A Continuing Dilemma.* Santa Monica, Calif.: The Rand Corporation, 1981.

__________. *The Laser-Guided Bomb: Case History of a Development.* Santa Monica, Calif.: The Rand Corporation, Jun 1974.

Del Papa, E. Michael, Dr. *From SNARK to SRAM: A Pictorial History of Strategic Air Command Missiles.* Omaha: Headquarters Strategic Air Command, Office of the Historian, 21 Mar 1976.

Dryden, H.L.; Pickering, W.H.; Tsien, H.S.; and Schubauer, G.B. *Technical Report—Guided Missiles and Pilotless Aircraft—A Report Prepared for the AAF Scientific Advisory Group.* Dayton, Ohio: HQ Air Materiel Command, Publications Branch, Intelligence T–2, May 1946.

Futrell, Robert Frank. *Ideas, Concepts, Doctrine: A History of Basic Thinking in the United States Air Force: 1907–1964.* Maxwell AFB, Ala.: Air University, 1971.

Glennan, Thomas K., Jr. *Policies for Military Research and Development.* Santa Monica, Calif.: The Rand Corporation, Nov 1965.

Harman, Alvin J. *Analysis of Aircraft Development*. Santa Monica, Calif.: The Rand Corporation, Mar 1973.

Klein, Burton H. *Policy Issues Involved in the Conduct of Military Development Programs*. Santa Monica, Calif.: The Rand Corporation, Oct 1962.

Perry, Robert L. *American Styles of Military R&D*. Santa Monica, Calif.: The Rand Corporation, Jun 1973.

__________. *Comparisons of Soviet and US Technology*. Santa Monica, Calif.: The Rand Corporation, Aug 1967.

__________. *Innovation and Military Requirements: A Comparative Study*. Santa Monica, Calif.: The Rand Corporation, Aug 1967.

__________. *The Antecedents of the X–1*. Santa Monica, Calif.: The Rand Corporation, Jun 1965.

__________. *The Interaction of Technology and Doctrine in the USAF*. Santa Monica, Calif.: The Rand Corporation, Jan 1979.

__________. *The Mythography of Military R&D*. Santa Monica, Calif.: The Rand Corporation, 1966.

__________. *Systems Development Strategies: A Comparative Study of Doctrine, Technology and Organization in the USAF Ballistic and Cruise Missile Programs, 1950–1960*. Santa Monica, Calif.: The Rand Corporation, Aug 1966.

Perry, R. L.; DiSalvo, D.; Hall, G. R.; Harman, A. J.; Levenson, G. S.; Smith, G. K.; and Stucker, J. P. *System Acquisition Experience*. Santa Monica, Calif.: The Rand Corporation, Nov 1969.

Perry, R. L.; Smith, Giles K.; Harman, Alvin J.; and Henrichsen, Susan. *System Acquisition Experience*. Santa Monica, Calif.: The Rand Corporation, Nov 1969.

Putnam, W. D. *The Evolution of Air Force System Acquisition Management*. Santa Monica, Calif.: The Rand Corporation, Aug 1972.

Simons, W. E.; Smith, G. K.; Ojdana, E. S., Jr.; Pei R. Y.; Purness, S. W.; and Wainstein, E. S. *Long Range Development Planning in the Air Force*. Santa Monica, Calif.; The Rand Corporation Sep 1976.

Stanley, Dennis J., and Weaver, John J. *An Air Force Command for R&D, 1949–1976: The History of ARDC/AFSC*. Washington: Headquarters, Air Force Systems Command, Office of History, 1977.

Stanley, William L. *Performance Advances in Fighter Aircraft: Measuring and Predicting Progress*. Santa Monica, Calif.: The Rand Corporation, Jul 1980.

Sturm, Thomas A. *The United States Air Force Scientific Advisory Board: Its First 20 Years, 1944–1964*. Washington: USAF Historical Division Liaison Office, 1967.

The Rand Corporation. *The Rand Corporation, The First Fifteen Years*. Santa Monica, Calif.: The Rand Corporation, Nov 1963.

Von Karman, Theodore. *Toward New Horizons—Science: The Key to Air Supremacy.* Washington: Defense Technical Information Center, Defense Logistics Agency, undated. (Contains memos dated 7 Nov 1944 and 15 Dec 1945.)

—————. "Where We Stand." Washington: AAF Scientific Advisory Group, 1946.

Regulations:

Department of the Air Force. AFM 1-2, *Air Doctrine: United States Air Force—Basic Doctrine.* Washington, Mar 1953.

—————. AFM 1-2, *Air Doctrine: United States Air Force—Basic Doctrine.* Washington, 1 Apr 1954.

—————. AFM 1-2, *Air Doctrine: United States Air Force—Basic Doctrine.* Washington, 1 Apr 1955.

—————. AFR 80-1, *Air Force Research and Development.* Washington, 8 Apr 1966.

—————. AFR 80-4, *Research and Development: Research Policies.* Washington, 1 Mar 1949.

—————. AFR 80-4, *Research and Development: Air Force Policy on the Support of Research.* Washington, 11 Apr 1966.

Departments of the Army, Navy, and Air Force. FM 100-5, JAAF, AFM 1-1, *Joint Action Armed Forces.* Washington, Sep 1951. (Department of the Army Field Manual, Department of the Navy, Department of the Air Force Manual.)

War Department. FM 100-20, *Field Service Regulations: Command and Employment of Air Power.* Washington, 21 Jul 1943.

Unpublished Works

Histories:

Department of the Air Force. "History of the Air Research and Development Command: 23 Jan–30 Jun 1951." Vol III. HQ ARDC, Office of Command Historian, Air Adjutant General.

—————. "History of the Air Research and Development Command: 1 Jul 51–31 Dec 52." Vol III. HQ ARDC, Historical Division, Office of Information Services. The supporting staff agencies, edited amd partially rewritten by Dr. Charles A. Johnson, Historical Division, Office of Information Services, HQ ARDC.

—————. "History: Air Research and Development Command: 1 Jan 53–31 Dec 53." Vol II: Supporting Documents. HQ ARDC, Historical Division, Office of Information Services.

__________. "History: Air Research and Development Command: 1 Jul 56–31 Dec 56." Vol III: Supporting Documents. Historical Division, Office of Information Services.

__________. "History: Air Research and Development Command: 1 Jul 56–31 Dec 56." Vol IV. Historical Division, Office of Information Services.

__________. "History: Air Research and Development Command: 1 Jul 57–31 Dec 57." Vol IV: Supporting Documents. Historical Division, Office of Information Services.

__________. "History of the Air Research and Development Command: 1 Jan–30 Jun 1954." Vol I: Narrative. HQ ARDC, Historical Division, Office of Information Services, 1954.

__________. "History of DCS/D: 1 Jul–31 Dec 1950."

__________. "History of the Air Research and Development Command: 1 Jan–30 Jun 1954." Vol II: Supporting Documents. HQ ARDC, Historical Division, Office of Information Services.

__________. "History: Air Research and Development Command: 1 Jan–30 Jun 1955." Vol I: Narrative. HQ ARDC, Historical Division, Office of Information Services.

__________. "History of the Air Research and Development Command: 1 Jul–31 Dec 1955." Vol I: Narrative. HQ ARDC, Historical Division, Office of Information Services.

__________. "History of the Air Research and Development Command: 1 Jul–31 Dec 1956." Vol I: Narrative. HQ ARDC, Historical Division, Office of Information Services.

__________. "History: Air Research and Development Command: 1 Jan 56–31 Dec 1956." Vol II. HQ ARDC, Western Development Division.

__________. "History of the Air Research and Development Command: 1 Jan–30 Jun 1957." Vol I. HQ ARDC, Historical Division, Office of Information Services.

__________. "History: Air Research and Development Command: 1 Jan–30 Jun 1957." Vol IV: Supporting Documents. HQ ARDC, Historical Division, Office of Information Services.

__________. "History: Headquarters, Air Research and Development Command: 1 Jul–31 Dec 1957." Vol I. HQ ARDC, Historical Division, Office of Information Services.

__________. "History of DCS/D: 1 Jul–31 Dec 1950."

__________. "History of the Deputy Chief of Staff, Development, Headquarters USAF, 1 Jul–31 Dec 1951."

__________. "History of the Directorate of Plans, Deputy Chief of Staff, Operations, Headquarters, USAF, 1 Jul 1950–31 Dec 1950." Vol I. Assembled and edited by Major J. C. Smith.

__________. "History of the Directorate of Plans, Deputy Chief of Staff, Operations, Headquarters, USAF, 1 Jan 1951–30 Jun 1951." Vol II. Assembled and edited by Captain Miller G. White, Jr.

__________. "History of the Directorate of Plans, Deputy Chief of Staff, Operations, Headquarters, USAF, 1 Jul 1951–31 Dec 1951." Vol IV. Assembled and edited by Captain Miller G. White, Jr.

__________. "History of the Directorate of Plans, Deputy Chief of Staff, Operations, Headquarters, USAF, 1 Jan 1952–30 Jun 1952." Vol IV. Assembled and edited by Captain Miller G. White, Jr.

__________. "History of the Directorate of Plans, Deputy Chief of Staff, Operations, Headquarters, USAF, 1 Jul 1952–31 Dec 1952." Vol V. Assembled and edited by Major James E. Lind. 1 Feb 53.

__________. "History of the Directorate of Plans, Deputy Chief of Staff, Operations, Headquarters, USAF, 1 Jan 1953–30 Jun 1953." Vol VI. Assembled and edited by Major James E. Lind. 3 Aug 1953.

__________. "History of the Directorate of Plans, Deputy Chief of Staff, Operations, Headquarters, USAF, 1 Jan 1954–30 Jun 1954."

__________. "History of the Directorate of Plans, Deputy Chief of Staff, Operations, Headquarters, USAF, 1 Jul 1954–31 Dec 1954."

__________. "History of the Directorate of Plans, Deputy Chief of Staff, Operations, Headquarters, USAF, 1 Jan 1955–30 Jun 1955."

__________. "History of the Directorate of Plans, Deputy Chief of Staff, Operations, Headquarters, USAF, 1 Jul 1955–31 Dec 1955."

__________. "History of the Directorate of Plans, Deputy Chief of Staff, Operations, Headquarters, USAF, 1 Jan 1956–30 Jun 1956."

__________. "History of the Directorate of Plans, Deputy Chief of Staff, Operations, Headquarters, USAF, 1 Jul 1956–31 Dec 1956."

__________. "Department of the Air Force Organization and Functions." HP 21–1, Hq Organization Chartbook, Oct 1967. 31 Oct 1967.

__________. "Organization and Mission—Departmental: Department of the Air Force Organization and Functions (Chartbook)." HP 21–1, Changes, 1968. 17 Mar 1969.

__________. "Department of the Air Force Organization and Functions Chartbook." HP 21–1. 31 Dec 1969.

__________. "Department of the Air Force Organization and Functions." "Organization and Mission— Departmental—Department of the Air Force Organization and Functions (Chartbook)." HP 21–1. 31 Aug 1970.

__________. "Organization of the Air Force." (Headquarters USAF Chart Book, 1964.) HP 21–1. 1 Jul 1963.

__________. "Organization of the Air Force." (Headquarters USAF Chart Book.) HP 21–1. Sep 1966.

__________. "Organization and Mission— Departmental— Department of the Air Force Organization and Functions Chartbook." (Hq Org Charts—1963–1965.) HP 21–1. 15 Sep 1966.

__________. "Organization and Mission— Departmental— Department of the Air Force Organization and Functions Chartbook." (Headquarters USAF Chart Book, 1961–1962.) HP 21–1. 15 Sep 1961.

__________. "Organization and Mission— Departmental— Department of the Air Force Organization and Functions Chartbook." (Headquarters USAF Chart Book Changes.) HP 21–1–1. 1 Dec 1964.

__________. "Organization and Functions of the Headquarters United States Air Force." (Hq Org Charts—1948.) 1 Dec 1948.

__________. "Hq Org Charts—1949." 1 Dec 1949.

__________. "Organization and Functions of the Headquarters United States Air Force." (Hq Org Charts—1950.) 1 Nov 1950.

__________. "Hq Org Charts—1955." Dec 1955.

__________. "Hq Org Charts—1956." Dec 1956.

__________. "Hq Org Charts—1959." Dec 1959.

__________. "Organization of the Air Force." (Hq Org Charts—1960.) HP 21–1–1. 15 Nov 1960.

Hollick, T. C., Lieutenant Colonel and Smith, John C., Captain. "History of the Directorate of Plans and Operations: Deputy Chief of Staff, Operations, Headquarters, USAF, 1 Jul 1949–30 Jun 1950." HQ USAF: Historical Office, 29 Nov 1950.

JCS History. "The Genesis of the JSOP/JSPD." Undated.

Wynn, Edward H., Colonel. "History: Directorate of Development Planning Office, Deputy Chief of Staff, Development: For the Period: 1 Jul 1955–30 Jun 1956." Colonel Wynn was Assistant Deputy Director of Development Planning.

Lectures:

Anderson, C. H., Colonel. "Lecture: Introduction to Planning (Parts 1 and 2)." Maxwell Field, Ala." Air Command and Staff School, Air University, 19 Sep 1946.

Department of the Air Force. "Study of the Air Force Board Structure: Directorate of the Air Force Board Structure: Office of the Vice Chief of Staff, HQ USAF."

Directorate of the Air Force Board Structure, Office of the Vice Chief of Staff, HQ USAF. "Study of the Air Force Board Structure."

Lincoln, G. A., Colonel. "Postwar Planning," Lecture delivered by Colonel G. A. Lincoln at the Air War College, 3 Nov 1947.

Lindsay, R. C., Major General. "Trends in Air Force Planning." Lecture/Air War College, 15 Jun 1949.

Spivey, Delmer T., Brigadier General. "The Mechanics of Planning: A Lecture Given Before the Air University." 8 May 1950.

Pamphlets/Reports:

Department of the Air Force. "Development Organization in the USAF (How A Piece of Equipment Evolves)." USAF Development Reports, Vol 1, May 1952.

__________. "Development Planning for Future U.S. Air Forces, The Development Planning Function in Headquarters USAF." DCS/Development, May 1955.

__________. "Project Hindsight: Final Report—Task I." Washington: Office of the Director of Defense Research and Engineering, 1 Jul 1967.

__________. "Report on Air Force R&D Organization with Particular References to DCS/D—ARDC Relationships." (Memorandum for General Putt.) 26 Nov 1951.

__________. "Semi-Annual Historical Report for the Deputy Chief of Staff, Development." 1 Jul 1952–31 Dec 1952.

__________. "The Current Research Program, and a Summary of Research Accomplishments." AFOSR 67–0300. Arlington, Va.: Air Force Office of Scientific Research, Office of Aerospace Research, USAF, undated.

Klusman, James E. "The Effect of Technology on Planning." Undated.

Smith, Joseph, Major General. "Air Force Planning." Tape No. 49–231. 5 Jun 1950.

Commentary

General Bryce Poe II, USAF, Retired

My old and respected friend Bill Holley has once again produced a thoughtful and well-reasoned paper that deserves close attention. Further, he has used his personal competence in both military and historical matters to give us something that is useful to today's military airman—that is, I believe, the most important thing of all.

Of course that does not mean that I would not quarrel with some of his deductions, but where we do differ it always comes down to arriving at different conclusions from the same facts—entirely matters of opinion.

For example, I would not grant the *Air Corps Newsletter* the importance he does. Although the in-basket of 1937 was undoubtedly not as stacked with trivia as today's, the increasing level of activity in the undermanned force might well have meant that a nonaction information item received only cursory attention.

It would also seem to me that General Arnold was handled a bit roughly, even allowing for the credit given him for later rehabilitation. The military professional is necessarily conservative in things relating to technology—witness those curious early flintlock muskets we see in museums, weapons with a just-in-case matchlock on the barrel as well. The higher the rank and the heavier the responsibility, the less likely one is to experiment at the cost of bringing known capability on line. It is often a matter of perceived priority and always subject to later criticism. The Civil War Springfield Arsenal commander, who resisted even consideration of repeating firearms so obstinately that one maker—Spencer—had to take his case to President Lincoln, clearly understood the value of such weapons. He knew, however, that the war could be won with the single-shot rifled musket and did not believe the Union Army could handle the increased logistic effort required to support the new weapons. Convincing arguments have been made to prove him either right or wrong. Even Messerschmitt's initial experimental jet fighter had a conventional piston engine installed in the gunner's cockpit in the interests of safety.

Just as persuasive a defense can be provided Arnold in this case. It may well be that he had his priorities right—stretching his limited resources in the early days to cover production of large numbers of able enough aircraft and trained crews and then shifting to a system more aligned to the future once the initial threat was in hand.

Finally, I might quarrel with the contention that earlier volume production of the Me–262 would have had the potential for disaster to the Allies. It certainly would have made the air war much more costly, and Allied air leaders were properly concerned, but even a year earlier would have been too late for the Luftwaffe. Perhaps their major problem was the extremely serious shortage of well-trained aircrews. The spectacular success of the Me–262 in fights such as those over Berlin on 18 March 1945, was accomplished by Steinhoff's elite 7th Fighter Group, and even their skill did little to blunt the damage caused by the 1,200 bombers in the attacking force. Once back on the ground, the jets were constantly attacked by waves of Mustangs and Thunderbolts.

The Allies would probably have been much more adversely affected had the Germans not made the decision in 1937 to halt all work concerned with four-engine bombers. Nevertheless, in fairness I must admit that both historian and airman are more likely to agree with Bill Holley than with me in this case.

Ritualistic nitpicking aside, I'd like to move on to the much more important and positive side of my review. In that light I would recommend the paper to anyone in our Air Force, from cadets here to the Air Staff. It is designed to make them think. As the author challenges, how do we stand today—would we make the same errors, miss the same opportunities? These are very pertinent questions, and the parallels are clear. There is much less difference between the concerns of the 1930s and those of the 1980s than one might think.

Heed the history of the reduction of effectiveness of both procurement and development when those two functions are combined. Remember the examples cited here, as well as others going right back to the separation of the two activities as a first order of business by Lloyd George in Britain at the beginning of World War I. Remember every time some politician or bureaucrat suggests, in the name of economy, combining Air Force Systems Command and

Air Force Logistics Command into a single unit as the Army's DARCOM, or the Navy's Materiel Command. Use this as a caution to watch carefully that the contractor's motive for profit in the civilian market does not dilute what you are paying him to do to support the military mission. Remember the lesson here when you think to make savings by holding the civil service grades of key technicians at unrealistically low levels.

Look carefully to the mix of technical and nontechnical education and training of military professionals. I say carefully because it may be that the pendulum already has swung too far in the technical direction. In the 1930s few men, in or out of the military, were technologically trained, but most good colleges and universities produced people who could write well and who knew something of the way men thought and could be expected to act. A case could be made that this has been reversed, to the detriment of those skills required for leadership and command.

To close, the most clear parallel is probably the current Air Force expansion into space. Today, the Chief of Staff is having to make extremely tough decisions as to whether to apply scarce resources to spare parts or CO_2 laser radar; fuel reserves or improvement of self-reinforcing plastics; hardening of overseas avionics facilities; or the specialized artificial intelligence that might develop software that could of itself produce software.

At the very least, General Holley's paper could comfort you with the assurance that none of your troubles were new; at best it could well stimulate you to better solutions of today's problems.

Colonel Gropman's detailed examination of a decade of Air Force plans was particularly interesting to me. He showed real courage in selecting the most complex period as regards the relationship between plans and technology and a real grasp of the intricate permutations and combinations of pressures brought about by the various military and civil bureaucracies involved. Each of us is the product of our own experience. Mine was in the field, in the tactical units, and in the Air Research and Development Command of the time. The paper often gave me the feeling of suspicions confirmed.

The author draws heavily on his own experience—a priceless advantage (I know of no one else with the background or access). Since he was a participant, however, a bit of prejudice may result. Or perhaps the reviewer, also a participant, is the one who is prejudiced.

For example, I sense that the entire subject of separation of Research and Development from the Materiel Command casts the commanders and staff officers of the latter, and their Air Staff counterparts, as Colonel Blimps, doggedly hanging on to their turf for no good reason. As I remember, the primary reason was given as a potential rival for resources. That was without question a significant concern, but there were others equally important. With the words "the future was subordinated to the present" the author—in my opinion—indicates that he has missed an important link between research, development, and acquisition on the one hand and procurement, maintenance, and supply on the other.

In the decade studied, almost half of the cost of ownership of a weapons system was accrued after delivery of the article to the using command—today that approaches 75 percent. Even before the final production design is approved, decisions have been made that cast in concrete the bulk of those post-delivery costs. Maintenance man-hours per flying hour, susceptibility to stress corrosion, fuel requirements, compatibility with ground support equipment, standardization of armament, and many other factors of the design past directly determine the cost of the logistics future. Testing done in the bright sunshine of Edwards or Holloman proves little as to the performance to be expected in Europe or Asia. The poorly written or sole-source contract for initial spares locks in costs for follow-on war reserve spares for years to come.

These were some of the reasons that motivated people like General Chidlaw to press for care in the transition. Evidence that their concerns were valid is easy to find. For example, from the split in command, right through to 1982, the amount of the research and development budget devoted to logistics support research—materials, corrosion control, fuel tank leaks, hot section turbine problems, etc., never reached three percent in any year. The problems festered until major actions were taken to bridge the gap, in particular establishment of the Acquisition Logistics Division in 1976 and its successor, the Acquisition Logistics Center, about a year ago. The continuing seriousness of the problem was highlighted most recently—17 September—by an unprecedented letter to all MAJCOMS, signed by the Secretary of the Air Force and the Chief of Staff, stating that reliability and maintainability were paramount in the acquisition process, in no way subordinate to cost, schedule, or performance. The letter directed action all across the Air Staff and the forces, with an initial deadline of a hundred days. While I do not believe this invalidates the general theme or conclusions of the paper

I feel it is a flaw that could have been readily overcome by a more balanced set of references.

The separation of the development and support functions was long overdue. Nothing would be worse than to combine them again, as is periodically suggested. Nevertheless, we learn more and will be prone to fewer future mistakes if we carefully examine both sides of the record.

Two other items of significance might have been addressed. The first relates to Rand. The establishment of that organization and its important contribution to Air Force planning is well set forth. What is missing is the sine wave of good-bad relations with the Air Force. By the end of the decade, Rand had become—to some senior uniformed personnel—the imperial Rand, very resistant to criticism or even comment. After a change in key personnel, things went back to normal, only to cycle again in the recent past. It takes nothing from the significant part Rand played to show that it too had its problems as a part of the Air Force hierarchy.

Finally, a small item but an intriguing one. The author remarks that planners found "it easier to make assumptions about the future than to live with ambiguity." Assumptions have been a part of military planning and problem solving throughout history—usually coming just after a "Statement of the Problem" and just before "Facts Bearing on the Problem." The difficulty is to always know what is an assumption and what is a fact, and too many military writers blissfully and dangerously flip back and forth without keeping track. My question would be—what alternative do we have to assumptions?

Enough said. We are in debt to Colonel Gropman for a very useful trip through the immense documentation covering one of the most difficult, yet fascinating, subjects I know. All those charged with planning, development, and even organization—perhaps *especially* organization—should read it and read it carefully.

Commentary

Richard H. Kohn

General Poe, Professor Holley, Colonel Gropman, ladies and gentlemen. This afternoon we have heard two fascinating and instructive presentations on technology and planning. The subject is of more than idle or momentary interest, for we live in an age dominated both by technology and by war. Our various eras in this century are often so characterized: the automobile age, the postwar era, cold war America, the nuclear age, the space age, the information age. The United States Air Force itself is the product of technological change: the introduction of flight to warfare, the movement of combat into the air, and the use of the area above the earth to affect conflict on the surface of the earth. There is no question in my mind that technology, more than any other single factor, has shaped our national security policy over the last generation, for the introduction of nuclear weapons and the rise of air power have put our nation at risk and ended over a century of relative safety from enemies that could threaten our existence as a nation.[1] We have been, and are, the leaders in the development and application of technology to war. It is no small irony that we ourselves "invented," if you will, airplanes and atomic bombs—the two innovations that ended our historic geographical security.

The two papers are quite different in focus and approach. One concentrates on planning, the other on technology. One emphasizes process (the means by which people acted), the other the substance of historical actions. One focuses on structure (the bureaucracy and institutions which did the planning—a macro approach); while the other is a case study of one particular change in technology, albeit a crucial one for air forces. The papers are united, however, in their criticism of both the process of planning and the result. For Colonel Gropman, planning is a process impossible to define or to encompass fully. At the beginning, he seemed to me unable to provide us with a precise portrait of who the planners were or what they were doing. He convinces us, however, that planning was beset with all sorts of difficulties, from the uncertainty of the political and international environment to the vagaries of bureaucratic structure, which not only cycled people through the various agencies too quickly but tampered with the arrangement of the agencies in such a way as to diminish the attention devoted to research and development at the headquarters level. For Professor Holley, the story of American aircraft engine development in the 1930s is one of missed opportunity. The effort was divided between the National Advisory Committee for Aeronautics and the Air Corps Materiel Division. Because the engineering talent focused more on testing than on basic research, and because the leadership of the Air Corps was by and large uneducated and unprepared in the areas of science and engineering, our research and development effort in the engine field lagged behind Germany and Britain in grasping the onrushing revolution in propulsion overtaking the airpower world. Holley concentrates on the decade before World War II and Gropman on the decade after, but in the different areas of technology and planning both draw essentially negative portraits. Both, by implication, blame the leadership of the Air Force for the sins of omission, misperception, and neglect, for it was the leadership which was ultimately responsible for all that went on in the service in those years.

While both presentations are real contributions to our understanding, they are focused on two relatively narrow subjects, and because they do not address the issues of technology and planning broadly, they can mislead us. Remember that this was, after all, the generation which created the largest and finest air force in the world, which defeated the German Air Force, destroyed the economies of Germany and Japan, leveled the cities of Japan, and supported our ground forces in one victorious campaign after another. This was the generation of American air leaders which failed neither in developing weapons and machines, nor in planning in Washington for our postwar security. Nowhere does Colonel Gropman show us that the very complicated process or the constantly realigning bureaucracy failed in any material way. Were the plans irrelevant or ill-conceived? Did the Air Force fail to keep abreast of technology or lack the most modern and effective aerial instruments of war? Of course, in the late 1940s, Vannevar Bush could justifiably criticize the way we decided to buy weapons. But Bush was not describing military planning but the process by which a democracy makes military policy, at a time when our military services were locked in an especially bitter struggle over roles and missions—their very existence.

Certainly the process of planning is messy, affected by bureaucratic structure and subject to the influence of rapidly changing events. Planners are harried people bedeviled by crises, enslaved by in-boxes. One very senior planner in the Pentagon told me recently that his most difficult problem is to find time—time for planning that will combine historical knowledge, the demands of the present, and the best projections of the future into sensible, structured, long-range and mid-range plans. Creating such plans is a very deliberate process to which we have devoted considerable resources in this country. But the issues come so fast and are so complex that there is virtually no time for study. The staffs are drawn off to, and become wrapped up in, the current problems which assume an irresistible urgency.[2] Another senior planner, describing the immediate postwar years of the 1940s in which he participated as Secretary of the Air Staff, drew an essentially identical picture.[3]

The very messiness and uncertainty of the planning process led the Air Force to create the Scientific Advisory Board and the Rand Corporation, institutions separated from the staff and command bureaucracies in order to keep the Air Force on the cutting edge of new technologies and to perform the research necessary to plan for future contingencies. By choosing to concentrate on the Air Staff rather than on the operating major commands, Colonel Gropman may have missed entirely the places where technology and planning were being integrated. Even in studying Headquarters Air Force, he focuses on the separate Air Staff directorates rather than on the Secretariat, the Office of the Chief of Staff, the Air Board or the Air Council, or other agencies where technology and planning would have been integrated. And I repeat: I don't think he has provided us the evidence for failure in result.

Professor Holley has no difficulty in this regard, because he chooses failure as the focus of his investigation. The case study approach in his talented hands is extremely instructive, but it can also blind us to the wider picture. The Air Corps was not, by and large, backward in technological development. One has only to cite the overall quality of American aircraft in World War II, the list of technical innovations developed by industry in the war, and the size of American aircraft production—itself a technological wonder which Professor Holley has elsewhere analyzed—to remember an institution which succeeded markedly in the world of science, research and development, and acquisition.[4] Holley is too hard on "Hap" Arnold, whose effort and attention were focused on organization, training, and production in the immediate prewar years. Arnold was the same leader who sponsored Theodore von Karman and created the Scientific Advisory Board at the end of the war. One reason the Air Corps may have neglected jet engine development was that, as an institution, it was focused like a cyclops in the late 1930s on bomber development, not fighters. Power, range, durability, reliability, and immediate production—not speed and not radical innovation—were the priorities for bombers at this time. And the U.S. Army Air Corps and Army Air Forces, in the B–17, B–24, and B–29, produced the finest bombers in the world.

We should also remember that technology can be unpredictable. We know that we can stretch technology and repeatedly we have succeeded, from the atomic bomb to the U–2 and SR–71, to the Atlas, Titan, and Minuteman ICBMs. But we know also that technology often follows its own logic. The Minuteman grew out of an unexpected discovery in fuel and engine development during the ballistic missile programs of the 1950s.[5] Planners and operators want to believe—perhaps even do—that military requirements drive technological change. They are right to a degree, for in broad outline the need to deliver firepower or ordnance over long distances with accuracy, to create greater explosive force, to be speedy, to see far, and to include a host of other characteristics of aerospace weapons systems, all shape development. War itself, after all, is the final arbiter of weapons. Yet we can cite instance after instance where technology arose unexpectedly, matured according to the laws of science and the practicalities of engineering, or sprang from the genius of an individual rather than the bureaucracy responsible for research and development. Even the cycle of development can be baffling. In an era of supposedly accelerating change, the life cycle of the B–17 from development to obsolescence was about a decade and that of the B–29 was even less, while that of the B–52 and the F–4, admittedly of a different era and partly shaped by political and budgetary limitations, will likely last fifty years—a half century. In the 1920s and 1930s, the major changes were airframe and propulsion, in the 1970s and 1980s, avionics and delivery systems. Technological change is often illogical or inexplicable, and people can be embarrassingly wrong. Admiral William D. Leahy, the President's Chief of Staff during World War II, repeatedly admitted in his memoirs that he did not believe that the atomic bomb would work. "This is the biggest fool thing we have ever done," he reputedly told President Truman in 1945. "The bomb will never go off, and I speak as an expert in explosives."[6]

In fact, the development of the atomic bomb illustrates very well the difficulties of connecting planning to technological change. Admiral Leahy was certainly not alone in doubting that the bomb would work. Even those who believed in the project could not predict when the weapon would be available, what difficulties would

be encountered in delivering it to a target, or the size and nature of
the explosion. Beyond these major uncertainties lay the great need
for secrecy, which virtually foreclosed any planning. While the
Army Air Forces prepared a unit to drop the weapon, and the Joint
Chiefs of Staff reserved some cities as possible targets, the Operations
Division of the War Department General Staff—responsible for
Army planning—was kept almost completely in the dark. In the
entire Operations Division, only "the three chief officers," all
generals, "gained some knowledge of the MANHATTAN DIS-
TRICT work," and only one was a planner.[7] All of the planning, in
fact, was based on the assumption that it would be necessary to
invade the Japanese home islands. In the spring of 1945, a young
officer named Andrew Goodpaster, recently assigned to the Operations Division, suggested to the Army's chief planner, Brigadier
General George Lincoln, that plans be developed for an occupation
in case Japan surrendered suddenly. Lincoln, although aware of the
bomb, had undertaken no such plan. He quickly agreed and
Goodpaster set immediately to work on plans that in modified form
guided American forces in the initial takeover of the Japanese
homeland.[8] Goodpaster, a young combat soldier just out of the
hospital, knowing nothing of the bomb, first suggested planning for
what eventually happened. Lincoln, a brilliant planner and the
Army's representative on the Joint and Combined Planning Staffs,
knew something about the bomb, but had not, prior to Goodpaster's
suggestion, paid much attention to a likely contingency.[9]

Neither of these papers, in my view, addresses an even more
crucial problem: the *relationship* between technology and planning.
Which drives the other? Which controls events? Which dominates?
The answer, I believe, is neither. The relationship is reciprocal and
situational; each is wedded to the other in a manner determined by
time, place, environment, and the specific technology and military
need. Furthermore, the relationship is blurry and unpredictable, just
as is the process of planning and technological change. We scholars
and military people swallow this with difficulty; our tendency is to
resist, to criticize, just as have Professor Holley and Colonel
Gropman. Scholars worship logic, reason, and order; military people
strive inevitably to organize and rationalize, to eliminate insofar as
possible the fog of war. Precision is at once a military goal and a
military impossibility.

It is possible, of course, to construct a paradigm to show the
relationship between technology and planning. Both are part of the
fundamental process by which a nation provides for its defense. As
the war colleges like to diagram it:

240

Goals—Policy—Strategy—Force Structure—Operations.

Governments decide upon their goals, formulate policy to achieve them, devise strategies to implement policy, construct forces to implement strategy, and use the forces in operations that will execute the strategy. Technology is a shaping force throughout and part of the environment. Technology is a constant, like the "threat." It is structural, like the economy. But it is less volatile than public opinion or some social issues. Planning, on the other hand, is part of the process by which goals, policy, strategy, force structure, and operations are developed. Planning is itself a process performed by staffs and bureaus, and it is a crucial one, for it links each step to the next, providing the logic and the system for formulating national security activity.

What I have just described, however, is theory—not the real world. In truth, the process is far more irrational, uncertain, and susceptible to momentary influences like chance events or personality. In the hypothetical world, the connecting link between technology and planning is doctrine, what Curtis LeMay has called "the central beliefs for waging war," the "network of faith and knowledge reinforced by experience which lays out the pattern for the utilization of men, equipment, and tactics."[10] Doctrine integrates the theory and experience of war with national policy and technology to furnish the planner with guideposts across the entire spectrum of military activity. And yet our record in the production of doctrine and in our construction of agencies to produce doctrine has been less than encouraging historically, as Professor Holley, the foremost student of doctrine in the Air Force, showed us ten years ago in his excellent Harmon Memorial Lecture.[11]

In the final analysis, we cannot adequately plan for technological change, for its pace and character are too accidental, too unpredictable, and military institutions have developed, historically, primarily to throw men into battle, not to research and develop weapons at the frontier of knowledge. Nor can one plan on the basis of technology if one cannot predict what weapons and systems are coming, what will work, how it will work, how many we will have, and when we will have them. In other words, I am not sure a nexus connecting research and development and plans, at the working levels on the Air Staff would be that helpful. As a matter of practicality, the two will usually connect, for the planner must ask almost always, "what can or what will we be able to do?" Likewise the scientist or engineer, in choosing a line of research or application, will want to ask, "what will the strategist or operator *want* to do?" Thus, to a degree, technology and planning drive each other.

For all of my skepticism, however, I find these two papers to be of tremendous value. Colonel Gropman reminds us that the "marriage between warriors and scientists," crucial to success in war, has been lacking in our history. Furthermore, he points out that planning is imperfect, occasionally poor, and sometimes dangerous; that the pressures and influences are sometimes so complicated and so changeable as to prevent sound results; and that the planning process—the bureaucratic structure—usually compounds the problem rather than helping with the solution. Professor Holley shows us that even in what we consider our strongest suit—technology—this nation of unparalleled wealth and ingenuity can commit costly mistakes. He demonstrates that even a generation of leaders whom we revere for their success in World War II can commit these mistakes.

Both of these papers can be tremendously disheartening if one wants order and rationality. I myself do not believe they are always possible or necessary. Professor Holley offers us the most realistic of solutions: we must people the process with men and women of broad education, wide vision, and great intellectual capacity. Free of presuppositions, they must be able to see and be comfortable with complexity and uncertainty. Above all else, they must be able to respond quickly to change, to recalculate the equation, to be flexible. An institution like the Air Force must search out such people, educate them to the challenge, and reward them if they succeed. This military history symposium makes a substantial contribution exactly to that solution.

Notes

1. The influence of technology is, of course, subject to continuing debate. See, for example, Ralph Sanders, "Technology in Military Strategy: A Realistic Assessment," *Technology in Society*, V (1983), 139–53.

2. Discussions with a senior planner on the Joint Chiefs of Staff, 8 Oct 1984, Washington, D.C.

3. Discussions with General Jacob E. Smart, USAF, Retired, 1 Jun 1984, Washington, D.C.

4. For technical innovations and American production, see *Wartime Technological Development: A Study Made for the Subcommittee on Military Affairs,* U.S. Senate, 79th Cong, 1st sess,(Washington, 1945); *Ibid, Supplement for 1944;* James Phinney Baxter 3d, *Scientists Against Time* (Boston, 1946); Irving B. Holley, Jr., *Buying Aircraft: Materiel Procurement for the Army Air Forces (United States Army in World War II, Special Studies)* (Washington: Office of the Chief of Military History, 1964).

5. For this point, I relied on Jacob Neufeld's history of the development of ballistic missiles in the USAF, a forthcoming volume in the Office of Air Force History's General Histories Series.

6. Quoted in Charles L. Mee, Jr., *Meeting at Potsdam* (New York, 1975). See also William D. Leahy, *I Was There*, reprint ed. (New York, 1979), pp 265, 269, 431, 432, 440–41.

7. "Military Use of the Atomic Bomb," (1946), pp 1–2, 27–28, George A. Lincoln Papers, Box 3, U.S. Military Academy Library, West Point, N.Y.

8. *Ibid*, pp 16, 19, 28–31; discussion with General Andrew Goodpaster, 11 Oct 1984, USAF Academy, Colorado.

9. General Goodpaster contradicts the following statement on page 8 of the official OPD account: "General Lincoln first (late July 1945) suggested to his own staff: 'We should start stacking up some studies on the assumption Japan quits, say 15 September. . .'." However the OPD account is internally inconsistent, claiming on page 15 that Lincoln had begun some similar planning in April

10. Quoted in Air Force Manual 1–1, "Basic Aerospace Doctrine of the United States Air Force," 5 Jan 1984.

11. I. B. Holley, "An Enduring Challenge: The Problem of Air Force Doctrine" (Harmon Memorial Lectures in Military History, Number Sixteen) (Colorado Springs: United States Air Force Academy, 1974), is only one of Holley's discussions of doctrine, which date back to his classic *Ideas and Weapons* in 1953 and run as recently as his "Concepts, Doctrines, Principles: Are You Sure You Understand These Terms?" *Air University Review,* XXXV (Jul-Aug 1984), 90–93.

General Bryce Poe, II, USAF, Retired, Moderator

Cargill Hall (Historical Research Center): I have a question for both of the authors. The commentator suggested that, despite the organizational disconnections and impediments in the postwar era, planning ultimately succeeded. Certainly we survived the period, and perhaps one cannot plan on the basis of technology—I think I'm paraphrasing Dr. Kohn correctly. It occurred to me that if you take the case of strategic bombers, an Air Force institution, the postwar bombers were largely designed and developed in terms of Arnold and von Karman's views; that is, they should fly higher, farther, and faster. If you think now for a moment about the B–52, the B–58, the B–70, and now the B–1. The B–52 and B–58 were conscripted ultimately to fly low-level subsonic missions, the B–70 was canceled, and the B–1 is left with a supersonic airframe and a subsonic mission. Does that represent the planning failure?

Gropman: We'll deal with the comment and the question I guess. Despite the disconnection, we survived Korea. If you're talking about major league AAA, AA, A, pony league, and little league, where do you put a Korea that stymied the United States of America for three years? And if you're proud of what we accomplished in the post-World War II period in planning and technology, you can cite the fact we survived Korea. You know if the Padres can't survive little league ball, then there's something wrong with the Padres. I don't know, I'm not so convinced. Tomorrow, Frank Futrell is going to comment about how the Air Force dealt with this particular period, our national policy, and nuclear madness. We start working production on conventional bombs in the fifties, and what do we produce? We produce an F–105 that became dogmeat in Vietnam for another little league country that we were dealing with. The Vietnam War starts in 1961 and the development of the weapons systems that we were using in that war came out of the era that I'm talking about. We haven't done very well. And as far as the criticism is concerned, it's the only way you advance. And what we might say to the press outside about the institution would be very different, but what we

244

say to each other is very necessary. Research and development—if you want to talk about research and development and planning, you've got to break research and development into its components. We do this when we budget: 6.1, 6.2, 6.3, 3.8, and 4, and so forth. Basic research, 6.1, should not be manipulated by planning. And the operators ought to stay out of that area, and the operators pretty much do; Systems Command tries to see to it. Basic research, fundamental research, is something that operators would probably mangle. Rand Corporation did a study they entitled *The Chef, Gourmet, and Gourmand*, which says the chef researcher prepares the menu of things for the gourmet. If the gourmet gets into the kitchen, he's not going to get anything other than indigestion. So they want the operators to stay out of the researcher's business. But development, that's a different story. And you see, when you go past basic research and you start talking about the 6.2, and 3, 3.8, 6.38, 6.4 development, now the operators must say: this before that, this before that—this is what I need to do my job, and that's what we're talking about. And there's the nexus that's missing, the one we're trying to develop. Somebody's got to guide it because we're talking about billions of dollars. Somebody's got to guide it, and actually the planners and the operators must be the ones that guide where the Air Force goes.

Tom Fabyanic (University of South Florida, Tampa): In both papers, Colonel Gropman's dealing with the postwar period and Dr. Holley's with the prewar period, it strikes me that a noticeable lack in both periods was the existence of conceptual thinking by the uniformed military officers. Now our good friend and colleague Dr. Kohn has offered us a solution. As I read him at the very end, he said, staff the system with bright articulate individuals who are broadly based men of vision. Now my question to you, Dr. Holley, and to you my good friend, Al Gropman, is this: would it make any difference?

Holley: Thanks, Tom. We've got to believe it does, and for those of us who are interested in developing the PME, the professional military education of officers, we've obviously got to believe it does. And whereas we think we've made tremendous strides over where we were pre-World War II, obviously there is enormous room for improvement in what we're doing. That doesn't imply catastrophic criticism of what we're doing now, but just steady building on from where we're at if I may use the vernacular. I hope that would be my central message and that I wouldn't be seen as, you know, engaging in character assassination. I'd like to use that as a point of departure for a good look at what happened to those men in World War II.

Before the war they lived rather provincial lives. You know people lived on post, and they talked with each other, and they didn't have many contacts outside. Well, the present Air Force is a very different Air Force. People don't live on post, and we lose something by that. We lose something of the unity, the cohesiveness, and so on, but on the other hand, we gain a lot of realism. We gain a great deal in terms of political sophistication and so on. So we have a different Air Force today—much more technically competent. There's much more emphasis on education. I guess what I'm driving at is that I think our professional schools should be more rigorous than they are. I don't know that I've answered your question, but I've given you some steer at what I was aiming at in the paper. Turning to Dick Kohn's comment about the successes of World War II, I think his answer would have been quite different if the narrow margins of success had tipped the other way. Suppose they had gotten numbers of jets into the air just that twelve months sooner and, therefore, Overlord didn't enjoy air superiority. One shudders at the thought of the casualties that might have been accrued. I think that we would have won in the long run, but my God what a cost, what a cost we would have had to pay. And so I think you can't look to the final success and say, therefore, all was well. I argue that's too close a margin of success not to be worried about it—the failure to look to the independence of the R outside of R&D. General Poe's brought out very effectively how important it is to have the D side, the development side, the logistical side, closely coordinated, but if you start meddling with the R side, the pure research, you're going to stultify it as we've demonstrated time and time again. Let's see, I've answered three criticisms on your one.

Poe: I have to break in on one thing. When you say, would it make any difference, I'm very much concerned with the fact that the world is different today than it was during the time we're talking about. Some of the most innovative things that were done by these people would seem very mundane. Dutch Kindelberger said that Arnold had gotten him to commit five times the net worth of North American to build airplanes without a single piece of paper. We would never be able to do that kind of thing anymore. I am terrified with the idea of trying to expand the industrial base under pressure and such as that. The innovator now is so bound up in public law, the media, and the rest of it, that I'm very much concerned about the fact you may have that right fellow, but whether he can go on with anything or not I'm not sure.

Holley: (Addressing Tom Fabyanic) Tom, may I add a footnote to that? General Poe made a point earlier by implication. We not only have to educate our professional officers, we've got to educate our Congressmen because over and over and over and over again, we see this business of them wanting to save money by combining systems and logistics and so on. That degree of education, that degree of enlargement of vision, is probably more important there, than it is in our professional officers.

Bob Cummings (USAFA Cadet): I have a question for Colonel Gropman. Sir, in Vietnam, as you alluded to in Korea, we fought a third rate country; we had the technology but perhaps the planning was deficient. I'm wondering how do mood swings effecting our nation, affect your job in planning. For instance, the Strategic Defense Initiative or Star Wars is coming at a time when people are more patriotic. So I wonder if you could comment on the mood swings of people and their effect on planning.

Gropman: You're referring to public opinion I guess. Well, obviously the people that work in ops and plans first of all are children of the culture to begin with. When the mood swings they swing with it. Around the Bolling swimming pool they look like everybody else in my neighborhood except for haircuts. You can always tell a GI around Fairfax County by his haircut but that's about the only way. He drives what other people drive, and he wears what other people wear, so he's a product of his particular times. That's a good thing about the United States military. Something that Bill referred to a few minutes ago is that we aren't isolated from our society; we see ourselves as citizens first and soldiers second, and it is very important that we do. One would hope, however, that as with the pet rock syndrome that so captured American people, (yellow ties now—I guess everybody's wearing yellow ties, a lot of them in this audience) the Air Force is beyond fads. We try to think down the road about twenty years, and we found it's foolish to try and predict what the mood is going to be in those twenty years. Lord Palmerston, the British Prime Minister in the mid–1800s said that we have no permanent enemies, we have no permanent friends, we have permanent interests, and it is our duty to secure those interests. That's an indirect quote because I don't have it in front of me. Well, the United States does too. Democrats and Republicans and the Carter PRMs (Program Memorandum) inherited by Reagan in 1981 looked suspiously like those of 1932 that we're following today. The language is a little bit different but the interests are permanent. The interests of the country are permanent and we need to maintain access to the resources of the world and so forth. We need to foment, for lack of a better word, democracy and human rights throughout the world. We need to be what we are, and we need to be true to what we are, and it doesn't make any difference if it's President Nixon or President Ford or President Carter or President Reagan—they stay pretty much the same. So the objectives, the overall objectives of this country remain the same over the longest period of time, and then within that comes the military's role in helping to secure those. Despite the mood swings as you call them, or the fashions of the particular day the military is out in front of those trying to see how in a changing world we can work to continue to secure those objectives. As I tried to say in the beginning, and I know Dick Kohn recognizes this and I hope you do too, it's a very difficult job—I wanted to start with that. Having done this for a long time in the Pentagon, I'm constantly amazed at how difficult and how challenging it really is. The mood swings don't really affect us terribly, because we're out in front of those. The English that we put on it perhaps is affected by what's going on at that particular time.

Military Planning and The Cold War

Introduction

Military planning grew even more difficult after World War II. America's new international role, its haunting fear of another great depression, its idealism and commitment to human freedom, its distaste for large standing armies, its atomic weapons, and its unwillingness to match commitments with national sacrifice all came together to make military planning exceedingly complex. The papers in Session III explore these problems from three perspectives—those of the Air Force, Navy, and the Joint Chiefs of Staff (JCS). As the focus moves into contemporary times, the reader will experience feelings of *deja vu*.

Frank Futrell, the dean of Air Force historians, argues that during the cold war period, air leaders overlooked the potential of aerial warfare in conventional conflict. The reasons were simple. Strategic bombing concepts from the 1930s combined with the promises of atomic weapons formed the basis for airpower thinking. Tight fiscal policies dominated the Truman and Eisenhower administrations, and because they believed the deterrent of nuclear weapons represented the cheapest and surest road to national security, conventional forces fell into neglect. With concentrated effort and resources going to Strategic Air Command, however, the tactical air arm lost capability and the Air Force sacrificed flexibility, a dimension all air leaders acknowledged as vital. By the late 1950s the use of nuclear forces in limited actions seemed more dubious, and strategic bombing became, in effect, a lone wolf component of the U.S. military, a point not made clear by the Korean War but certainly brought home by the Vietnam conflict.

If the Air Force bound itself to strategic bombing, the Navy was equally dedicated to Mahan's concepts. Tom Etzold contends that Americans failed to notice flaws in the concept as it applied to the United States because of great World War II successes, and in fact concepts of insularity were inappropriate for the United States in the postwar period. Too often the Navy looked with suspicion on questions from the outside, and too often the assumptions upon which it planned were not shared by other military services or the civilian leadership. To compound the problem, the Navy could not hold its own in national security debates of the early and mid 1970s because of misapplied methods of analysis and arguments. The time has come, Etzold argues, for the Navy to work with assumptions common to the services and the civilian leadership and to invest in ideas for the long term without regard to budget submissions.

Professor Schandler considers the experience of yet a different type of institution, the Joint Chiefs of Staff. A center of controversy in recent years, the Chiefs are tasked to give the President military advice while acting as heads of their respective services, a difficult task at best. As early as 1964, the military and civilian leadership clashed over the proper action to be taken in Vietnam, and in 1965 the Chiefs recommended aggressive and ambitious actions not condoned by the Secretary of Defense. At the same time, civilian leadership did not provide clear guidelines or directions to the military. The pattern continued throughout the war.

At issue was what level of military force should be applied? The President's policy was a classic application of limited war theory which the military viewed as negative and ineffective. The President's unwillingness to mobilize the nation for warfare should have sent a message to military leaders regarding the extent to which he would task the nation over Vietnam. Although the JCS should have realized the political realities Johnson faced, they continued to argue for measures the President judged unacceptable. Organization in this case was not a factor, Schandler argues; the heart of the difficulty lay in the lack of clarity on national objectives provided by the national leadership.

In each of the three examples, the relationships, direction, and teamwork necessary between the political leadership and its military was lacking. Poor coordination is certainly not new in military history, but its disastrous results must be apparent to those entrusted with national strategic planning.

The Influence of the Air Power Concept on Air Force Planning, 1945–1962

Robert F. Futrell

If this paper had a subtitle it would be: "A Funny Thing Happened to the Air Force on the Way to the Holocaust." The title mentions air power. In historical usage this term has had varied meanings. General William "Billy" Mitchell said it was "an ability to do something in or through the air." In 1945–1962, however, the U.S. Air Force equated air power with strategic air striking power—bombs on target—preferably nuclear bombs on enemy heartland targets. The years 1945–1962 were the days of glory for the U.S. Strategic Air Command (SAC). How this came about and its effect on Air Force plans provides a significant vignette of military experience. Lest anyone miss it, my overall conclusion is going to be that the revolutionary strategic power enthusiasts—who focused on developing flight for independent military actions—overlooked a real worth of air activity in a synergy of total military power, as a cooperative permitter, expeditor, and force multiplier in a total scenario of war. Acceptance of a bombs-on-target concept of air power strapped the Air Force into a lone wolf configuration poorly prepared for the requirements of war and confrontation in the years following the Cuban missile crisis of 1962.

At the beginning of World War I, Colonel Billy Mitchell was Chief of Air Service, AEF, in France, and thus the first U.S. tactical air force commander. Late in 1917, he published a paper titled "General Principles Underlying the Use of the Air Service in the Zone of Advance, A.E.F." Here he wrote that the outcome of war depended primarily on the destruction of the enemy's military forces in the field. No one of the Army's offensive arms could win complete victory. The mission of the Air Service was to help other arms in their appointed missions. Mitchell divided aviation into two classes: tactical aviation operating in the immediate vicinity of friendly troops and strategic aviation usually operating more than 25,000 yards in advance of friendly troops, its object being "to destroy the means of supply of an enemy army, thereby preventing it from employing all of its means in combat."[1] By 1922, however, Mitchell had been favorably impressed with the independent air bombardment striking force concepts of Giulio Douhet.[2] These showed in Mitchell's 1926 testimony in Congress, when he explained his modern theory of making war. A hostile army in the field was no longer the main objective since its purpose was only to defend an enemy's vital areas. "Now we can get today to these vital centers," he said, "by air power.... So that, in the future, we will...go straight to the vital centers, the industrial centers, through the use of an air force and hit them. That is the modern theory of making war." But Mitchell was not in favor of eliminating the Army and Navy entirely. The Navy and its air service could be "just the way it is...," he said, "for work on the high seas." Of 100 percent national defense, he said, 50 percent should be air power, 30 percent land forces, and 20 percent sea forces.[3]

Especially at the Air Corps Tactical School (ACTS) in the 1930s, perception of Mitchell's strategic theory was sharpened by the development of all-metal bombers while the technology of smaller aircraft—most notably pursuit planes—tended to stagnate for several years. School instructors developed a concept of the industrial fabric of a nation and the effects that its destruction from the air would have on the enemy's war effort.[4] Of this period, General W. W. "Spike" Momyer has recalled: "I think our preoccupation with the strategic concept of war did more to frustrate any thinking on the employment of other aspects. If you will look at our pre-World War II writing, it's almost all devoted to the employment of strategic aviation against the heartland of a nation."[5] In 1941, four Army Air Forces officers in the Air War Plans Division drew on their ACTS background and, in nine days, prepared AWPD–1, a statement of Army Air Forces (AAF) mobilization requirements for World War II, which, in effect, became the AAF wartime plan. These men professed an inability to state requirements without a strategy, and they proposed all-out strategic air campaigns against Germany and then Japan to be possibly followed if necessary by surface war.[6] AWPD–1's bid for first priority war production of strategic bombers was not accepted, but Army Chief of Staff General George C. Marshall nevertheless gave the AAF very high priority within the War Department and accepted a remarkable buildup of AAF strength at the expense of the numbers of Army divisions mobilized. In World War II the U.S. Army mustered 89 divisions rather than the 215 originally specified as necessary to defeat the Axis. The AAF's maximum attained strength of 269 tactical groups remarkably matched AWPD–1's statement of requirements—239 air groups and 108 observation squadrons.[7]

Where AWPD–1 had presupposed an orderly war whereby Air Force forces would first conduct strategic bombing and afterward perhaps support Army forces, World War II was not like that, and distinctive strategic and tactical air forces emerged. In the initial months after December 1941, American and British bombers served in lieu of a Grand Alliance second front. During the winter of 1942–1943 American forces were bloodied in North Africa, and from this experience came War Department Field Manual 100–20, *Command and Employment of Air Power*, published in July 1943. Predicated on the principle that "Land power and air power are coequal and interdependent forces; neither is an auxiliary of the other," the manual authorized establishment of tactical air forces for cooperation with land forces through attainment of air superiority, isolation of the battle area, and close air support of ground troops.[8] The tactical air force was tested and validated in Italy and came to full stature in France and Germany. By March 1945, in the judgment of General Dwight D. Eisenhower's Chief of Staff, Lieutenant General Walter B. Smith, "the tactical coordination of air and ground forces has become an instrument of precision timing."[9] In the strategic air war against Germany, General Carl Spaatz fought his forces *both* to destroy Germany's will and economic capability to wage war *and* to prepare for the very chancy Allied invasion of Normandy coming up by ensuring the Luftwaffe was destroyed.[10] "The Normandy invasion," Eisenhower explained in November 1945, "was based on a deep-seated faith in the power of the air forces, in overwhelming numbers, to intervene in the land battle. ...Without that air force, without the aid of its power, entirely aside from its anticipated ability to sweep the enemy air forces out of the sky, without its power to intervene in the land battle, that invasion would have been fantastic.... Unless we had faith in the air power to intervene and make safe that landing, it would have been more than fantastic, it would have been criminal."[11]

Except for the shock of the atomic bomb in the final days of World War II, it is entirely probable that the airpower lesson of World War II would have been that air power—although not independently decisive—while employed in a new combination with land and sea power, and in overwhelming force, was incontestably a primary factor in the defeat of both Germany and Japan. The victory that was looming before the atomic bombs in August 1945 was a triphibious victory.[12] In 1944 an article in the *New York Times,* alleging that air power needed a Mahan, drew a riposte from an old line Air Corps commander, Major General Follett Bradley, who wrote: "We do not need a Mahan of air power so much as an oracle of combined operations—triphibious, if you will. The true expositor of military things to come. . .must evaluate correctly the effect of air power in combination with land and sea power on a battle, a campaign, and a war, and he must know something of the technique by which that effect is produced."[13] In the last year of the war in Europe, when strategic bombing was notably successful, the success of the bombing aided surface exploitation, but the surface battles contributed to the strategic air campaign. The pinch of logistics used up in surface fighting, in combination with destruction of production facilities from the air, exhausted Germany's economy. The forward movement of Allied ground armies uncovered forward airfields in France permitting easier fighter cover for the bombers making the final kill of Germany. In thinking back on wartime outcomes, General Spaatz noted: "Japan was a peculiar situation, being an island empire. . . . But when you are up against a continental empire you have the problem of winning against great masses of people with great internal resources. . . . We had established almost complete air superiority over Germany at the time of the invasion, but it took a considerable amount of fighting to subdue Germany after air superiority had been established."[14]

In the U.S. War Department, postwar planning commenced in 1943 and shaped up around General Marshall's belief that the United States would not maintain large standing military forces in peacetime. At the end of 1943, Marshall bucked back plans offered him with the marginal note: "I think maintenance of sizable ground expeditionary forces probably impracticable except on a basis of allotment of fillers after six months. Having air power will be the quickest remedy."[15] When plans for a 105–group and then a 78–group Air Force were rejected, Lieutenant General Ira C. Eaker, Deputy Commander Army Air Forces, ordered on 25 August 1945, that 70 tactical groups with 400,000 men would be the bedrock minimum strength objective. This was the strength needed to maintain D-Day forces and to have people and bases for mobilization of a million and a half men in a year. Replacement aircraft for this size force would keep national aircraft production in being.[16]

In the new Air Force the AAF Postwar Plans Division wanted a single Continental Air Forces (CAF) to provide initial strategic bombing and then to support exploitation forces. Consequently Headquarters, CAF, began to operate at Bolling Field on 1 April 1945, and on 8 September 1945, Major General Samuel E. Anderson, CAF Chief of Staff, asked for authority to provide a global striking force, to furnish tactical air for cooperative training with the Army and Navy, to plan U.S. air defenses, and to train replacement units and crews for overseas rotation.[17] Chief of Plans, Major

General Lauris Norstad, had come to prominence as a tactical air commander, and in regard to the postwar organization planning, he had long believed that the tactical air force was the outstanding development of World War II, except now the atomic bomb had possibly made the tactical air force "as old fashioned as the Maginot Line."[18] General H. H. Arnold passed the CAF proposal on to General Spaatz as his successor to the command of the AAF. General Eisenhower had become Chief of Staff of the Army, and in January 1946 after conversation with Eisenhower, Spaatz elected to organize the Air Force combat elements into a Strategic Air Command, Tactical Air Command, and Air Defense Command.[19] In air plans, General Norstad nevertheless rationalized that strategic air and air defense would be required at war's outbreak while tactical air would await a general mobilization.[20] In the explosive demobilization of 1946, combat effectiveness fell off to next to nothing, and General Spaatz had no choice but to give first priority to "the backbone of our Air Force—the long-range bomber groups and their protective long-range fighter groups organized in our Strategic Air Command."[21]

In 1946 an aggressive Soviet Union was identifiable as the most likely threat to the free world at the very time U.S. military forces were in complete disarray. At the end of 1946 the Strategic Air Command had only one effective B–29 group—the 509th Composite Group with 27 aircraft modified to carry the bulky "Fat Man" atomic bombs. By mid–1947 SAC kept about 160 B–29s on operational status, most being intended to drop conventional bombs. The size of the U.S. atomic warhead inventory was the best kept top secret in American history, so secret that some with need to know were unable to find out. Only in recent years has it been disclosed that the size of the atomic stockpile was 2 warheads in 1945, 9 in 1946, 13 in 1947, 50 in 1948, and 250 in 1949. Only President Truman could authorize use of an atomic bomb, and he gave no assurance until April 1949 that he might do so, and then he said it would be only "if necessary." Prevailing conditions such as these led Lieutenant Colonel Harry Borowski to describe U.S. strategic power before 1950 as "a hollow threat."[22]

Early in 1946 the Joint War Plans Committee of the Joint Chiefs of Staff began a series of studies code named PINCHER to provide a concept of operations for joint war planning. The progress of this classified story is told to us by Robert Little, John T. Greenwood, Thomas H. Etzold, John Lewis Gaddis, and especially David A. Rosenberg. These historians have traced plan HALF-MOON, becoming FLEETWOOD, becoming DOUBLESTAR.

Meanwhile back in 1946, in the AAF Plans Division (AC/AS–5) and on the basis of PINCHER, an air plan—MAKEFAST— provided that, within the four months after D-Day, six B–29 groups would be flying from bases in Britain and Egypt. This force would destroy the Soviet Union's petroleum production within nine months and the mobility of Soviet ground and air arms within a year. In the winter of 1947–1948, the Air Force Directorate of Intelligence gave intensive study to atomic targeting. Since the U.S. Strategic Bombing Survey had concluded that city bombing was ineffective, the target shop plotted industrial systems in the Soviet Union only to find these individual targets clustered in and around seventy Soviet cities. A concept followed that the objective of atomic air strikes would be to destroy government control, industrial capacity, and support potential rather than specific industrial objectives. The concept was called, "To kill a nation." Thinking on this order appeared in SAC's Emergency War Plan 1–49 that was added as an atomic annex to the HALFMOON emergency war plan. When the Joint Chiefs of Staff put more reliance on atomic weapons, they requested the Atomic Energy Commission to expand the atomic stockpile, which, as seen already, grew to 250 warheads in 1949.[23]

In the winter of 1947–1948, General Spaatz looked to a specially appointed Heavy Bomber Committee for advice on the plane the Air Force should buy to replace the B–29 and the B–50, an improved version of the B–29. The candidates were the mammoth B–36, conceived in 1939 when it seemed Britain might go under, and two new jet bomber prototypes in development, the B–47 and the B–52, neither of which had intercontinental range without aerial refueling. The SAC Commander, General George C. Kenney, disliked the B–36, but the committee received enough information about aerial refueling to believe it would be a feasible way of extending the jet bomber range. In World War II aerial refueling had not been practical for planes that carried iron bombs, but planes that carried atomic arms could feasibly have their ranges so extended. Before retiring on 30 April 1948, General Spaatz accepted the committee's recommendation to continue B–36 development and to hasten aerial refueling activity. Now, General Hoyt S. Vandenberg, Spaatz' successor as Chief of Staff, USAF, inherited the problem of what to do about SAC and also confronted a new problem in that President Truman was imposing an austere $14.4 billion on total requests for national defense for fiscal year 1950.[24]

At this juncture, Borowski's inside story is that there was dissatisfaction about how SAC was being run in high places, including stories that General Kenney was essentially a tactical air

258

commander in the Pacific during World War II. According to Borowski, General Norstad, while serving as acting vice chief of staff in mid–1948, advised Vandenberg that Kenney should be replaced by Lieutenant General Curtis E. LeMay, an aggressive and experienced World War II bomber commander.[25] On 19 October 1948, LeMay took command of SAC and quite shortly announced that "the fundamental goal of the Air Force should be the creation of a strategic atomic striking force capable of attacking any target in Eurasia from bases in the United States and returning to the points of takeoff."[26] Under what was called the "14.4 billion concept" the Air Force could no longer try to have seventy groups and would have to retrench to forty-eight groups. A USAF board of senior officers advised that the air atomic offensive must have priority, and on 1 December 1948, General Vandenberg reduced the Air Defense Command and the Tactical Air Command to a status of operational headquarters with units assigned to a new Continental Air Command. These forces assigned to ConAC would be used as required either for air defense or for tactical air support.[27] Looking back at this, General Momyer would later observe: "If anything, it reflected the basic philosophical split within the Air Force on how people looked at future war. In essence the two functions that you really got down to were these: one was the prosecution of the strategic offensive against the enemy, and the other was the denial of his offensive against you. You needed an air defense force, but you didn't really foresee a traditional air-ground campaign."[28]

In preparing the National Military Establishment budget requests for fiscal year 1950 in late 1948, the Army, Navy, and Air Force, for the first time, based their programs on what was euphemistically called "a correlated and integrated" strategy that in no way seems to have patched up distrust between the Navy and the Air Force.[29] Called back to Washington from retirement by President Truman, General Eisenhower worked to promote interservice harmony and also recorded his thoughts in his diary. U.S. Navy briefings on 2–3 February 1949 confirmed his impression that the Navy viewed its main mission as "projection of American air power" and that control of the seas was not a primary concern. On 9 February, Eisenhower found General Vandenberg jaundiced on aircraft carriers. "Van," Eisenhower recorded, "will not agree Navy needs any carrier larger than escort type. I feel that in first months of war a few big carriers might be our greatest asset. I want to keep ten in active fleet—about six to eight of which would always be in operation. Van thinks I'm nuts, but I'm convinced I'm right, at least as long as we have them."[30] In March 1949, Louis Johnson replaced Secretary of Defense James V. Forrestal, and in April Johnson announced discontinuation of production of the Navy's super aircraft carrier, the *United States*.

In mid–1949 the United States joined the North Atlantic Treaty and Alliance. To support this activity President Truman sent Congress a request for a military assistance appropriation for countries vital to U.S. security. In explaining why the Joint Chiefs of Staff were supporting the assistance package, General Omar Bradley outlined the going U.S. strategic concept. The United States would be charged with strategic bombing, and first priority in defense would be the ability to deliver the atomic bomb. The U.S. Navy and Western Union naval powers would conduct essential naval operations, including keeping sea lanes open. The hard core of the ground power in being would come from Europe, aided by other nations. England, France, and the closer countries would have the bulk of short-range attack bombardment and air defense. The United States would, of course, maintain its own defense and tactical air support forces for its ground and naval arms.[31]

At the same time the Joint Chiefs of Staff voiced support for military assistance, they assumed the U.S. defense request for fiscal year 1951 would equal the $14.4 billion President Truman had been willing to request for 1950. But with no warning in July 1949, Truman called defense officials to his office and told them to reduce the fiscal 1951 request to $13 billion, a reduction that by plan or circumstance equaled the military assistance package. For the U.S. Navy this cut promised further aircraft carrier reductions in addition to the *United States*. From April through August, a Navy propaganda office attacked the B–36 program and the growing reliance on long-range strategic bombing. In this same season, sometime between 26–29 August, the Soviet Union exploded an atomic device several years before U.S. strategists had expected.[32]

The "Revolt of the Admirals" brought two House of Representatives Armed Services Committee investigations in August-October 1949. The committee quickly exonerated Air Force leaders of insinuations of irregularity in B–36 procurement, but in regard to strategy, the final committee report advocated preservation of a plural defense establishment. The committee held that "military air power consists of Air Force, Navy, and Marine Corps air power, and of this, strategic bombing is but one phase." Regarding strategy, the committee stated: "the basic reason for this continuing disagreement is a genuine inability for these services to agree, fundamentally and professionally, on the art of warfare."[33] All this lingering in-fighting over the years necessarily affected strategic contingency planning.

After surveying the 1945–1950 time frame, Robert Little concluded: "The number of strategic plans of every type overtaken by events or time was legion. Short-range plans that gained approval were typically and admittedly infeasible and hardly more than a beginning was made on intermediate and long-range plans, or on mobilization plans. . . . Although the Korean War was perhaps not foreseeable, its planning had to proceed virtually from scratch, barely ahead of implementing actions and operations."[34] Major General John A. Samford, Director of Air Force Intelligence, had an additional thought: "Since it has been stated that military men are unable to reach any fundamental agreement on the art of war, it seems very probable that civilian thought will go to work to help them."[35]

On 30 January 1950 President Truman, who had leaned more and more on the assurance of the atom bomb during the Berlin blockade, directed the Atomic Energy Commission to proceed with development of a technically feasible immensely more powerful thermonuclear weapon. That same day, he directed the Secretaries of State and Defense to prepare a basic review of the national political and military strategy of the United States in the light of the Soviet atomic explosion. The result of this review, National Security Council 68 (NSC–68), 14 April 1950, recommended the United States initiate an immediate and large-scale buildup of American and Allied military and general strength in order to develop an adequate shield under which the United States could both resist local Soviet aggression and deter general war, until it could develop means short of general war to bring about a modification in Soviet behavior. The National Security Council handled the paper for costing and estimated that the expanded military program would come to about $50 billion annually for a number of years. President Truman had been attempting to limit total military spending to not more than $15 billion a year and preferably less. The fiscal 1952 budget request in early 1951 was another $13 billion.[36]

When the North Koreans invaded South Korea on 25 June 1950, the United States had no plan for the defense of the Republic of Korea; in fact, the ROK lay outside the declared U.S. defense perimeter in the Pacific. Nevertheless, resisting the attack required expanded defense capabilities above and beyond the level recommended in NSC–68. Especially in the first months of the Korean war, the judgment at highest U.S. levels held that the Korean invasion was the first stanza of World War III. NSC–68 had estimated that the Soviets would possess a fission bomb stockpile of 200 warheads by mid–1954. The year 1954 looked like a year of maximum danger to the United States and Western Europe because

Soviet production of new weapons would peak. For one moment, when the Chinese Communist armies were attacking in mass, it appeared that President Truman might authorize emergency use of an atomic weapon. This intimation, however, brought Britain's Prime Minister Clement Attlee posthaste to Washington on 4 December 1950, and in the end a communique noted: "The President stated it was his hope that world conditions would never call for the use of the atomic bomb." In the winter of 1950–1951, General Douglas MacArthur called for the use of atomic bombs against China, even though he later disclosed that he did not know the size of the stockpile. It would appear that at mid–1950, the U.S. stockpile numbered 299 and a year later, at mid–1951, it reached 447 warheads. Given this stock and the need to maintain deterrence of the Soviet Union, it is easy to see why the Joint Chiefs of Staff were not eager to use atomic bombs in Korea or against China. General Vandenberg described his organization as a shoestring air force in view of its global commitments. It could not sacrifice its deterrent capabilities for the sake of pecking at the periphery of Communist power in Manchuria and China.[37]

In the push-and-counterpush battles on the Korean peninsula, the synergism of air-ground defense fought the far larger Communist ground forces to a standstill, and military armistice negotiations began in mid–1951. Early in October 1951, the Joint Chiefs of Staff were able to complete planning for stabilized forces. The program projected an army with 20 divisions; a navy with 409 major combat ships, including 12 modern aircraft carriers, 3 marine divisions, and 3 marine air wings; and an air force with 143 wings, including 126 combat and 17 troop carrier wings. President Truman approved this military buildup on 28 December 1951, but he directed the program be stretched out in order that the armed forces budget, including military assistance for fiscal 1953, would fall below $60 billion.[38] In February 1952, the North Atlantic Treaty Organization (NATO) nations meeting in Lisbon yielded to American urging and established a goal of 96 divisions by 1954, 40 to be in permanent readiness and 56 to be capable of becoming operational within 30 days. The Truman strategic doctrine thus implied that the United States and NATO would be prepared to fight a nonnuclear war of whatever size an adversary might elect. In the U.S. atomic program, however, expanded warhead production doubled the stockpile from mid–1951 to mid–1952, increasing the stored warheads from 447 to 832. New technology was turning out bombs of small and convenient design that could be carried by fighter aircraft. The arrival of the atomic-capable tactical 49th Air Division in England on 5 June 1952 added realism to the SHAPE defenses. Taking into consideration the growing nuclear weapons availability, European allies were less enthusiastic about large conventional defenses. The British chiefs of staff argued that the advent of nuclear weapons justified a primary reliance on atomic air power and a substantial reduction in expensive surface forces. On a visit to Washington in July 1952, Air Chief Marshal Sir John Slessor argued that the Lisbon force goal placed too great a strain on fragile European economies and recommended a strategy of nuclear deterrence based upon American and British nuclear air power.[39]

In January 1952 General Eisenhower, Supreme Commander Allied Powers in Paris, expressed dismay in his diary with press reports that the United States crash military armament program would soar to $65 billion. He was skeptical that 1954 was a year of maximum danger. "There is no greater probability of war today than there was two years ago; and no one can say for certain that there is any greater probability of deliberately provoked war at the end of this year or of next year than there is now." "If we do not, as American citizens," he continued, "weigh this situation and reach a reasonable answer in this year's appropriations, we will be so committed to a possibly unwise military program that either we will begin to go far more rapidly down the inflation road or we will again have to accomplish a sudden and expensive contraction in that program. In this latter case, much of this year's appropriations would have, of course, gone down the drain."[40] In the autumn of 1952, the successful presidential candidate Eisenhower promised economy in government. to concentrate on bringing the stalemated and increasingly unpopular Korean War to an end, and to make a personal trip to Korea to learn how best to serve American interests. At the time the United States was electing a new president, the successful detonation of a thermonuclear test device in Operation IVY on 1 November 1952 promised an almost incalculable increase in strategic bombing power. In mid–1953, the size of the nuclear stockpile reached 1,000 warheads. During the spring of 1953, the Eisenhower administration was able secretly to threaten to use atomic weapons if the United Nations did not soon get an honorable military armistice in Korea. The armistice came on 27 July 1953, and Secretary of State John Foster Dulles offered a cogent reason why the Communists agreed to the armistice: "The fighting was stopped on honorable terms because the aggressor, already thrown back to and behind his place of beginning, was faced with the possibility that the fighting might, to his own great peril, soon spread beyond the limits and methods he had selected."[41]

As soon as the Korean conflict was ending, the Eisenhower administration abandoned the crisis year 1954 planning concept and reduced planned defense funding to a long haul into the future. The goal of the Air Force was trimmed from 143 to 137 wings, which parenthetically it reached for one brief moment thanks to some programming legerdemain in mid–1956, only to find that it could not program support for a force of this size. Eisenhower named a new slate of Joint Chiefs of Staff headed by Admiral Arthur W. Radford and requested a fresh view of the defense budget. In statements during 1953, Eisenhower referred to the need for the services to integrate new weapons more effectively into their planning. A new basic national security policy was drafted in NSC 162/2, and reportedly, at the suggestion of Admiral Radford, the new JCS proved willing to accept budget cuts and force reductions provided they could be assured of being able to use nuclear weapons across a wide range of possible military conflicts. On 9 December Admiral Radford gave Secretary of Defense Charles Wilson a memorandum containing the JCS views on an appropriate military strategy to implement NSC 162/2. The JCS stated that emphasis should be placed "upon the capability of inflicting massive damage upon the USSR by our retaliatory striking power as the major deterrent to aggression, and a vital element of any U.S. strategy in the event of general war." They also recommended "the provision of tactical atomic weapons for U.S. or allied military forces in general war or in a local aggression whenever employment of atomic weapons would be militarily advantageous."[42]

At Supreme Headquarters Allied Powers Europe (SHAPE), it became evident in 1963–1964 that the NATO allies were not going to meet the Lisbon goals of ninety-six divisions, and it appeared possible that the allied structure could crumble before it was built. In a new assessment of defense requirements stated in Military Committee document MC 14/2, the NATO Council in December 1954 resolved that member nations would plan to use nuclear weapons from the outset of a war, and that this decision to stockpile nuclear warheads readily available in time of need would permit a reduction in the size of the ground forces previously considered necessary. Under this statement of NATO strategy, the forward defense forces would constitute a shield or a trip wire while atomic strikes flown by theater aircraft, the Strategic Air Command, the United Kingdom Bomber Command, and American naval forces would provide the sword. U.S. strategic forces were targeted for a Romeo (retardation), Bravo (blunting), and Delta (destruction) mission in the event of aggression in Europe. In order to have the mass necessary to penetrate hostile defenses with high assurance of necessary survival, the United States required something on the order of 1,000 nuclear delivery aircraft (land-based and sea-based).[43]

Most assessments of the New Look and massive retaliation have been blurred by the rhetoric often employed by Secretary Dulles and Admiral Radford, not to mention Secretary Wilson's "more bang for a buck." On the other hand, General Andrew J. Goodpaster, writing on the basis of six and one-half years in the White House as staff assistant to President Eisenhower and a later tour as Supreme Allied Commander in Europe, has set forth some better judgmental standards to evaluate both the Eisenhower defense policy and indeed any military policy—this by pointing to the importance of military power in terms of defense, deterrence, or detente. Defense equals employment of armed forces in combat operations or the preparation of such forces. Deterrence is the persuasion of an adversary not to use or threaten to use force. Detente is aimed at the values of arms for reducing tension between adversaries.[44]

As it happened, General Goodpaster also set down the contemporary memorandum record of President Eisenhower's high level conference of 22 December 1954. At this meeting, Eisenhower pointed out that the two categories of military force that he was emphasizing—forces for retaliation and continental defense—would not be sufficient to give the United States a war winning capability if deterrence failed and a major war broke out. Because assessments of Soviet atomic capability suggested that the United States could "be knocked out within the first thirty days of combat," the major mission of American forces at a war's beginning would be "to blunt the enemy's initial threat—by massive retaliatory power and ability to deliver it, and by a continental defense system of major capability." The New Look would provide the forces for what Eisenhower called the aversion of disaster phase. A war's second phases would be when we would go on to win, clearing sea lanes and assembling ships, men, and equipment for a World War II-type war. Eisenhower believed that the New Look would deter the Soviets and since lowered defense spending was of utmost importance, the New Look's admitted operational shortcomings were an acceptable risk.[45]

The years of the New Look were heady years for the U.S. Air Force and its essentially simplistic concept of air power as massive strategic bombing. At the National Press Club on 29 November 1957, Air Force Chief of Staff General Thomas D. White declared that the U.S. Air Force was "synonymous with airpower." Air doctrine called for machines that would fly higher, faster, farther. According to open sources, the U.S. nuclear stockpile swelled from

1,750 weapons in 1954 to 26,500 in 1962 (and would peak at 32,000 in 1967), the greatest increase between 1955 and 1965, when almost 30,000 weapons were added, more than 11,000 between 1958 and 1960 alone. Air Force wing strength peaked at 137 wings in mid–1956 and then had to be reduced, mostly in tactical fighter wings to meet financial constraints. In the several years after 1956 the 11–wing B–52 force expanded to 14 wings, with a compensatory reduction of shorter range B–47s. By all military standards the Strategic Air Command under General LeMay stood at a state of readiness, discipline, and efficiency seldom before known in world history. It was LeMay's intention in the event of war with the Soviet Union to deliver the Air Force's nuclear allocation in one cataclysmic salvo, blasting Romeo, Bravo, and Delta targets not progressively but in one supreme effort. The development of strategic striking power was accompanied by a denigration of tactical air forces and air mobility forces. It was said that the USAF Tactical Air Command got SACercized. In a me-too activity in mid–1955, TAC developed a nuclear CASF, a composite air strike force with a mission of readiness to deploy to any world trouble spot. TAC's new F–105 Thunderchief tactical fighter was built to drop nuclear bombs; it was completely unsuited to air combat, but the going belief asserted that air superiority and the destruction of an enemy air force would be accomplished by nuclear strikes on hostile airfields. Under extreme financial pressure in 1957, a cold war conference of senior Air Force commanders agreed that the Air Force should cross the nuclear Rubicon: it should measure its high-explosive ordnance capability and retain it, should not increase it, and should eliminate it when national policy permitted. Sometime in the mid–1950s, General Theodore R. Milton was one of a small group who reviewed a movie produced for SAC for the edification of civic groups. The movie, Milton recalled, showed "in a wonderfully simplistic way, how a bomber or two made superfluous all the other excessive paraphernalia of war: the troops, the ships, the fighter planes, were all neatly crossed out. The strategic bomber, majestic and unopposed, would take care of things." Again in 1957, General LeMay conceived that the U.S. Army ought to provide its own organized firepower support within a combat zone and that the Strategic Air Command and Tactical Air Command should be reorganized into one "Air Offensive Command" under a single commander. Given a combination of SAC and TAC, LeMay thought that the Air Force could more logically "take a united stand in pursuit of its ultimate objective of achieving unified control of all air offensive forces, regardless of service, under a single air commander."[46]

As long as there was an asymmetrical technological imbalance on the part of the Soviet Union, the New Look's emphasis on nuclear air power as a deterrent force was viable, but what American technology gave, Soviet technology eroded. One factor overlooked in airpower thought, moreover, was that aerial technology and weapons effects do not necessarily provide overweening utility in a war if one follows the premise of Air Marshal Slessor that to win a war means to create "world conditions more favorable for oneself than would have been possible if there had not been a war."[47] In an article published in September 1957, Secretary Dulles waffled on massive retaliation in favor of mobile tactical nuclear weapons around the Soviet perimeter to give an effective defense against full-scale conventional attack. The greatest shock came in October 1957, when the Soviet Sputnik portended a possible intercontinental ballistic missile knight's gambit. Here the explosion of the ten-megaton hydrogen thermonuclear device in Operation IVY had opened for the United States the avenue for development of still not too accurate ICBMs since a small multimegaton warhead—even with a circular error probable (CEP) of five miles—would be an effective blow to urban-industrial targets. The Soviets seized the same opportunity. In response to this technological challenge, President Eisenhower, in September 1955, accorded the highest national priority to the USAF's ATLAS ICBM program, this without—as Colin Gray points out—an exact rationalization of the strategic significance of such an intercontinental ballistic missile. The growing reluctance to depend on actual usage of nuclear weapons was evidenced in the Lebanon-Taiwan Straits Crisis in 1958. In the Taiwan area, the contingency war plan called for use of nuclear bombs against Chinese Communist airfields in Fukien Province in case Taiwan was invaded. But as U.S. forces were gathering toward Taiwan, President Eisenhower doubtlessly noted a Soviet threat; a nuclear strike against China would be the same as an attack on Russia. In any event, Eisenhower directed that nuclear weapons would not be used at the outset of a Chinese Communist attack.[48]

At the height of the U.S. presidential campaign in 1960, John F. Kennedy found time to review Liddell Hart's *Deterrent of Defense* and to agree with its grand theme that "the West must be prepared to face down Communist aggression, short of nuclear war, by conventional forces." "The notion that the Free World can be protected simply by the threat of 'massive retaliation,' " Kennedy added, "is no longer tenable." In office as President, Kennedy directed that he have choices between holocaust and humiliation.[49] Following a visit to Omaha for a SAC strike plan briefing, the new Secretary of Defense Robert S. McNamara would explain that in the early 1960s he already believed—using italics for emphasis—that *"nuclear weapons serve no military purpose whatsoever. They are totally useless—except only to deter one's opponent from using them."*[50] The Kennedy administration gave emphasis to a buildup of general purpose forces as well as missile forces, the latter increase—according to McNamara later on—being rather more than was needed because of a lack of more accurate information about Soviet missiles. The test of the Kennedy defense strategy came in the Cuban missile crisis of October 1962, when the United States was able to flex far superior strategic power over the Soviets and was also able to ready general purpose invasion forces in Florida for movement to Cuba. To General LeMay the Cuban crisis was an outstanding example where superior strategic power, coupled with a manifest willingness to employ it, was decisive. "Certainly. . ., " LeMay explained, "we had the conventional forces to go in and take care of the missiles in Cuba or any other conventional Russian forces that were there. Our strategic superiority gave us the option of whether we would go or not. The choice was made that it was not necessary to go because the Russians removed the missiles."[51] But Secretary McNamara thought differently, pointing out that "perhaps more significantly, the forces that were the cutting edge of the action were the nonnuclear ones. Nuclear force was not irrelevant but it was in the background. Nonnuclear forces were our sword, our nuclear forces were our shield."[52] General LeMay's influence and the old ideas about air power would continue to be felt in the Air Force for a couple or more years, but the insistence on the transcendent decisiveness and utility of strategic bombing mellowed rapidly. In 1965 Secretary of the Air Force Eugene M. Zuckert described a new climate of thought where Air Force leaders were willing to abandon their old disbelief that "there was any war which couldn't be won by air power alone," but they still rightly knew that air power was "the supreme deterrent to general war" and "that there was no war which could be won *without* air power."[53]

It is very easy in an all-knowing present to be clever about the historical past. What I have said here reflects a new environment of interservice cooperation forced in no small part by the strategic necessity of raising the nuclear threshold while simultaneously coping with the military power of the Soviet Union. The major thrust of renewed interest in the tactical air force reflects the cogent work of the TAC-TRADOC (U.S. Army Training and Doctrine Command) connection in renovation of air-land battle as well as the USAF maritime operational cooperation now being undertaken with U.S. Navy forces. But even though it may be unsporting to scoff at the past, it goes without saying that the historical 1940s and 1950s laid the groundwork for the 1960s and thereafter. Thus if this survey of air planning is to be more than mere buff-stuff, some observations drawn from the past yet possibly of ongoing pertinence deserve mention, as much to get thought as anything else.

Air Force planning in 1945–1962 was partly produced and partly drawn from national military planning. The plans of the era were not based upon the whole aspect of war as an institution that comes in many different characterizations. The emphasis of air planners was in making war fit a weapon—nuclear air power—rather than making the weapon fit a war. Theirs was a weapons strategy wherein the weapons determined the strategy rather than strategy determining the weapons. The pertinent observation here is that sound military planning must be based on a study and appreciation of war in its broadest aspects, not only in modern times but throughout history.

We know that all plans are inevitably based upon assumptions, either stated or implicit. In 1945–1962 air planning notably failed to make correct assumptions. One fatal assumption was that a President was going to authorize use of nuclear weapons for anything but deterrence. Here planners would have done well to have recognized that the use of nuclear bombs would have been a political rather than a purely military decision, and sound planning should have developed alternate strategic hedges against the possibility that nuclear escalation might prove politically unacceptable. Air planners also incorrectly assumed that all wars would be metropolitan wars against highly integrated societies built around vital centers; that the United States would have a long-lasting atomic monopoly; and that the United States would have a long-time superiority in technology. Too little thought was given to the fact that strategy can outwit technology; note the guerrilla who cautiously refuses to provide aiming points for advanced firepower. One may also speculate that for technology to be decisively decisive, it must be vastly superior, possibly on the order of western gunboats versus aboriginals in colonial times.

Air Force planners did not grasp distinctions between the defense, deterrent, let alone detente usages of military power. Air planners rationalized that the deterrent capabilites of strategic bombing would be readily convertible into war-fighting defense capabilities, which was not proven. Despite Air Force contentions it was untrue that forces for large wars could win small wars.

A final observation returns to my initial assertion that Air Force planners failed to appreciate the need to develop and apply air power in a synergy of military power. Flexibility has long been cited as a desirable characteristic of air power, yet the lone wolf strategic bombing Air Force of the 1950s was anything but flexible. It is true that extreme flexibility can equal dissipation of what will always be essentially scarce and always expensive aerospace resources. It is also true—to paraphrase old War Department Field Manual 100–20— that land power, air power, and sea power are equal and interdependent forces, and in unity there is a strength not found separately in land, sea, or air forces.

Notes

1. Lieutenant Colonel Wm. Mitchell, "General Principles Underlying the Use of the Air Service of the Zone of the Advance A.E.F.," *Bulletin of the Information Section AEF*, vol 3, no 132, 10 Apr 1918. Robert Frank Futrell, *Ideas, Concepts, Doctrine: A History of Basic Thinking in the United States Air Force, 1907–1964* (Maxwell AFB, Ala., 1974), p 12.

2. Alfred F. Hurley, *Billy Mitchell, Crusader for Air Power* (Bloomington, Ind., 1974), p 75 and *passim*.

3. Hearings before the Committee on Military Affairs, House of Representatives, *Department of Defense and Unification of Air Service*, 69th Cong, 1st sess (Washington, 1926), pp 397–98; Futrell, pp 28, 30.

4. Robert T. Finney, *History of the Air Corps Tactical School* (Maxwell AFB, Ala., 1955), *passim*.

5. Richard H. Kohn and Joseph P. Harahan, eds., *Air Superiority in World War II and Korea, An Interview with Gen. James Ferguson, Gen. Robert M. Lee, Gen. William Momyer, and Lt. Gen. Elwood R. Quesada* (Washington, 1983), p 18.

6. James C. Gaston, *Planning the American Air War: Four Men and Nine Days in 1941, An Inside Narrative* (Washington, 1982), *passim*.

7. Kent Roberts Greenfield, *American Strategy in World War II, A Reconsideration* (Westport, Conn., 1979), p 86. Futrell, p 62. Haywood S. Hansell, Jr., *The Air Plan that Defeated Hitler* (Atlanta, 1972), *passim*.

8. W. D. Field Manual 100–20, *Command and Employment of Air Power* (Washington, 1944), p 1. This manual is reproduced as appendix in Kohn and Harahan, *Air Superiority*.

9. Walter Bedell Smith, *Eisenhower's Six Great Decisions: Europe 1944–45* (New York, 1956), p 144.

10. William Geffen, ed., *Command and Commanders in Modern Warfare, The Proceedings of the Second Military History Symposium, U.S. Air Force Academy* (Washington, 1971), pp 282–83.

11. Hearings before the Committee on Military Affairs, U.S. Senate, *Department of Armed Forces, Department of Military Security*, 79th Cong, 1st sess (Washington, 1945), p 360.

12. This conclusion is well stated by the late great U.S. Army historian, Kent Roberts Greenfield, *American Strategy in World War II*, p 86.

13. "A Mahan of the Air," Letter to the Editor from Follett Bradley, Great Neck, N.Y., 1 Apr 1944, in *The New York Times*, 9 Apr 1944.

14. Hearings before the Subcommittee of the Committee on Appropriations, House of Representatives, *Military Establishment Appropriation Bill for 1948*, 80th Cong, 1st sess (Washington, 1947), p 619.

15. Memo for CS Army from Major General Thomas T. Handy, Asst CS Operations Division, subj: Outline of Post-War Permanent Military Establishment, 28 Oct 1943; marginal comments by G. C. M. See also the definitive history on the organization of the postwar Air Force, Herman S. Wolk, *Planning and Organizing the Postwar Air Force, 1943–1947* (Washington, 1984).

16. Futrell, pp 102–03. Perry McCoy Smith, *The Air Force Plans for Peace* (Baltimore, 1970), pp 73–74.

17. Futrell, p 104.

18. *Ibid*, p 90.

19. Interview with Spaatz by Brigadier General Noel Parrish and Alfred Goldberg, 21 Feb 1962.

20. Futrell, pp 101–02.

21. *Military Establishment Appropriation Bill for 1948*, p 600.

22. Harry R. Borowski, *A Hollow Threat: Strategic Air Power and Containment before Korea* (Westport, Conn., 1982). This book provides an excellent summary of the state of Air Force deterrence posture at the cold war's beginning. For once highly classified data on the U.S. nuclear warhead stockpile year by year see Thomas B. Cochran, William M. Arkin, and Milton M. Hoening, *Nuclear Weapons Databook*, vol I: *U.S. Nuclear Forces and Capabilities* (Cambridge, Mass., 1984), pp 14–15. See also David MacIsaac, *The Air Force and Strategic Thought, 1945–1951*, The Wilson Center Security Studies Program Working Paper, No 8, 1979.

23. Robert D. Little, *Organizing for Strategic Planning, 1945–1950: The National System and the Air Force* (Washington, 1964); Thomas H. Etzold and John Lewis Gaddis, *Containment: Documents on American Policy and Strategy, 1945–1950* (New York, 1978). Futrell, p 122.

24. Futrell, pp 123–24.

25. Borowski, pp 135–49.

26. Futrell, p 125.

27. *Ibid*, p 125.

28. Kohn and Harahan, p 63.

29. Futrell, p 127.

30. Robert H. Ferrell, ed., *The Eisenhower Diaries* (New York, 1981), pp 156–57.

31. Hearings before the Committee on Foreign Affairs, House of Representatives, *Mutual Defense Assistance Act of 1949*, 81st Cong, 1st sess (Washington, 1949), pp 69–72.

32. Futrell, pp 129–30.

33. Report of the Committee on Armed Services, House of Representatives, *Investigation of the B–36 Bomber Program*, 81st Cong, 2nd sess (Washington, 1950), pp 33; A Report of Investigation by the Committee on Armed Services, House of Representatives, *Unification and Strategy*, 81st Cong, 2nd sess (Washington, 1950), pp 33, 53–56.

34. Little, p 76.

35. Major General J. A. Samford, "Identification of Strategic Concepts," Lecture, Air War College, Maxwell Air Force Base, 21 May 1951.

36. See NSC–68, in Etzold and Gaddis, pp 382–442. Futrell, pp 144–45.

37. Futrell, pp 145–53.

38. *Ibid*, pp 160–67.

39. *Ibid*, pp 174, 215; M. J. Armitage and R. A. Mason, *Air Power in the Nuclear Age* (Urbana, Ill., 1983), pp 184–91.

40. Ferrell, pp 209–13.

41. Futrell, pp 176–77. In an interview on 18 September 1966, Eisenhower disclosed that he would use whatever was necessary, not excluding nuclear weapons, to end the fighting in Southeast Asia. Congressional Quarterly Service, CQ Background, *China and U.S. Far East Policy, 1945–1967* (Washington, 1967), pp 198–200.

42. Samuel F. Wells, Jr., "The Origins of Massive Retaliation," *Political Science Quarterly*, Spring 1981, pp 31–52.

43. Armitage and Mason, pp 188–91; Futrell, p 215.

44. General Andrew J. Goodpaster, *For the Common Defense* (Lexington, Mass., 1977), pp 53, 102–03.

45. A. J. Goodpaster, "Memorandum of Conference with the President," 22 Dec 1954, cited in Wells, p 39.

46. Futrell, pp 215–27; Alfred F. Hurley and Robert C. Ehrhart, eds., *Air Power and Warfare*, The Proceedings of the 8th Military History Symposium, USAF Academy (Washington, 1979), p 301.

47. Sir John C. Slessor, "Has the H-Bomb Abolished Total War?" *Air Force*, May 1954, pp 24–26, 48.

48. Colin S. Gray, *Strategic Studies and Public Policy, The American Experience* (Lexington, Ky., 1982), pp 43–44. Futrell, pp 304–09.

49. John F. Kennedy, "Book in the News, B. H. Liddell Hart, *Deterrent or Defense,*" *Saturday Review,* 3 Sep 1960, p 17.

50. Robert S. McNamara, "The Military Role of Nuclear Weapons, Perception and Misperceptions," *Foreign Affairs,* Fall 1983, pp 79–80.

51. Hearings before a Subcommittee of the Committee on Appropriations, House of Representatives, *Department of Defense Appropriations for 1964,* 88th Cong, 1st sess (Washington, 1963), pt 2, p 503.

52. Futrell, pp 358–60.

53. Eugene M. Zuckert, "Some Reflections on the Military Profession," *Air University Review,* Nov-Dec 1965, p 4.

The Navy and National Security Policy in the 1970s

Thomas H. Etzold
Arms Control and Disarmament Agency

Then Arthur learned, as all leaders
are astonished to learn, that
peace, not war, is the destroyer
of men; tranquillity rather than
danger is the mother of cowardice;
and not need but plenty brings
apprehension and unease.

Le Morte d'Arthur

For any military organization, the challenges of peacetime are as strenuous as those of war, and often as consequential. To be sure, those challenges take on different form in peace, and sometimes, therefore, remain unperceived and unmet. War asks manifestly for great deeds; peace, less evidently, calls for great thoughts. War places a premium on decision and action; peace permits the posing of more fundamental questions and, more troubling still, admits the possibility of doubt, disagreement, discussion, and delay.

As the U.S. Navy finally discovered in the 1970s, peace transforms fighting organizations into bureaucracies. "A peacetime navy. . .is moored to civilian life. Doctrine, precedent, routine, and habit take hold. Money is scarce and cruising is costly. The Navy may contend with a hypothetical enemy in annual maneuvers, but its most pressing engagement is the battle of the budget. To get its share it must deal effectively with other elements of government and with influential public groups through the political process. The more it engages itself, the more it is bound by other institutions."[1] The habits of mind and the patterns of behavior appropriate to the conditions of war become ineffectual in less exigent circumstances. The result may be lack of preparedness for peace and its ventures, a weakness seldom appreciated to the same extent as unpreparedness for war.

In addition to those ailments common to all navies in peacetime, the U.S. Navy in the 1970s suffered from a more exclusive malady: prolonged success. It had, after all, been the fortunate possessor of a popular and persuasive ideology, the bearer of wartime glories, the custodian of long-lived assets remaining at war's end. Unfortunately, ideology, glories, and assets all became less dependable underpinnings of the Navy in those years.

Thus, in the middle 1970s, the Navy became aggrieved and resentful at the raising of ordinary and legitimate peacetime questions about the Navy's purpose and utility. Former Secretary of Defense James Schlesinger used to say that "There are no embarrassing questions, only embarrassing answers." During 1970s debates over budget shares, national strategy, and mission allocation among the services, the Navy produced many such answers, evident when on several occasions the Secretary of Defense and the Chief of Naval Operations published planning guidance that in some ways conflicted, and when the President vetoed a large defense authorization, principally to avoid building a nuclear carrier much wanted by many uniformed Navy leaders.

In the late 1960s and early 1970s, the Navy had difficulty conceptualizing the value of naval forces in terms that carried conviction within the national security community. In a related development, naval strategic thought for a time focused primarily on technical, logistical, and tactical problems, with far too little attention to the political context that makes strategic thought meaningful and purposeful. Naval strategic thinking revolved around fantasies of nuclear war at sea, or proxy war at sea, or still other scenarios built without regard to practical political experience or sensibility. Naval strategy seemed, at least for a while, mainly a function of the momentum of force structure and modernization, so that the strongest arguments for new ships seemed to be that the old ships were old, due to retire.

Thus, by mid-decade, the U.S. Navy faced a peacetime challenge of considerable dimension. Administration guidance on strategy and programming seemed to be forcing the Navy in directions other than those preferred by naval leaders. The Navy and others in the national security community disagreed on assumptions about current political structure, trends in international relations of import for political-military planning, and consequently the basis for threat analysis. These disagreements became most acute at a time when the Navy's ideology of sea power—once potent—had become platitudinous, if not irrelevant. Unprepared for the impertinence of peacetime debate, the Navy approached its peacetime challenges in part with inappropriate methods of argument. Each of these subjects— diverging Navy/national security community assumptions, the ideology of sea power, and Navy methods of argument—deserves careful discussion.

One principle reason for the Navy's mid–1970s difficulty in defending its strategic ideas and force planning was a divergence between the political-military assumptions of Navy leaders and those of others in the national security community—that ill-defined cluster of National Security Council (NSC), White House, Defense, State, and congressional staffers, and academic hangers-on. Several such disagreements became obvious in written and spoken exchanges of views. Many more, however, remained obscure even to those people tangled in disagreement. It is useful to identify those points more precisely, more to identify areas of disagreement than to determine who, or what, is right. On this premise, the essay presents individual points in contention with deliberate brevity, in which some oversimplification is unavoidable.

Through the later 1960s and early 1970s, the Navy and others in the national security community disagreed on the general slope of the trends in international affairs—whether, in aggregate, world affairs were developing favorably or unfavorably for American interests and values. Assumptions as fundamental as these rarely reach articulation in policy and strategy discussions, which is unfortunate. For the conviction that the environment will permit one to prosper—or conversely, foreclose that possibility—shapes other assumptions and decisions probably more than any other single factor of psychology.

There was in the 1970s widespread agreement that the international environment was tending toward political pluralism and economic diversity, with the number of important power wielders increasing, and the ability of great powers to exert influence beyond their borders decreasing. There was less agreement on whether these and associated trends were promising or threatening. Though demanding, complex, and perhaps even chaotic, in the Carter administration's view, such a world was wholesome from the standpoint of American institutions. This view was related to that expressed some thirty years ago by George F. Kennan, then head of the Policy Planning Staff in the Department of State. American foreign policy and domestic institutions, he believed, had been founded on the confidence that the United States and the American people could thrive in a diverse, pluralistic world. This characteristic in fact distinguished the United States from its ideological adversaries, especially the Soviet Union. Unlike the Communist governments of the world, the United States did not need to control everything of import or interest to it. Instead, the United States needed leaders wise enough to define and refine ideas of American national interest in consonance with evolving international conditions and the legitimate aspirations or need of other states.

In contrast, Navy leaders saw a menacing world marked by adverse tends, especially in basic power relationships and in American economic dependence, or, somewhat less pejoratively, interdependence.

The Navy and others in the national security community disagreed on the extent to which American national interests might be susceptible to, and in need of, redefinition. Community policy analysts believed that a number of international and domestic factors either permitted or required the United States to conceive its interests in less sweeping and less burdensome terms in coming years. In this regard, and against the preferences of a naval establishment still committed to a larger view of American national interest and a more traditional view of American commitments, the Carter administration developed strategy and guidance intended to realize lines of policy indicated, though unexecuted, in the Nixon years. The primary meaning of the Nixon Doctrine, for instance, was that the time had come to scale down American commitments so as to permit a reduction of force structure. The United States had become overextended materially in attempting to make containment an effectual, worldwide policy and strategy principally by material means: commitments, aid, deployments. When Nixon left office, American commitments were larger than American capabilities. There were two possible approaches to this problem. One was to increase force structure and thus capability. The other was to reduce commitments. The Carter administration chose to continue the downward revision of commitments, largely through the euphemism of prioritizing regions and contingencies. The naval establishment, and probably other military leaders, had hoped to spur the growth of force structure to meet commitments rather then the reduction of commitments to accord with capabilities.

The Navy and others in the national security community disagreed on the relative promise of diplomatic maneuver versus political-military coercion in attaining national objectives in coming years. In pursuing American national interests, the Carter administration apparently intended to rely more on diplomatic maneuver than on the threat or use of military force. In contrast, Navy leaders, when pressed, were likely to admit the conviction that, over the years, the gunboats have proven just as effective as diplomats, and often a good deal more effective.

The Carter administration believed, at least from all appearances, that it was at once less easy to get one's way by the resort to force externally and more difficult to support a resort to force domestically. In recent moments of political tension, some of the smallest and weakest countries in the world denied bunkering to warships of the United States, surely a sign of the times. Correspondingly, as in the cases of Vietnam and Angola, neither the American public nor its elected representatives in the middle and latter 1970s hesitated to end administration involvements in foreign military or clandestine operations. There was no difficulty in finding places where one could fight traditional enemies for important stakes. But it seemed more difficult than ever to find places where one could do so with reasonable confidence that results would be favorable, significant in terms of larger American interests, and likely to obtain the requisite support in Congress and from the public. Thus the interest of the Carter administration in retaining worldwide interventionary-coercive-power projection forces or capabilities reached its lowest point since the Korean War.

The Navy and others in the national security community disagreed on the extent to which American political-military problems grow out of differences with allies or differences with enemies. The Carter administration adopted the view that many American problems lay in relations with allies rather than with enemies. With allies, presumably, it was necessary to proceed by bargaining and maneuver rather than coercion—a view not always held by American leaders, to be sure.

The Navy, in contrast, continued to emphasize American problems with enemies, and to suppose that problems with allies were of a lesser order in proportion to overall national interest and national security calculations. Parenthetically, one must note that the Navy and others in the national security community disagreed not only on the proportion of problems as between friends and enemies but even on the extent to which real conflicts of interest, whether with friends or with enemies, might be resolvable by increases in coercive capacity. This reflected basic differences on ideas concerning the definition of power, in which the administration appeared to hold somewhat broader ideas than did the Navy about what power is and how to use it.

The Navy and others in the national security community disagreed about the desirability and likely consequences of general balance in the U.S.-Soviet strategic arms relationship. From the Carter administration's point of view, a strategic arms agreement was highly desirable even if it fell somewhat short of U.S. hopes and needs in certain technicalities. Carter administration policy reflected the assumption that advantages to be found in certain political factors in SALT might outweigh specific technical liabilities and even justify the taking of some risks. Even an imperfect SALT agreement, it was argued, would make deterrence more reliable and less vulnerable to erosion through developments in technology or force structure. A SALT agreement would widen the possibilities for a diplomacy of maneuver, which would be to American advantage in the long run for reasons alluded to above: the view that the United States was fundamentally more capable of thriving and operating effectively in such conditions and with such methods than was the Soviet Union.

Conversely, a strategic arms agreement that contained technical shortcomings or appeared to involve significant American concessions was unwelcome to Navy and other military leaders. They assumed that a flawed agreement would make deterrence less reliable. Further, they tended to believe that deterrence, even when it worked, led not to increased maneuver policy but to an increase in the use of limited war—in the little wars so much discussed by strategic theorists of the latter 1950s. In the view of many military leaders, either to maintain reliable deterrence or to cope with the lesser conflicts permitted in a deterrent framework would impose on the United States a requirement for increased military expenditures and a larger force structure, both strategic and conventional.

The Navy and others in the national security community disagreed in selecting the enemies against which to size and configure American naval forces. It was obvious to everyone that the most capable possible enemy of the United States was the Soviet Union. But the Carter administration stressed its convictions that maneuver and not coercion would likely predominate in relations with principal powers; that deterrence would be effective; that the Russians did not, and would not, consider war an attractive option; and that Russian and American interests converged rather than conflicted on a number of current and coming issues. All this made the prospect of Soviet-American war seem remote to administration analysts. Thus the consolidated defense guidance for fiscal 1980, issued early in 1978, emphasized that the Navy should concentrate on "localized contingencies outside Europe."[2]

In contrast, the Navy's leaders preferred to estimate requirements and develop strategy on the basis of scenarios involving sustained conventional war against the Soviet Union, fought on a global scale with multiple fronts. They insisted that a Navy able to handle the worst case could cope with anything else. Higher government echelons did not readily accept that argument. The Carter administration was thus unwilling to fund a shipbuilding program large enough to support the Navy's strategy—at least, until the invasion of Afghanistan and the 1980 election campaign.

The Navy and others in the national security community disagreed over the imminence of conflict. As mentioned, the Carter administration believed that conflict, especially with the Soviet Union, was by no means impending. In this regard, it is particularly important to understand the significance of the Carter administration's investment in pre-positioned military supplies in the NATO Central Region. This was not, as some might think, a quick fix undertaken in the expectation that confrontation and war were likely, or near, or otherwise to be expected. Instead, the administration's investment in the NATO Central Region has to be understood as part of its approach to problems with allies, especially the problem of alliance confidence in the United States during great change in the American global policies and posture. It was also related to the general American drive to motivate alliance members to higher contributions and more efficient efforts in alliance military planning and preparation. Finally, that investment reflected a determination, perhaps overdue, to repair the physical effects of neglect in Europe during the Vietnam War, as well as the deficiencies in equipment resulting from hasty American aid to Israel in 1973.

The Navy continued to discuss strategic and program planning reflecting a higher sense of urgency and of the likelihood of conflict than held by the administration, and the Navy justified these approaches in part on the basis of a misreading of the administration's activity in relation to the NATO Central Region.

The Navy and others in the national security community disagreed on priorities of various regions and contingencies both as bases for force planning and for war strategy. The Carter administration gave first priority to Europe, second to the Middle East, with the rest of the world ordered more by the pressures of the moment than by any other criterion. In the Navy's view, Northeast Asia deserved higher peacetime investment and wartime priority than it received; so also with the Mediterranean, the Persian Gulf, and certain sea lines of communication that Navy analysts considered indefensible with present and projected force levels. As noted above, it is important to remember that the Carter administration used regional and contingency priorities to some extent as a device for the continued reduction of American commitments.

These were associated, though distinct, arguments over two points: the number and nature of contingencies to use as the basis for estimating aggregate military requirements for the United States, and the question of whether, or how, to limit a possible war with the Soviet Union. The Carter administration decided that the Navy, at least, should concentrate on preparing principally for two of the smaller contingency cases commonly used in requirements estimating, and favored a much more circumscribed approach to early phases of any potential war with the Soviets than did the Navy leadership.

The Navy and others in the national security community disagreed on the likely duration and nature of a possible war in NATO's center. The Carter administration decided to anticipate, at least for a time, a war that was short, intense, and likely nuclear. The Navy believed it wiser to prepare for one that might be sustained and predominantly conventional. The administration postulated the short war in Central Europe as the principal planning case for the NATO area; correspondingly it emphasized the buildup of pre-positioned stocks for the land battle and invested in increasing the power of the army and tactical air forces. Navy leaders believed that reliance on the assumption of a short war foreclosed allied opportunities dependent on planning and preparing for more extended conflict.

As one might expect, the foregoing divergencies in assumptions left members of the national security community and the Navy thinking of one another in somewhat less than complimentary terms.

In the Navy's view, some members of the community underestimated the size of the threat, the potential imminence of serious military embroilment, the likely duration and scale of major conflict, and the magnitude of the Navy's possible contribution to deterring war or fighting under anticipated conditions. Further, Navy leaders considered the Carter administration view of potential military needs too inhibited geographically. In this they held an attitude akin to that of General Douglas MacArthur, who in the latter 1940s similarly attempted to convince his superiors to devote more resources to his Far East Command. "The problem," MacArthur wrote, "insofar as the United States is concerned is an overall one. . . . For if we embark upon a general policy to bulwark the frontier of freedom against the assaults of a political despotism, one major frontier is no less important than another, and a decisive breach of any will inevitably threaten to engulf all."[3]

In the view of others in the national security community, the Navy proved unresponsive to political guidance, overly fixated on the Soviet threat, unrealistic about the possibilities of sustained, conventional war without escalation to nuclear exchange, wedded to traditional force structure despite changing political and technical environments, and more concerned with organizational prerogatives than with military efficiency. Thus, in the middle and latter 1970s, the Navy and others in the national security community remained at an impasse, their assumptions unreconciled.

A second problem for the Navy in the mid–1970s debates over strategy, force structure, and budgets was its reliance on a theory of sea power that in some respects had become less effective than supposed. Time was when the doctrines of Alfred Thayer Mahan, aspirations for empire, and ebullient confidence epitomized in the mixture of ideas known as social Darwinism all spared the Navy any excessive effort in explaining its importance. In the 1970s, however, long-ignored flaws of theory, altered American self-images, changing views of national interest and international circumstance, and a transformed climate for naval warfare increased the Navy's burdens in this regard.

In certain respects, the classical theory of sea power, both in terms of its influence upon history and its prescriptions for naval warfare, had always been imprecise and time-bound. Trade did not usually follow the flag, for instance, as in the familiar formula. More often, things worked the other way around: the flag followed in the wake of intrepid individuals and confident companies. In all likelihood, there never had been a relation between economies of mother countries and those of colonies such as that postulated in classical economic and naval theory of the latter nineteenth century, as economic historians demonstrated after World War II. Of course, such theoretical misapprehensions and misstatements of theory correspond to, when they are not actually the product of, contemporary theories of national power.

No part of Mahan's theories was more time-bound than that dealing with naval warfare. It is something of an irony that, within a few years of Mahan's elaboration of the doctrines of offensive fleet action, technical developments should have invalidated that doctrine. In Mahan's day the great ships, the dreadnoughts and super dreadnoughts, were virtually invulnerable to smaller ships. But with the World War I submarine and the 1920s bomber came the fundamental technical revolution of modern naval warfare: Small platforms acquired the capability to engage and to destroy much larger ones. Later, this same revolution did away with the absolute need for naval platforms to destroy other naval forces. The technical basis for Mahanian tactics and, to a large extent, Mahanian strategy, crumbled, though for years the dimensions of this problem would go unrecognized, as in some respects they remain today.

In the 1970s, the self-images, power theories, and strategic outlooks that permitted some enduring flaws in naval thought altered. Several of the flaws uncovered in this process merit individual discussion because of their part in continuing debates on navies and national strategy.

In the 1970s, it became questionable whether Americans perceived more than an indirect and tenuous connection between the free use of the seas and the existence, size, or exact capabilities of the U.S. Navy. In earlier years, such a connection had been easier to credit. At the nation's birth, international piracy still posed a considerable hazard to ocean commerce. In the nation's earliest wars, and during those of the French Revolution and Napoleon, American ships and citizens had to admit the liabilities they faced in contesting the views of maritime law held by Great Britain and France. For many decades American trade, notably in the Far East, relied on gunboat diplomacy to maintain access to ports and trade, even though those gunboats more often belonged to one of the European powers than to the U.S. Navy. In the 1970s, of course, pirates and gunboat diplomacy of that old tradition were both gone, neither lamented.

In peace, Americans tended to view the free use of the seas as customary, not particularly dependent on the Navy. In war, they recognized—sometimes, to be sure, reluctantly—that at best the Navy would be able to use and protect only the major reinforcement and resupply routes to one or two theaters. In war against a formidable adversary, there would be no approximation of peacetime maritime traffic. In either case, the connection between the navy and the nation's use of the sea was somewhat other than the ideal enshrined in Mahanian slogans out of the last century.

Americans in the 1970s did not consider insularity a compelling determinant of U.S. strategic requirements or an apt description of

American circumstances. Of all the traditional ideas prominent in current naval discussions, that of insularity was one of the most misleading. Navy enthusiasts consistently underestimated the need to rethink the strategic meaning of insularity in a time of great political and technical change.

Traditionally, the idea of insularity referred to three related, though distinct, points concerning strategy and navies. The first and most encompassing of these ideas of insularity was the thought that American national development and in particular the sources of American national power and potential, could resemble those of Great Britain. Such an idea was well and good in an age of unabashed imperialism. It is important, in fact, to remember that for Mahan and his contemporaries there was no embarrassment, no shame, in straightforward advocacy of imperial conquest and exploitation of less advanced regions and societies. This idea of Britain as a model was also more popular, and thus more potent, before modern British development had reached a stage of post-industrial prostration. It was easier to credit the model of imperial and colonial success when Americans still believed almost without reservation in the superiority and exportability of western democratic political ideas and institutions. Mahan and others probably were careless in exaggerating the extent to which other states could imitate the British formula for national greatness. Certainly the admirers of Mahan and other propagandists of new navalism at the turn of the century overstated the extent to which the United States *should* emulate the island empire, a model that in the last two decades has dismayed rather than encouraged American observers.

Secondly, as a corollary of the idea of Great Britain as a model, the idea of insularity suggested that, because of small territory and resource bases, a state of certain characteristics can find power and greatness only in reliance on the sea. This idea readily coupled itself to two other vigorous ideas in the late nineteenth and early twentieth century American milieu: the twin drives for territorial and commercial expansion, the latter in part a dynamic of the early industrialization of both Britain and the United States.

It is evident, of course, that in several important features the foregoing image was distorted. The United States never possessed so small a territory or resource potential as to make comparison with England apt. By the turn of the century, its population (to mention still another point of comparison) outnumbered that of England and Wales by two to one, a proportion that steadily increased in favor of the United States. By the turn of the century, the United States had become a real, though still inactive, land power. As such, it had at best a marginal need for distant and diminutive colonies, as many critics of American imperialism perceived at the time of the Spanish-American War. Economic arguments concerning the need of industrial economies for foreign markets then as now are in part specious, based on fallacious assumptions about the saturation of domestic markets in these industrial states. Those arguments relied as well on faulty econometric analysis of the supposed profits of the imperial-colonial extractive process, work now discredited for some twenty years.[4]

In all, it was an error to think that, like England, the United States lacked an adequate national power base, needed colonial markets, and therefore depended on the sea to export administrative and commercial acumen and finished products, and then to import raw materials. It was at best a partial explanation of a much different aggregate economic and political reality. But that idea remained the heart of familiar 1970s refrains concerning America's dependence on lifelines, vital sea lines of communication, arteries of American commerce, highways to markets, routes of supply and of access to esssential—or better yet, strategic—resources.[5] There was enough truth in the idea to make it durable and appealing. But, as just argued, there was enough untruth to make it a faulty and unconvincing basis for describing the United States as an insular nation.

Thirdly, insularity has connoted isolation, a connotation both geographical and political. Several generations ago, it was still possible to conceive of the oceans as barriers, natural defenses against distant adversaries. In that context it used to make sense to think of the Navy as the first line of defense. After World War II, however, advancing technology and the increasing strategic reach of potential adversaries such as the Soviet Union progressively eroded America's natural defenses. Indeed, the military operations of that war foreshadowed an end to America's geographical invulnerability. In the primary strategic revolution of the cold war, the United States became vulnerable to direct attack. This fact permanently altered the significance of any concept of geographical insularity, as well as of associated concepts of naval strategy.

The political element of insularity as isolation also owned a significant strategic dimension, perhaps best summarized in the classical axiom that an insular power with a navy could "take as much or as little of a war as it will." This traditionally was touted as a chief ingredient of modern British statecraft.

But, in contrast to traditional British politics, the United States after World War II acquired peacetime military commitments to more than forty nations (the number has fluctuated with political tides), most of them quite distant from its borders. Theoretically, the United States retained that much-prized commodity, freedom of action; no one could compel the United States to fulfill its obligations. In fact, however, in acquiring its many commitments, the United States surrendered the classical strategic advantage of geographical isolation for the sake of rendering calculable the reactions and relations, under certain circumstances, of a number of the world's other states. Further, as Steven T. Ross has observed, Great Britain in its splendid isolation was only twenty miles from the French coast. "When England wished to conclude alliances, she could still keep her army at home in time of peace. Proximity reassured actual or potential friends. Obviously the United States is a long way from Europe, and Europeans are aware of America's isolationist past. America needs allies to preserve the status quo but must reassure and sustain them with real and effective military presence."[6] All this is to say nothing about the comparative logistic burdens of war some twenty miles distant by sea and war some eight thousand miles removed.

In sum, the idea of insularity always applied to the United States less than assumed in classical naval theory. In the 1970s, it became manifestly inappropriate, and as employed in arguments about the dependence of the United States on ocean lifelines to vital sources of supply, and on the Navy to defend those lifelines, the idea seemed inverted, if not perverted. For in classical naval theory, insular and coastal states of certain characteristics went to sea to augment meager power bases. Overseas connections were to become sources of strength and to increase national power, not to become strategic vulnerabilities or long-term liabilities on the national power and resources on the home country. In the 1970s, it was a near thing to judge whether American reliance on the sea constituted a strength or a weakness. Certainly it did not in itself connote insularity.

Through the 1970s, the environment for naval warfare contin ued to change in ways that undercut the usefulness of classical dicta concerning the uses of navies and the operations of naval forces in war. The usability of naval forces in contemporary political and technical circumstances became more doubtful as to result and more complicated as to practice. The ability of small platforms to destroy large ones was the underlying dynamic in at least two important trends. One was the trend towards increasing outreach of land powers into ocean areas and, in particular, the ability of land-based systems to engage sea-based systems at considerable distances from shore. Sea forces in the 1970s no longer benefited to the same extent as formerly from their traditional advantages of mobility, concealment, surprise, mass, and initiative in engagements against foes restricted to the land. A second trend of note, reflecting the same basic issue, was the decreasing usability of conventional power projection forces in areas of high intensity threat or against enemies armed with modern combat aircraft, antiair weapons, and cruise missiles.

The larger implications of these trends, or tendencies, deserved in the 1970s and demand now both clear recognition and sober reflection. Most important, perhaps, the trends mentioned have gradually forced more and more constricted definitions of naval missions, especially those of sea control. Mahan held an idea of command of the sea that was virtually unlimited, in which by definition the possessor or winner of command of the sea needed fear no strategically significant uses of the sea by adversaries. Sir Julian Corbett, more cautious and systematic, prepared the way for the more restrained understanding that command of the sea might be limited in time and space, though still strategically significant. Corbett's latterday successors, Admiral Stansfield Turner and Admiral James L. Holloway, III, redefined the idea of command of the sea to its present doctrinal status as "sea control. . .the capability to use selectively those portions of the seas essential to U.S. interests."[7] In the 1970s, the definition of this classical idea became so restrictive that some naval authorities considered it inhibiting, an actual liability in carrying forward debates about the possible uses, and therefore requirements, of the Navy.

It is also important to note that changing political circumstances seemed to many individuals in the 1970s to be producing relatively novel tasks for naval forces, with the potential to alter traditional understandings of the uses of navies and therefore of force structure and requirements. Protection of offshore facilities and resource claims became an issue as did the maintenance of rights of passage through straits and other confined sea areas. There was a widespread tendency inside the Carter administration as well as outside it to think that in these changing circumstances sea power was less and less separable from land power—that, in fact, certain types of land-based power might be partially interchangeable with sea forces.

For strategic analysis, deficiencies of naval theory in a way can be more serious than deficiencies of force structure. For without an adequate theory of sea power and the use of the sea with prevailing concepts of national power and international circumstances, it is impossible to perceive accurately the real correlation of world forces. Without integrated and usable theories of naval and national power, one can never know accurately his own strengths and weaknesses or those of his allies and adversaries. This is an essential element of judgment in national security affairs. Henry Kissinger, for one, stressed the high test of statesmanship involved in being able both to "recognize the real relationship of forces and to make that knowledge serve (one's) ends."[8] The inability to understand sea power in this precise sense was Napoleon's underlying weakness as a strategist. His inability to grasp the fundamentals of the theory of sea power in his day consistently doomed him to miscalculate Great Britain's ability to oppose his own great power.

In this same sense, the Navy in the 1970s needed to reconsider—and to refine—its classical theory of sea power. The questions that national security managers asked, and to which Navy leaders had to respond, could not be answered without a surer grasp of fundamentals. There was a natural desire to fix such problems in time for the next iteration of the budgeting and programming cycle. But a theory in shreds could not be so easily or rapidly rewoven.

In addition to assumptions divergent from those of others in the national security community and a dated theory of sea power, a third problem attenuated Navy ability to hold its own in national security debates of the early and middle 1970s: misapplied methods of analysis and argument. As most people know, it is possible to be right and still to lose, whether in formal debate or in the less formal, but deadly serious, arena of political-military decisionmaking.

One weakness of technique affecting Navy debating results was the general perception that the Navy's many communities did not, and could not, agree on an ideal force structure and strategic outlook. This perception was without doubt truer at some times and on some issues than others. In 1978–79, for instance, the Secretary of the Navy and the Chief of Naval Operations differed over whether another carrier should have a nuclear or conventional power plant. Alternative views on the most promising technologies, ideal force structure, naval missions, or budget and strategic priorities were relatively easy for congressional staffers and reporters to discover amongst the Navy's aviation, surface, subsurface, and nuclear power officers. The effect was to weaken the ability of the leadership to advance any particular program without fear of opponents armed with contrary views of equally professional and competent naval authorities.

A second liability in 1970s Navy discussions of strategy and requirements showed in the tendency to exaggerate the consequences of being right or wrong about trends in power relationships and force structure investment decisions. This was a particularly tricky problem. It is natural, and by no means exclusively a Navy sin, to augment failing arguments with fateful auguries. Thus in discussions of Navy force structure, as shipbuilding programs diminished, the Navy's warnings heightened: the nation was on the verge of having a navy too small to defend national interests; soon the United States would forfeit maritime superiority to the Soviet Union; soon the U.S. Navy would be NUMBER TWO, no longer number one.

Unfortunately, and as suggested earlier in the present essay, the 1970s divergence on national security assumptions rendered the Navy's intimations of coming calamity useless, or worse, self-defeating. There was no agreement on the exact extent of American national interests and what they might require in the way of defense; there was no general understanding of what maritime superiority might be and what benefits it could confer on the United States; there was no common concept of the political and strategic implications of having either the first or second navy in the world, nor even any common standard for measuring one navy against another. In this situation, suggestions of imminent or ultimate doom robbed the Navy of credibility; they did not win fundamental or budgetary arguments.

A third defect in Navy approaches to 1970s national security debates was an over-reliance on scenario building. To be sure the devising of scenarios had and has a place in strategic analysis. But it is an extremely weak debating tool when discussing political expectations, likely next events, or future conditions. The reason for its weakness lies in its accessibility: anyone can play, and everyone does. It is impossible to invent a scenario, introduce it into discussion, and prevent its being altered in ways large and small, often as not to the disadvantage of its sponsor. There neither are rules of evidence nor rules of engagement adequate to prevent the recasting of assumptions, the postulating of alternative results.

Scenario building can be a way of formulating ideas about the future; it can never be a method of validating them. Scenario building is most useful in preparing cost and feasibility studies, but even in this, such scenarios often are not sufficiently distinguished from the business of anticipating the future. It is possible by scenario building or game playing to test the ability to cope with various eventualities; it is impossible to prove in such ways that those eventualities will come to pass. The presumption that scenarios used for cost and feasibility studies may actually approximate real world politics and circumstances often leads to inept efforts to exaggerate their meaning. In this sense, scenario building may blur political judgment.

Another failing of technique showed in the Navy's continuing uncertainty over the exact composition of the target audience it should be addressing in national security debates. For several years the Navy mistakenly focused its efforts principally on winning in the Office of the Assistant Secretary of Defense for Program Analysis and Evaluation (PA&E), with secondary attention to gaining more direct influence with those people holding higher office in the Defense Department. On other potential audiences in academia, the public, the congressional, White House, and National Security Council staffs, and the media, the Navy in the 1970s expended relatively scant and undifferentiated effort. This was a mistake. Far from being a citadel of analytic purity in which logic, quantitative analysis, and objective reality hold sway, PA&E like most agencies of government—was and probably should be—subject to political influence and political direction. There would be something wrong if such offices were not susceptible to political guidance. But this means that the Navy's problems with PA&E were not about some objective reality and the number crunching that surrounds it. Instead, those problems were about present and future circumstances assumed to be realities of varying likelihood and varying importance in budgetary and program planning. In this sense the arguments were political, not analytical in any quantitative sense except in the most minute—and still conjectural—details. The Navy needed to win more influence within the national security community, which can control the assumptions even of outfits like PA&E.

Another weakness of Navy methods in national security debates in the 1970s was the overemployment or inappropriate use of systems analysis and force structure analysis. The Navy had—and in some measure retains—a regrettable tendency to talk hardware and hulls to politicians. Temporarily, at least, the Navy seemed to have lost sight of the uses of systems analysis as a method of evaluating decisions on the margin, rather than in the center, and it was encouraging to see Navy leaders such as Under Secretary R. James Woolsey attempt to restore perspective on this analytical method.[9] The problem, of course, reached far beyond the Navy for a time, perhaps as a result of the exaggerated importance of the systems analysts themselves in the Department of Defense.

Inappropriate reliance on systems analysis reduced Navy effectiveness in national security debates of the 1970s in two related ways. First, the need to deal on time with the planners and programmers in each budget cycle encouraged the Navy's—perhaps any bureaucracy's—tendency to put means before ends. This is a classic error, one perhaps possible in the Navy in that time only because of shortcomings mentioned earlier: the overconfidence in an enfeebled theory, and relative inattention to people in the national security community holding the power over assumptions. Second, the Navy attempted to use force structure and systems analysis to prevail in arguments about essentially political assumptions. This effort miscarried, for obvious reasons. Such planning could have been quite useful for internal guidance and for dealing with budgeteers and programmers once there was agreement on assumptions. But even at its best, it was ill-suited for dealing with the problems of assumptions, images, and purposes outlined in the present essay and prominent in the Navy's troubled 1970s environment.

This would be a sad and sobering tale if it were not for the fact that, in the latter 1970s, as the problems here described made themselves felt, the Navy's leadership responded. Admiral Thomas B. Hayward, Chief of Naval Operations in the latter 1970s, and Admiral James D. Watkins, his successor in the early and middle 1980s, recognized and addressed precisely the difficulties here outlined. I leave it to future meetings or other historical inquiries to set these out; having played a personal role in these efforts, I can scarcely claim the impartiality necessary to describe or assess the efforts and their results. Nevertheless, I would like to offer some simple concluding observations.

First, the services do not hold the power, or even, in many cases, much power, over assumptions in the national security community. This being the case, they must make their way by solid argument, not through stolid self-confidence or subterranean bureaucratic manipulations. Although it is tempting to consider the problems in terms of the annual tactics and timing of budgets, which must certainly be attended to, over time a broader and more fundamental addressal of underlying issues is not only desirable but necessary.

Concerning problems of theory, the Navy like other services must recognize its need to invest in ideas for the long term just as it invests in research and development or in platforms. The revival, or revision, of theory is not so much a problem of finding new ideas, although a few would be welcome. As one young naval officer fresh from a tour in Washington once told me: "In Washington, there are no new ideas. Everything you can think of has been thought of before." To the extent that may be true, the problem is to identify the old ideas of diminished relevance and effectiveness, and to cease relying on them. The purpose of a reconsideration of theory cannot and must not be to reaffirm the institutional commitment to present force structure and strategy.

Finally, it is essential to approach divergent national security assumptions with the firm realization that the principal issues between the services and other members of the national security community tend to be more political than technical. In addition to the possibility that it is not always right, the Navy, like its sister services, must face the fact that being right often has little to do with winning arguments. In politics, especially, issues are often decided not on their merits but in spite of them. Military leaders and institutions need the pliability to develop and advance their convictions in a political framework that requires compromise and permits error. Acceptance of such views can lead to an unconstructive cynicism, one that hardens individuals and institutions to the misconstrual of disagreements and the misuse of analytic methods. But this is particularly to be avoided in a time of continuing public skepticism regarding the professional military.

The present generation of military leaders has the opportunity to shape the ideas that will guide their successors for many years. The ideas of the next few years will be more important than any of the other assets passed from one generation to another, for ideas outlive hardware, and often institutions. How our military leaders respond will determine whether later generations regard the early 1980s as a time of opportunity grasped or opportunity lost.

NOTE: Dr. Etzold was not present to read his paper or to comment.

Notes

1. Waldo H. Heinrichs, Jr., "The Role of the United States Navy," in Dorothy Borg and Shumpei Okamoto, eds., *Pearl Harbor as History: Japanese-American Relations, 1931–1941* (New York, 1973), pp 197–98.

2. "The Navy Under Attack," *Time*, 8 May 1978, p 18.

3. This quotation comes originally from a message from MacArthur to Congressman Charles Eaton, 3 March 1948, and was repeated in a telegram to General Albert Wedemeyer on 20 Nov 1948, in *Declassified Documents Quarterly & Reference System*, 75: 258C.

4. Some of the original errors occurred in the work of British political economist, J. A. Hobson, in his influential book, *Imperialism*, published in 1902 (republished by the University of Michigan Press, Ann Arbor, 1965). Hobson's work inspired further errors culminating in Lenin's famous pamphlet, *Imperialism: The Highest Stage of Capitalism*, written in 1916 and published in 1917 (modern editions available with various publication dates from International Publishers, New York). The most thorough critic of these writings has been David K. Fieldhouse. For a brief statement of his critique, see his "The New Imperialism: The Hobson-Lenin Thesis Revised," in George H. Nadel and Perry Curtis, eds., *Imperialism and Colonialism* (New York, 1964).

5. The navy's most extensive efforts to set out this view appear in *U.S. Lifelines: Imports of Essential Materials—1967, 1971, 1975—and the Impact of Waterborne Commerce on the Nation.* Washington, OpNav—09D–PIA (Jan 1978).

6. "Blue Water Strategy Revisited," Naval War College Review, XXX, No 4/ Sequence 267 (Spring 1978), p 66.

7. *CNO Report: A Report by Admiral James L. Holloway III, U.S. Navy, Chief of Naval Operations, Concerning the Fiscal Year 1979 Military Posture and Budget of the United States Navy* (Washington, Mar 1978), p i. Admiral Turner's thought saw its fullest expression in his article in the Mar-Apr 1974 issue of the *Naval War College Review.*

8. *A World Restored* (Boston, 1957), p 325.

9. "Planning a Navy: The Risks of Conventional Wisdom," *International Security*, III, No 1 (Fall 1978), pp 17–29.

JCS Strategic Planning and Vietnam: The Search for An Objective

Herbert Y. Schandler

By law, "...the Joint Chiefs of Staff are the principal military advisers to the President, the National Security Council, and the Secretary of Defense." They are also charged with preparing strategic plans and providing for the strategic direction of the Armed Forces.[1]

In recent years, the organization and structure established to enable the Joint Chiefs of Staff (JCS) to carry out these important functions has been subjected to much critical analysis. Serious organizational deficiencies have been alleged. The major organizational problem, it has been charged, stems from the dual responsibilities as members of the JCS and as chiefs of their respective services. This means, according to many critics, that the Joint Chiefs of Staff are incapable of providing impartial strategic advice divorced from service interests. This dual responsibility, according to these critics, tends to reduce military advice to a lowest common denominator of service, and branch biases make it difficult even to get unvarnished professional military advice on military strategy and operations.[2]

An examination of JCS strategic advice to the President and the Secretary of Defense during the Vietnam War might be useful in determining the truth of these charges. The Vietnam War involved all of the services. It was clearly a limited war on the part of the United States to be fought with limited resources and for limited objectives. It was a war in which the President often sought the advice of his military chiefs, but did the President receive wise professional counsel from his military chiefs? Was the military strategy recommended a strategy designed to accomplish the aims of policy? Did service and parochial interests unduly influence policy recommendations?

U.S. strategic military planning for the use of ground forces in the defense of Indochina can be traced to the days following the signing of the Geneva Accords and the establishment of the Southeast Asia Treaty Organization in 1954. These contingency plans reflected U.S. combat experience in Korea, to include the U.S. view of the Chinese threat to Southeast Asia. They also reflected the New Look military doctrine of the Eisenhower Administration with its emphasis on U.S. air, naval, and nuclear supremacy.[3]

U.S. contingency plans for the defense of South Vietnam provided for countering a conventional enemy offensive by North Vietnamese or combined North Vietnamese-Chinese forces. South Vietnamese troops would occupy blocking positions while American forces, generally those already based in the Pacific Command, would secure major air and sea facilities in South Vietnam and would then deploy to occupy these blocking positions north and west of Saigon.

After the invasion had been contained, a counteroffensive would be undertaken, featuring an ambitious joint airborne, amphibious, and ground attack into North Vietnam.

To support these plans, provisions were made for selecting potential targets for nuclear strikes, for occupying key cities, and for interdicting the enemy's critical lines of communication (LOC). These plans anticipated and were based upon a mobilization of U.S. reserve units.[4]

Contingency plans did not change markedly during the 1955–1965 time period. The escalating threat posed by the Viet Cong and President John F. Kennedy's interest in counterinsurgency appear to have been only superficial distractions to the military planners. In general, they had difficulty translating counterinsurgency doctrine and strategy into plans and tactics for use of American combat forces in Southeast Asia. As they were unsure how to deal conventionally with an insurgency, they tentatively proposed to train indigenous forces for this mission. Under this scheme, American units would continue to occupy blocking positions to stop the invading North Vietnamese forces while South Vietnamese internal security forces would take on the Viet Cong.[5]

The U.S. military training mission in Vietnam during the period 1954–1960 tended to concentrate on building a South Vietnamese army in an image of an American army and geared to resist attack from the North. In fact, responsibility for training and equipping paramilitary and internal security forces was not vested in the military at all, but in other U.S. agencies, which differed radically in their views of the proper mission, composition, coordination and employment of those forces.[6]

Thus, U.S. efforts to create an effective South Vietnamese military force during this period were critically affected by perceptions of the threat, by exaggerated estimates of the value of American military standards in responding to the threat, and by fragmentation in determining and administering the overall program of assistance to Vietnam.

From the time of the overthrow of the Diem government in 1963 to the end of the winter in February and March of 1964, it became increasingly clear that the South Vietnamese had, despite significant American aid, not been able to achieve political stability. As the realization in Washington grew that an ally on whose behalf the United States had steadily increased its commitment was in a state of political and military collapse, the President undertook a determined policy reassessment of the future American role in Vietnam.

Attention focused initially on positive action against North Vietnam. The controversial Tonkin Gulf incident, on 4–5 August 1964, precipitated the first U.S. reprisal against North Vietnam and provided the President with a broad congressional resolution of support. The precedent for U.S. military action against North Vietnam had been established.[7]

Throughout the remainder of 1964, recommendations were made by the Joint Chiefs of Staff to continue retaliatory raids against North Vietnam, but they were resisted by the President. On 13 February 1965, after a series of Viet Cong attacks on American installations and servicemen, President Johnson finally approved a program for measured and limited air action against selected military targets in North Vietnam. Although the program, dubbed ROLLING THUNDER, evolved into a regular, continuing, and militarily significant effect, the President, through his Secretary of Defense, continued to keep this air effort under strict and careful control. Within this framework of political control, the ROLLING THUNDER program was allowed to grow in intensity, in geographic coverage, and in assortment of targets.[8]

The decision to use military power against the North, in the end, seems to have resulted as much from a lack of alternative proposals as from any compelling logic advanced by the military in its favor. Getting North Vietnam to remove its support and direction of the insurgency in the South was the basic objective, but there was no general agreement as to the likelihood of the result or of a strategy to attain it. And the President's reluctance to approve these actions was based upon a hope that the South Vietnamese government would be able to make itself more effective and thus preclude the necessity of American action.

The alternative of withdrawing American support from a Saigon government demonstrably incapable of pulling itself together and organizing a stable government in its own defense was briefly considered. However, the JCS objected forcefully to this alternative. President Johnson had previously considered this course of action and at the September 1964 policy review had asked whether any of his advisors doubted that "Vietnam was worth all this effort." All had agreed that the loss of South Vietnam would be followed, in time, by the loss of all of Southeast Asia.[9]

Despite official hopes that the ROLLING THUNDER bombing campaign would rapidly convince Hanoi that it should agree to negotiate a settlement to the war in the South, or that it should cease to support the insurgency in the South in exchange for a halt in the bombing, these hopes were not realized. After a month of continued and regular bombing, the North Vietnamese showed signs of adjusting to the bombing campaign and preparing for a long siege while they continued to support the Viet Cong in South Vietnam. By the middle of April 1965, it was generally recognized that in order to bring Hanoi to the bargaining table, some evidence that the Viet Cong could not win in the South would also be necessary.

On the morning of 8 March 1965, a United States Marine Corps battalion landing team splashed ashore at Da Nang in South Vietnam. A companion battalion landed by air later the same day. Although there were already over 20,000 American servicemen in South Vietnam, this was the first time that an organized ground combat unit had been committed. The mission assigned these two battalions was to secure the airfield and U.S. supporting installations and facilities.

The landing and mission assigned these forces had been recommended by General William Westmoreland on 22 February 1965. He was concerned about the ability of the South Vietnamese to protect the base, from which American aircraft were conducting air strikes against the North and providing air support missions in the South.[10] Thus the air strikes against the North were directly related to the initial deployment of ground forces.

As the buildup of American forces continued throughout 1965 and as they were authorized to conduct offensive options at the request of the field commander, General Westmoreland, it became clear that an overall strategic plan was required to clarify the national purposes and objectives these additional forces were meant to serve. President Johnson, in his message to the American people announcing the deployment, had indicated that these forces were to resist aggression in South Vietnam and to "furnish assistance to support South Vietnam...to bring Communist aggression and terrorism under control."[11] General Westmoreland had stated a more ambitious objective, to defeat and destroy enemy forces in South Vietnam.

Therefore, in order to establish a basis for future force requirements and for overall conduct of the ground war, the JCS set out to develop a strategic concept for U.S. military operations in Southeast Asia. By the end of August 1965, they had developed a concept that contained their basic assumptions and goals, and they pressed this concept on the civilian leadership with single-minded intensity in the following years.

The Joint Chiefs of Staff saw three equally important military tasks to be accomplished by the U.S. in Vietnam:

1. To cause the Democratic Republic of Vietnam (DRV) to cease its direction and support of the Viet Cong insurgency;

2. To defeat the Viet Cong and to extend Government of Vietnam (GVN) control over all of South Vietnam;

3. To deter Communist China from direct intervention and to defeat such intervention if it should occur.[12]

The military tasks recommended by the JCS to achieve their self-imposed objectives were extremely ambitious. Aggressive and sustained military action, the military chiefs stated, would allow the United States to hold the initiative in both North and South Vietnam. North Vietnam's war-supporting power would be progressively destroyed and the Viet Cong defeated. To achieve this, they visualized that the following military actions would be required:

> ... to intensify military pressure on the DRV by air and naval power; to destroy significant DRV military targets; to interdict supporting LOCs in the DRV; to interdict the infiltration and supply routes into the RVN; to improve the combat effectiveness of the RVNAF; to build and protect bases; to reduce enemy reinforcements; to defeat the Viet Cong.... The physical capability of the DRV to move men and supplies through the Lao

corridor, down the coastline, across the DMZ, and through Cambodia must be reduced...by land, naval, and air actions....a buildup in Thailand to ensure attainment of the proper U.S.-Thai posture to deter CHICOM aggression and to facilitate placing U.S. forces in an advantageous logistical position if such aggression occurs.[13]

The Secretary of Defense, of course, did not approve this ambitious program which raised such controversial and far-reaching policy issues as blockading North Vietnam, involving U.S. ground forces in Laos and Cambodia, and building up U.S. forces in Thailand. But he did not reject it either. Indicating that an overall approval was not required at that time, the secretary merely agreed that "recommendations for future operations in Southeast Asia should be formulated" as the occasion necessitated.[14]

Left with no other guidance from their civilian superiors, the Joint Chiefs of Staff continued to formulate recommendations for future operations along the same lines. Their recommendations continued to take the form of requests for additional American troops in South Vietnam and for expanded operations authority outside South Vietnam. Since the President and the Secretary of Defense had failed to provide them with any national objectives, missions, or strategic concepts other than the very general ones of "resisting aggression" or "insuring a non-Communist South Vietnam," the military leaders adopted their own concept for conducting the war and continued to press for its approval.

Each request for additional deployments from the field commander was forwarded by the JCS along with their recommendation to involve U.S. land forces in Laos and Cambodia, to blockade Haiphong, to increase the bombing effort against North Vietnam while reducing geographic restrictions, and to mobilize U.S. reserve forces.

And always these recommendations were disapproved by the President, while force levels and deployments which could be supported without a mobilization were approved. A planning process was initiated which accommodated the JCS pressure for increased operating authority with the desire of the President to retain the support of his military chiefs within a limited war.

This planning process has been described by General Westmoreland as follows:

I customarily developed plans for the troops that I thought were needed based upon my projection of the situation. This was normally done on a calendar year basis. This request was studied, analyzed, and costed by the

Department of Defense, JCS, and the services. After this process had taken place, there was always a personal conference between Secretary McNamara and me, at which time we discussed the matter in detail, examined all alternatives, and came to an agreement on the troops that should be organized and prepared for deployment. The matter would then be discussed by us with the President, who would make a decision.[15]

And so the American commitment of force in Vietnam grew in an *ad hoc* fashion to accommodate divergent views of U.S. objectives there.

By the end of 1966, Secretary of Defense McNamara began to question the premises under which the U.S. had committed major combat forces to Vietnam. In a report to the President subsequent to his visit to Saigon, the secretary recommended changing the emphasis of U.S. strategy. Rather than defeating the enemy by offensive action, as had been consistently recommended by the military commanders, McNamara wanted to return to a rather defensive posture, "by getting ourselves into a military posture that we credibly would maintain indefinitely—a posture that makes trying to 'wait us out' less attractive to the North Vietnamese/Viet Cong." To achieve this, the secretary recommended a five-part program far different from the war plan envisaged by his military commanders:

1. Barring a dramatic change in the war, we should level off at the total of 470,000 (U.S. ground forces).

2. An infiltration barrier should be constructed across the neck of South Vietnam near the 17th parallel and across the infiltration trails in Laos.

3. Stabilize the ROLLING THUNDER program against the North at present levels.

4. Pursue a vigorous pacification program.

5. Increase the prospects for a negotiated settlement of the war.

Even if these steps were taken, however, McNamara foresaw no great probability of success in the near future. The solution, as he saw it at the time, was to prepare openly for a longer war in order to "give clear evidence that the continuing costs and risks to the American people are acceptably limited, that the formula for success has been found, and that the end of the war is merely a matter of time."[16]

This remarkably somber and pessimistic document gave an answer, finally, to the demands of the military chiefs for an approved strategic concept for U.S. operations in Vietnam. That answer, however, was a clear no to their proposals to defeat North Vietnamese forces through major increases in U.S. forces in South Vietnam and expanded bombing in the North. McNamara's concept provided an alternative strategy and criterion for success, as well as new assumptions about the meaning of winning, against which future military recommendations could be measured.

The JCS, as could be expected, disagreed with McNamara's strategic alternative. They reiterated their previously developed, but unapproved, strategic concept of maximum pressure on the enemy at all points free of most political restraints, in order to achieve U.S. objectives in the shortest possible time and at the least cost in men.[17]

However, in approving the deployment of a 1967 end-strength of U.S. military personnel of 470,000, McNamara posed the strategic dilemma and seemed to resolve it finally:

> We now face a choice of two approaches to the threat of the regular VC/NVA forces. The first approach would be to continue in 1967 to increase friendly forces as rapidly as possible, and without limit, and employ them primarily in large scale seek out and destroy operations to destroy the main force VC/NVA units.... The second approach is to follow a similarly aggressive strategy of seek out and destroy, but to build friendly forces only to that level required to neutralize the large enemy units and prevent them from interfering with the pacification program. It is essential to this approach that such a level be consistent with a stable economy in SVN, and consistent with a military posture that the U.S. credibly would maintain indefinitely, thus making a Communist attempt to "wait us out" less attractive. I believe it is time to adopt the second approach for three reasons: (1) if MACV estimates of enemy strength are correct, we have not been able to attrite the enemy forces fast enough to break their morale and more U.S. forces are unlikely to do so in the foreseeable future; (2) we cannot deploy more than 470,000 personnel. . .without a high probability of generating a self-defeating runaway inflation in SVN, and (3) an endless escalation of U.S. deployments is not likely to be acceptable in the U.S. or to induce the enemy to believe that the U.S. is prepared to stay as long as it is required to produce a secure non-Communist SVN.[18]

The turn of the year saw the policy debate over basic U.S. tactics in South Vietnam continue as it became increasingly clear that the nature of our objectives, the political basis of our commitment, the desirable magnitude of our presence, and the ground and air strategy to be pursued were still not crystallized or carefully delineated within the administration.

The underlying controversy over the military strategy to pursue in Vietnam was soon brought into the open again. On 18 March

1967, General Westmoreland submitted an analysis of his additional force requirements projected through June of 1968. Westmoreland indicated that although he had not strongly objected to the 470,000–man ceiling established earlier, reassessment of the situation had made it clear that that force, although enabling the United States to gain the initiative, did not permit "sustained operations of the scope and intensity required to avoid an unreasonably protracted war."[19]

The Joint Chiefs of Staff formally reported to the Secretary of Defense on 20 April 1967 that additional forces were needed to achieve the objectives they considered the United States to be pursuing in Vietnam. The JCS request reaffirmed the basic objectives and strategy that had been contained in each troop request since 1965, but which had now become a point of issue within the administration. The military leaders repeated their view that the U.S. national objective in South Vietnam remained the attainment of a stable and independent non-Communist government.

They indicated that the military missions necessary to achieve that goal were:

a. To make it as difficult and costly as possible for the NVA to continue effective support of the VC and to cause North Vietnam to cease direction of the VC insurgency.

b. To defeat the VC/NVA and force the withdrawal of NVA forces.

c. Extend government dominion, direction, and control.

d. To deter Chinese Communists from direct intervention in SEA.

They then listed the three general areas of military effort that they felt were necessary in pursuit of those missions:

1. Operations against the Viet Cong/North Vietnamese Army (VC/NVA) forces in SVN while concurrently assisting the South Vietnamese Government in its nation-building efforts.

2. Operations to obstruct and reduce the flow of men and materials from North Vietnam (NVN) to SVN.

3. Operations to obstruct and reduce imports of war-sustaining materials into NVN.

The military leaders indicated that U.S. efforts were inadequate in each of these areas. In South Vietnam, insufficient forces prevented the establishment of a secure environment for the people. In North Vietnam, an expanded bombing campaign was required to reduce infiltration of men and supplies to the South, and in the third area, relatively little effort had been permitted.

Therefore, in addition to the deployment of additional ground forces to South Vietnam, the Joint Chiefs of Staff strongly recommended increased effort against the enemy's strategic supply lines into North Vietnam. Again, the JCS reiterated their belief that a reserve call-up and extension of terms of service were "the only feasible means of meeting the additional FY 1968 requirements in the stipulated time frame." And in another plea for an approved strategy for the conduct of the war, something they had been seeking since the first troop deployments in 1965, the military leaders recommended that their "military strategy for the conduct of the war in Southeast Asia. . .be approved in principle."[20]

The Defense Department attacked directly the strategic concept upon which the request was based. The defense civilians argued that a limit to the number of U.S. forces had to be imposed, thereby stabilizing the ground conflict. The JCS, of course, fought back, declaring that this position would not permit early termination of the war on terms acceptable to the United States, provided little capacity for initiating new actions or maintaining momentum, and presented an alarming pattern of realignment of U.S. objectives and intentions in Southeast Asia.

The arguments about strategy went on throughout the summer and fall. At a White House luncheon on 12 September the President had asked his military advisors to recommend additional actions, *within existing policy limitations*, that would increase pressure on North Vietnam and accelerate the achievement of U.S. objectives in South Vietnam. Here, again, however, the military chiefs showed neither flexibility nor creativity. In their reply, on 17 October 1967, the JCS indicated, in rather a resigned tone, that they considered the rate of progress to have been, and continued to be, slow, largely because U.S. military power had been constrained in a manner that had significantly reduced its impact and effectiveness. Military operations had been hampered in four ways, they argued:

a. The attacks on enemy military targets have been on such a prolonged, graduated basis that the enemy has adjusted psychologically, economically, and militarily, e.g., inured themselves to the difficulties and hardships accompanying the war, dispersed their logistic support system, and developed alternative transport routes and a significant air defense system.

b. Areas of sanctuary, containing important military targets, have been afforded the enemy.

c. Covert operations in Cambodia and Laos have been restricted.

d. Major importation of supplies into NVN by sea has been permitted.

Pessimistically, the Joint Chiefs of Staff indicated that progress would continue to be slow as long as these limitations on military operations continued. The military leaders then listed a series of steps they believed could be taken. Their recommendations again included removing restrictions on the air campaign against all militarily significant targets in NVN; mining NVN deep water ports and NVN inland waterways and estuaries north of 20° N; extending naval surface operations north of 20° N; increasing air interdiction in Laos and along NVN borders; eliminating operational restrictions on B–52s in Laos; expanding ground operations in Laos and Cambodia; and expanding and reorienting NVN covert programs.[21]

But once again what should have been a fundamental argument as to American purposes in South Vietnam was reduced to the single issue of what force buildup could be supported without mobilizing the reserves. The Joint Chiefs of Staff again failed to get agreement on a strategic concept for fighting the war. Indeed, a change in concept or in objectives was not even mentioned in the decision to allocate additional limited ground forces to the war.

By the end of 1967, however, it finally appeared that the military chiefs had accepted the political restrictions imposed upon them by the Commander in Chief. On 27 November 1967, in response to another presidential request to recommend military action in Southeast Asia over the next four months, the military chiefs reiterated their pessimistic analysis, "There are no new programs which can be undertaken under current policy guidelines which would result in a rapid or significantly more viable increase in the rate of progress in the near term."[22]

Acceptance by the Joint Chiefs of Staff of these political restrictions was short-lived. The Tet Offensive of 1968 appeared to provide the JCS with one last opportunity to implement their all-out concept for war in Vietnam while mobilizing to reconstitute the strategic reserve.

The President was anxious to send whatever additional forces were needed by his field commander in Vietnam to prevent a politically damaging defeat. Faced with this fact and with Communist threats in Korea, Berlin, and possibly elsewhere in the world, the Joint Chiefs of Staff saw Tet as an opportunity to force the President's hand and to achieve their long-sought goal of a mobilization of reserve forces.

But again the President was not prepared to make that decision and held the JCS at bay. However, the decisions that had been avoided in past years could no longer be avoided. Additional American deployments to Vietnam could not be met or sustained without a large reserve call-up and severe economic adjustments. Further, there was no assurance that the manpower requirement would not grow larger in the future. There were also strong indications that large and growing elements of the American public had begun to believe the cost had already reached unacceptable levels.

The political reality that faced President Johnson in 1968 was that more of the same in South Vietnam, with an increased commitment of American lives and money and its consequent impact on the country, accompanied by no guarantee of victory in the near future, had become unacceptable to major elements of the American public. After the shock of the Tet Offensive, the military reports of success no longer rang true. The impression grew that progress in many ways had been illusory. The possibility of victory had become remote, and the cost had become too high, in both political and economic terms.

The road to ending the war in Vietnam, it finally became clear to American leaders, depended at least as much on South Vietnamese political and military development as it did on American arms. This realization, then, made it possible to return to the original purpose for which American forces were sent to South Vietnam, that of preventing the defeat of the South Vietnamese government.

The decisions at Tet to limit U.S. troop levels and to place more reliance on the South Vietnamese represented a long-overdue rationalization of the American effort in Vietnam and a return to the basic principles that had been used to justify American intervention in Vietnam in the first place.

The American failure in Vietnam, then clearly stems from obvious difficulties in our decisionmaking processes at the highest levels of government. At the highest level, the cold war and the successful defense of South Vietnam was seen by President Johnson as essential to the domestic political well-being of the United States.

Vietnam itself initially was not seen as of great strategic importance to the United States. Rather it was seen as an integral part of the cold war and a test of the United States' military commitments to its allies around the world, as a vital clash of wills between communism and the system of alliances established by the United States after World War II. It was the testing ground where the challenge of Communist wars of national liberation would be met by counterinsurgency warfare.

Not to intervene and assist a beleaguered ally, the President felt, meant that communism would spread throughout Southeast Asia, other United States commitments would be called into question, and the nation would be split by a vicious internal debate as to the wisdom of the policy adopted. President Johnson has been quoted as saying as early as 1962: "I am not going to be the President who saw Southeast Asia go the way China went."[23]

The long-term goal was a political settlement that would allow the South Vietnamese to determine their own future without outside interference. In a speech at Johns Hopkins University in April 1965, the President laid out for the American people what would be done in Vietnam: "We will do everything necessary to reach that objective (that the people of South Vietnam be allowed to guide their own country in their own way). And we will do only what is absolutely necessary."[24]

Thus, the President's policy objectives translated into doing the minimum amount militarily to prevent a South Vietnamese defeat while convincing Hanoi that it would not succeed in its aggression.

To the President and his Secretary of Defense, then, this meant a war for limited purposes using limited resources in a geographically constricted area to achieve a diplomatic purpose. The allocation of American manpower, resources, and materiel would not be allowed to reach the point where the war would unduly affect the civilian economy or interfere with the burgeoning programs of the Great Society. Operations would be restricted geographically so as not to incite Soviet or Chinese intervention.

The objective would not be to win, either in North or South Vietnam, but rather to convince the North Vietnamese (and their Soviet and Chinese sponsors) that the cost of continuing the war in South Vietnam would be, over time, prohibitive to them and that they could not succeed.

Thus, the President's policy translated into a classic application of limited war theory. Military force was to be applied in ways which would provide signals to the enemy, signals of American resolve which would convince the North Vietnamese that they could not win and that a diplomatic settlement would be desirable.[25]

The President's strategy, then, was defensive in nature and, in effect, left the decision as to when to end the war in the hands of the North Vietnamese. The administration saw the conflict in South Vietnam simply as a Communist aggression on the cold war model— a challenge to a free nation by expansionist international communism. The questionable legitimacy and inefficiency of the fledgling South Vietnamese government, and the anticolonial traditional and nationalist credentials of North Vietnam were overlooked. Thus, the enemy was much too simply described and the Saigon government had ascribed to it by Washington capabilities and qualities which it never possessed.

The President's principal military advisors saw the White House's limited political objective as essentially negative and ineffective. This no-win approach, they felt, yielded the initiative to the enemy and ultimately placed primary reliance upon the fragile and undependable South Vietnamese armed forces. If the U.S. was to go to war, the Joint Chiefs of Staff felt that a more ambitious objective was necessary, that of defeating the enemy both in North and South Vietnam. They advocated the classic doctrine that victory depended upon the rapid application of overwhelming military power through offensive action to defeat the enemy's main forces.

The Joint Chiefs of Staff continued to request additional American troops for South Vietnam, increased bombing of North Vietnam, and expanded authority to strike in Laos, Cambodia, and North Vietnam. They felt that any U.S. effort to win the war in the South was thwarted by the availability to enemy troops of crucial sanctuaries and supply routes in Laos and Cambodia, where they would refit, reequip, and escape destruction by American ground and air power.

Further, the constraints on the use of air power in North Vietnam, they felt, allowed the enemy to adjust to the bombing campaign so that its pressure did not become unacceptable. Of equal consequence and concern to the military chiefs was the fact that the White House decision not to call up U.S. reserve units depleted American active forces outside of Vietnam to the point where the nation might not be able to respond to overseas military contingencies elsewhere.

As the war developed, the debate within the administration concerning the level of American effort in South Vietnam, in fact, came to revolve around this one crucial issue of mobilization. When the President searched for the elusive point at which the political costs of the effort in Vietnam would become unacceptable to the American people, he always settled upon mobilization—that point at which significant members of reservists would have to be called up to provide enough manpower to support the war.

This domestic constraint, with all its political and social implications, not any argument concerning long-range military strategy, appears to have dictated American war policy. Lyndon Johnson saw reserve mobilization as the threshold at which the nation would see itself as being on a war footing. His top priority continued to be the passage by Congress of the social programs of the Great Society. He would not be a wartime President. This debate behind closed doors concerning the limited strategy advocated by the President and his civilian advisors and the more forceful strategy advocated by the military chiefs continued throughout Lyndon Johnson's presidency.

Thus, fundamental differences between military and civilians at the national level concerning the war in Indochina were never resolved. There was no agreed, coherent strategy to achieve American objectives and, indeed, no agreement as to those objectives. Decisions concerning the allocation of American resources to Vietnam were made on the basis of what was the minimum additional effort that could be made while maintaining congressional support for (or acquiescence in) the administration war policy and for the programs of the Great Society. There was to be minimum disruption of American life. As late as 1966, President Johnson declared to the Congress, "I believe we can continue the Great Society while we fight in Vietnam."[26]

The President made at least eight separate decisions concerning United States manpower levels in Vietnam in 1964–68. The issues addressed and the decisions that were made were always tactical and short-term in nature. The only alternative policies examined involved different force levels or alternative bombing campaigns.

Although Lyndon Johnson was determined to wage a limited campaign with limited resources for limited political purposes as opposed to military victory, these operational and resource constraints were not made specific to his military chiefs. President Johnson continued to buy time for his domestic programs and to buy the support of his military chiefs by temporizing, by avoiding decisive action, and by getting agreement at the lowest level of intensity he could to meet the current situation in Vietnam, not to derail his legislative program, and to maintain the support of the American people.

The role of the Joint Chiefs of Staff in this circumstance raises many pertinent questions concerning their influence, usefulness, and effectiveness in the national decisionmaking process. As chief military advisers to the President, they are bound to give him their best military advice unconstrained by political considerations. But at some point, it would seem essential that they salute, accept the political limitations imposed upon them by civilian authority, and plan military operations to achieve national objectives within those political limitations, or inform political leadership of the limitations of military force within given policy restraints.

The Joint Chiefs of Staff, however, seemed incapable of accepting these political limitations, and, indeed, seemed incapable of, or unwilling to, accept the necessity of conducting a limited war with limited resources in Vietnam, in which military actions were designed specifically to elicit a diplomatic, and not a military, outcome. Some have accused them of dusting off and attempting to implement old contingency plans even though conditions had changed drastically.[27]

The JCS made no independent analyses of what manpower levels would be needed to achieve White House objectives (denial of Communist victory) within the restraints placed upon the military operations in Vietnam by the President, or of what military gains actually could be achieved within those constraints. Their advice on how to win was always predictable: "Do what General Westmoreland asks, lift the political and geographical restraints under which our forces operate, and increase the size of the strategic reserve."[28] But this was advice which the President was never willing to accept.

310

On the other hand, it does not appear from the available documents that any of the senior military leaders threatened or even contemplated resigning to dramatize his opposition to the limitations on the conduct of the war insisted upon by the President and his advisors. Far from seeking to present their views in public, each member of the JCS, who (with the exception of the chairman) was also chief of his respective service, sought to protect the position of his service and his own status inside the administration while striving to change White House policy from within. The ventilation of disagreements with presidential policies did not become a high priority for the senior members of the military establishment during the entire period of U.S. involvement in Vietnam.

President Johnson was aware of the possible political repercussions of such a military defection, and he temporized over the years in order not to push his loyal military leaders to such a point. At a conference in Honolulu in 1966, he told Westmoreland, "General, I have a lot riding on you. . . I hope you don't pull a MacArthur on me."[29]

Although the President never approved the military strategy that the JCS continued to recommend, he never explicitly ruled it out either. He allowed the military chiefs gradual increases in their combat forces in Vietnam and held out the possibility of greater operational leeway in the future. He pointed out the political and fiscal realities that he felt prevented his meeting all of their requests while never rejecting completely all of those requests. He slowly increased the resources and authority of General Westmoreland in a process of gradual and reluctant escalation.

Although political public relations on the home front is not among the normal tasks of a field commander, the President employed Westmoreland in this role three times in 1967 alone. Each time the general voiced his encouragement with the way things were going in Vietnam, and confirmed that he was receiving all the troops and support he had asked of the President and was getting them just as fast as he needed or could absorb them.

In his book, *A Soldier Reports,* General Westmoreland later reflected:

> In my press conferences and public appearances. . .I recognized that it was not the job of the military to defend American commitment and policy. Yet it was difficult to differentiate between pursuit of a military task and such related matters as public and congressional support and the morale of the fighting man, who must be convinced that he is risking death for a worthy cause. The military was thus caught in between and I myself as the

man perhaps most on the spot may have veered too far in the direction of supporting in public the government's policy, an instinct born of devotion to an assigned task even more than to a cause and of loyalty to the President as Commander in Chief.[30]

Denied a strategic concept and the military freedom they felt was necessary to win the war, the military chiefs were pacified by gradual increases in force levels and in bombing targets and, eventually, by the replacement of a Secretary of Defense who had become anathema to them. But these increases in military authority and resources were always within the President's guidelines. Lyndon Johnson retained the political constraints upon military action and, in effect, determined his own strategy. And so the military chiefs, while each sought a larger role for his own service, in effect became sophisticated yes men for the President's policies, assuring the public, as did General Westmoreland, that every request from the field commander had been met, and seldom raising in public their view of the eventual military consequences of the President's restrictions.

The consequences of this failure to develop a precise, clear military strategy were certainly unintended by President Johnson. They included a costly bombing campaign against North Vietnam and the commitment of half a million American troops to a ground war in Asia without any fundamental agreement within our government as to how success was to be achieved, or what really represented success.

Thus, the effort in Vietnam was piecemeal, indecisive, contradictory, and misdirected. Each decision in Washington represented a compromise between a President determined to preserve his domestic programs while defending freedom in Southeast Asia with the least possible disruption in American life, and the Joint Chiefs of Staff who saw no alternative but an American takeover of the war and an all-out military effort against a dangerous and tenacious enemy, while mobilizing to maintain American military capabilities to deal with contingencies in other parts of the world.

By presenting a facade of unanimity concerning the conduct of the war and of the objectives being pursued, the President and the Joint Chiefs of Staff, in effect, inhibited rational national debate within the American body politic concerning United States objectives in Southeast Asia and the forces and resources to be devoted to the attainment of those objectives. When this debate did come, it was initiated by scattered groups of antiwar protesters and their congressional allies who offered no workable policy alternatives.

In the short term, Lyndon Johnson displayed the attributes of a successful political leader. He compromised in order to retain the continued support of his military leaders which he felt was necessary to maintain support within the nation for his objectives and actions in Vietnam. He never changed his objectives while maintaining, he felt, the pace of the action and the conduct of operations in the war within the political limits he felt to be necessary. But he was not a good Commander in Chief. He never made clear his objectives, the resources to be allocated to the achievement of those objectives, and the political restraints which were to be maintained upon military operations. He never insisted that his military advisors constrain their military advice within the political and resource constraints he had established but which he had never communicated to them explicitly. He never insisted that any of the chiefs who did not agree with his policy restrictions step down. And when it became clear that his military chiefs did not accept these political constraints, and insisted on recommending that national policy be changed so as to fight the war on their basis rather than on that of the President, he never removed them—as his predecessor, Harry Truman removed a field commander under somewhat different circumstances. Lyndon Johnson's greatest fault as a national leader was that he chose not to choose between the Great Society and the war in Vietnam. Instead he sought a series of pragmatic solutions for avoiding what he believed would be a divisive national debate over that choice.

The question, then, remains as to how to make the advice of the Joint Chiefs of Staff pertinent to the needs of the President and his Secretary of Defense. It does not appear that any organizational changes would preclude the inadequacies of military advice as occurred during the Vietnam period.

Clearly, a primary requirement is clarity and consistency in the statement of national objectives which military force is designed to support or implement. It is important that his determination of objectives be the result of prior, conscientious deliberation, rather than of default, of wishful thinking, of unilateral goals or determinations, of assumptions or impressions as occurred during the Vietnam conflict. Once established, these objectives should be frequently subject to scrutiny and debate within the administration to insure that policy goals remain consistent with external conditions and with domestic and regional political realities.

Other Presidents have wrestled with the problem of developing military advice within the constraints of political limitations and realities. President John F. Kennedy early in his administration admonished the JCS to ". . .base their advice not on narrow military considerations alone but on broad gauged political and economic factors as well."[31] But clearly, it is not the role of the Joint Chiefs of Staff to recommend political and economic policy, and there is not evidence that they followed President Kennedy's directive.

Looking at the war in Southeast Asia during the 1960s, one can conclude that there seemed to be little common understanding between the civil and military leaders. Military goals were not developed to accomplish the objectives of a declared policy. The policy aims almost directly precluded the changes of success of the military strategy implemented.

And so again, we come down to personalities, leadership, and mutual respect. In the end, it is the President and the Congress who must determine and enunciate national objectives and the role of force in achieving those objectives. But the military, in accepting and working within those national objectives, must realistically define the capability of force to achieve those policy objectives, to not overstate the capabilities of its forces, and to make it clear to civilian authority just what force can accomplish, and cannot be expected to accomplish, in a given situation and within specific policy guidelines.

Notes

1. JCS Publication Number Four, 1 Jul 1969.

2. David C. Jones, "Why the Joint Chiefs of Staff Must Change," *Armed Forces Journal International* Mar 1982, pp 62, 64–68, 72. Edward C. Meyer, "The JCS—How Much Reform is Needed?," *Armed Forces Journal International*, Apr 1982, pp 82, 84–90. Robert F. Ellsworth, "JCS Reform—and More: A Long Overdo Initiative," *Armed Forces Journal International*, May 1982, pp 69, 76.

3. Historical Division, Joint Secretariat, Joint Chiefs of Staff, *The History of the Joint Chiefs of Staff. The Joint Chiefs of Staff and The War in Vietnam: History of the Indochina Incident, 1940–1954,* Vol I, 20 Aug 1971. (Top Secret downgraded to Unclassified.)

4. BDM Corporation, *A Study of Strategic Lessons Learned in Vietnam; Volume 5, Planning the War* (McLean, Va., 4 Apr 1980), pp 3–1 to 3–2.

5. Alexander S. Cochran, Jr., "American Planning for Ground Combat in Vietnam, 1952–1965," *Parameters, Journal of the U.S. Army War College*, Vol XIV, No 2 (Dec 1983), p 65.

6. Ronald Spector, "The First Vietnamization: U.S. Advisors in Vietnam 1956–1960," pp 109–15 in Joe C. Dixon, ed., *The American Military and the Far East,* Proceedings of the Ninth Military History Symposium, U.S. Air Force Academy, 1980 (Washington, 1980); *U.S.-Vietnam Relations, 1945–1967* (Washington, 1973). IVA (4), pp 1.1–5.1.

7. Eugene G. Windchy, *Tonkin Gulf* (Garden City, 1971), p 317; Joseph C. Goulden, *Truth is the First Casualty—The Gulf of Tonkin Affair; Illusion and Reality* (Chicago, 1969), pp 37, 48–79. U.S. Congress, Senate, Committee on Foreign Relations, *The Gulf of Tonkin, the 1964 Incidents,* 90th Cong, 2nd sess, 20 Feb 1968.

8. Johnson, *The Vantage Point* (New York, 1971), p 130; Taylor, *Swords and Plowshares* (New York, 1972), p 337; *U.S.-Vietnam Relations,* IVC (3), pp 48–51.

9. *U.S.-Vietnam Relations,* IVC (3), p 79.

10. Johnson, *The Vantage Point,* p 120.

11. *Public Papers of the Presidents Lyndon B. Johnson 1965 Volume I,* (Washington, 1966), p 319.

12. JCSM 652–65, Aug 27, 1965, Subject: Concept for Vietnam, quoted in *U.S.-Vietnam Relations,* IVC (6) (a), p 14.

13. *Ibid.*

14. *U.S.-Vietnam Relations*, IVC (6) (A), p 15.

15. Personal interview with General Westmoreland, 16 Sep 1973.

16. *U.S.-Vietnam Relations*, IVC (6) (a), p 81.

17. *Ibid*, pp 93–100.

18. *Ibid*, pp 108–10.

19. *U.S.-Vietnam Relations*, IVC (6) (b), pp 61–67.

20. *Ibid*, pp 74–76.

21. *U.S.-Vietnam Relations*, IVC (6) (b), pp 222–23.

22. *Ibid*, pp 225–26.

23. Tom Wicker, *JFK and LBJ: The Influence of Personalities on Politics* (New York, 1968), p 208.

24. *Public Papers of the Presidents: Lyndon B. Johnson 1965, Vol 1*, p 395.

25. Stephen Peter Rosen, "Vietnam and the American Theory of Limited War," *International Security*, Fall, 1982, pp 84–87.

26. Johnson, *The Vantage Point*, p 326.

27. Cochran, *op cit*.

28. Alain C. Enthoven and Wayne K. Smith, *How Much is Enough? Shaping the Defense Program, 1961–1969* (New York, 1971), pp 299–300.

29. Westmoreland, *A Soldier Reports*, p 159.

30. *Ibid*, p 417.

31. Theodore Sorensen, *Kennedy* (New York, 1969), p 605.

Commentary

Melvyn P. Leffler

The papers by Futrell, Schandler, and Etzold are stimulating and thought provoking. They should prompt civilian and military authorities to think more seriously about improving the planning process.

Futrell shows that tactical and air mobility capabilities were pretty much disregarded in the quest to develop overwhelming strategic air striking power. More importantly, he argues that this mix of forces "strapped the U.S. Air Force into a lone wolf configuration poorly prepared for the requirements of war and confrontation in the years following the Cuban Missile Crisis of 1962." In short, Futrell criticizes Air Force planners for emphasizing capabilities that were not well designed for the types of conflicts in which the U.S. was to become embroiled. We had enormous capabilities, but they were not well geared to achieve many of the nation's overall objectives. The reason, says Futrell, is that weapons and technology determined strategy rather than vice versa.

Schandler's paper takes a different approach. He focuses on objectives during the Vietnam War. He emphasizes the ambiguity of American goals and the inherent discord that emerged between Johnson and McNamara on the one hand and Westmoreland, Sharp, and the JCS on the other hand. In sum, he suggests, we had objectives that were unrealizable given the constraints imposed by the President and the unwillingness of military planners to establish a viable strategy within those constraints.

The Futrell and Schandler papers stress a mismatch between means and ends, between available forces and national objectives. Yet according to a recent JCS handbook, military strategy "is the art and science of employing the armed forces to secure the objectives of national policy by the application of force or threat of force."[1] Why, then, have military planners not done a better job of reconciling means and ends; why have they not been able to configure forces and design tactics more capable of achieving vital national objectives? It is in this regard that Etzold's paper is very instructive. Poor naval planning in the 1970s, he suggests, emerged from an unwillingness of naval leaders to tackle basic assumptions, to define objectives, to rethink antiquated theories of sea power, and to debate frankly with top civilian officials their differences over means and ends. Good planning, Etzold emphasizes, is more than a nuts and bolts exercise, much more even than sophisticated systems analysis. What he has to say is illuminating and significant. But the requirements of effective planning demand both leadership from civilian authorities as well as a bolder conceptualization of their task by military planners. It is ironic yet suggestive that one can look at military planning during the very onset of the cold war and locate many of the factors that have beleaguered the planning process ever since.

Let us step back for a moment to August 1945. Atomic bombs had been dropped on Hiroshima and Nagasaki, the Japanese were about to surrender, and the Joint Chiefs of Staff were turning their attention to the postwar era. Influential officers on the Joint Strategic Survey Committee (JSSC), the Joint War Plans Committee (JWPC), the Joint Planning Staff (JPS), and the Joint Post War Committee (JPWC) agreed to focus immediate attention on devising both a postwar strategic concept and a detailed list of overseas base requirements. They also decided to undertake a comprehensive study of the basis upon which to formulate postwar military policy.[2]

Staff officers on the JCS committees started with the assumption that military policy was supposed to uphold national policy. At this point, they encountered their first dilemma: civilian officials had not yet provided clear guidelines on what constituted vital interests or foreign policy priorities. For the time being, the planners took the liberty to define these objectives for themselves.[3]

But neither the JCS nor James Forrestal, the Secretary of the Navy, felt content with this initial effort. In their view, technological developments *and* the economic requirements of total war necessitated a comprehensive study of national security requirements by a specially appointed presidential board.[4] At the same time the JSSC completed a new report on the Soviet Union and requested, as a priority matter, a new assessment that would define where the United States could and should draw the line to deter future Soviet expansion. The JCS concluded that this new study must be submitted to the Secretaries of War and Navy and reconciled with the views of the State Department before submission to the President.[5] Although Secretary of War Robert P. Patterson had misgivings about some of these initiatives, he was alarmed by the pace of demobilization and its prospective impact on occupation goals in Germany, Japan, and elsewhere. Accordingly, on 1 November 1945, Patterson sent Secretary of State Byrnes a list of questions, the answers to which might underscore the close linkages between military strength and policy objectives and thereby not only slow down the pace of demobilization but also provide a more coherent context for planning itself.[6]

The response of the White House and State Department to these initiatives are revealing. President Harry S Truman turned down the request for a special study of national security requirements. At the Secretary of State's staff committee meeting on 13 November, Byrnes' closest aides expressed widespread dissatisfaction with the JCS study that tried to establish a framework for formulating postwar military policy. State Department officials clearly were uncomfortable with attempts to lay out and rank national interests. At about the same time, they also refused to delineate critical regions in Asia where the use of American military forces might be warranted. And Secretary of State Byrnes responded to Patterson's questions on demobilization in an equally unforthcoming manner. Noting that neither 200,000 nor 400,000 troops would suffice to achieve political goals in Europe, Byrnes remarked that the country must have sufficient military strength to manifest a determination to back up national policies everywhere.[7] The problem that Byrnes obscured, of course, was that planners felt they had neither the manpower nor the financial resources to manifest such a determination. This was especially true during the late autumn of 1945 when State Department officials were defining objectives in a more and more expansive manner. They were already advocating policies to revive the economies of Western Europe, contain the revolutionary left in Italy and Greece, deter Soviet expansion in Turkey and northern Iran, establish a trusteeship in all of Korea, support a united, democratic, and pro-American government in China, and elicit Soviet acquiescence to some modest form of equal commercial opportunity and democratic government in eastern Europe.[8]

During the winter of 1945–46, military planners became alarmed by the absence of meaningful collaboration with State Department officials and by the emerging gap between foreign policy goals and military capabilities. At meetings of the Joint Planning Staff, Navy, Army, and Air Force planners emphasized and reiterated that objectives exceeded capabilities, that vital interests were not being distinguished from secondary and tertiary interests, and that State Department officials were not willing to delineate where military force should be used to uphold national interests. It was difficult to conduct intelligent planning without this information. To help clarify some of the imponderables, planners pleaded for an official political estimate of the Soviet Union upon which to base their initial war plans.[9]

By the time military planners received this estimate, the State Department had taken a strong public stand to secure the removal of Russian troops from northern Iran, and Truman privately had ordered Byrnes to assume a tougher posture in all negotiations.[10] Yet some of Byrnes's closest assistants, like Ben Cohen, worried that the diplomatic posture of the U.S. might be too intransigent. The Secretary of State, therefore, requested a JCS analysis of Soviet demands regarding the Dardanelles and Tripolitania, and Cohen sought out the advice of General George Lincoln, the Army planner. Significantly, military advice was unequivocally to make no concessions; the growth of Soviet influence and/or power in Asia Minor or North Africa could not be permitted.[11] Despite all their apprehensions about the gap between capabilities and objectives, the planners and the JCS encouraged a definition of goals that far exceeded available means.

So in the formative years of the cold war, planners found themselves in a terrible bind. During 1947–49, they continued to observe civilian officials assuming an ever widening set of objectives and commitments. The Truman Doctrine implicitly committed the United States to Greece and Turkey; the Marshall Plan and German rehabilitation led to NATO; the reconstruction of Western Europe demanded assured access to Middle East oil; and the reverse course in Japan accentuated the importance of containing communism and revolutionary nationalism in Korea and Southeast Asia. Planners had serious reservations about Korea, but for the most part they defined American goals in a similar, all-encompassing fashion. Moreover, they realized that the pursuit of these objectives, including a revitalized Germany and Japan, might provoke Soviet countermeasures and lead to war. Looking at the $14.4 billion they would have available in the 1950 budget, planners felt they could not even meet the initial strategic undertakings in their war plans. The JCS informed Forrestal that the prospective budget left the nation unprepared for war, should it erupt. The JCS also reviewed all American commitments and objectives and insisted once again that they far exceeded capabilities.[12]

In general, planners recognized the United States had no strategy, that is, insufficient military assets to reconcile means and

320

ends. The emphasis on air power and atomic weaponry was the best they could do, given the fiscal constraints that Futrell correctly stresses. Although this military posture was largely disconnected with the pursuit of national security objectives throughout much of the globe, it did provide a deterrent to threatening Soviet behavior in absolutely critical areas, like central Europe.

The White House and State Department generally shrugged off the rising discontent of the planners. Civilians, of course, were disgusted by the bitter rivalry between the Air Force and Navy. The pursuit of organizational self-interest among the services discredited the larger problems planners were raising, that is, their inability to design plans capable of achieving national objectives, fulfilling commitments, or assuring readiness at the onset of conflict. State Department officials, however, remained confident that the Soviet Union would avoid war. Had not the Russians pulled out of Iran, refrained from intervention in Greece, and avoided conflict over Berlin? And the men at Foggy Bottom also believed that elsewhere American objectives could be achieved through a mixture of economic, military, and technical assistance. In short, they thought war unlikely; they defined the nature of the threat in terms of socio-economic chaos and revolutionary nationalist turmoil; and they conceived of solutions primarily in nonmilitary terms. They remained reluctant to define vital interests or assign priorities to foreign policy goals in a world that was so completely interconnected. All of this was apparent in NSC 20/4, adopted in November 1948.[13]

After the Soviet explosion of the atomic bomb and the fall of China, attitudes at Foggy Bottom began to change. State Department officials were the strongest proponents of NSC 68. But in June 1950 fiscal conservatives and budget balancers still were fighting to contain big military spending. Truman had not made up his own mind when the 38th parallel in Korea was crossed.[14]

That the United States was ill-equipped to fight the war in Korea was not primarily the fault of military planners. The White House and the State Department continually had broadened American interests and had incrementally vested American prestige in Korea, yet had been unwilling to define what areas were worth fighting over. They had circumscribed military spending and had denied planners the means to defend peripheral areas which, they, the civilians, subsequently sought to defend militarily.[15] The mismatch between military capabilities and national objectives did not stem simply from new technology, but from grandiose objectives, tight budgets, imprecise priorities, and an inchoate understanding of the threat policymakers and planners were struggling against.

After the Korean War the situation did not improve. Since many government documents for the post-Korean era still remain classified, historians must tread carefully. Yet one thing is for certain, the American nuclear threat was no longer a hollow one in the 1950s. In a pathbreaking article, David Rosenberg has depicted the unprecedented buildup of American warheads and delivery vehicles, especially in the late 1950s. Moreover, Rosenberg shows that Eisenhower himself, despite his considerable skill and understanding, could not control the buildup or get the planners to clarify the strategy upon which the buildup was based. Exactly why and how this happened is not yet clear, for Eisenhower refrained from using nuclear weapons, although he never ruled them out, to achieve American objectives in third world areas where the cold war was increasingly being waged. He preferred to rely on covert operations, which in his initial years as President proved so successful in Iran and Guatemala. But the worsening situation in Laos and Vietnam and the subsequent Bay of Pigs fiasco illustrated the limits of CIA operations. Yet strategic air power seemed equally unsuited to deal with revolutionary nationalist turmoil and guerrilla insurrections. Nevertheless, military planning, as Futrell demonstrates, continued to focus primarily on war-fighting against the Soviet Union rather than on developing capabilities and tactics to support overall foreign policy objectives.[16]

The gap between planning and objectives is seen to be equally wide when one takes note of Eisenhower's interest in limiting the arms race. Yet the immense proliferation of warheads and delivery vehicles created a poor context for convincing the Soviets that arms control was a serious American objective. From Rosenberg's article we now have a better understanding of why Robert McNamara acknowledged several years ago that Soviet planners had good reason to fear that the United States was developing a preemptive capability.[17] This may not have been the intent of planners, but it was a consequence of their actions. And it underscores the apparently narrow context in which planning took place; a context that emphasized war-fighting with the Soviet Union at the expense of all other national objectives.

In this regard, Schandler's paper is of particular interest because it focuses on objectives, rather than capabilities during the Vietnam War. I agree with his emphasis, but not with some of his analysis. I do not think the evidence demonstrates that Johnson, Rusk, and

McNamara had a different goal in Indochina than did the JCS. For Westmoreland and the JCS, the objective was to preserve an independent non-Communist South Vietnam. When Johnson, Rusk, and McNamara stated that their aim was to convince the enemy to abandon the military struggle and go to the bargaining table, they still expected to get an independent, non-Communist South Vietnam through negotiations. Notwithstanding George Ball and a few other dissidents, the goal of the Johnson administration was to prevent the loss of South Vietnam. "Your mission," Johnson wrote Henry Cabot Lodge in March 1964 "is precisely for the purpose of knocking down the idea of neutralization wherever it rears its ugly head." McNamara was more circumspect, but he defined a favorable outcome as one which maintained an independent, non-Communist, and hopefully pro-American government in South Vietnam.[18] Military leaders clearly grasped the fundamental objective, but could not achieve it.

They failed to achieve it not simply because of inadequate means, but because the goal had been so poorly conceived ever since it became a foreign policy issue in the 1940s. The opposition to Ho Chi Minh reflected an all-consuming desire to defeat international communism everywhere without defining areas of priority, without delineating relationships between the Kremlin and Communist or revolutionary nationalist movements, without examining local and regional circumstances, without assessing costs, risks, and benefits, and without dissecting the threat being thwarted. The goal may now seem obscure only because the reasons for it, and the circumstances surrounding it were so incoherent. But I would submit that the goal itself was clear and consistent for over two decades. The problem was that it was not susceptible to military solution, especially given the constraints, so adeptly emphasized by Schandler. From his and other accounts we can discern that planners could neither assure victory within the limitations imposed by Johnson nor convince him to jettison these limitations.[19] Why, then, did the planners not call for a reassessment of the objective?

Strategy calls for the linkage of tactics and goals. Throughout most of the cold war, civilians have defined objectives that far exceeded American capabilities. They have been reluctant to rank goals and have not seriously planned for the role of force in achieving goals until crises were underway and American prestige embroiled. Meanwhile, military planners, as Futrell and Etzold show, have preferred to focus on fighting wars against the Soviet Union and in ways that relate primarily to organizational rather than national self-interest. Relatively small amounts of time and effort have been spent developing tactics and assets geared to the diverse goals of policymakers. In my view, Schandler and Etzold, therefore, are correct when they emphasize that objectives, interests, and assumptions must be continuously subject to scrutiny.

Yet they provide very little guidance on how to define these interests and goals. Too frequently, it is assumed that the national interest will simply evolve from the interplay of pressure groups and bureaucracies rather than from careful analysis of evolving national and international circumstances. Goals must emerge as a result of thoughtful assessments of vital interests and sustainable capabilities over time. Planning requires a shrewd assessment of these interests, a subtle examination of other nations' intentions, and an astute appraisal of threat as well as an imaginative configuration of forces and selection of tactics. When all of this occurs, we will have military planning that approaches a strategy. Since civilians sometimes have defaulted most egregiously in this linkage of means and ends, perhaps military planners might lead the way.

Notes

1. Quoted in Harry G. Summers, *On Strategy: A Critical Analysis of the Vietnam War* (Novato, Calif., 1982), p 4.

2. See, for example, the materials in Record Group (RG) 218, Records of the Joint Chiefs of Staff (JCS), CCS 381 (5–13–45), sect 1, National Archives (NA); also see James F. Schnabel, *The History of the Joint Chiefs of Staff: The Joint Chiefs of Staff and National Policy, 1945–1947* (Wilmington, Del., 1979), 1:135–45.

3. JPS 633/6, "Basis for the Formulation of a Post-War Military Policy," 20 Aug 1945, RG 218, CCS 381 (5–13–45), sect 1, NA.

4. See, for example, William Leahy to Secretaries of War and Navy, 24 Oct 1945, Harry S Truman Papers (HSTP), President's Secretary's File (PSF), box 158, Harry S Truman Library (HSTL); Memorandum to the President, by Forrestal, 8 Nov 1945, *ibid.*

5. JCS 1545, "Military Position of the United States in Light of Russian Policy," 8 Oct 1945, RG 218, CCS 092 USSR (3–27–45), sect 1, NA.

6. For Patterson's concern about the impact of demobilization, see, for example, Patterson to James F. Byrnes, 1 Nov 1945, Department of State, *Foreign Relations of the United States, 1946* (Washington, 1972), 1:1111–12, hereafter cited as *FRUS.*

7. For Truman's action, see Truman to Forrestal, 29 Nov 1945, HSTP, PSF, box 158, HSTL; for the staff committee meeting, see *FRUS*, 1946, 1:1119–28; for Byrnes' response to Patterson and State Department views, see *ibid*, pp 1128–33.

8. See Melvyn P. Leffler, *American National Security, 1945–50*, chapter one (manuscript in preparation for The University of North Carolina Press).

9. For the meetings of the Joint Planning Staff (JPS), see JPS, 236th meeting, RG 218, CCS 092 USSR (3–27–45), sect 4; JPS, 238th meeting (late Jan 1945), *ibid*, sect 5; JPS, 240th meeting, 6 Mar 1946, RG 218, CCS 381 USSR (3–2–46), sect 1, NA. For the JCS request for a political estimate of the Soviet Union, see Memorandum for the Secretary, JCS, by George Juskalian (14 Mar 1946), RG 165, Records of the Army's Operations Division (OPD), OPD 350.05 TS, NA.

10. "Adequate Governmental Machinery to Handle Foreign Affairs" (no signature), 13 Mar 1946, RG 319, Records of the Army's Plans and Operations Division (P&O), P&O, 092 TS, NA. For Truman's instructions to Byrnes, see diary entry, 28 Feb 1946, HSTP, Eben A. Ayers Papers, box 16, HSTL.

11. See, for example, Byrnes to JCS, 6 Mar 1946, RG 218, CCS 092 USSR (3–27–45), sect 5; JCS 1641 series, "U.S. Security Interests in the Eastern Mediterranean," Mar 1946, *ibid*, sect 6; Memorandum for the Record, by Lincoln, 16 Apr 1946, RG 165, Records of American British Conversation (ABC), ABC 336 Russia (22 Aug

1943), sect 1–c; Lincoln to Hull, 16 Apr 1946, *ibid*, ABC 092 USSR (15 Nov 1944); Howard C. Petersen to Patterson, 22 Apr 1946, RG 107, Records of the Office of the Secretary of War, Robert P. Patterson Papers, safe File, box 1, NA.

12. Melvyn P. Leffler, "The American Conception of National Security and the Beginnings of the Cold War," *The American Historical Review*, 89 (Apr 1984): 369–78.

13. *Ibid*, pp 346–81; for an excellent discussion of the impact of the Iranian, Greek, and Berlin crises on decisionmaking, see John R. Oneal, *Foreign Policy Making in Times of Crises* (Columbus, Ohio, 1982). NSC 20/4, adopted in Nov 1948, constituted the definitive statement of overall American foreign policy until NSC 68. NSC 20/4 may be found in John L. Gaddis and Thomas Etzold, *Containment: Documents on American Policy and Strategy, 1945–1950* (New York, 1978), pp 203–11.

14. John L. Gaddis, *Strategies of Containment* (New York, 1981), pp 92–95. For the continuing opposition of budget balancers to NSC 68 and for Truman's hesitation, see Robert Pollard, "The National Security State Reconsidered: Truman and Rearmament, 1945–50," paper delivered at the Harry S Truman Centennial Symposium, The Woodrow Wilson International Center (Washington, 1984).

15. See, for example, William W. Stueck, *The Road to Confrontation: American Policy Toward China and Korea* (Chapel Hill, N.C., 1981); Charles M. Dobbs, *The Unwanted Symbol: American Foreign Policy, the Cold War, and Korea, 1945–1950* (Kent, Ohio, 1981).

16. David Alan Rosenberg, "The Origins of Overkill: Nuclear Weapons and American Strategy," *International Security*, 7 (Spring 1983) 3–71; Stephen Ambrose, *Ike's Spies: Eisenhower and the Espionage Establishment* (Garden City, 1981).

17. Robert Scheer, *With Enough Shovels: Reagan, Bush, and Nuclear War* (New York, 1982), pp 218–19; for Eisenhower, the arms race, and test ban negotiations, see Robert Divine, *Eisenhower and the Cold War* (New York, 1981), pp 110ff.

18. Gareth Porter (ed.), *Vietnam: A History in Documents* (New York, 1981), pp 271, 318; Larry Berman, *Planning A Tragedy: The Americanization of the War in Vietnam* (New York, 1982).

19. For an excellent summary of the literature, see George C. Herring, "American Strategy in Vietnam: The Postwar Debate," *Military Affairs* 46 (Apr 1982), pp 57–63.

Discussion and Comments

General A.J. Goodpaster, USA, Retired, Moderator

George Grosskopf (U.S. Navy, Retired): I would like to direct my question to Dr. Schandler please. I served a year in Vietnam, and the question I'd like to put to you I put to others when I was in-country, but I haven't had the opportunity to ask someone at your level. I didn't, and I still don't, understand this morbid body count approach. Even a sailor understands that continual gain of territory means something. Can you tell me if in the past such statistics were ever used in any war or police action?

Schandler: Again, I think this goes back to objectives. In Vietnam there were no geographical objectives that you could take, and I don't want to put the whole blame on the military either—Vietnam was a political war, and part of our objective should have been winning the hearts and the minds of the people, pacification, building a South Vietnamese government, an army capable of defending their country so that we could get out of it. The military really had very difficult ways or no ways, really, of measuring progress in Vietnam other than this approach and the strategy adopted was really a conventional military strategy in Vietnam. This was the objective of defeating the enemy, and I think this was adopted basically as a way of showing that we were defeating the enemy and even as a psychological device on the enemy, showing him that he couldn't win. Military operations were never, it seems to me, coordinated with the political objectives of winning the hearts and minds of the people, so we were unable to show that we had made progress on the ground. We developed a whole province advisory system, a measurement system, and a hamlet evaluation system to attempt to show progress. But in a war in which you are really trying to wear the enemy down psychologically, you are trying to show him that he can't win. There really were no other ways of measuring this. I think the strategy adopted on the ground or the tactics adopted on the ground (I don't know if you can call it a strategy or not), really were based upon continuing American increases. In fact the tactics on the ground were based upon the removal of these restrictions at some point by the President. As I indicated in my paper, the fact that they were never going to be removed while President Lyndon Johnson was in office anyhow, really precluded the success of the military operations in Vietnam. We weren't going about it in the right way. We were never going to get the resources needed to achieve what the objectives were on the ground over there. I think basically this was derived as a means of measuring progress the same way in the air war in the north. The way you measured progress was by tons of bombs dropped, sorties, and missions, whether they hit anything or not. Whether they were helping to achieve the objective or not, was very difficult to measure. I remember, and I say this really in sadness, reading the CINCPAC 1967 evaluation of the air war in North Vietnam. Admiral Sharp wrote this great report talking about the number of sorties, number of bombs dropped, number of bridges destroyed, railcars destroyed, roads destroyed; and then at the end, he said by a prodigious effort and by the diverting resources, the transportation system in North Vietnam at the end of 1967 was slightly improved over what it was at the beginning of 1967. And it's funny, but that was in his official report to the President. Looking at this, one could say, "My God, can't we figure out a cheaper way to improve the transportation system in North Vietnam than the way we're doing it." So it was very difficult to measure progress in this kind of a war.

Goodpaster: I think I owe it to the audience to step out of my role as chairman in relation to the question and discussion, because this is a question of fact which I was in position to observe as deputy commander in Vietnam from mid–1968 to mid–1969. During that period, we did indeed have ways of measuring our progress. General Abrams was the commander and I, as deputy commander, and Bob Komer, subsequently Bill Colby, together defined a set of criteria— outputs rather than inputs—that would indeed measure progress. One of them, referring to the hearts and minds, was to see how far the accelerated pacification campaign launched by President Thieu (with great courage I might say) in the fall of 1968—how far that was able to go—what parts of the populated area were brought back under control and under safe conditions for the conduct of the normal activities of government. Along with that, there was, as an output, a determination of the location of the main force units that were being employed against us. The idea being to get them back into the high jungle area where they could not maraud and damage the accelerated pacification plan. I won't go into more detail except to suggest that those of you who are interested in this ought to give careful attention to that year of operation and to the year that followed, a year in which a ceiling had been placed on the American forces. Indeed, we were engaged in the process of Vietnamization of the war. Reach your judgments on analysis of the facts as developed during that period. And now I will step back into my proper role as chairman.

Schandler: Let me respond for just a moment if I may sir, because my remarks were intended to go through the period of the Tet Offensive of 1968. During the Tet Offensive and in the recommendations made thereafter, a limitation was put upon American forces. The restrictions on the forces were generally accepted. It was seen that we would have to increase the Vietnamese forces and withdraw, and this was really a rationalization of our system in the period after 1968. After Tet came a rationalization, a dependence upon the Vietnamese, a concentration on the pacification program, a complete change in our objectives there.

William Pickett (Rose-Hulman Institute of Technology): This question is for Dr. Schandler and also General Goodpaster, I wondered if you have come across any information about President Eisenhower's role as an advisor to LBJ, and if you know his opinion of LBJ's approach in Vietnam?

Goodpaster: I'll answer that. The documents have now been released, as you may know, and they are accessible—I've seen a set of them. I served at President Johnson's request as liaison with former President Eisenhower from 1964 until I went to Vietnam in 1968. At President Johnson's request, I kept President Eisenhower informed of the progress of the war. He talked with President Johnson a number of times by phone; very often he would send advice and counsel, and on one occasion privately met with Johnson and his leaders in the cabinet room to discuss the conduct of the war. It would be too much for me to attempt to summarize it here except perhaps to use one figure of speech which Eisenhower used repeatedly, and that was to avoid the tactics of gradualism, to decide what it was he wished to do, and then to use, in the military term, adequate and superior force in order to accomplish that. He said if my enemy holds a hill with one battalion and I attack with two and I know my business, I probably will be able to take that hill—it may take me a while and the losses may be heavy on both sides. The interesting thing is if I attack with five battalions, and I know anything about my job, I'll certainly be able to take it. I'll probably take it with much smaller losses and in a much shorter period of time.

Schandler: May I make one comment on that sir?

Goodpaster: Yes, please.

Schandler: Because Johnson didn't go to Eisenhower for military advice, he used President Eisenhower basically as a political leader, as I said, to gain political support for his objectives. Eisenhower was a Republican, a military man, a leader of the Republican Party, and this was basically a political tactic by LBJ; he maintained throughout that he was merely following what other administrations had done in Vietnam, that there was nothing new, that he was supporting the policies of Eisenhower, of Kennedy, and so on. This consulting with Eisenhower insofar as he got military advice might have been useful but it was a political tactic by LBJ again to gain public support for the war.

Goodpaster: The follow-on question, as to whether I agree—I would see quite a lot more to it than that. (*laughter*)

Tom Fabyanic (University of South Florida at Tampa): My question is for Dr. Frank Futrell. The implications of the trends that you outline from 1945 to 1962 are rather profound. Would you be willing to extend your analysis to the Vietnam period?

Futrell: The extension of my analysis to the Vietnam period—in the first place I don't think Vietnam was a military problem. I worked on the advisory phase of the Vietnam problem as you know. I tried to conceal that, and the book didn't turn out too well. Neither did the war. But what could we have done? We had modeled air power after a fight against a metropolitan enemy who had vital centers. How do you use technology against an enemy who does not admit his vital centers to your attack? Therefore, can you settle a problem as Vietnam militarily? I think I've closed a circle—there was no military solution for Southeast Asia. Of course you realize that Vietnam was only one portion of Southeast Asia. As long as we left the frontier on Laos wide open, the frontier on Cambodia wide open, the military rules could not apply; neither could air power or technology apply to that. Early on, there was an Air Force plan by Colonel Grover Brown, who subsequently became a general officer, that the solution to the problem in Vietnam was not conventional military forces, as we were trying to build there, but was rather the quick mobility on the part of the South Vietnamese constabulary that would respond very quickly nationwide to Viet Cong attacks. That would not then involve a metropolitan type use of war. Now I've closed the circle and talked all around it, the simple fact is, I don't know.

Goodpaster: I'm afraid we've run out of time. I'm going to provide one minute to our speakers. If they would care to make a statement in the order in which they spoke initially. Professor Futrell.

Futrell: I would add to the consideration of body count—early on body count originated with the Diem regime, reflecting the desire on Secretary McNamara's part to quantify—Secretary Brown had stated at one time that it was one of the great disappointments of Secretary McNamara in Southeast Asia that he could never find a way to quantify. And thus I would go back and modify my whole statement and my paper that one of the greatest things you need in terms of military experience is to learn how to evaluate effectiveness of military operations.

Schandler: Yes, just one comment. Professor Leffler indicated that I stated our goals in Vietnam were not obtainable, and I'm not sure that that is correct. Perhaps our goals were obtainable if we could have figured out what our goals were and then applied the resources to those goals. But we chose only the military defeat of the enemy, which seemed to be an obtainable goal, and we did not apply military forces in a way which would have assisted in pacification, would have built up the South Vietnamese government, in ways which would have made our goals obtainable. Political science gives no prescription for building a democratic regime in a former colonial country short of qualified manpower in the midst of a war. So I don't know if we could have done that or not; the point is we never really tried.

Goodpaster: Dr. Leffler?

Leffler: Nothing further.

Goodpaster: I think that we have exhausted our time, and I will avoid every temptation to step out of my role as chairman again, and simply say that there still remains much in the Vietnam story that is yet to be told. I am happy to be here with historians. I think historians have a very vital role. I think history can serve often as the test of policy, as the test of strategy. To see outcomes, to in effect relate output to input, to see outcomes and to relate and evaluate those outcomes against the intentions, against the policies, against the strategy or lack of strategy, of those who bore the responsibility for leadership. And on that note may I say that it has been a particular personal pleasure to be with you and to turn over the podium to Major Harvey.

SESSION IV

Planning and Limited Conflict
1945–1980

Introduction

Because of the Vietnam War, Americans view limited war with great apprehension. How then should military planners address the matter of contingency planning for limited war in regions of the world most likely to produce conflict involving U.S. interests? To look at this issue, the Eleventh Military History Symposium dedicated its last session to the topic of military planning for limited warfare after Vietnam.

As planning for the symposium developed, Latin America loomed large in the minds of Americans. The United States invaded Grenada and made its economic assistance and military presence known in Central America. The American public warned against extensive involvement and asked what exactly were U.S. interests in this region. To provide a historical foundation for this key question, Professor Child agreed to analyze our military planning efforts as they concerned Latin America over the past fifty years.

The United States, he tells the reader, has always taken Latin America for granted, and government agencies have usually given the region low priority until an immediate problem surfaced threatening U.S. interests. Then planning progressed along on an *ad hoc* basis. Historically, our dealings with Latin American countries have been seldom those of equal partners; U.S. interests centered primarily on the availability of resources and potential bases in the region while denying the same to potential adversaries. With the advent of the cold war, for example, the United States instituted military assistance programs and President Kennedy made national development and civic actions a large part of U.S. assistance to Latin America in exchange for multilateral and bilateral agreements between the United States and Latin American countries.

The year 1965 and the Dominican Republic crisis marked a high point in U.S.-Latin American relations regarding military planning, but as the Vietnam War commanded more U.S. attention, cooperation fell off. As the Cuban revolution appeared less danger-ous, U.S. agencies further lost interest, and the Congress was more reluctant to grant military assistance to Latin American nations. The drift continued with human rights issues during the Carter administration. As Latin American countries found sources of assistance elsewhere and relied less upon the United States, the climate around joint military cooperation and planning changed. At the time of the conference, it was clear that the basis for strong joint military planning with regard to Latin America was not historically strong and could take any number of turns.

Alexander Cochran's more contemporary paper examines how well the U.S. military has been planning for another limited conflict. Nations and their armies have responded differently to defeats: Jena spurred the Prussians into a military system that brought great success in the nineteenth century; the French adopted a defensive frame of mind after the Great War; Japanese attitudes toward its military altered dramatically after August 1945. How would the United States respond to its negative experience in Vietnam? In 1984 the consensus among military officers and scholars seemed evenly divided over the matter of impact. Some held the Vietnam legacy was nonexistent after a decade; others were less sure and believed such a dramatic experience had to leave some mark. While Cochran's task was made more difficult by the shortage of historical documents, he describes the turmoil within the Army following the U.S. departure from Vietnam.

The U.S. Army, he argues, faced many problems after Vietnam—demobilizing, implementing the All Volunteer Force concept, resolving the status of reserves, and modernizing NATO forces. Within the context of these problems, Army officers examined their service carefully in books and professional journals, first finding fault with their institution and developing, in Cochran's words, a "crisis in confidence." By the end of the decade, however, their attitudes shifted toward the idea that the Army was not totally at fault; the will of the American people had much to do with war's outcome. While they never came close to adopting a stab-in-the-back thesis reminiscent of 1930 Germany, they concluded that "wars of the future must be perceived as popular by the people, winnable by the military, and allowed to be won by the politician." Healthy discussions continued over doctrine, and a new AirLand Battle concept for NATO emerged. But the impact on planning for limited war seems to be manifested in caution. Army leaders, for example, were less enthusiastic about entering Lebanon in 1983 and in taking part in the Grenada operation than their civilian counterparts. This attitude seems healthy within the context of Clausewitzian thinking, but its potential dangers are apparent. If a nation's army holds grave reservations about fighting limited actions unless it feels their efforts

336

are solidly supported by its public, that nation's military loses some of its value as a political arm. On the other hand, utilizing warfare as a tool of national policy is, as Clausewitz tells us, the gravest of all decisions and restraint in making such choices cannot be unduly criticized. It remains for the reader and later historians to draw their own conclusions about the impact of the Vietnam War on U.S. planning efforts for limited wars. The basis for judgment may come in Latin America where our record is mixed.

Postwar U.S. Strategic Planning for Latin America (1945–1976): from "Rainbow" to "IDAD"

Jack Child

I. Introduction.

This paper examines United States strategic planning for Latin America in three post-World War II periods: 1945–1961 (cold war benign neglect); 1961–1967 (the *focos* and Internal Defense and Development—IDAD); 1967–1976 (strategic divergence, neglect, and system fragmentation).

The analysis will focus on the following themes:

—the tendency of U.S. strategic planners to take Latin America for granted and to give it low priority unless a significant threat is identified; in which case a specific *ad hoc* crisis response is generated to face the threat.

—the interplay of unilateral, bilateral, and multilateral U.S. strategic approaches, and the different political and military facets of these approaches.

—the bureaucratic political struggle (especially between the U.S. military and State Department) involved in this interplay.

—the creation, functions, and fate of the institutions established to implement U.S. strategic planning for Latin America.

A brief summary of U.S. strategic planning for Latin America prior to 1945 is presented here as an introduction to planning in the postwar period. The first coherent U.S. strategic planning for Latin America dates back to World War I, and focused on the closest Latin American neighbor, Mexico. U.S. relations with Mexico were strained during the war and through the whole 1910–1920 period of greatest instability of the Mexican Revolution. Copies of the 1919

338

"General Mexican War Plan" in the National Archives of the United States reveal the general features of strategic planning in this period: U.S. forces would be made available to seal the Mexican border and protect U.S. interests along the border; should conditions require it, expeditionary forces would blockade Mexican ports and seize the principal oil and coal fields in northern Mexico. The 1919 plan was superseded by the first of the so-called color plans: Green, which dealt with various contingencies in Mexico and built on the previous plan. Green was the most elaborate and detailed of all the color plans, and existing copies (of several thousand pages each) contain detailed instructions for subordinate units down to the smallest logistical detachments.[1]

Other color plans in the 1920s and 1930s were less elaborate and broader in scope. They ranged from those dealing with specific contingencies (such as Tan for intervention in Cuba and White for Panama Canal defense) to more sweeping plans (such as Gray) for blockading and landing in the remaining Caribbean and Central American countries. In the late 1920s a rather imaginative (and indeed almost incredible) series of Purple plans was drawn up by the U.S. War Department for the invasion of each South American country (except the land-locked nations of Bolivia and Paraguay).

The chief characteristic of the color plans of the 1920s and 1930s was that they were unilateral U.S. plans, reflecting an era of blatant U.S. military intervention in the Caribbean and Central America. The color plans contained no consideration of forming coalitions with the Latin American nations as allies. At most, there were some cases in which the plan called for the establishment of post-invasion constabulary forces under U.S. tutelage. The color plans had a strong geographic focus on the Caribbean and were linked to a unilateral strategic concept which envisioned the Caribbean as a U.S. lake.

All this was to change with the coming of the Good Neighbor Policy and the abandonment of U.S. unilateral intervention in favor of multilateral approaches to hemisphere security and diplomatic problems. The color plans were quietly shelved (although highly classified contingency plans remained for special situations in Panama, Mexico, and Brazil), and in the late 1930s the strategic planning effort went into a series of global plans known as the Rainbow plans.[2] These Rainbow plans integrated U.S. Latin American strategic planning into the global World War II allied effort and steered away from any implication of unilateral U.S. intervention in Latin America. Although they did not envision military operations with Latin American nations, they did focus on the need for U.S. bases and access rights in certain key countries (most notably Brazil, Mexico, Panama, and Ecuador). Unlike the color plan approach, these bases and access rights were to be obtained through cooperative efforts within the framework of Pan American solidarity in the war. Rainbow 1, 2, and 3 employed the concept of defending a "Quarter Sphere" (i.e., half of the Western Hemisphere) down to the northeastern bulge of Brazil, while Rainbow 4 provided for sending U.S. forces as far as the southern part of South America, and thus incorporated the broader concept of hemisphere defense.

The relationship between the quarter sphere and the hemisphere defense approaches of the various Rainbow plans was an important one. Hemisphere defense was primarily a political and diplomatic concept stressing the unity of all the nations of the hemisphere in the face of an outside threat. It was the strategic facet of the Good Neighbor Policy, and had long historical roots going back to the original Monroe Doctrine and the ideas of the Latin American Liberator Simon Bolivar. As a result, it was consistently advocated by the U.S. State Department as the strategic concept which would best ensure Latin American cooperation in economic, political, and diplomatic spheres. The U.S. military, in contrast, stressed the more limited and bilateral quarter sphere approach on the pragmatic grounds that the scarcity of resources made it impossible to defend the whole hemisphere. Further, the military departments tended to favor bilateral arrangements with selected allies (principally Brazil and Mexico) over multilateral military arrangements, which they saw as a waste of time and the source of possible security leaks to the Axis.

II. 1945–1961: Cold War Benign Neglect.

A. Overview.

U.S. strategic planning for Latin America for most of the 1945–1961 cold war period can aptly be characterized as benign neglect. The period began with encouraging signs that the attention devoted to hemisphere defense matters in World War II would be carried over into a permanent relationship through the institutionalization of a multilateral inter-American defense system. However, cold war crises in Western Europe and Korea soon distracted the United States from this goal, and Latin America was relegated to being a low-priority area with a distinctly secondary role.

General statements of U.S. strategic objectives can be found in recently declassified JCS and NSC documents.[3] These objectives included:

—Latin American political support of U.S. objectives in international fora.

—internal stability in Latin American nations.

—cooperation in eliminating Communist and other anti-U.S. subversion.

—assistance in securing hemisphere air and sea lanes.

—access to bases required by the U.S. for hemisphere defense as well as for operations outside the continent.

—standardization of Latin American military organization, training, doctrine, and equipment along U.S. lines.

U.S. military planners consistently viewed Latin America as an economy of force area whose greatest security contribution was to provide raw materials in an environment of internal and international stability. This stability would make minimum demands on U.S. strategic assets, which could be then safely diverted to higher priority areas of the globe. The world was strategically divided into a primary space where the superpowers contended for supremacy, and a secondary space (which included Latin America and most of the third world) whose principal role was to support the superpowers. Should the U.S. come under a nuclear attack, Latin America would play a vital role in providing survival and recovery commodities to the United States.[4]

The standardization objective mentioned above was the offshoot of a World War II concern that the Latin American military establishments had historically come under excessive European influence, and that in the early days of the war, the Germans and Italians were able to achieve political and strategic goals through this influence. Thus, the major U.S. objective of standardization of the Latin American military along U.S. lines implied keeping out European suppliers by giving or selling the Latins' surplus U.S. World War II equipment. Aggressive military sales activities by outside nations, even if they were NATO allies such as the British and French, were opposed by U.S. strategic planners during this period.[5]

The strategic geography of Latin American imposed its own set of priorities. A 1957 JCS document defined the areas of particular strategic importance to the United States as: the Panama Canal and its approaches; Mexico; Caribbean approaches to the United States; Venezuelan oil and iron producing areas; bauxite sources in the Guianas and Jamaica; northeast Brazil; Straits of Magellan and Cape Horn passages; and the mineral producing areas of Chile, Bolivia, and Peru.[6]

B. Early Postwar Strategic Planning.

The early postwar period (1945–1948) can be seen as a transition from the *ad hoc* arrangements made during the war to a permanent set of plans and institutions for security in the hemisphere. This transition involved a series of decisions which tended to bring out differences between the United States and Latin America as well as disagreements within U.S. policymaking circles. A further issue was the relative priority of Latin America in the global postwar strategy of the United States, and the way in which this priority would influence economic and military assistance.

From another perspective, this period was one in which planners sought a replacement for the wartime Rainbow plans for continental defense. Here the issue was whether to develop a multilateral hemisphere defense plan which would be the logical extension of Rainbow 4, or a series of bilateral approaches linked to key countries which would be closer to Rainbow 1, 2, and 3. In terms of institutions, this dichotomy meant deciding whether the U.S. strategic planning effort would emphasize multilateral military institutions such as the World War II Inter-American Defense Board, or, in contrast, stress the value of special bilateral defense commissions (such as those with Brazil and Mexico) and bilateral military assistance missions.

These years also witnessed some bitter bureaucratic infighting between the State Department and the U.S. military. During the war years the State Department had seen its influence diminish in Latin American policymaking as the U.S. military gained a free hand in the hemisphere on a broad range of matters frequently extending beyond the purely military ones. The problem was compounded by the significant political role played by many Latin American military institutions, and especially in those countries where the president was a military officer. These generals/presidents frequently held little respect for U.S. diplomats, and preferred to deal with senior

U.S. military officials if they could. Predictably, the professional U.S. diplomats deeply resented this arrangement, and welcomed the end of the hostilities as the appropriate moment to restore their prewar domination of inter-American policymaking.[7]

The first battleground for this struggle was the attempt to secure congressional approval of a major postwar transfer of U.S. weapons to Latin America (the Inter-American Military Cooperation Act). This legislation would replace the World War II Lend-Lease Act and would ensure standardization and continued U.S. military influence in Latin America. To the State Department, this was an unwarranted perpetuation of a situation barely tolerable under wartime emergency conditions. In the end the State Department prevailed, the bill failed, and U.S. military planners suffered a major setback.[8]

In February 1945 representatives of the American Republics met in Chapultepec, Mexico, for the Inter-American Conference on Problems of War and Peace, the stated purpose of which was to plan the postwar transition of the inter-American system, to include its security arrangements and institutions. However, because it took place just before the San Francisco United Nations Conference, it also became the arena for airing U.S.-Latin American differences on the relative importance of regional and universal international organizations. The Latin American delegations understandably wanted to protect their carefully nurtured regional system, and were anxious to create strong conflict-resolution and security instruments within this system. Specifically, there was a proposal to strengthen and make permanent a successor institution to the World War II *ad hoc* Inter-American Defense Board. In contrast, the United States wanted to avoid the creation of powerful regional institutions which might interfere with the effectiveness of the security instruments of the United Nations, and therefore opposed this Latin initiative.[9] The outcome of the Chapultepec Conference was a compromise which allowed the Board to continue, and left it to two subsequent conferences (Rio, 1947, and Bogota, 1948) to determine the fate of a permanent multilateral military organ within the inter-American system.

There was considerable irony in these opposed U.S. and Latin American positions at Chapultepec, in that three years after the 1945 conference, both the U.S. and Latin America reversed their positions. For the United States, the reason for the reversal was the reality of the cold war and the Soviet veto in the U.N. Security Council, which greatly reduced the value of that organization as a military instrument for enforcing peace and supporting U.S. strategic objectives. Thus, the United States increasingly saw the value of regional security arrangements, such as NATO and SEATO, which would serve to contain the Soviet Union and its allies. The inter-American system was viewed by U.S. policymakers as one more such containment alliance. For Latin America the reversal of positions after Chapultepec was due to a reluctance to get involved in the cold war and a disillusionment with the United States as it turned its attention to Western Europe and never came through with the hoped-for "Hemisphere Marshall Plan." Latin America was also returning to its traditional fear of U.S. interventionism, which had only been temporarily dissipated during the Good Neighbor period. There was Latin concern that strong multilateral military instruments under U.S. influence could be used as a guise for U.S. intervention in Latin America.

Thus, U.S. strategic planning for Latin America in the early years of this postwar period increasingly stressed the value of multilateral security arrangements and institutions in the form of a collective security treaty and the continuation of the Inter-American Defense Board or a successor under strong U.S. control. The State Department pressed this multilateral approach on somewhat reluctant War and Navy Departments, which continued to emphasize the value of bilateral relationships based on arms transfers and military training missions. The outcome of these two currents was a compromise under which the multilateral instruments would function as a symbolic cover for the real institutions of security, which would continue to be the bilateral ones favored by the military establishment. In practice, priority was given to the bilateral commissions between the U.S. and the key nations of Brazil and Mexico, as well as other countries with a high strategic significance such as Venezuela and Panama.

C. The Rio (1947) and Bogota (1948) Conferences.

The Rio Conference (the mission of which was to draft the collective security treaty) was scheduled to meet soon after Chapultepec, but problems between Argentina and the United States caused a series of delays. Unfortunately, these delays increased the gaps between U.S. and Latin American positions on security issues and made it less likely that meaningful agreement would be reached.

By 1947 the United States was well into the cold war and had become increasingly disenchanted with the United Nations as a global security instrument. Thus, a primary objective at the 1947 Rio Conference was to obtain a strong treaty which could be effectively used as an alliance against the Soviet Union and its allies. Further, the United States sought a treaty that would require the minimal diversion of U.S. strategic assets to the hemisphere. The U.S. military also was interested in obtaining access to bases in Latin America which might be useful to support and defend logistic links to other theaters such as Europe and the Far East.[11] The Latin American delegations at the Rio Conference (led aggressively by Argentina) resisted these U.S. objectives, arguing that the inter-American system was much more than a security system, and stressing the economic, political, and cultural dimensions of the relationship.

What emerged from the Conference was a weak Inter-American Treaty of Reciprocal Assistance (the so-called "Rio Treaty") which did not even require the American nations to provide military forces to aid an attacked nation. Further, the treaty did not create any of the essential alliance infrastructure, and in fact does not mention the Inter-American Defense Board or any similar military coordinating instrument. Although some delegations argued that these points would be brought up at the 1948 Bogota Conference, which would deal with the charter of the inter-American system, it seemed clear that this weak security treaty was setting the stage for an impotent multilateral military organization.[12]

U.S. planning in the interim period between the Rio and Bogota conferences focused on what permanent military organ would be lodged in the Charter of the Organization of American States to be drafted at the Bogota Conference. This planning brought out further differences between U.S. military and diplomatic circles. The U.S. War and Navy Departments wanted to insure that any permanent military organ that was created would be under firm U.S. military control, and that it would not be in a position to impose restraints on U.S. strategic planning.[13] The State Department felt that to insist on strong U.S. control would offend the Latin delegations and limit the organization's political value.

The Latin American-U.S. differences, and the internal U.S. disagreement on strategic planning and institutions, led to what can appropriately be called the elegant and emasculating compromise on the issue of an effective permanent military organ at the Bogota Conference. What emerged from the conference, as embodied in the

Chapultepec Conference, 1945.
U.S.—Latin American disagreements over
the regionalism—globalism issue.

NORTH ATLANTIC OCEAN

MEXICO

Castro comes to power, 1959.
Bay of Pigs invasion, April 1961.
Cuban Missile Crisis, October 1962.

CUBA

Dominican intervention, 1965.
OAS creates an Inter—American Peace
Force after U.S. unilateral actions.

DOMINICAN REPUBLIC

HONDURAS
GUATEMALA
EL SALVADOR
NICARAGUA
CARIBBEAN SEA

Guatemalan crisis, 1954. Leftist
government overthrown by
covert means.

COSTA RICA
PANAMA

VENEZUELA
GUYANA
SURINAME
FRENCH GUIANA

Inter—American Conference, Bogota, 1948.
Produces an OAS Charter with weak
security organs.

COLOMBIA

Korean War. Reluctant Latin American support.
Colombia is the only nation to send troops.

ECUADOR

BRAZIL

PERU

PACIFIC OCEAN

Rio Conference, 1947.
Produces a weak
collective security
treaty (Rio Treaty)

BOLIVIA

Che Guevara's "focos" guerrilla
campaign, 1966—1967.

PARAGUAY

CHILE

ARGENTINA
URUGUAY

SOUTH ATLANTIC OCEAN

Charter of the Organization of American States and a series of continuing resolutions, was a weak and *ad hoc* Advisory Defense Committee. This committee would have no permanent existence and would be convoked for specific purposes at the whim of the organization's political council (in fact, the Advisory Defense Committee has never been convoked, although it remains on paper in the OAS charter to this day). At the same time, the existing Inter-American Defense Board was permitted to continue its activities by means of a resolution separate from the charter, thus considerably weakening it from a juridical point of view.

The net effect of these three conferences from 1945 to 1948 was to create a weak but permanent multilateral security arrangement within the formal inter-American system and the Organization of American States. While the result did not totally satisfy any one of the parties involved, all could derive some comfort from the arrangement. The Latin Americans were satisfied that the weakness of the multilateral instrument would make it difficult for the United States to use it for intervening in the hemisphere. The U.S. State Department was pleased that it had kept U.S. military influence low in what it regarded as primarily diplomatic matters. And the U.S. military felt that they had avoided being unduly restrained by multilateral arrangements, and could still pursue their strategic goals through bilateral means, and unilateral ones if necessary. Further, for the U.S. military establishment, the multilateral instrument offered possibilities as a justification and facade for these other channels.

The compromises of Chapultepec, Rio, and Bogota also ushered in a period of U.S. strategic benign neglect for Latin America as attention was drawn to cold war crises in Berlin, Western Europe, and the Far East. More than anything else, U.S. strategic planners in this period wanted a tranquil and stable Latin America which would provide an uninterrupted flow of strategic materials and be an area of strategic economy of force for the United States.[14]

D. Latin America and the Korean War.

The Korean War had an important impact on U.S. strategic planning toward Latin America. The failure to obtain strong inter-American security instruments in the early post-war period, and the benign neglect of 1948–1951, led to a disappointingly low level of

Latin American political, economic, and military support of U.S. efforts in the Korean War. This, in turn, caused the Joint Chiefs of Staff to reassess the U.S.-Latin American strategic relationship and conclude (not surprisingly) that it had been weakened because of the lack of U.S. arms and training for Latin America. The prescribed solution (which was partially implemented) was to establish a series of bilateral military defense assistance agreements and an increased military assistance program for Latin America.

U.S. strategic objectives for Latin America during the Korean War were basically the old goals of economy of force and access to raw materials and lines of communication.[15] The Joint Chiefs of Staff had little interest in seeing Latin American military contingents fight in Korea, arguing that their levels of military preparedness and standardization on U.S. lines was low, and that they would probably be more trouble than they were worth. The State Department wanted to see a broad range of Latin American participation for political reasons and attempted to persuade the JCS to accept even the smallest Latin American contingents, to include squad-size medical teams and individual volunteers. The JCS successfully countered that the smallest Latin American participation would have to be a complete battalion.

In any case, there were few serious offers of Latin American military support at any level. In the end, only Colombia sent troops to Korea (one infantry battalion and a frigate). The reasons for limited Latin American enthusiasm seemed clear; Korea was a long way off, and there was little interest in getting involved in what seemed to be mainly an American cold war problem.[16]

At the multilateral level during the Korean conflict, the U.S. was successful in convening a Meeting of Consultation of the hemisphere's foreign ministers (the fourth, in 1951), which produced some expressions of support for the United States. The meeting also approved a resolution which gave the Inter-American Defense Board added authority to plan for hemisphere defense, although the board's recommendations still had only advisory power. The board dutifully drafted a new "General Military Plan for the Defense of the Hemisphere" under heavy U.S. guidance. This new plan reflected JCS priorities: it was broad and conceptual in nature, and called for bilateral implementing plans among Rio Treaty nations to provide for technical and military assistance. This provision gave the JCS the vehicle it needed to strengthen the bilateral arrangements for military assistance to the Latin American nations.[17]

348

E. The Military Assistance Program and U.S. Strategic Planning, 1951–1961.

The military assistance program which grew out of Korean War concerns came to dominate the U.S.-Latin American military-to-military relationship during the next ten years, and was the principal vehicle for U.S. strategic planning for the hemisphere in this period.[18] The resulting inter-American military system could be represented by a model in which the U.S. military assistance program was the hub of a wheel; the spokes of the wheel represented the bilateral agreements with individual Latin American nations. But the wheel had no rim, since the Latin American nations had few strategic or military contacts among themselves other than those provided through the bilateral military system dominated by the United States.

The 1951 Mutual Security Act provided the legislative framework for the series of bilateral mutual defense assistance agreements, which were signed with most of the Latin American nations between 1952 and 1954 (Argentina and Mexico were two exceptions). Toward the end of the 1950s the military assistance program involved U.S. military missions (MILGroups) in eighteen countries, with almost 800 assigned U.S. military personnel. It also included extensive training programs in U.S. bases in the Canal Zone and the continental United States, almost monopolistic sales and grants of U.S. military equipment, an active exchange of visits by senior military officers, and a regional command headquarters (US-SOUTHCOM—Southern Command) in the Panama Canal Zone.[19]

Despite the impressive growth of the military assistance program during these years, U.S. strategic planners fretted over the limits placed by a frugal Congress, and the generally low priority given to the area in this period. They were also alarmed by the inroads made by outside arms sellers (mainly European) and warned that if the goals of standardization were jeopardized, U.S. influence in the area would decline.[20]

The general U.S. strategic approach to Latin America in this period continued to be the cold war primary/secondary space concept under which Latin America was to be denied to the strategic adversary, but was also to be an economy of force area requiring relatively little attention from the United States. A 1957 JCS paper described a strategic division of labor under which the United States would protect the hemisphere perimeter and its external sea lanes of communications, while the Latin American nations would provide the U.S. with necessary bases to this end, and would maintain internal security and defense of close in sea lanes.[21] In the late 1950s the military assistance program came under increasing criticism, among other things because of the way it tended to associate the U.S. with dictatorial Latin American regimes. To counter that criticism an additional role was given to the Latin American nations: that of providing antisubmarine warfare defense in support of the larger goal of keeping the naval approaches to the hemisphere open.[22]

In this period U.S. strategic planners also floated the concept of an Atlantic triangle. Under this plan Latin America (or selected Latin nations) would be linked to NATO in some type of security arrangement which would form the third leg of the Atlantic triangle. The other two legs, already in existence, were NATO (linking Canada, the U.S., and Western Europe), and the Rio Treaty (linking the United States and Latin America). However, in light of Latin America's historic reluctance to get involved in cold war conflicts, it was not surprising that the idea received little support. Indeed, there was some resentment over the manner in which this concept reaffirmed the U.S. tendency to see the Rio Treaty as an anti-Communist security alliance. This U.S. view was in considerable contrast to the Latin perception that the Rio Treaty was primarily a diplomatic and political instrument for conflict resolution and protection against intervention.

This period also witnessed a security crisis which produced some interesting reactions on the part of both Latin America and the United States. The crisis was the increasing influence of leftist elements in Guatemala from 1952 to 1954, which peaked with the arrival of a shipment of Eastern bloc weapons in 1954. The United States was not particularly successful in obtaining the support of the multilateral elements of the inter-American system in countering what it perceived to be a dangerous Communist inroad in the hemisphere. The Tenth Inter-American Conference of 1954 addressed the issue, but did little more than grudgingly support an anti-Communist resolution proposed by the United States. The more effective channels used by the U.S. were covert ones which were both unilateral, and bilateral with Guatemala's anti-Communist neighbors (Nicaragua and Honduras). The disappointing performance of the multilateral security system, and the perceived success of covert methods, reaffirmed the tendency of U.S. strategic planners to support these approaches, and may have been an important factor in the Bay of Pigs fiasco seven years later in Cuba.[23]

III. 1961–1967: The *Focos* and Internal Defense and Development (IDAD).

A. Overview.

The period from 1961 to 1967 saw a major shift in U.S. strategic planning for Latin America in the face of a significant perceived security threat in the region. This threat involved the possibility that the Cuban revolution of Fidel Castro could be exported and repeated in other nations of the hemisphere. This threat greatly increased the strategic priority of Latin America to the United States, and led to the focusing of a great deal of attention, energy, and funds to the area and its security problems. Old military institutions were revitalized, and a number of new ones were created, to the point that the inter-American military system reached its historic apogee in this period.

From the perspective of U.S. strategic planners during these years, Latin America was the testing ground for a new concept which was believed to hold promise as an evolutionary response to the destructive violence of revolutionary warfare. The concept linked internal defense to development (IDAD) and stressed that in an insurgency environment the military had to play key roles in both the development and defense of its nation. The implementation of this concept radically changed U.S. strategic planning for Latin America, and was a factor in shifting the orientation of the military in several Latin American nations in ways that were unforeseen at the time.

However, this period of high strategic priority for Latin America was a brief one. Within six years the sense of urgency over the insurgency threat declined markedly among U.S. strategic planners, chiefly because of the death of Che Guevara and the discrediting of his theory of guerrilla warfare. Moreover, the deepening U.S. involvement in Vietnam in the mid and late 1960s quickly diverted the attention of these planners from Latin America toward the Far East. Despite its brevity, this period is an important one because of its relevance today, a relevance that affects current insurgencies in the area as well as the political and military roles of the Latin American military.

B. The Threat: Focos.

Unlike prior revolutions in Latin America, Fidel Castro's

developed a strong internationalist thrust and aggressively sought imitators in Latin America by attempting to export itself.[24] In part this was due to the personalities of the key leaders of the revolution, and in part to a very favorable response among certain leftist sectors in Latin America. The attempt to export the Cuban revolution in the early and mid 1960s was also linked to a strong belief in the mystique of Marxist-Leninist guerrillas and the inevitable triumph of wars of national liberation.[25]

In the 1960s the threat of insurgencies in Latin America was increased not only by political and logistical support from Cuba, but also by a specific theoretical concept: that of the *foco*. The Spanish word *foco* is a medical term referring to the point at which an infection enters the human body (it was perhaps not a coincidence that the chief proponent of the *foco* theory, Che Guevara, had been trained as a medical doctor). The idea was to insert a small cadre of highly trained and motivated guerrillas (the *foco*) into the body politic of several Latin American nations. These *focos*, acting like germs in a human body, would multiply, spread, and start the larger engine of the revolution in each one of these countries. The end result would either be a series of Cubas in the hemisphere or, if the United States intervened, "one, two, many Vietnams." As Che Guevara stated in the first page of his primer on insurgency: "It is not always necessary to wait until all the conditions for the revolution are present; the insurrectional *foco* can create them."[26]

For the reformist Kennedy administration in 1961 there was another threat to its plans for Latin America beyond the revolutionary menace of the *focos*: the Latin American military itself. There was considerable concern that the new administration's projects for development and democracy in Latin America (embodied in the Alliance for Progress) would be blocked by reactionary military officers who might respond to the *foco* threat with repression and direct military rule.

C. The Strategic Response: Internal Defense and Development (IDAD).

The strategic response of the Kennedy administration to the threat of the *focos* in Latin America must be set in the broader context of the new administration's global strategic shift from massive retaliation to flexible response. This latter concept suggested that the United States and its allies must be able to counter a variety of threats (ranging from nuclear confrontation to wars of national liberation) with appropriate responses. Thus, massive nuclear retaliation was not a suitable or credible response to Third World insurgencies, which could be defeated only by attacking their root causes as well as by directly confronting the guerrillas.

Within the continental strategic context there was a growing feeling that the old hemisphere defense concept was increasingly obsolete and irrelevant to the needs of the 1960s. Just as the Roosevelt administration needed hemisphere defense as the strategic concept to support the Good Neighbor Policy, so too did the Kennedy administration need a new strategic concept to support the Alliance for Progress reforms, deal with the Latin American military, and confront the *foco* threat.[27]

The answer was the IDAD concept: an integrated approach to internal defense and development.[28] It was seen by Kennedy administration planners as both therapy (to counterinsurgencies), and prophylaxis (to isolate the guerrillas by depriving them of fertile ground); it was also presented as a vehicle to keep the Latin American military out of politics. Latin America was viewed by these politico-military strategists as a pilot model in which this IDAD concept would be tested before being applied to other areas of the world which were also facing Marxist-Leninist wars of national liberation.[29]

The clearest early articulation of the Kennedy administration's IDAD concept came in a January 1961 Policy Planning Staff paper appropriately titled "A New Concept for Hemispheric Defense and Development."[30] The paper persuasively argued that faced with this new challenge to security in the hemisphere, the United States should turn the Latin American military establishments away from obsolete continental defense roles and towards the new concept of defense through development. Two specific concepts were offered to implement the basic IDAD idea: counterinsurgency and civic action.

Counterinsurgency was presented as that body of proven tactics and techniques which had permitted the defeat of several insurgencies, such as the Malayan and the Huk, thus demonstrating that guerrillas were not invincible. For the Latin American military this would involve abandoning the conventional organization, tactics, and heavy equipment associated with World War II and the Korean conflict. Instead, it would emphasize decentralized operations, effective communications, light equipment, better intelligence, aggressive small unit patrolling, greater mobility, and much more flexibility and imagination on the part of the small unit commander directly involved with hunting down the guerrillas.

Civic action was the innovative idea that military establishments in Third World nations should have an important role in nation-building as well as defense. Proponents argued that most military units have the technical capacity to participate in projects which would make a direct contribution to development, such as road building, food distribution, well digging, literacy education, medical and dental care, etc. This was a particularly attractive concept to the strategic planner not only because of its direct contribution to national development, but also because it was a way of showing the peasant in isolated areas that his government cared about him and was willing to help him progress. Backers of the idea anticipated that the peasant would respond by supporting the government and denying assistance to the guerrilla. Thus, civic action had the power to turn around Mao's dictum and separate the fish (the guerrilla) from the water (the people) who must support him if he were to succeed in his insurgency. In the context of the historically high political role of the Latin American military, there was also the hope that by shifting military units from the major cities to the countryside, and by absorbing their energies in nation-building projects, they would perhaps be less likely to become involved in coups or exert political pressure on elected civilian governments.

Documentation from the early Kennedy period[31] establishes that the IDAD concept and the changes it brought to the military assistance program were quite consciously linked to the Alliance for Progress, and that by late 1961 this link had become the principal rationale for military assistance to Latin America. A November 1961 Memo from the Chairman of the JCS to the President outlined steps by which the U.S. Armed Forces and its military programs could contribute to the achievement of U.S. national objectives in Latin America in support of the Alliance for Progress. The memo noted the shift from hemispheric defense to internal defense and development, and commented in reference to nation building and civic action: "The nation building role of the indigenous military force includes, first, the nation protector mission, and second, the use of military skills and resources in ways contributing to the economic development and special progress of the nation, i.e., civic actions. When the military and the people become close to each other there is no place for the enemy to hide."[32]

D. Implementing IDAD.

The process of implementing IDAD in 1961–1967 was made much easier by the high priority assigned to Latin America, by a relative lack of bureaucratic infighting on this issue in the Kennedy administration, and by a fairly harmonious coordination of the unilateral, bilateral, and multilateral institutions and policies which supported the concept.

The IDAD concept from its birth was one of those rare policies which generated enthusiastic support from most of the bureaucratic elements involved in implementing it, or which could have placed obstacles in its way. For the U.S. military, the idea represented a credible replacement for the now obsolescent hemisphere defense concept, and this period saw a considerable increase in military funding and programs for Latin America based on IDAD concepts. For the State Department, the traditional nemesis of activist U.S. military programs in the hemisphere, the idea was seen with enthusiasm because of its contribution to development, and the intriguing possibility that civic action might make the Latin American military less political. This latter possibility even led a number of American academics and liberals to support the concept. Lastly, the Congress generally approved military assistance which could be linked to the Alliance for Progress.[33]

Implementing the IDAD concept led to an unprecedented expansion of the somewhat dormant inter-American military institutions of the prior period.[34] The U.S. Military Assistance Program shifted its emphasis sharply in 1961–1967, and expanded its personnel and funding levels. IDAD concepts were taught to the Latin American (and U.S.) military in all the educational institutions of the inter-American military system, such as U.S. military schools in Panama and the United States. IDAD became the basis for a new institution: the Inter-American Defense College, founded in 1962 as part of the Inter-American Defense Board. The Board itself was revitalized as it addressed a series of projects related to IDAD. A number of channels were established to enhance inter-American military coordination, to include radio and telecommunications networks, intelligence sharing, annual conferences of service chiefs, and periodic tactical exercises. In the Isthmus the United States was instrumental in creating the Central American Defense Council (CONDECA), which was envisioned as the first of a series of subregional coordinating bodies under the loose supervision of the Inter-American Defense Board. One ambitious project which ran into difficulties was the proposal to create a standby multilateral

Inter-American Peace Force which would be available under OAS Rio Treaty control to assist a country threatened by subversion or aggression. The proposal ran into Latin American fears that it might be used by the United States for intervention; it also generated some opposition from the U.S. military, which was not too interested in placing its units under OAS control. As we shall see below, even though an Inter-American Peace Force was indeed created during the 1965 Dominican Republic crisis, the circumstances of its creation tended to confirm Latin American fears and made it very unlikely that such a force would be approved in the future.

Within the context of the *focos* and the Alliance for Progress, the IDAD concept and its operational aspects can be seen in a positive light. The *focos* were in fact defeated, although a strong case can be made that the principal factors in this defeat were basic errors made by the guerrillas rather than the contributions of the IDAD idea. The inter-American system and its security components functioned fairly effectively (although not with unanimous Latin American support) as an anti-Castro alliance in the early and mid 1960s. There was, for example, rather strong Latin American support of the United States during the Cuban missile crisis, and most of the Latin American nations supported the attempt to isolate Castro. On the negative side, the Bay of Pigs represents a dismal failure of a unilateral United States effort (with some bilateral support from a small number of Central American nations).

The Dominican crisis of 1965 represents a high point for the inter-American military relationship in this period, but it was also the beginning of its downfall. The creation of an Inter-American Peace Force (IAPF) had long been a priority objective of U.S. strategic planners, as long as the force was under effective U.S. control. However, attempts to create a standby force had failed, and it was not until the OAS was faced with the 1965 crisis that it reluctantly took action. The 1965 IAPF was created over considerable Latin American opposition, an opposition that reflected concern over the original unilateral U.S. intervention. There was also much resentment over the way the United States was turning to the OAS to provide a multilateral cover for the sizable contingent of U.S. combat troops in Santo Domingo.[36]

This period in postwar U.S. strategic planning for Latin America ends with the death of Che Guevara in a Bolivian schoolhouse in October 1967. Guevara went to Bolivia in a futile effort to prove the validity of his *foco* theory, but his death proved that even he could not start the engine of revolution if local conditions did not favor it. With his death the first period of the Cuban revolution's attempt to influence other revolutions ended, and Cuba entered a decade in which it seemed to turn inward or away from Latin America. Accordingly, U.S. strategic planners, increasingly concerned with Vietnam, dropped the high priority given to Latin America in the 1961–1967 period and returned it to its traditional status as a tranquil area of economy of force. The hemisphere was about to enter another period of U.S. strategic benign neglect.

IV. 1967–1976: Strategic Divergence, Neglect and System Fragmentation.

A. Overview.

The period from 1967 to 1976 (and indeed beyond) was one not only of U.S. strategic benign neglect for Latin America, but also one of divergence in threat perception and geopolitical approaches, decline and drift in security cooperation, and fragmentation in the inter-American military system and its institutions which had been built up since early World War II.

In a general sense these negative trends reflected the strains and drifting apart that characterized U.S.-Latin American relations in many fields during this period. However, the decline seemed to be more obvious and damaging in the security field. As had happened often in the past, Latin America was being taken for granted and given a low priority in the absence of any significant threat to U.S. interests in the area. But this time Latin America was much more independent than in the past, and much less inclined to accept this dose of benign neglect with passivity. As U.S. strategic planners directed their attention elsewhere and created a security vacuum, certain Latin American nations moved to fill that vacuum in ways not anticipated by their North American counterparts.

This period was also one in which the U.S. military planners lost several bureaucratic battles, not only with their rivals in the State Department, but also with a bureaucratic adversary which had not previously posed major obstacles—the U.S. Congress. A series of congressional restrictions on military assistance began to severely limit the U.S. military's ability to use this historic vehicle for cementing military-to-military relationships, a process which culminated in the 1976 legislation specifically linking the provision of foreign aid with human rights performance.

At the institutional level most of the organizations created in the previous thirty years survived, but many saw their activities and influence severely diminished as a result of U.S. strategic benign neglect. This process was most evident in the decline of the military assistance and arms transfers which formed the hub of the inter-American military system.

B. Divergences in Threat Perceptions.

A basic cause for the decline in U.S.-Latin American strategic relationships in this period was a fundamental divergence in the perceived security threats in the area. This situation was in considerable contrast with the period of World War II and the *foco* threat of the early and mid 1960s. Many of the Latin American governments shared a feeling of relief when Che Guevara was killed and when it seemed that Cuba had played out a short-lived attempt to export its revolution. Other Latin American nations (especially Uruguay, Brazil, Guatemala, and Argentina) did not share this view as they saw the *focos* reappear in an urban guise which in some cases seriously threatened the central government. Some of these nations saw themselves becoming involved in a long and bloody dirty war in which their military establishments put down the leftist guerrillas with brutally repressive methods.

Another important element in the divergence was the return to classical military threat perceptions involving strains with neighbors. Several factors account for this. For one, many of the Latin American military establishments were frankly looking for a new role to justify their budgetary and personnel demands after the *focos* were defeated. Some military officers also felt that the IDAD concept, and especially its low level civic action aspect (i.e., road construction, ditch digging, food distribution) were demeaning and incompatible with their basic role of defending the motherland.[37] Thus a return to the classical mission of protecting the nation against foreign invaders (the most credible ones being close neighbors) was seen by many Latin American military officers as a way of restoring their honor and dignity which had become somewhat stained during the period of guerrilla warfare. Latin America has a long history of border tensions between neighbors, but these conflicts in the past had been kept at manageable levels by limited warmaking capabilities and by the conflict resolution capacity of the inter-American system and the United States. Thus, in the period after 1967 we can observe an increase in border tensions between various Latin American nations, and a buildup of conventional weapons by the military using these tensions as justification. The period saw an outright war between Honduras and El Salvador (1969), shooting incidents between Peru and Ecuador, and tensions between Guatemala and Belize, Argentina and Chile, and Peru and Chile.

The Cuban military involvement in Angola in 1975 (and other parts of Africa shortly afterward) gave rise to another threat perception which was shared by a few hemisphere nations: that Cuba might once again become involved more actively in hemisphere military adventures. This could happen by supporting guerrilla movements, or by employing an Angola-like intervention by consent scenario whereby one party in a Latin American interstate conflict invites Cuban assistance. This type of scenario was raised in terms of possible invitations by Peru (in case of war with Chile), Panama (confrontation with the U.S. over the Canal), Belize (conflict with Guatemala) and Guyana (with Venezuela).

C. Divergences in Strategic and Geopolitical Vision.

As might be expected from the divergences in perceptions of security threats, this period is one which also saw considerable diversion in strategic and geopolitical vision.

There is little evidence of any coherent U.S. strategic or geopolitical view of Latin America in this period. As a low-priority security area, the main emphasis fell on maintaining the status quo and the economy of force aspect. There also was a noticeable geographic retrenchment back to the Caribbean basin, suggesting an abandonment of the South American Southern Cone and a retreat to those close-in areas of greater importance. Strains with Panama over the Canal, renewed interest in the Caribbean's oil-producing nations, and several attempts to improve relations with Cuba indicated a much greater attention to the Caribbean than to the Southern Cone of South America.

In contrast, the Southern Cone nations were very active in generating strategic and geopolitical ideas in this period. In part this reflects the neglect and low priority assigned the area by the United States, but it also represents evidence of a more mature, independent, and active set of Latin American nations no longer willing to accept the U.S. lead in strategic matters. The ABC countries (Argentina,

Brazil, and Chile) were particularly active in generating and publishing geopolitical ideas and strategic doctrine on topics such as competition and cooperation in energy projects, influence in the smaller states of the area, and control of the Southern territories (to include Antarctica and the Malvinas/Falklands Islands).[38]

The possible emergence of Brazil as a twenty-first century superpower was another topic of this current of strategic and geopolitical analysis, and it inevitably generated discussion of the probable reactions of cooperation or competition by other South American states (especially Argentina). One example of this type of strategic-geopolitical thinking was the discussion of a possible South Atlantic Treaty Organization (SATO) which would permit the Southern Cone nations to join efforts in extending their influence into the South Atlantic. SATO was seen as potentially important in terms of South America's oil shipping lanes, the access to the Southern passages (Magellan and Drake), and the control of the Southern Islands (Falklands/Malvinas, South Georgia, Sandwich, Orkney, and Shetland), and ultimately Antarctica.

D. The Latin American Response.

The Latin American response to the sense of divergence and neglect in strategic relations was to take advantage of the situation and assert a greater independence in this field.

This period saw important changes in the political, social, economic, and ideological outlook of the Latin American military, especially in the southern part of South America.[39] Some of these changes were due to the geopolitical currents mentioned above. Others were a reflection of a current of reformism which influenced a large number of military officers in countries such as Brazil and Peru. These officers had observed the ambitious plans formulated by civilian reformers (U.S. and Latin American) in the early years of the Alliance for Progress, and had seen these plans bog down for a number of reasons. At the same time, these officers were concerned over the threat posed by guerrillas and felt that reforms were necessary in order to avoid more violent revolutionary change. The IDAD concepts pushed by the United States in the early 1960s further contributed to these changes among the military by sensitizing them to the implications of underdevelopment in their nations, and the opportunities it presented to Marxist-Leninist subversion. In a number of South American countries in this period, the national war colleges took on a key role as catalysts for analyzing national problems of defense and development and coming up with what seemed like appropriate solutions. These solutions began to take form in countries such as Brazil, Argentina, Chile, and Uruguay under what was called the national security state doctrine. What emerged from these currents was a sense among key military officers that civilian reform attempts were destined to fail, and that they, the military, would be more effective and patriotic reformers and therefore should take direct control of their nations' destinies.[40]

The typical military reformist movement in South America in this period turned out to have strongly nationalistic, state-centered and authoritarian tones. The national security doctrine also had close links to currents of geopolitical thinking. To the surprise of many in the United States, the military reformers' deeply held nationalistic feelings frequently focused on what was perceived to be an excessive dependency on the United States. Thus, one of the basic policies of the military reform movement in Latin America was to reduce this dependency in all fields, to include military relationships as well as economic, political, and cultural ones.

The attempts to diminish military dependency on the United States involved seeking arms from sources other than the United States by turning towards Europe and the Soviet Union as well as by stimulating their own arms industries.[41] Apart from reducing technological and arms dependency on the U.S., the military reformers also moved to reduce their reliance on U.S. tactical doctrine and the U.S. domination of the inter-American military system. The net result was to weaken further the philosophical bases and institutions for hemisphere strategic cooperation precisely at a time when the United States was paying very little attention to them.

E. The United States Response.

As suggested previously, the U.S. strategic planning response to these changing realities in Latin America was one of drift and neglect as attention was directed elsewhere. With the exception of the report which Nelson Rockefeller wrote in 1969 after his analysis of inter-American relations, there was little in this period that can be called strategic planning of new security approaches toward the changing realities in Latin America.[42] The driving forces in U.S. strategic relations with Latin America seemed to be, on the one hand, Latin America's push for reformism and independence, and, on the other, several attempts by the U.S. Congress and State

Department to limit the military assistance programs which were the foundation of hemisphere security relations.

Bureaucratic politics was thus a major factor in this period. As has been noted, the State Department has historically viewed the military-to-military links emanating from the military assistance program with some suspicion, and has not hesitated to attempt to exercise greater control of the program whenever possible. In the late 1960s and early 1970s, such an opportunity presented itself as Latin America was given a low strategic priority and the economic and political channels of inter-American relations increased their importance over the security ones.[43] With the decline of the Alliance for Progress and the *foco* threat, the U.S. military had a difficult time defending assistance programs on the basis of the IDAD concept, and a return to the old hemisphere defense rationale was not especially credible. The military assistance program also got caught up in a battle between the executive and legislative branches over the conduct of foreign policy, which became especially bitter as a result of the Vietnam conflict. In the early and mid–1970s the key foreign relations committees in Congress moved decisively to restrict the size and funding of the military assistance programs by limiting the personnel ceiling in the military groups, and by terminating a good many of the military missions abroad.[44]

The Congress also passed legislation restricting military assistance in specific circumstances. These included the Hickenlooper amendment (suspending aid in cases of nationalization), the Conte amendment (prohibiting the transfer of sophisticated weapons), and the Fulbright amendment (placing ceilings on military aid to Latin America). Although each of these restrictions could be defended as being well intentioned and aimed at particular situations, when taken collectively they represent a body of restrictions which were seen by Latin American nations as paternalistic and demeaning. Thus, they tended to reinforce the Latin American move away from the United States as an arms supplier and toward European or local sources. The resulting decline in the military assistance program significantly diminished the ability of the United States to influence Latin America in security matters.

But the legislative provision which had the greatest impact on U.S.-Latin American security relations was the linking of military assistance to human rights performance. For many years there had been concern that security assistance programs had tended to associate the United States with repressive military regimes which had little regard to democratic norms or the basic rights of their peoples. This concern grew as the IDAD concept and supporting military assistance programs focused on counterinsurgency and internal security. The fear that the U.S. had become unwittingly involved in helping the violators of human rights seemed especially acute for the nations involved in fighting brutal dirty wars against leftists in the nations of the Southern Cone. The relevant legislative safeguard was inserted into the 1976 International Security Assistance and Arms Export Control Act and stated that the U.S. should not supply security assistance to any country which consistently and grossly violated internationally recognized human rights.[45] The legislation included a provision that the U.S. government collect and publish data on the human rights situation in each country involved. The reaction from many Latin American nations was swift and indignant: they regarded these provisions as unwarranted intrusions into their internal affairs, and several canceled existing security arrangements with the United States rather than submit to these procedures.

There are few indications of U.S. strategic planning in Latin America during this period. U.S. military planners and policymakers seemed more concerned with limiting the damage to inter-American security relationships, and produced little in the way of original planning or justification for existing institutions and arrangements. Much more influential were the legislative restrictions described above and the ideas contained in analyses such as those of the Linowitz Commission ('The Americas in a Changing World," 1974; "The U.S. and Latin America: the Next Steps," 1976) and the Institute for Policy Studies ('The Southern Connection," 1977); these were to have a considerable impact on the U.S.-Latin American security planning in the Carter Administration.[46]

Notes

1. War Plans Color, Record Group (RG) 407, File 1920–1948, U.S. National Archives (NA). For a discussion of these plans, see the author's article, "From 'Color' to 'Rainbow': U.S. Strategic Planning for Latin America, 1919–1945" in *Journal of Inter-American Studies and World Affairs*, 21, no 2, (May 1979), 233–59.

2. *Op cit*, pp 247–49. Also Stetson Conn and Byron Fairchild, *The Framework of Hemisphere Defense* (Washington, 1960). For a typical Rainbow Plan, see Rainbow 1, 11 Jul 1940, RG 407, File AG 361, Entry 365, NA.

3. For example: NSC 144/1, 18 Mar 1953 in *Foreign Relations of the United States (FRUS)*, 1952–54, 4:615. NSC 5432, 3 Sep 54 in FRUS 1952–54, 4:81–87. JCS 1233/2, RG 218, NA.

4. See note from Secretary of Defense George C. Marshall to the Secretary of State, 10 Jan 1951 in FRUS, 1951, 2:990–91. NSC Report 21, 27 May 60 in *Declassified Documents* (Washington, 1982), item 1207.

5. NSC 5613/1, 11 Sep 1957 in *Declassified Documents, 1980*, item 334B.

6. JCS 1976/204 (p 2353), 28 Feb 1957 in *Declassified Documents, 1980*, item 151A.

7. Laurence Duggan, *The Americas, The Search for Hemisphere Security* (New York, 1949), p 181. Ellis Briggs, *Anatomy of Diplomacy* (New York, 1968), p 103. U.S. Department of State, Memo: Certain Activities of War Department and Army Officers in Other American Republics, 21 Nov 1944, RG 353, SWNCC Box 139, NA.

8. The basic document is JCS 1419, RG 218, NA. See also Circular Telegram, 6 Oct 1945, FRUS 1945, 9:256–57. Memo (Braden), 16 Dec 1946, FRUS 1946, 9:108–10. Spruille Braden, *Diplomats and Demagogues* (New Rochelle, 1971), p 364.

9. JCS 1233/2, RG 218, NA. Inter-American Defense Board, *Historia de la Junta Interamericana de Defensa* Document S–558 (Washington, 1961).

10. Defense Department Memo, MAP Program for FY 1950, 1 Feb 1949, in *Declassified Documents 1978*, item 363A.

11. JCS 1233/2, RG 218, NA. FRUS, 1947, 8:78–79. JCS 570/51, RG 218, NA. War Department, OPD, Memo for Lieutenant General Ridgway, 20 Mar 1947, RG 43 (Rio Conference, 1947), NA.

12. Memo (Braden to Acheson), 29 May 1947, FRUS, 1947, 8:2–3. *Historia de la Junta, op cit,* pp 91–97.

13. Memo from the Secretary of State, FRUS, 1948, 9:11.

14. NSC–56; JCS 1976 series; JCS 1852/2; RG 218, NA.

15. JCS 1670/48; JCS 1976/25, RG 218, NA. Also FRUS, 1951, 7:990–91.

16. FRUS, 1950, 1:642–46, 672–75. FRUS, 1951, 7:1008–10, 1212–16, 1476–77. JCS 1670/48; JCS 1976/62; JCS 1976/46. Personal interview with Major General Robert L. Walsh (Chairman, IADB, during the Korean War period), Washington, Jul 1977.

17. *Inter-American Defense Board Yearbook for 1951* (Washington, 1952). FRUS, 1951, 2:925 and passim, pp 990–91.

18. NSC 56/2; JCS 1976/27; RG 218, NA. Hearings before the Foreign Relations Committee, Senate, *Mutual Security Program for 1952*, 82nd Cong, 1st sess (Washington, 1951), p 39. FRUS, 1951, vol II, p 1004–06.

19. Hearings before the Committee on Foreign Relations, Senate, *Mutual Security Act of 1951*, 81st Cong, 2nd sess (Washington, 1950), p 394, 398. Hearings before the Committee on Foreign Relations, Senate, *United States and Latin American Relations*, 86th Cong, 2nd sess (Washington, 1960), Document 125, 1960, pp 38–39. Hearings before the Committee on Foreign Relations, Senate, *Mutual Security Act of 1959*, 85th Cong, 2nd sess (Washington, 1958), pp 538–39.

20. FRUS, 1952–1154, 4:171. Memo, 7 Mar 1956, *Declassified Documents, 1979*, item 135C.

21. JCS 1976/204, 28 Feb 1957 in *Declassified Documents, 1980*, item 151A.

22. Hearings before the Committee on Foreign Affairs, House of Representatives, *Mutual Security Act of 1959*, 85th Cong, 2nd sess (Washington, 1958), p 744. Hearings before the Committee on Foreign Relations, Senate, *Mutual Security Act of 1959*, 85th Cong, 2nd sess (Washington, 1958), pp 207, 560. U.S. Navy Brief OP–001, 23 Jun 1959, *Declassified Documents, 1978*, item 54A.

23. FRUS, 1952–1954, 2:151, 279, 1018–19, 1041–43, 1449–51. Top Secret annex to NSC 144, 6 Mar 1953, *Declassified Documents, 1981*, item 331B.

24. Jay Mallin, "Phases of Subversion: the Castro Drive in Latin America," *Air University Review*, Nov 1973, pp 54–62. Ernest Evans, *Rift and Revolution: The Central American Imbroglio* (Washington, 1984), pp 167–93.

25. State Department, Subcommittee on Cuban Subversion, Memo, 12 Nov 1963, *Declassified Documents, 1980*, item 290A.

26. Che Guevara, *Guerra de Guerrillas* (Montevideo, Uruguay, 1968), p 1. Central Intelligence Agency, Note re: Che Guevara's Statement, 3 Dec 1962, *Declassified Documents, 1975*, item 49B.

27. Walter LaFeber, *Inevitable Revolutions: The United States in Central America* (New York, 1983), pp 148–53.

28. Department of State, "A New Concept for Hemispheric Defense and Development," 15 Jan 1961. In the author's possession; declassified by Freedom of Information section, 21 Jan 1977.

29. JCS Summary Report, 21 Jul 1962, *Declassified Documents Retrospective, 1975*, item 242C. White House Staff Memo, 16 Jan 1963, *Declassified Documents Retrospective, 1975*, item 902A.

30. Department of State, "A New Concept for Hemispheric Defense and Development," 15 Jan 1961 (see footnote 27 supra), pp 1, 3. Defense Department Memo, May 1964, *Declassified Documents, 1977*, item 99D.

31. Hearings before the Committee of Foreign Affairs, House of Representatives, *The Internal Development and Security Act*, 87th Cong, 1st sess (Washington, 1961), p 424. State Department Report, 18 Oct 1961, *Declassified Documents Retrospective 1975*, item 698B.

32. JCS Memo JCSM–832–61, 30 Nov 1961 to the President, Military Actions for Latin America, *Declassified Documents, 1981*, item 166A.

33. White House Memo (Maxwell Taylor), CounterInsurgency, Establishment of the Special Group, 2 Jan 1962, *Declassified Documents Retrospective, 1975*, item 900C.

34. See the author's *Unequal Alliance: The Inter-American Military System* (Boulder, 1980), especially pp 154–68.

35. Department of State, "A New Concept for Hemispheric Defense and Development," 15 Jan 1961 (see footnote 27, supra), p 11.

36. James R. Rose, *An Inter-American Peace Force within the Framework of the OAS* (Metuchen, N.J., 1970), pp 29–30. Horacio Luis Veneroni, *Fuerza Militar Interamericana* (Buenos Aires, 1966), pp 129–31, 139–40.

37. Colonel Augusto Rattenbach, "Estados Unidos y la Venta de Armas a America Latina," *Estrategia*, 28 (May 1974), 18–19.

38. Jack Child, "Geopolitical Thinking in Latin America," *Latin American Research Review*, 14, no 2, (Summer 1979).

39. See the author's *Unequal Alliance* (footnote 34, supra), especially pp 190–206.

40. Department of State Research Memorandum RAR–26, "The New Militarism in South America: Agent for Modernization?," 28 Aug 1969, *Declassified Documents, 1981*, item 214B.

41. Department of State Research Memorandum RAAS–2, "Latin America: The Outlook for Arms Spending," 5 Mar 1973, *Declassified Documents, 1981*, item 216A.

42. Lester D. Langley, *The U.S. and the Caribbean in the Twentieth Century* (Athens, Ga., 1980), pp 269–70.

43. Charles D. Corbett, *Inter-American Security and U.S. Military Policy* (Carlisle Barracks, Pa, 1977), pp 3–5.

44. *Washington Post*, 7 Jul 1969. U.S. General Accounting Office, *Assessment of Overseas Advisor Efforts of the U.S. Security Assistance Program* (Washington, 31 Oct 1975), p 35.

45. Hearings before the Committee on International Relations, House of Representatives, *International Security Assistance and Arms Export Control Act of 1976*, 94th Cong, 2nd sess (Washington, 1976), pp 20–22.

46. Commission on U.S-Latin American Relations (the Linowitz Commission), *The Americas in a Changing World* (Washington, 1974) and *The U.S. and Latin America: the Next Steps* (Washington, 1976). Institute for Policy Studies, *The Southern Connection* (Washington, 1977).

Bibliographic Comment

The principal primary sources used in this paper are quite different for each of the three periods under consideration because of the time frame in which classified documents have been made available. For the first period (1945–1961) there is an extensive declassified documentation, especially in the National Archives (Record Groups 165, War Department; 407, Adjutant General's Files; 218, Joint Chiefs of Staff; 59, State Department; 43, International Conferences), and in the *Foreign Relations of the United States* series through 1954. Few of these sources have declassified their documents for the second period (1961–1967), but for this period the *Declassified Documents* series (Carrolton Press, later Research Publications, Inc.) provide numerous documents, especially from the relevant presidential libraries. Very few declassified documents exist for the the last period (1967–1976), and here the paper relies on public statements and reports as well as selected interviews. More detailed information on sources is contained in the author's *Unequal Alliance: The Inter-American Military System* (Boulder, 1980).

The Impact of Vietnam on Military Planning, 1972–1982: Some Tentative Thoughts

Alexander S. Cochran, Jr.

In a recent article, I analyzed American military planning for ground combat operations in Vietnam from 1952 through 1965. My basic conclusion argued that the commitment of ground combat units to Vietnam in 1965, both Army and Marine Corps, and their initial missions were not hasty or reactive, as claimed by some historians of the Vietnam War, but rather the product of sustained military planning over the preceding decade.[1]

Based upon subsequent research, I am now further persuaded that the conduct of military ground operations in Vietnam through the rest of 1965 and well into 1966 was very much dictated by the military planning of the preceding decade. Indeed I would argue that the perceptions held by the military planners of the late 1950s and the early 1960s, and the organizations designed by force developers to carry out those plans, directly influenced the initial phases of American combat participation in that conflict.

I have now shifted my research to the period following the withdrawal of American units from Vietnam, examining the relationship between the American military experience in the Vietnam War and military planning during the following decade. In doing so, I have been interested in how my earlier conclusion concerning 1965 actions in Vietnam and prewar decade planning might apply to the postwar decade planning, and in how Army planners might be relating to their own perceptions of the Vietnam experience.

I am indebted for the suggestions of three Army officers who participated in both Vietnam and Army planning, Robert T. Frank, Lewis Sorley, and Thomas Ware, and the critical comments of David R. Petraens, Robert K. Griffith, Jr., and Ronald H. Spector, who have studied the period from different perspectives. However, the views expressed are mine alone and do not necessarily reflect those of the Department of Defense, the Department of the Army, or the U.S. Army Center of Military History.

In my research of the pre-Vietnam era, I was able to use the actual military plans, thanks to the publication of *The Pentagon Papers*, routine declassification of critical documents, and the conclusion of the war for which the plans were made. Such had not been true for my analysis of the post-Vietnam era. Most specific details of and rationale for military plans remain—and justly so—classified. As a result, I have turned to other sources, none of which have proven as satisfactory. Broad policy statements were more often issued for information and do not provide historical perspective. Information provided to the various interested congressional committees was structured primarily for budgetary justifications. A great deal of internal and external deductions by defense analysts and contemporary commentators were made for other reasons. In my earlier work, I discovered that attitudes and perceptions of upper and middle level planners were critical, but, for the 1972–1982 period, most participants would only talk in generalities, reluctant to discuss the specifics of planning. While some high level retirees have vented personal frustrations on various aspects of military planning in articles, letters to the editor, or, in a few instances, memoirs, quite often these proved dangerously skewed by personal bias. In other words, as an historian, I lacked adequate sources.

I have filled some of these evidential voids with personal knowledge. As one who spent two and one half years in Vietnam as a soldier, an equal amount of time in the 1980s studying the war as an historian, and time in between observing planning trends and talking with planning participants, I have been able to construct what I considered to be a relatively valid picture, though it certainly will be revised with release of the actual plans. Until recently, I considered anything after World War II as current events and the province of the political scientist, and I am even more conscious of this when I deal with the 1970s.

The theme of this conference has been military planning. Presumably by now, our conversations have led to a definition of just what we mean by military planning. Obviously, it involves resources and requirements, strategy and budget allocations, doctrine and capabilities. It also involves planners. In this paper, I have focused upon them. In my judgment, they are the ones who must match resources with requirements, bring strategy into line with budget allocations, and assure doctrine conforms to capabilities.

I have focused my attention upon the planners of the sustained land combat service, the U.S. Army. I did so for several reasons. Vietnam was essentially a ground war fought by Army troops and led by joint command dominated by the Army. More than 3,000,000 servicemen and women served in Vietnam to include offshore waters from 1965 through 1973, of which more than 50 percent were in the Army. If one includes the members of the other ground combat force, the U.S. Marine Corps, this percentage rises to about 75 percent.[2] Of the 350,000 casualties sustained during the war, the U.S. Army suffered more than 66 percent.[3] Army career officers who were vital participants in the military planning procedure of the postwar decade served two and sometimes three one-year tours in Vietnam during the war. Thus, I assumed that if any military service was influenced by the Vietnam experience, it would have to be the U.S. Army.

Under my definition, military planners were responsible for matching resources with requirements. In terms of personnel resources, the Army underwent a drastic reduction during the early 1970s. Its peak strength dropped from 1,500,000 soldiers organized into nineteen plus full strength divisions in mid–1969, to less than 800,000 organized into thirteen undermanned divisions by 1973, a reduction of almost 50 percent and the Army's lowest strength since the outbreak of the Korean War. Likewise, its annual percentage of the Department of Defense budget fell from a high of 32 percent in 1968 to a low of 21 percent in 1974.[4]

To complicate matters, planners had to deal with the reality that the prospect of having adequate soldiers to man divisions and to staff necessary support organizations was bleak. During this period, not only did the number fall, but the draft was discarded. The Nixon administration committed the Army to achieving an all-volunteer force by June 1973—an event that might have taken place earlier without the conflict but was certainly tied to popular discontent with Vietnam. By 1974, the goal of an all-volunteer force had been achieved, but, in the following year, strength and quality proved difficult to sustain. Simultaneously, a reduction in force of junior and middle level officers was necessary, and many Vietnam veterans were forced out. The Army was thus seeking volunteer soldiers while dismissing commissioned officers.

Planners also had to consider the impact of budget allocations upon military strategy. Here too they were strapped. An army is machines—tanks and artillery pieces, trucks and helicopters. During the Vietnam War, priority understandably went to the procurement of current weapons and transportation systems needed for that conflict, largely at the expense of research and development. With reduction in funds available for equipment procurement after the war, Army planners now faced a new problem. Not only were there insufficient amounts of equipment, but they also perceived some to be outmoded systems as compared to those of the Warsaw Pact. With this logic, long standing projects such as a new main battle tank, infantry carrier, and transportation helicopter were either canceled or stretched out.

They likewise confronted confusion over the future status of a vital element of their forces. Traditionally the Army had always relied upon the militia in wartime emergencies. But, for the first time in its history and primarily for political reasons, the reserve components had not been called for help in Vietnam except for a minor callup after Tet 1968. The failure to mobilize the militia proved a disastrous decision. To avoid Vietnam service, many young men eligible for the draft sought assignment to national guard and reserve units. Simultaneously, these units were stripped of equipment for the war to replace combat losses in Vietnam and to provision newly activated units bound for the war. Overall readiness of the reserve components plummeted. The end of the war and the draft brought more problems. When the personnel situation predictably reversed itself, the waiting line of potential members was replaced by unit vacancies. By 1976, National Guard and Army Reserve assigned strength was at a fourteen-year low point. In that year, the Army formally admitted that "inadequate strength has replaced lack of equipment as the most critical factor in inability of the reserve components to meet readiness objective."[5]

Equally important was the resentment among professionals in the reserve component units. While official reports mildly mentioned "the ambiguities of mobilization policy in the mid–1960s," concerned regulars and reservists alike were more opinionated. Some observers merely cited administrative problems and personnel and equipment shortages, implying a rosier future once corrected.[6] But others were more pointed in professional journals, as the title of some articles explicitly indicated. "Can the Reserve Components Make It?," asked one regular closely associated with the reserves, while a reservist wondered about, "The Other Military: Are U.S. Reserve Forces Viable?" Another reservist pondered, "The Reserves: Cause for Optimism or Concern?" while a retired officer and defense analyst asked, "The Army's Reserve Components: Ready for What?" A career reservist wondered, "What are U.S. Reserve Forces Really For?" while a retired general officer announced, "Being Regular is not Enough!" All the authors played to the same implicit theme. Many professionals in the reserve components deeply resented being left out of Vietnam and now questioned their future. As one analyst of this recently concluded, "the growing involvement of the Army Reserve could well have been the key to what might well have been a different course for the Vietnam War."[7]

More importantly, military planners were concerned with the role of the active Army in future strategy. And likewise, there were questions among many here on its future role and mission. Confused by the erosion of public confidence concerning Vietnam and frustrated at the increasing evidence of failure in that war, many Army officers now turned inward. Their outlets were the professional journals where an impressive debate on the future of the Army began to evolve.

Direction in their search for a purpose came from many sources. One was provided by an outside journalist, Ward Just, who in *Military Men* used a series of essays to document unnamed Army officers questioning not only the Army's past role in Vietnam, but also its future in civil-military relations.[8] Hard on the heels of this revelation came two studies on military professionalism conducted by the U.S. Army War College.[9] These proved even more traumatic as they documented promotion oriented practices by senior officers during the Vietnam era and confirmed an erosion of ethical disposition and military professionalism throughout the entire Army.

The effect upon morale within the Army officer corps was devastating. Forced inward by the tragedy of events in Vietnam, they now could only point fingers at themselves. The net result was what General Robert Gard called at the time "an identity crisis," what Dr. Ronald Spector has more recently described as "a collective nervous breakdown," and what I think can more accurately be designated as "a crisis in confidence."[10]

Basically, the Army had lost confidence in itself. Significantly, some officers published books with the same conclusions concerning this problem. Colonel William L. Hauser in his work *American Army in Crisis: A Study in Civil Military Relations*, and Colonels Zeb B. Bradford and Frederic J. Brown in their report, *The United States Army in Transition*, painted a bleak picture, but they outlined programs for recovery. However, Reserve Major Richard A. Gabriel and retired Lieutenant Colonel Paul L. Savage in their study, *Crisis in Command: Mismanagement in the Army*, were downright pessimistic, proclaiming that "there is a sickness in the soul of the Army."[11] The shock continued when several years later a retired Army general, Douglas Kinnard, polled fellow general officers who had served in Vietnam and confirmed that they had long harbored reservations over the policy and strategy of the Vietnam War as well as overall Army leadership during the Vietnam era. And then an anonymous officer writing under the pseudonym of Cincinnatus blasted the Army in a book appropriately entitled *Self-Destruction: The Disintegration and Decay of the United States Army during the Vietnam Era.*[12]

Thus, immediately after the Vietnam War, Army planners were hard pressed to make reality out of expectations with personnel and material resources being dramatically reduced and traditional roles being assailed. Their problem was partially solved by a change in national strategic orientation. Reacting to policy direction from the Nixon and Ford administrations, policy subsequently confirmed by the Carter administration, Army planners gladly returned their attention and priorities to that area of the world where they had been prior to 1965, which more than coincidentally had been the scene of the Army's greatest successes in the 20th Century. As topical articles in *Army Magazine* indicated, interest in Vietnam was quickly replaced by a sharp focus upon Europe.[13] But here also the units were in shambles. The Army in Germany had served as a sustaining base for Vietnam during the war, and its units had been racked with personnel turnover and equipment shortages, not to mention the other social problems of the 1960s such as drug abuse, racial tensions, and antimilitarism.[14]

Still there was hope for the Army, as its first Chief of Staff in the post-Vietnam period was perceived by many as the ideal leader to pull the pieces together. General Creighton Abrams was a hard but fair leader who generated admiration, respect, and even awe from his subordinates with his pragmatic approach to problems during his career and especially during the final years in Vietnam. Faced with dwindling personnel and equipment resources and urged on by congressional pressure, he ordered a dramatic bite the bullet reduction of support to combat unit ratios of the 1973 Army, to reconstitute its thirteen divisions into sixteen, even though only ten were then considered combat ready. To create more combat troops, he supervised the reduction of headquarters staffs and broke up the monolithic Continental Army Command (CONARC), a move that angered many senior officers.[15] And just when it appeared that he was turning things around, he tragically died in office; and the Army's confidence took another nose dive.

What the Army needed to force it out of self pity and to face reality was a jolt, and the Arab-Israeli War of 1973 provided that. It

374

showed Army planners several things. It revealed the increased lethality of the modern sophisticated battlefield. It resurrected the proper and vital role of the reserve components as part of the total force structure. And it illustrated the critical importance of the first battle. But it also revealed a confusion in doctrine. Planners were concerned with bringing theoretical doctrine in line with unit capabilities. It became obvious that their own current Army tactical doctrine envisioned a protracted war based upon mobile defense.[16] It was obvious that a revision was in order.

Doctrinal revision was entrusted to General William E. DePuy, Commanding General, U.S. Army Training and Doctrine Command. DePuy, characterized by David Halberstam in *The Best and the Brightest* as "one of the Army intellectuals, . . . considered by most civilians in the Pentagon the brightest general they had ever met," was a tough and savvy infantryman who had commanded a division during the early days of the Vietnam War. He had developed strong opinions about future doctrine and had bypassed many senior to him with his recent promotion. For those in search of purpose and confidence, he provided a glimmer of hope as he took personal interest in and direction of this major effort.[17]

Critical to those involved with this doctrinal review was the current intellectual internal finger pointing going on within the Army, the debate that started from the spirit of Colonels Hauser, Bradford, and Brown and was now waged on the pages of the Army's professional journals.[18] There many senior officers sought to forget totally Vietnam, instead staking their futures on World War II-type battles in central Europe. But junior, midlevel, and retired officers refused to let the Vietnam experience fade away. They now sought substantive lessons from Vietnam, a search made all the more bitter when South Vietnam fell in conventional battle to the North Vietnamese Army. As more read, more wrote, and a consensus emerged that the Army had lost the war not only because of a lack of professionalism and a decay of ethics, but also because it had used the wrong strategy, doctrine, and tactics.[19] Counterinsurgency doctrine had failed in Vietnam, their argument went, because it was too imprecise. In the next war, when the outcome might very well be determined at the first battle, as suggested by the Arab-Israeli War, the Army could not afford such vagueness. New doctrine had to be specific.

The doctrine as developed by DuPuy for Army planners was precise. It was based on specific knowns. The enemy would be the Soviets. The battlefield would be central Europe. The Soviets, with a preponderance of combat power, would attack in echelons. To counter, the outnumbered American Army would conduct an active defense and prevail by a combination of maneuver and attrition.[20] These notions were a startling contrast to the counterinsurgency doctrine used by planners for Vietnam where the enemy and his tactics were unknown, the battlefield was the world, the Army assumed overall combat superiority, and the decisive blow was through massive firepower. Thus the doctrine was a total rejection of Vietnam.

The doctrine was given to planners with the publication of the new FM 100–5, "Operations," in mid–1976, the capstone volume for the Army's new How-to-Fight manuals.[21] The manual was controversial even before publication. Civilian critics attacked its basic assumption of winning the first battle though outnumbered. There were vague charges of the doctrine being ramrodded through by General DePuy, and there were rumors of official squelching of valid criticisms to be published in a specific military journal.[22] One retired general branded the whole matter as "typical Pentagonese bullshit."[23] The Army did not help things by issuing the manual in a loose leaf notebook to indicate the ability for change. Some in the field took that to indicate tentativeness.

Promulgation of FM 100–5 initiated the most heated doctrinal debate in the Army since discussions of the ill-fated pentomic reorganization of the 1950s. Initial reception from both within and outside the Army was good. Particularly hailed was the doctrine's historical base and clear definition. But soon other words were heard. Some lamented reliance upon defense at the expense of offense. Others charged it was old wine in new bottles. How about application in battlefields other than in central Germany? Were the right Soviet tactics considered? But most important, the debate began at the height of internal dissolution over Vietnam.[24]

Those involved in the debate had concluded that Vietnam era ticket punching included pleasing superiors to insure promotion, even when the facts or situation demanded otherwise, a sort of don't make waves approach. Debate over FM 100–5 did not follow the trend. Now middle level officers expressed doubts on the viability of active defense and the ability to win the first battle. They openly challenged approved doctrine on the pages of professional journals. Perhaps the ultimate came in 1984 when a United States Military Academy cadet expressed his reservations on the doctrine in *Military Review*, pointing out the striking similarities to German Army doctrine from 1917 through 1945.[25]

Resolution was helped by the retirement of General DePuy. His replacement, General Donn Starry, held a different perspective. While DePuy was an infantryman, Starry was an armored officer, and he saw the debate in a different light. He pressed his doctrinal specialists to address the reservations and to make adjustments as necessary. A three-day conference was held during which pros and cons were aired in an academic atmosphere.[26] The net result was a consensus that the planners needed doctrine that was more flexible and broader based.

Criticisms were considered, and, in August 1982, a revised FM 100–5 appeared.[27] The authors now gave their revised doctrine a new title, "AirLand Battle Doctrine." They placed more emphasis upon offensive action and expanded the battle area. The debate on the correct doctrine continues today. But of importance to military planners, this revision of theoretical doctrine was the result of unit capabilities, something that had been lacking in the Vietnam period.[28]

While active defense had been revised for AirLand Battle doctrine, planners also modified tactical organizations to fulfill the new doctrinal expectations and incorporated the reserve components into active planning considerations. Concurrent with the doctrinal debates of the late 1970s were planning discussions for a new division structure, Division 86. The result was a heavy division structure with supporting corps units specifically designed to defeat the Soviet threat on the plains of northern Europe. As the Army planning priorities remained on NATO, those units not specifically targeted for European contingencies were also modified under the Division 86 concepts.[29] Army planners had expanded their fighting forces from thirteen to sixteen divisions through affiliation programs and the ROUNDOUT concept where national guard battalions and Army reserve units became part of regular army divisions and support units for planning and training. CAPSTONE, the grouping of active, reserve, and national guard units into preorganized mobilization packages with specific missions, furthered this notion. As planners now realized, the decision not to use the reserve components during Vietnam was a political one. Now their plans deliberately included the militia to preclude the omission in the future. As one senior Army planner candidly admitted recently, "The Army's capability to fight a war without the Reserves is zero."[30]

Reaction by Army planners to Vietnam led to a major reexamination of the Army's role in civil-military relations. Its roots lay in the early 1960s when John Kennedy urged all "to pay any price, bear any burden, meet any hardship, support any friend, oppose any foe to assure the survival and success of liberty." A generation of younger Army officers marched off to Vietnam perceiving themselves as freedom fighters saving that country from communism, only to have the roof cave in on them in 1975. To the thoughtful ones, the lesson was that the "can do, sir" attitude needed modification. Somehow this might provide an explanation for the loss of Vietnam.[31]

They gained valuable assistance from Colonel Harry Summers, a Vietnam veteran who had also witnessed the final embarrassing days of the U.S. Army in Vietnam as a member of the U.S. delegation of the Four Party Joint Military Team, Vietnam. Summers then worked for General Fred Weyand, who had the unenviable task of following General Abrams as Chief of Staff of the Army. General Weyand was vitally concerned with the public's perception of the future role for the Army.[32] From this assignment, Summers went to the Army War College as a strategist with the Strategic Studies Institute.

He was assigned to take an open, critical, unclassified, and unofficial look at the lessons of Vietnam. The study had begun several years earlier at the instigation of the Army's Vice Chief of Staff, General Walter T. Kerwin, and its chief planner, Lieutenant General Edwin C. Myer, and against much senior opposition. The result was his important book, *On Strategy: The Vietnam War in Context*.[33] Viewing the war as a tactical victory, but a strategic defeat, he analyzed its conduct at both the civilian and military level in a Clausewitzian context. "How," he asked, "could we have succeeded so well, yet failed so miserably?" One reason, he felt, was that the Vietnam conflict was never clearly understood by either the American public or its army. Midlevel Army officers saw this failure to communicate the real war to the American people as a breakdown in the Army's role in civil-military relations. They sought to replace the "can do, sir" attitude with one of candor. Others rationalized the loss of the war as a failure of American will rather than that of the American military. But they all concluded that future wars must be perceived as popular by the public, winnable by the military, and allowable by the politicians.

General Edward C. Meyer, who was instrumental in support of the study, became Army Chief of Staff from 1979 through 1983 and expanded this attitude into a wider context. Writing shortly after assuming the Army's top post, he noted,

> Our perception of the national need may clash with the often confused
> and conflicting messages which percolate from the grass roots of the
> nation . . . . Our focus must be on a sensible posture over time, as opposed
> to the 'today' orientation of the politician.[34]

Army planners now envisioned a strategy of popular and winnable wars, and they sought to implement it through the tact of candor. Thus on the joint scene, they purposely sought noninvolvement in Lebanon, consistently preached caution with regard to Central America, and only accepted a sure-win confrontation in Grenada. Likewise in professional journals, they urged reality in overall strategy and noted the pitfalls of current joint planning. This attitude is evident in the recent recommendations by the Sidle Commission to include now the media, their primary scapegoat during the initial post-Vietnam debate, in all military planning.[35]

In summary, Army planners emerged from the Vietnam experience with a crisis in confidence and an unsureness of purpose. Faced with dwindling personnel and equipment resources, they were hard pressed to bring resources into line with requirements. Budget allocations dictated strategy, and doctrine ran counter to capabilities. The dual shocks of the Arab-Israeli War and the final fall of South Vietnam provided the requisite therapy. From rigorous internal questioning came a new intellectual strength among concerned officers, the courage to challenge without fear of penalty and a willingness to accept risks. Planners were given a new doctrine based upon knowns and not assumptions and revised in response to intense debate. Tactical organizations were reorganized to fit the doctrine, and the alienated reserves were finally reincorporated. And a more candid role by the Army in civil-military relations was outlined. The post-Vietnam period for Army planners was a rocky one as they sought to make reality out of expectations. Indeed as a recent cover story in *Newsweek* makes clear, doubt on the Army's capabilities persists at the highest leadership level, particularly over whether the correct strategy, organization, and doctrine has been chosen.[36] The current furor over the adoption of the light infantry division provides evidence of this skepticism at the midlevel.[37]

The impacts of Vietnam upon Army planning were wide and important. While definitive assessment must await the availability of historical evidence, I would project that the experience of Vietnam will continue to influence military planning for the remainder of the twentieth century. Traditionally military historians have chided military planners for using the last war to plan for the next; however, I suspect that this will not be the case with Vietnam. Planners now

I suspect that this will not be the case with Vietnam. Planners now candidly admit that Vietnam was a strategic loss, and they are not anxious to plan for a repeat performance.

Notes

1. Alexander S. Cochran, Jr., "American Planning for Ground Combat in Vietnam," *Parameters*, Summer 1984, pp 68–69. Some historians who make this claim are Larry Berman, Leslie Gelb, Richard Betts, George Herring, and Dave Palmer.

2. Figures are on file at The U.S. Army Center of Military History, Washington, DC, hereafter CMH. Also see Shelby L. Stanton, *Vietnam Order of Battle* (Washington, 1981).

3. *Department of the Army Historical Summary: Fiscal Year 1973* (Washington, CMH, 1977), p 4.

4. Statistical information on the Army contained in this and subsequent paragraphs was taken from the applicable fiscal year *Department of the Army Historical Summary* (Washington, CMH). Additional budgetary and personnel information came from annual budget discussions in *Army* and *Armed Forces Journal*. Also see *Department of Defense Annual Report for Fiscal Year 1968* (Washington, 1971) and *Secretary of Defense Melvin R. Laird's Annual Defense Department Report, Fiscal Year 1973*.

5. *Department of the Army Historical Summary, Fiscal Year 1977* (Washington, CMH, 1979), p 75.

6. Irving Heymont, "Today's Citizen Soldier: Ready for Tomorrow's War?," *Army*, Apr 1974, pp 16–22; Gailon M. McHaney, "And These are Reserves, by God," *ibid*, Apr 1974, pp 25–28; Eric C. Ludvigen, "The Guard and Reserve Move Out," *ibid*, Aug 1974, pp 12–16; and T. G. Westerman and Wayne C. Knudson, "Bold Thinking is Needed to Revitalize the Ready Reserve," *ibid*, May 1976, pp 35–37.

7. Benjamin L. Abramowitz, "Can the Reserve Components Make It?," *Military Review*, May 1976, pp 58–64; Roy A. Werner, "The Other Military: Are U.S. Reserve Forces Viable?," *ibid*, Apr 1977, pp 21–36; Joseph H. Spina, "The Reserves: Cause for Optimism or Concern?," *ibid*, Sep 1977, pp 28–31; John T. Fishel, "The Army's Reserve Components: Ready for What?," *ibid*, Nov 1978, pp 22–35; George H. Gray, "What are U.S. Reserve Forces Really For?," *ibid*, Jun 1975, pp 87–91; J. McKinely Gibson, "Being Regular is Not Enough," *Armed Forces Journal*, Jan 1975, pp 17–19. Quotation is from James T. Currie, "The Army Reserve and Vietnam," *Parameters*, Fall, 1984, pp 75–84. For a critical assessment of the reserve components in the Vietnam era, see Richard B. Crossland and James T. Currie, *Twice the Citizen* (Washington, OCHR, 1984), pp 193–210.

8. Ward Just, *Military Men* (New York, 1970).

9. U.S. Army War College, "Study on Military Professionalism," 30 Jun 1970, and "Comprehensive Report: Leadership for the 1970s. USAWC Study for the Professional Soldier," 20 Oct 1971, CMH Files.

10. Ronald H. Spector, "Vietnam and the Army's Self-Image," paper presented at The Second Indochina War Symposium, Nov 1984. Robert G. Gard, Jr., "The Military and American Society," *Foreign Affairs*, Jul 1979, p 689.

11. William L. Hauser, America's Army in Crisis: *A Study in Civil-Military Relations* (Baltimore, 1973); Zeb B. Bradford, Jr., and Frederic J. Brown, *The United States Army in Transition* (Beverly Hills, 1973); and Richard A. Gabriel and Paul L. Savage, *Crisis in Command: Mismanagement in the Army* (New York, 1978).

12. Douglas Kinnard, *The War Managers* (Hanover, N.H., 1977); and Cincinnatus, *Self Destruction: The Disintegration of the United States Army During the Vietnam Era* (New York, 1981). "Cincinnatus" claimed to be an active duty officer who saw Vietnam service but later proved to be a chaplain in the reserves who had not been to Vietnam.

13. During the period 1968–1970, *Army Magazine* had forty-nine articles on Vietnam and only six on Europe. By 1976–1978, there were fourteen articles on Europe and only four on Vietnam. I am indebted to David R. Petraens for these figures.

14. James H. Polk, "The New Short War Strategy," *Military Review*, Mar 1976, pp 58–64, and L. James Binder, "'Real Success Story': The U.S. Army Europe Puts It All Together," *Army*, Aug 1974, pp 6–10.

15. James E. Hewes, Jr., "Innovation versus Tradition: Department of the Army Headquarters Organization and Management, 1961–1981," CMH Files.

16. C. N. Barclay, "Learning the Hard Way: Lessons from the October War," *Army*, Mar 1974, pp 25–29; T. N. Dupuy, "The War of Ramadan: An Arab Perspective of the October War," *ibid*, Oct 1974, pp 22; and Fred C. Weyand, "First Battle is Crucial: Our Strategy is Readiness," *ibid*, Oct 1975, pp 16–18. Also see Jefferey Record, "The October War: Burying the Blitzkrieg," *Military Affairs*, Apr 1976, pp 29–31, and Colin S. Gray, "Blitzkrieg: A Premature Burial?," *ibid*, Oct 1976, pp 15–18.

17. David Halberstam, *The Best and the Brightest* (New York, 1969), pp 541–42. Information on the TRADOC development of the new doctrine was taken from John L. Romjue, *From Active Defense to AirLand Battle: The Development of Army Doctrine, 1973–1982* (Fort Monroe, Va., USATRADOC Historical Office, 1984). Also see "Conversations with General William E. DePuy," Senior Officers' Debriefing Program, U.S. Army Military History Institute, Carlisle Barracks, Pa.

18. Samuel R. Williamson, Jr., "Quo Vadis: The Army After Vietnam," *Army*, Sep 1973, pp 10–15.

19. See, for instance, David R. Holmes, "Some Tentative Thoughts After Vietnam," *Military Review*, Aug 1977, pp 84–87; Lloyd J. Matthews, "'Farewell the Tranquil Mind': Security and Stability in the Post-Vietnam Era," *Parameters*, 1972 pp 2–13; and John M. Collins, "Vietnam Postmortem: A Senseless Strategy," *ibid*, Mar 1978, pp 8–14.

20. William E. DePuy, "Technology and Tactics in Defense of Europe," *Army*, Apr 1979, pp 15–33, and "FM 100–5 Revisited," *ibid*, Nov 1980, pp 13–17.

21. *Department of the Army Field Manual 100–5, Operations* (Washington, 1 Jul 1976).

22. John Patrick, "Banned at Fort Monroe, or the Article that Army Doesn't Want You to Read," "TRADOC's Reply," and Philip A. Karber, "Dynamic Doctrine for Dynamic Defense," *Armed Forces Journal*, Oct 1976, pp 23–29.

23. George P. Seneff, "TRADOC's B.S.," *ibid*, Dec 1976, p 5.

24. Dan G. Loomis, "FM 100–5, Operations: A Review," *Military Review*, Mar 1977, pp 66–69; William S. Lind, "Some Doctrinal Questions for the United States Army," *ibid*, Mar 1977, pp 56–65; Donald B. Vought, "Preparing for the Wrong War," *ibid*, May 1977, pp 16–34; Zeb B. Bradford and Frederic J. Brown, "Implications of the Modern Battlefield," *ibid*, Jul 1977, pp 3–11; David Schlacter and Fred J. Stubb, "Special Operations Forces: Not Applicable?," *ibid*, Feb 1978, pp 15–26; Ralph C. Rosenberg, "Relative Combat Power," *ibid*, Mar 1978, pp 56–67; Calvin C. Seybold, "We Could Fight Outnumbered—Offensively—and Win!," *ibid*, Jun 1978, pp 35–40; Archer Jones, "The New FM 100–5: A View from the Ivory Tower," *ibid*, Feb 1978, pp 27–36; Donn A. Starry, "A Tactical Evolution—FM 100–5," *ibid*, Aug 1978, pp 2–11; Floyd V. Churchill, "To Win the First Battle," *ibid*, May 1979, pp 60–69; Richard Hart Sinnreich, "Tactical Doctrine or Dogma?," *Army*, Sep 1979, pp 16–19; and William E. DePuy, " 'One Up and Two Back': Reexamining an Old Law," *ibid*, Jan 1980, pp 20–25.

25. Stephen W. Rickey, "The Philosophical Basis of the AirLand Battle," *Military Review*, May 1984, pp 48–53.

26. "Abstracts from the U.S. Army Combined Arms Center and the Inter-University Seminar on Armed Forces and Society Symposium on Tactics and Military Posture, 30 March–1 April 1978," *Military Review*, Jul 1978, pp 33–47.

27. *Department of the Army Field Manual 100–5, Operations* (Washington, 20 Aug 1982).

28. John M. Oseth, "FM 100–5 Revisited: A Need for Better Foundations Concepts," *Military Review*, Mar 1980, pp 13–19; William Staudenmaier, "Some Strategic Implications of Fighting Outnumbered on the NATO Battlefield," *ibid*, May 1980, pp 38–50; Richard M. Swain, "On Bringing Back the Principles of War," *ibid*, Nov 1980, pp 4046; Wayne A. Dowling, "U.S. Army Operations Doctrine: A Challenge for the 1980s and Beyond," *ibid*, Jan 1981, pp 64–73; Clyde J. Tate and L. D. Holder, "New Doctrine for the Defense," *ibid*, Mar 1981, pp 2–9; Donn A. Starry, "Extending the Battlefield," *ibid*, Mar 1981, pp 31–50, and "The Principles of War," *ibid*, Sep 1981, pp 2–12; John C. F. Tillson, "The Forward Defense of Europe," *ibid*, May 1981, pp 66–67; Anthony M. Coroalles, "Maneuver to Win: A Realistic Alternative," *ibid*, Sep 1981, pp 35–46; C. Lanier Deal, Jr., "The Key to the Deep Battle," *ibid*, Mar 1982, pp 51–54; John S. Doerfel, "The Operational Art of the AirLand Battle," *ibid*, May 1982, pp 3–10; L. D. Holder, "Maneuver in the Deep Battle," *ibid*, May 1982, pp 54–61; Huba Wass de Czege and L. D. Holder, "The New FM 100–5," *ibid*, Jul 1982, pp 53–70; James M. Dubik, "FM 100–5: Comparing the Operational Concept and the Defense," *ibid*, Dec 1982, pp 13–19; James C. Barbara and Robert F. Brown, "Deep Thrust on the Extended Battlefield," *ibid*, Oct 1982, pp 21–32; and Holland E. Bynam, "Where Have all the Foreverisms Gone?," *Army*, Jan 1982, pp 18–24.

29. Stephen N. Magyuera, "Troubleshooting the New Division Organization," *Military Affairs*, Jul 1977, pp 53–60; Paul A. Bigelman, *Army*, Jun 1981, pp 22–33; and William R. Richardson, "Winning on the Extended Battlefield," *ibid*, Jun 1981, pp 34–42.

30. Lieutenant General William R. Richardson, Oct 1982, as quoted in Crossland and Currie, *Twice the Citizen*, p 211.

31. Robert K. Griffith, Jr., "Beyond Vietnam: Turbulence, Decline, Reorientation, and Recovery," CMH files; Marc B. Powe, "The U.S. Army After the Fall of Vietnam: A Contemporary Dilemma," *Military Review*, Feb 1976, pp 3–17; Andrew P. O'Meara, "Civil-Military Conflict within the Defense Structure," *Parameters*, Mar 1978, pp 85–92; "The Democratic Army and the Nation State," *ibid*, Jun 1978, pp 35–44; and Alfred H. Paddock, Jr., "Does the Army Have a Future?: Deterrence and Civil-Military Relations in the Post-Vietnam Era," *ibid*, Sep 1978, pp 51–57.

32. H. G. Summers, Jr., "Why an Army: The Public Needs to Know," *Army*, Dec 1974, pp 9–14; and Fred C. Weyand and Harry G. Summers, Jr., "Serving the People: The Need for Military Power," *Military Review*, Dec 1976, pp 8–18.

33. Harry G. Summers, Jr., *On Strategy: The Vietnam War in Context* (Carlisle Barracks, Pa., U.S. Army War College, 1981).

34. Edward C. Meyer, "Toward a More Perfect Union in Civil Military Relations," *Parameters*, Jun 1979, pp 76–83.

35. William O. Staudenmaier, "Military Strategy in Transition," *Parameters*, Dec 1978, pp 28–36; Richard L. Lunsford, Jr., "Defense Planning: A Time for Breadth," *ibid*, Mar 1978, pp 15–25; and Alwyn H. King, "U.S. Global Retrenchment and the Army of 2000," *ibid*, Jun 1979, pp 47–55. On the Sidle Commission, See Richard Halloran, "A Pentagon Panel Favors Reporters at Combat Scenes," *The New York Times*, 24 Aug 1984, p 1.

36. "The Top Brass: Can They Fight a Modern War?," *Newsweek*, Jul 1984, pp 32–51.

37. Dale K. Brudvig, "The Division May Be 'Light', But Can It Fight?," *Army Times*, 10 Sep 1984, p 65.

Commentary

James R. Leutze

It is a great pleasure for me to be here and to have the opportunity to review the two papers you have heard as well as to offer some commentary of my own.

What I have just said indicates the manner in which I propose to approach my task. That is, first I shall review both papers, then make my observations and comments on the period, and finally draw some lessons that might apply to the future. However, before turning to the individual papers, there is a comment I wish to make which applies to both. I was generally disappointed that neither author defined what he meant or interpreted to be meant by the term "limited conflict." Obviously, this either seemed unnecessary or inappropriate, but in fact the failure to address this issue led to a certain imprecision or lack of focus which distracted the reader. At a later point I'll return to this issue.

But first, let me turn to the papers. The first, "Postwar U.S. Strategic Planning for Latin America: from 'Rainbow' to IDAD,'" by Jack Child of The American University, I found to be very comprehensive, thorough and thought provoking. Clearly the author has done extensive work in this subject area and is familiar with the secondary sources as well as primary materials including recently declassified record groups. He seems to me to have correctly identified the pendular movement of U.S. policy toward Latin America; we pay constructive attention to the area only when there is a real or perceived problem or when our attention is not occupied elsewhere. As has become painfully obvious, our periodic ministrations are not enough to solve the long term, endemic problems of the region. I found his application of the term "benign neglect" to be particularly appropriate during the cold war period.

On the other hand, it seemed to me that he did not adequately address the issue of how the war in Vietnam affected our reaction to developments in Latin America, particularly in the Caribbean and

Central America. The author does acknowledge that the Vietnam affair preoccupied American planners in the 1961–67 period but does not go on to assess how the failure in Vietnam influenced those same planners *after* 1968 when we made the decision to accept something less than victory in Southeast Asia. Although I would be quick to point out the many differences for a planner thinking of fighting a limited conflict in Latin America, there would have been many shocking analogies to fighting and losing such a conflict in Vietnam. The termination of the one war must have sent seismic reverberations through the offices of the plans Mafia and sounded like, if not the clap of doom, at least an alarm bell at Southern Command in Panama. Surely studies were done and possibly even some changes recommended in the curriculum at the U.S. Army School of the Americas to reflect how what had been learned in Vietnam could be applied to other areas. Perhaps no such information is available in the public domain, but it certainly would be relevant and most instructive when discussing strategic planning in the post-Vietnam period.

In this regard, it seemed to me unfortunate that the author did not provide any detailed information about planning for any of the military or quasi-military actions during this 1945–76 period. The U.S. did send troops to the Dominican Republic in 1965; the CIA was intimately involved in planning the Bay of Pigs operation in 1961; and there must have been planning for an invasion of Cuba before and after the missile crisis. In each of these instances, the planning that went into these operations would seem to merit examination in the context of this subject. Some might even argue that actions, such as the CIA-backed coup in Guatemala (1954) and the Cuban missile crisis (1962), deserved more attention than they received. The one specific military campaign discussed, the effort to isolate the *focos*, is dealt with only superficially. Apparently the author believed that to deal with all of these topics would hopelessly dilute his paper, but I believe that these operations are relevant and fully as deserving of examination as are the Rio and Bogota conferences.

However, in summation, I believe the paper was well written, exhaustively researched, informative, and fills an important gap in our knowledge. The author did a good job given the period of time he chose to cover. My primary complaint, in fact, is that by choosing to survey a period of thirty-one years in thirty minutes, he forced himself to be too general. At the same time, I found myself wishing that he had specifically addressed some more current issue like Grenada and planning for El Salvador.

Next, to Alexander S. Cochran's paper, "The Impact of Vietnam on Military Planning, 1972–1982: Some Tentative Thoughts." This paper was not as sweeping as the last, but it contains, in my view, more unrefined nuggets. Unfortunately, it does not deal in adequate detail with these subjects, nor does it come to grips with what I conceive to be the major issue. Unlike the last paper, there is a problem with documentation. Most of the sources are professional journals with virtually no primary sources cited. The author confronts this subject at the beginning by saying that most official sources are not yet available, and that those he could get access to seemed unsatisfactory. He also alludes to the fact that subjects so close to the present are almost current events. Given these understandable problems, I am interested in knowing why he chose to go on to 1982 rather than stopping in 1976. The source difficulties could only increase the closer he comes to the present.

Now, to more specific observations. Although the author explains why he did so, I thought it unfortunate that he confined himself to discussing the Army and its reactions to Vietnam. The other services were also strongly affected by the reversal of our fortunes and their reactions might provide useful insights and balance.

In broader terms, I found that much of the paper dealt with what seemed initially to be nongermane issues. For instance, considerable time was spent in examining the Army's "crisis in confidence" and its morale. While this is an important topic and a clear outgrowth of the Vietnam experience, the author does not explicitly connect it with planning for limited conflicts. The same is true in the discussion of the debate over AirLand Battle that led to the publication and then the revision of FM 100–5. This debate over AirLand Battle arose out of the determination by certain high-ranking officers in the Army that the "enemy would be the Soviets" and the "battlefield would be central Europe." Whether in fact these are knowns, as the Army assumes, is really not the issue here. The issue is that this battle would not be a limited conflict even if one discusses it as a conventional war, ignoring the escalation possibilities. While the suggestion that younger officers refused to meekly accept a new doctrine because they had grown suspicious of ticket punching in Vietnam and, therefore, insisted that FM 100–5 be revised is interesting; it still does not tell us anything about the conflicts we are addressing. Be that as it may, it is in the latter stages of the paper that we get to the important issues and the unrefined nuggets that I referred to previously. For instance, I was particularly taken with the comments on civil-military relations on page 378.

Underlined in red on every senior planner's desk pad should be the phrase "wars of the future must be perceived as popular by the public and winnable by the military and allowable by the politicians." In the final paragraphs the author also comes to grips with other illuminating and responsive points. The most intriguing of these can be found in his final sentence: "Planners now candidly admit that Vietnam was a strategic loss, and they are not anxious to plan for a repeat performance." This important observation may be the key to some of the problems I encountered earlier in the paper. Can one infer that the reason the Army occupied itself with planning AirLand Battle was because they could not face or imagine fighting another Vietnam? It would not be the first time that paralysis followed failure. Was this mental paralysis the result of the "crisis in confidence" the author mentioned? Unfortunately these issues are not discussed, but they are very important and I would now like to use them as a springboard for beginning the next section of this presentation.

As I indicated initially, in this section I would like to extend my commentary beyond the papers and make some observations about how I think this topic of planning for limited conflicts might be fruitfully addressed. Presumably when this topic was chosen, the intent was that by historically surveying this period and learning how planners had shaped strategy for limited conflicts, lessons could be learned that would provide guidelines for the future. Part of my difficulty with both of these papers was that the authors failed to define what they interpreted to be a strategy for limited conflict; consequently, each seems to approach the subject in a distinctly different manner and to a certain extent neither comes to grips with the primary assignment.

What we need, therefore, is a definition of what we mean by "limited conflict." Happily, Robert Osgood (in his book *Limited War Revisited*) has come up with at least a start toward a satisfactory definition. "Limited wars," he writes, "were (are) to be fought for ends far short of the complete subordination of one state's will to another's, using means that involve far less than the total military resources of the belligerents and leave the civilian life and the armed forces of the belligerents largely intact."[1] While I realize that Osgood and Thomas Schelling and others who wrote about limited war in the pre-Vietnam era are not universally approved, it would be a mistake to disregard *in toto* the theories that were developed.[2] Moreover, there are other useful, theoretical studies that might provide keys to future success.[3]

Be that as it may, although we used the term limited conflict instead of limited war, in my view the purpose of this session is to examine instances during the 1945–1976 period in which military force was used or in which plans were made for using military force within the context of Osgood's definition.[4] To me this implies that we are not concerned with plans or confrontations in which the United States would range itself directly opposite the Soviet Union or the Warsaw Pact. Instead we are invited to look for instances in which the United States used or planned to use military force in some peripheral area such as the Caribbean, the Middle East, or Southeast Asia and to fight something other than a war intended to bring about total victory. These are wars hedged about with political, diplomatic, and even economic restraints. They are what have been referred to as half wars. The two most obvious instances in the period are Korea and Vietnam. Korea, I believe, deserves very serious study, especially in light of Colonel Harry Summers' provocative suggestion that we drew the *wrong* lessons from that war, because we mistakenly "saw our limited victory in Korea as a kind of defeat" instead of as a victory in a limited war.[5] Vietnam, on the other hand, has already drawn considerable analytical attention. Of particular value in the search for lessons are Timothy Lomperis' *The War Everyone Lost—and Won: America's Intervention in Viet Nam's Twin Struggles*; the Woodrow Wilson Center's *Some Lessons and Non-Lessons of Vietnam*; Colonel Summer's *On Strategy*; Osgood's *Limited Wars*; and the previously noted *Lessons from an Unconventional War*.[6] Any contingency planning based on that war should also consider the following points:

a. We need to be cautious about applying historical lessons where they *don't* apply. Vietnam *wasn't* Czechoslovakia, El Salvador *isn't* Vietnam.

b. We need reliable intelligence on the enemy we are fighting. What is their history, their culture, their societal background? What is their connection with other enemies, particularly major opponents or blocks? What is their pain threshold, their economic vulnerability, the price they are willing to pay? What are they willing to negotiate on? Are there internal schisms or weaknesses that can be exploited?

c. We need improved techniques for controlling the actions of the group or country we are presumably helping.

d. Our ability in the area of civil-military relations must be improved. The public must be provided with facts, not body counts, and they must be won over through logic not rhetoric. (I don't, by the way, feel that excluding the press from reasonable access is a good way to go about this.)

e. If we are to be able to logically explain why we are doing something, there must be a logic in it. Before we engage in limited conflict, we should carefully define our strategy and how military force fits into that strategy and how success will be defined.

As if this were not enough, I think that in surveying this period (1945–1976) for lessons, we are tempted to address another question. Is it possible to successfully wage limited conflicts? This is an important question because there seems to be a post-Vietnam consensus that we cannot. While first reminding my listeners that this is a logical outgrowth not just of Vietnam *but of the entire postnuclear search for a mission by the U.S. services*, I will fall back on my academic specialty. As an historian my initial reaction is to suggest that we should *not* confine ourselves to the post-World War II period when asking whether limited wars can successfully be waged. For instance, in the American experience, the War of 1812, the Mexican War, and the Spanish-American War might offer some ideas. We also should look at the experience of other countries ancient and contemporary. The Falklands War, for instance, is particularly illuminating.

My next reaction is to wonder if the problem of searching for lessons may not be complicated by the definition we have accepted for limited conflicts. My suspicion is that Osgood's, and probably most other definitions, are not precise enough. This suspicion arises out of the conviction that the basic problem with Vietnam was that it was a limited war that outgrew its limited status. Any war that goes on for twelve years, costs $139.6 billion, and involves more than 2,000,000 men is not by my definition a limited war.

Therefore, I suggest that boundaries—in terms of numbers and duration—be placed upon the wars we consider as limited. For sake of discussion I suggest 1,500 to 50,000 men and from six months to two years in duration. While I am dubious that right now the public would enthusiastically support a deployment, even the deployment of the size and duration I mention, I am quite certain that that public attitude will change.

Furthermore, this type of military commitment to a Third World or peripheral area is the most likely mission for the modern military services. For that reason there should be accurate, realistic, historically sensitive planning for this kind of conflict. In this regard, if future operations are to be successful, the military and civilian areas of the government will neglect, at their peril, the Clausewitzean principle that "war is an extension of state politics by other means." What I take that to mean is that the civilian leadership needs to find ways to smoothly incorporate the use of military forces into their grand strategic designs; that the military must see that victory is more than winning tactical successes; and that the public must come to realize that successfully conducted international relations include military power as well as the more familiar economics, diplomacy, and politics.

Notes

1. Robert Endicott Osgood, *Limited War Revisited* (Boulder, Colo., 1978), p 3.

2. For negative commentary see Richard K. Betts "Misadventure Revisited," *The Wilson Quarterly* (Summer 1983), pp 95–110, especially p 103; also Stephen Peter Rosen "Vietnam and the American Theory of Limited War," *International Security* (Fall, 1982), pp 83–113. Rosen does include a useful section on "Redefining the Theory," pp 103–113.

3. See Richard A. Hung and Richard H. Shultz, Jr., eds., *Lessons from an Unconventional War* (New York, 1982), especially pp 191–221; also David Tarr, "The Strategic Environment, U.S. National Security, and the Nature of Low Intensity Conflict," in Sam Sarkesian, ed., *Non-Nuclear Conflicts in the Nuclear Age* (New York, 1980).

4. See, for example, General James M. Gavin, *War and Peace in the Space Age* (New York, 1958) and Maxwell Davenport Taylor, *The Uncertain Trumpet* (New York, 1960).

5. Harry G. Summers, *On Strategy: A Critical Analysis of the Vietnam War* (Novato, Calif., 1982) p 59.

6. Timothy L. Lomperis, *The War Everyone Lost—and Won: America's Intervention in Vietnam's Twin Struggles* (Baton Rouge, 1984); "Lessons and Non-Lessons of the U.S. Experience in Vietnam," in Peter Braestrup, ed., *Vietnam as History: Ten Years After the Paris Peace Accords* (Washington, 1984); Summers, *On Strategy*; and Osgood, *Limited War Revisited*.

Discussion and Comments

Admiral Noel A.M. Gayler, USN, Retired, Moderator

Jerry Cantwell (HQ Air Force Reserve): I need to ask Dr. Cochran to drop the other shoe. The Air Force clarified the status of its air reserve forces, guard and reserve, after Southeast Asia, by accepting unreservedly on the one hand Public Law 9168 from the Congress, and on the other hand the total force concept from Rand and sold both to the Office of the Secretary of Defense. My question is: both vehicles have been available to the U.S. Army; has it made equal use of them?

Cochran: Yes, I think the CAPSTONE II program in operation right now effectively integrates the reserves and the national guard into not only armed forces structuring but also planning. You see things like the light division which are now being created. If you look at it one third of those forces come from the guard and the reserves. Without answering more specifically and from what I read and what I understand, yes we are. The Army is getting the reserves more actively involved in the planning.

Colonel Ken Alnwick (Strategic Concepts Development Center, National Defense University): I'm going to break your rule a little bit sir, but you'll love it anyway. Dr. Leutze to help you help Dr. Cochran, I have a footnote on the impact of Vietnam on Air Force planning and doctrine. Zip. And I would suspect that the same applies to the Navy. And now to Dr. Child, I would ask you to comment on the political-military planning that is exercised by the CINC in his current role in the Southern Command, the CINC as a regional military planner. Thank you.

Child: I would have to say that I have been somewhat out of contact with the information that would allow me to answer your question accurately. I think it's good to put it in historical perspective. For many many years the position of Commander in Chief Southern Command was seen as, shall we say, not the highest priority assignment. It was a good assignment to go to just before your retirement. Panama was seen as a very tranquil place, a lot of golf, good swimming, snorkeling, and so forth. General Nutting arrived there at a time when all this changed very clearly. I worked for General Nutting for many years. Most dramatically the current CINC South, General Gorman, has assumed a very significant role. Let me be candid and say, I think in many cases he is driving much of the equation. Although I don't know him personally, I do have an area specialist bias against an individual with General Gorman's qualifications who comes in with no area knowledge, picks it up very quickly, and charges very very hard. I'm a little bit leery and more than a little nervous about that to be perfectly honest. I would hope that some of the initiatives that I see coming out of SouthCom are tempered by the area specialist knowledge, the deeper sense of the history of the U.S. interventions in the area, and the price that we might pay if we did get involved more deeply in the area. I accept what General Gorman is trying to do, but I hope it will be balanced by this deeper sense of history and the culture, particularly of the U.S. relationships with the countries in this area. As a specific example, I think the Sandinistas in Managua would love to see a U.S. intervention. It would give them an excuse for a number of their failures, it would allow them to revert back from the role they're playing now that they're a little uncomfortable in—that is playing the role of bureaucrats—and it would allow them to pick up their rifles, go back into the hills, and again play the role of Sandino which they can play best.

Gayler: That *is* a perception.

Tom Wiltsey (Ninth Air Force): I'd like to pick up on a comment alluded to in the commentary and direct it to both speakers. Although we're not planning to repeat our defeat in Vietnam, through your research do you sense any kind of traumatizing of planners for the next wars in the sense the French were traumatized by their World War I experience?

Cochran: Maybe I could answer this in the context of a discussion we had at lunch with Jack Child about my perception of what Army planners feel about Latin America, which I became aware of last summer and last spring in Washington. For the first time in my life, I watched military planners parade up to the hill and actively lobby against an administration position. At that time I was studying the early period of the Vietnam War, and it struck me that this was a 180–degree turn. I personally believe that Army planners are very leery about Latin America primarily because of the Vietnam experience. I think this very much conditions the way they go about planning. Now, the big question is: how much impact do those planners have at higher levels of decisionmaking? I'm not too sure on that point.

Child: I think there was a double trauma and it depends upon where you're coming from ideologically. If you're coming from the right, the trauma might be expressed very simply as let's do it right this time, let's not make the mistakes of Vietnam. If you're coming at it ideologically from the left, I suppose it could be reduced simplistically to never again should we allow ourselves to get sucked into something like that. Both are traumatic and paralyzing, and I think will cause us to pay a significant price in the future. I would hope that there is considerable middle ground between those extremes. Let me comment again on a somewhat personal level. In 1962, I was one of that first group of 16,000 advisors about whom Maxwell Taylor said, "That's all we need in Vietnam." And I felt I was part of Camelot. This is something that Sandy referred to a few minutes ago. I felt it was either that or the Peace Corps, and they were essentially two sides of the same coin. I went to Vietnam the first time with the feeling that—we were doing something right, proper, and significant. My second tour in Vietnam ten years later was obviously a quite different circumstance that doesn't particularly need to be looked into, except that I would share with you in retrospect a vignette that suggests to me the moment I realized that we were losing the Vietnam War—the end of my first tour, at the end of the Camelot phase. I had spent the tour up country in the Da Nang area as an advisor to the Vietnamese Second Infantry Division. Something I saw coming out to the Saigon airport on my way home should have told me we were losing the war. We were building barracks and putting air conditioners in them for our people. And I think that was the key moment—our technology of air conditioning isolated us from the environment in really terrible ways. I didn't realize it at the time, but looking back, I think it was a key moment.

Peter Vigor (Soviet Studies Research Centre): My question is to Dr. Leutze. If unlimited war is the state using all its resources, and if we are to adopt your definition of limited war with very small resources over a short period of time, what do we call Vietnam?

Leutze: I take your point. I call Vietnam an unlimited war but falling between those two definitions. It obviously isn't a total war in which we're using all of our resources, and we're not trying to destroy the enemy totally. But I think we were using such extensive forces and over such a long period of time, I can—well, you shake your head.

As I say, I consider a force of 600,000 men not an unlimited force, and the point is the American public came to consider it as an unlimited war and that really was a large part of the problem. And I don't think the American public is going to change in that perception. I think they will continue to view that kind of war as more of a war than they are willing to fight, unless they can see, as I also suggested, the political-military strategic objective involved more clearly than they could in the Vietnam War. But Vietnam sort of comes out as neither fish nor fowl, which maybe is part of the problem.

Gayler: I don't think that any of the military commanders involved would believe that the Vietnam War was unlimited from our standpoint. The limitations on what we could do were pervasive; they caused us to operate sometimes in contravention of every one of Clausewitz's principles of war. So we have to find some other wording, some other semantics which conveys your view. It was much too big to be treated in the way in which it was, and yet the military reality was we really did have one hand tied behind our back.

Dean Allard (Naval Historical Center): May I address the question to you, Admiral? Could you comment on the impact of Vietnam upon Navy planning?

Gayler: I think it is more general than what I've heard described both for the Army and the Air Force, general in the sense that the Navy shared the trauma of all the military in the loss of confidence by the country. We were not so seriously threatened, and as a matter of fact, except in the air and the brown water navy, not so directly involved. So I don't think we had quite the traumatic feeling of failure. From my experiences as a unified commander, however, I think I would bring another conclusion to you. It is simply not true that in that war, military capabilities could not have been effective. I recall, for instance, the quarantine of Hanoi and the mining of Haiphong harbor in December 1972 both of which in fact were spectacularly successful military operations and forced an armistice. I think we all realized that it was much too late in a political sense. The one extraordinary characteristic of the mining of Haiphong harbor, which was arguably one of the most effective military operations of the war, in that it denied, together with the bombing of the railroad yards and the mining of the canals, supply, was that nobody ever got killed on either side. Now that I think is something that we as military commanders and military historians should think about more. It's the effective application of power with minimum casualties. We think about that quite often in the Navy, but in general we were not as traumatized as the other services except for those who served in the brown water navy.

Cochran: Sir, may I comment on a comment?

Gayler: Certainly.

Cochran: One of my more recent responsibilities to the Center of Military History has been to go to the Army staffs and start asking them, "What do they want from us as historical works go?" To complement what Dr. Leutze has said, the feedback we are getting from staff officers and Army planners is we want to know more about what happened in local, limited wars like Korea. So I would think this is something of a comment on a comment—the impact is to redirect Army planners to think about their roles in limited wars.

Gayler: I think that would be very useful.

Richard Kohn (Office of Air Force History): It occurs to me that among the many dilemmas planners must face, programmers, military leaders and political leaders also, is the dilemma between planning for the most dangerous or planning for the most likely. In that context I'd ask, first you Admiral Gayler, if you could comment on the possibility that planners are now paralyzing themselves by retreating into planning for the most dangerous because it seems to avoid the dilemma of public support. I worry about that a bit because if the military establishment only recommends certain courses of action with public support beforehand, we may be eroding our deterrent posture.

Gayler: Well, I think that's a very perceptive comment, and I think I agree there is a major danger of that. If you confine your constellation of potential plans to those which you are assured in advance will command public support in all circumstances, you may not be doing what you should. I think further, and I don't think its any secret to anybody who knows me, that we are far too preoccupied with planning for and providing for nuclear war which is a discontinuity from all other military operations, a discontinuity from all other previous military thought, and so enormous that in my judgment it should be treated as a special case. Speaking of treating, I won't treat you all to the way I think it should be treated as a special case, but I will just say I think it should be very different from what we are doing now, and that our preoccupation with it has been a major factor in our not directing attention to our real problems. As an illustration, I will give you my impression that the mutual nuclear deterrent between ourselves and the Soviet Union is going to continue because it is so clearly in the interests of the Soviet Union and ourselves that we not go to nuclear war. Underneath this nuclear standoff is where the action is going to take place, just as it did in Hungary, just as it did in Czechoslovakia, and just as it did in Cuba. The action is going to be determined by the usable military forces on the scene. Whether they be land, sea, air, or whatever combination. So that's the sort of thing toward which we should direct our attention. I believe I'm agreeing with you.

Unidentified Speaker: This question is addressed to Mr. Child. I believe for a long time we've been engaged in a war of ideas, and I believe ideas are weapons. Having resided in Latin America before the war, I was appalled at the lack of men in our major universities who could teach courses in areas and languages. I would ask you what has happened since World War II to rectify what it seems to me was a singular error in the academic community?

Child: I think you could almost draw a parallel to the periods of concern and benign neglect that I traced in a different context. I think your point is a very good one. There was generally a sense of not much concern for it in the thirties; during the war there was a tremendous interest in Latin America. Offices like Nelson Rockefeller's did a great deal to awaken cultural understanding. The fact that I grew up in Latin America, I think, was part of that general sense of interest and concern in Latin America, I think, it declined rather markedly after the Second World War. I think that little incidents like Vice President Nixon's trip to Latin America, which was a real shock, showed the depth of ignorance that we had toward the area. I think in the period of the Alliance for Progress we saw again a renewal, a rebirth of studies of Latin America, area studies. Again anecdotally, the Army sent me for a marvelous one-year, all-expenses-paid tour to earn a master of arts degree in Latin American studies which was a great experience for me. It really changed my life in many ways and that's a reflection of this interest in Latin America. If I could continue anecdotally, I then turned around after Vietnam and asked the Army "Would you like me to try for a Ph.D.?" and they said, "No there really isn't any need for Ph.D. specialists in Latin America in the Army." Anyway, I see now a renewal of interest in Latin America, for the wrong reasons I might add, but the interest is there. Enrollments in Spanish and Latin American studies courses at my university, at least, are certainly up—I think that's true in a good many other places. There is a famous quotation by a *New York Times* journalist who said that,

"North Americans are willing to do anything for Latin America, invest money, blood, effort, except read about it and learn about it." And I think that captures the essence of your question. I think it's very unfortunate.

Summary Remarks

John W. Shy

By tradition closing remarks at conferences are positive and upbeat. The critics have had their say, the detailed discussions have been held, and at the end everyone ought to feel good, consider what they have learned, and fly away feeling it was all worthwhile.

Alas, I am obliged to begin these closing remarks by sounding downbeat—saying that we may have been too parochial (or provincial) in our collective concern, and adding that this whole subject is fairly depressing.

The depressing nature of the subject is surely obvious and hardly needs emphasis. The story of military planning in the twentieth century, as we have heard it told, is overwhelmingly a story of failure—of planners who did not plan, or could not plan, or whose plans were ignored, or were disastrously wrong. In only a few cases—notably Etzold's account of U.S. Navy planning in the 1970s, and Cochran's account of the U.S. Army's response to Vietnam—was there anything positive or successful. And even in these two cases, perhaps because they are so very close to us in time, I detected a certain skepticism in the audience as to whether things were really going as well as these two papers indicated. Time of course will tell. A very small but recent and relevant incident suggests the need for some caution in concluding that the Army, traumatized by Vietnam and fixated on the central European battlefield, has its planning act together. The assault companies of the 82nd Airborne Division at Grenada did not have access to their organic 81–mm mortars because worst-case planning for a different kind of battle made them virtually unavailable for the first phase of this surprising little venture in the Caribbean, where it was not clear until the last moment whether the assault elements from Fort Bragg would be air dropped or air landed. In this case, fortunately, it had no unhappy military consequences. But those 81–mm mortars were prepacked for one contingency, not the other, and—as usual—Murphy's law prevailed.

The variety of approaches to our subject demonstrates that even the simple word, planning, apparently so clear, in fact refers to a number of quite different activities. Organization, doctrine, technology, strategy, operational decisionmaking—all have a planning dimension. No neat definition of the word that ignores any of these dimensions can capture the process that concerns us. What those dimensions have in common—if I may attempt my own definition— is anticipating the future with all its uncertainties, while defining and preparing to reach specified objectives. Ideally the plan will enable us to reach those objectives as quickly, cheaply, and safely as possible. The planner, if he can outguess the future and be clear about objectives—each a formidable task even when not treated as interactive with each other—must then minimize delay, cost, and risk. Staggering! Depressing!

No one can blame the organizers or participants of the symposium for the depressing nature of the subject. Nor is our provincialism a matter for criticism; this is an American conference, strongly oriented toward the current concerns of the American military, and it is not surprising that so much of its effort has dealt with more recent, especially more recent American, experience. After Professor Deutsch's account of German military planning before the two World Wars, and our first session devoted to French, Soviet, and Japanese planning going into the Second World War, we have spent the rest of our time on events in our own country, in our own lifetimes—if you are my age or older, that is. By sacrificing something in scope we have achieved depth.

How else, except by taking the time and giving the details, could we understand why the people at Wright and Langley Fields in the 1930s were so oblivious to the possibilities of jet propulsion, or why two separate parts of the Air Staff were planning the next war in the 1950s with little or no contact between them, and with virtually no effect on the chief war-fighting part of the Air Force—SAC. Brief treatments of these two cases would, almost certainly, have made the actors look like fools. But as presented by Professor Holley and Colonel Gropman, we can easily see how competent, diligent, intelligent Americans found themselves making what now seem to be serious planning mistakes.

Now it is at just this point that the limited scope of our inquiry does begin to trouble me. As described so elegantly by Professor Cairns, French failure before 1940 is truly a classic case in which a host of factors converged to produce a military and national disaster. Nazi, Soviet, and Japanese planning look better, but not much.

Professors Deutsch and Coox tell us how German and Japanese planners pushed their nations into unwinnable wars, and—according to Peter Vigor—only German planning mistakes and consequent losses make Soviet planning, in retrospect, look passably good. So why hasn't American planning—informed by these unhappy mistakes of others and facilitated by our famous energy, ingenuity, and flexibility (so unlike the authoritarian Nazi, Stalinist, and Japanese planning performances, and also free of the rigidities and relative weakness of the French in the 1930s)—been demonstrably better? What's wrong with us? We have heard Futrell on the Air Force, Etzold on the Navy, Schandler on Vietnam, and Child on Latin America; taken all together, they sound like variations on the theme of planning failure. Not only is the whole subject depressing, but I sense a certain gloominess about the American capacity ever to get it right.

My own response to this gloom is directly related to the scope of the inquiry. If we had the week, or several weeks, needed to be truly comprehensive, to read, hear, and discuss the detailed research findings of fifty or sixty experts instead of a dozen short papers, I suspect the atmosphere would change as our perspective on the subject changed. The recent American experience, once set more firmly in the broadest historical context, would appear less peculiar and less discouraging. The truth, I think, is that planning, which we would all agree is a Good Thing, a vitally important virtue of true military professionalism, and a vital aspect of national security, is an almost impossibly difficult thing to do well. Not planning is Bad, we know: witness the rapid defeat of the great French Army in 1870, famed for its ability to improvise, defeated by a weaker enemy who had a plan. We also know that a rigid, worst-case plan can be as bad as no plan at all: witness the notorious Schlieffen Plan, which first eliminated German diplomatic options in 1914 and then demanded that the German Army knock out its Western enemies in six weeks—possible perhaps, but very, very unlikely in the conditions prevailing. So we know that Good Plans are contingency plans— worked out in a crisply rational way, matching military resources and capabilities to political commitments and objectives, thoroughly developed but never rigid, each contingency assigned an estimated probability of occurrence, all elements of all plans reviewed and adjusted in response to changing circumstance. But we all know—or we should know (after Richard Kohn told us yesterday)—that it never, ever happens that way. And we should know, as historians, that the irrational, frustrating, messy (Kohn's word) real world of military planning is not some American disease but a fundamental condition of the whole process. Even the huge gap between the impossibly tidy concept of planning and the repulsive reality of what almost always happens in actual planning, is a part of the historical—and contemporary—problem. More than one of these papers and comments, so critical of some historical planning failure, imply that better, wiser people—ourselves, for example—might have come closer to that crisp, cool, rational, ideal world of Good Planning.

I very much doubt it. If we broke out of our preoccupation with recent and American experience, and considered carefully all the cases of modern military planning since about 1850, when steam power, rifled weapons, and electrical communications had begun to change the nature of warfare, I think we would be convinced how dauntingly difficult the task really is, no matter who is doing it, whatever the situation, the organization, or the techniques. The most detailed of these papers suggests why this is so. Conflict between civilian and military values and viewpoints is part of the problem but may be overrated. Surely bureaucracy—bureaucratic fragmentation, bureaucratic inertia, bureaucratic politics, and the politicization of bureaucracy—is truly crippling. Colonel Gropman has said that there are about 300 people on the Air Staff involved in planning. No research, just a little imagination, is needed to see the bureaucratic problems such numbers must create. And yet to separate planning from administration and operation usually means making the planning function weak and irrelevant, as suggested by Colonel Gropman's story. Separating the best estimates of the future from a firm grasp of the present seems intellectually, organizationally, and psychologically impossible. And yet to merge the two is inevitably to make the future hostage to the urgencies of here and now. Professor Holley's wonderful little story of what happened at Wright Field is a parable of the planner whose priorities are set by the immediate needs of development and operations. Doing what it had learned to do so well—developing air-cooled engines and neglecting alternative forms of propulsion—the small, dedicated Wright Field staff eventually gave birth to a thirty-six-cylinder, four-row, 5,000–hp, air-cooled engine—a brilliant achievement but a virtual dinosaur in the military situation of 1945.

To emphasize this dilemma is not a message of despair. It is meant instead to be a message of realism, both for historians who are apt to be hypercritical of human and institutional failure, and for military professionals who are apt to be impatient and hasty when results do not match expectations. Planning is essential, no question about it; but satisfactory planning, unless aided by good luck and enemy blunders, is simply too hard. Too much conflict and too much uncertainty are built into the process for the achievement of consistently good results.

Dr. Harry Ball, Colonel, USA, Retired, in an informal conversation between sessions, made an important point that I am going to steal, a point that General Goodpaster alluded to when he said that, over his long and distinguished career, there was a noticeable correlation between the quality of planning effort and the quality of operational results. To put it a bit differently, and in Dr. Ball's own terms, one of the most important effects of planning may be educational—to make military planners (and those they work for and with) think through their problems—their future tasks, their options in responding to those tasks, and their resources (actual and prospective) in pursuing each option. As with the famous COLOR and RAINBOW plans of the United States before 1941, none of the preconflict plans may in the event be implemented, but the continuing, intensive exercise of working through the American strategic future proved to be invaluable.

All this of course, is one historian's opinion. But maybe the real value of the symposium lies less in a specific conclusion, mine or any other, than in opening up the whole difficult subject, through the consideration of a variety of case studies, done from a variety of viewpoints. The upbeat message, by way of conclusion, is that all of us—historians and planners—have been made by the two days of this symposium, more realistic, a little more objective, rational, and comparative, when we next must deal in our professional work with a particular military planning problem.

Let me close, speaking for all of us, in thanking Lt. Colonel Borowski, Major Harvey, and all the others at the Air Force Academy, from General Scott to the cadets who checked off our names at the motel, for a superbly and congenially run symposium. If we needed some evidence that effective American military planning is possible, then Colonel Reddel and his team have provided that heartening confirmation.

Thanks, for all of us.

Speeches
and
Memorandum

Introduction

The Eleventh Military History Symposium featured two speeches addressing current and future planning considerations. These presentations and the following commentary provide a fitting end to the proceedings as they link present and future concerns with past.

General Albert C. Wedemeyer, United States Army, retired, served as one of General George C. Marshall's principal planners during World War II and has been described as the man who planned its victory. Involved with military planning throughout his long career but unable to attend the symposium, General Wedemeyer offered the following remarks. He suggested the United States create a national strategy council—an advisory group of experts from all fields directly related to national strategy and independent of direct political pressures—to assist the government in planning. While some elements of his proposal existed in the old State Department Policy Planning Staff or in the current National Security Council, this new group would enjoy greater resources at its disposal, and they would not deal with the day-to-day operational concerns that current planners must face. This body would aim to incorporate many of the lessons developed during the symposium sessions.

Major General Davis C. Rohr, United States Air Force, currently Deputy Commander, United States Central Command, agreed to share with the symposium the current problems and structure of this new military organization. The Iranian crisis of 1979–81 sparked the drive for creating this new command as the United States came to realize its influence in the Middle East hardly matched its vital interests in the region—specifically, western access to Persian Gulf oil and Arab/Israeli peace. His command is not the first in U.S. history tasked to be ready to deploy on short notice to a distant part of the world, and as in the past, air and sea transportation and logistics give him the most difficulty. The issue again arises: to what extent will the national leadership and public opinion support the command with the resources necessary to meet the task, and in the absence of sufficient resources, how do his planners respond?

Admiral Bobby Inman, United States Navy, retired, took the symposium into the future with a preview of new technologies and events likely to affect planning in the next century. His remarks forced the audience to recognize again the problems planners will encounter in trying to incorporate new and often unproven technology into military planning. No solutions to the problems are clearly evident except to give the very important job of planning to the very best minds. In several decades history will show how well our nation responded to this important endeavor.

Memorandum on a National Strategy Council

General Albert C. Wedemeyer, USA, Retired

For forty years and more, I have been concerned about the adequacy of our national policymaking machinery to deal with the challenges of an increasingly turbulent and complex world.

My first clear awakening in this regard occurred back in 1941 in the months before Pearl Harbor. I was a staff officer in the War Department charged with drafting a broad plan (later known as the Victory Program) for the mobilization and employment of U.S. resources in a possible global war with the Rome-Berlin-Tokyo Axis. The American public was sharply divided in its attitudes toward the conflicts raging in Europe and elsewhere. A babble of voices urging various degrees of involvement or noninvolvement arose on all sides. Torrents of foreign and domestic propaganda sought to sway opinion. The nation's fate and future unquestionably were at stake in a world drifting ever closer toward general war.

It is perhaps not surprising that in this situation official Washington seemed as confused and divided as the nation itself. However, it was the task of the small group of strategic planners, of which I was a member, to chart and propose a specific course. Before long I rediscovered the obvious: a journey can be charted only with a destination in mind, and *strategy* can be plotted only with goals or aims in mind. I accordingly set out to discover what the objectives of U.S. involvement might be—other than the physical destruction of the forces which might then be arrayed against us. What were our country's true interests? How could those interests best be protected and advanced? What kind of world did we wish to emerge from the cataclysm of another terrible war?

To my consternation, I could find few if any concrete answers to these vital questions. So far as I could discover, no systematic official attention had been given them. No mechanisms for considering them in an orderly and informed way existed within the government. Indeed, I found little awareness or acceptance of the notion that supreme issues of war and peace *required* thorough analysis in the top echelons of the national government. An uneasy feeling came over me that the ship of state was rudderless in the storm; or, if the rudder were still intact, there at least were no charts and orders on the bridge to guide the navigator.

And so, when war came, we embarked on a great crusade to slay the dragons which then confronted us. Plunging emotionally into the conflict, we endured much bloodshed and suffering (and imposed even more on others), expended untold treasure, and helped wreak destruction on large portions of the earth's surface. When the smoke of battle lifted, we spent billions more to restore the damage that had been done. Then, to our sorrow, even the idealistic slogans (e.g., the Four Freedoms) that had inspired and sustained the crusade were mocked by the rise of new tyrannies, new wars, and a flood of new problems that dwarfed the old ones. Instead of ridding the world of tyranny, we found that, in destroying one set of tyrants, we had simply paved the way for the rise of other more dangerous ones.

After World War II, a few promising steps were taken in Washington to improve the mechanisms of interagency coordination. I am thinking here of the establishment of such agencies as the National Security Council and the Policy Planning Staff at the State Department. But it is my considered opinion that those steps have long since proven inadequate. In general we have continued to follow the previous patterns of expediency. New policies unfold from year to year and from administration to administration in response to external events or to the shifting requirements of domestic opinion and partisan opportunism. In foreign affairs we have observed since 1945 alternating patterns of *realpolitik* and fuzzy idealism, containment and detente, irresolute engagement and confused withdrawal. At home we have seen an endless patchwork of economic policies, fiscal policies, military policies, social policies—and these too frequently have developed haphazardly, in response to particular pressures, with little concern for the harmony of the whole, the conservation of resources, the advancement of our national aims and objectives, or the good of the country.

Let me briefly illustrate the effects of this fateful state of affairs on foreign policy. In the years immediately following World War II, U.S. leaders awakened to the realization that the Soviet Union, far from being the cooperative postwar partner they had led themselves to expect, was in fact embarked on a relentless course of territorial and ideological self-aggrandizement. In response they embraced the much-touted policy of containment. Whereas this policy appeared at first to reflect a needed sharpening of Uncle Sam's eyesight, and a stiffening of his spine, it soon degenerated (in the absence of strategic vision) into an excuse for unilateral intervention everywhere. It meant the almost automatic commitment of American resources wherever a threat appeared—in Western Europe, Greece, Turkey, Korea, Lebanon, and Vietnam. It meant the frequent shedding of American blood. It meant not only the early abandonment of our faith in collective security, but even of our insistence that others play a primary role in defending themselves. It thus meant the gradual shifting of many of the security burdens of the non-Communist world onto the shoulders of the United States. It meant the constant dissipation of American resources. The debacle of Vietnam provided an indescribably tragic climax to this process. The Kremlin, it will be noted, has quite consistently conserved its resources and retained its freedom of maneuver. The Soviet strategists are playing a patient game in which the objective balance of forces is shifting gradually in their favor. The scolding once administered to the ancient Athenians by one of their public men can thus be directed most appropriately at present-day Americans: "Shame on you Athenians," Demosthenes exclaimed,

> for not wishing to understand that in war one must not allow oneself to be at the command of events, but to forestall them. You Athenians are the strongest of all the Greeks, in ships, cavalry, infantry and revenue, and you do not make the best of them.

> You make war against Philip like a barbarian when he wrestles—if he suffers a blow, he immediately puts his hand to it. If he is struck again he puts his hand there too, but he has not the skill or does not think of parrying the blow aimed at him or of evading his antagonist. You, likewise, if you hear that Philip has attacked the Chaeronea, you send help there; if he is at Thermopylae, you run there, and if he turns aside you follow him, to right or left, as if you were acting on his orders. Never a fixed plan, never any precautions—you wait for bad news before you act.

I am not so naive as to believe that all the ordeals America has experienced over the past thirty-five years could have been avoided or even alleviated. I have some appreciation of the complexity and intractability of historical forces. I have some appreciation of the difficulties of governing a free society, and I concede the necessity—indeed the high wisdom—of basing all public policy in America on the solid foundation of popular consent. I do believe, however, that with more effective means for guiding the development of coordinated national policies, and with more coherent strategies in pursuing those policies, the record could have been much brighter.

My present concern arises not only from the conviction that our governmental machinery and methods are little improved over those of the past, but also from the knowledge that today's world is a far more dangerous one than that of yesteryear. We could get by in World War II with what we had and with what we did. Our security and prosperity in the future, I am positive, will require more.

It is commonplace to note that the relatively secure, isolated inward-looking world of the founding fathers is long gone. Modern communications and transportation have shrunk the world to the dimensions of an eighteenth century township. Events in the remotest corners of the globe now can, and often do, affect conditions everywhere. Improved nutrition and medicine have swollen the earth's populations, introducing an era of intensified struggle for space, power, and resources. Intense ideological conflicts divide nations and peoples. Traditional values and authority are everywhere besieged. The rise of ultradestructive weapons (biological and chemical as well as nuclear) has jeopardized life. Access to these weapons by small, irresponsible states—or even terrorist groups—has introduced an incalculably destabilizing and dangerous element into human affairs.

To compete in this struggle and to meet successfully these challenging conditions, our government must introduce elements of foresight and forehandedness into the management of affairs that have not heretofore been compelling. As in 1941, the American people are sharply divided today on issues of defense and foreign policy. They are probably more divided than in 1941 on so-called social issues. The babble of voices arising from the media, institutions of learning, think tanks, countless private organizations, action groups, lobbies, etc., far surpasses in volume and variety the clamor during the months preceding World War II. This uninhibited expression—although seldom fully informed, often misinformed, and sometimes mischievous—is a sign of social and intellectual vitality; it must continue as the primary engine of our democratic system.

However, the clash of private views and interests (as expressed in the political process) is in itself no longer an adequate method for development of sound and foresighted national policies in this age of perpetual crisis. The efforts of the existing branches and department of the government to develop and guide policy simply *must* be supplemented. In my opinion, we sorely need *an official agency of the government* to serve as a steadying gyroscope to the ship of state. We need what I would call a *National Strategy Council*—which I will hereafter briefly describe.

412

May I emphasize that I am *not* using the term *strategy* in its usual military connotation. In fact, I would subordinate the military connotation of strategy in a much broader and comprehensive interpretation, emphasizing the political, economic, cultural, and psycho-social forces as instruments of national policy. Strategy, I would define, as: *The art and science of developing and employing all the political, economic, and psycho-social resources of a nation together with its armed forces in the ongoing struggle to ensure the security and well-being of the people.*

This comprehensive interpretation of strategy would give U.S. policy a measure of coherence and stability it has not had, and does not now possess, but which is utterly mandatory if our republic is to meet the challenges of the future. It would encourage the integration of matters (for example, economic and military programs) which too often have been treated in isolation, and thus unrealistically or unwisely. It is my conviction that if *all* the instruments of national policy are employed imaginatively, and in a timely and coordinated manner, the frequency of occasions requiring a resort to military force would dramatically decline. We would not find ourselves—as we so often have done in the past—backing into wars, or being obliged to employ naked military force because opportunities to pursue peaceful options were either unperceived or neglected.

To return to the National Strategy Council—although the idea of yet another agency of government may be viewed by some with skepticism, I unequivocally urge its favorable consideration, and soon. May I summarize my concept of the nature and functions of a National Strategy Council. I visualize a relatively small, continuing council of perhaps eleven distinguished citizens who would devote their full time and talents to studying and formulating recommendations concerning national strategy in its broadest aspects. This body would possess *advisory* functions only. It would regularly provide advice for the enlightenment and guidance of the legislative and executive branches of the government—and indeed, when appropriate, for the American people. The council would have semiautonomous status comparable to that of the Federal Reserve Board. The members would have access to all sources of official and unofficial information and strategic intelligence, and possess the experience, expertise, and time required to evaluate basic policy in the foreign and domestic fields. The council would be in a position to judge the significance of international developments, especially the implications of such developments for U.S. interests, and to weigh the mutual effect of domestic policy proposals on each other and on foreign policy.

Members of the council, like Supreme Court Justices, would be appointed for life by the President with the advice and consent of the Senate. To the degree that such qualities could be identified, men and women of wisdom and vision would be sought. They would be chosen as individuals of unquestionable patriotism and mature judgments. They would be drawn from the practical as well as academic fields of politics, economics, history, law, business, and the military. A small secretariat would be provided to support the council. Further, a small professional staff would be provided for each member, as in the Supreme Court. Members would be free from the heavy administrative duties that burden department heads. I would hope that, in time, the council would so establish itself in the public mind as an objective, nonpartisan agency of such extraordinary competence that it would be accorded the prestige and authority (although not the formal power) now enjoyed by the United States Supreme Court. Indeed, I believe that this council would be in a position to contribute more to the future prosperity and well-being of this nation than any other single agency, arm, or organ of the government.

One further suggestion—to highlight the shift of strategic emphasis from military to the broader, comprehensive policy concerns, I propose that the National Strategy Council be established physically in the buildings presently occupied by the National War College at Fort McNair. I would call this location the National Strategy Center. The word war would be eliminated from the name of the institution and the place. Although war in its narrower military aspects would continue to be studied by the armed services, the focus of the National Strategy Center would be on coordinated employment of all the instruments of national policy. Varying circumstances would suggest the application of one or another combination of such instruments in particular circumstances. At times, one combination would be indicated; at other times, another. Force and the use or threat of force would always play a role in national strategy. But force should be employed only in coordination with other instruments and only when those instruments, by themselves, are unable to achieve national aims and objectives.

In summary, let me again emphasize the following crucial points:

1. The contemporary world presents our nation with challenges that are truly unprecedented.

2. Our traditional patterns of national policymaking have become increasingly inadequate; they are dangerously inadequate today.

3. The crying need of the future is for strategic vision and for the instruments through which sound national strategy can be developed and directed.

Never in my career as soldier or civilian have I written in greater concern for the future of our country, or with greater conviction of the need for reforms of the sort I have herein tried to describe.

Forging New Paths of Military Planning:
Challenges of the Middle East/Persian Gulf

Major General Davis C. Rohr, USAF

Good afternoon. I appreciate your kind introduction. This is an emotional experience for me to return to the Academy twenty years after leaving the Department of History. Thank you for the invitation. This noon I'd like to spend a few moments talking about the planning challenges facing our nation's newest unified command, the Central Command, presently based at MacDill AFB, Florida, near Tampa. The command's geographic area of responsibility (AOR) encompasses nineteen nations in the central region beginning with Egypt, extending south and east across the Horn of Africa, the Arabian Peninsula, through Iran, and as far north and east as Afghanistan and Pakistan.

Yesterday, during your seminar on "Technology and USAF Planning," Al Gropman provided a classic definition of planning as that "systematic process of formulating objectives for the future and developing strategy and resource allocation alternatives for reaching these goals." The problem in the central region is that while objectives can be relatively easy to formulate, the development of strategy and definitive allocation of resources is made extremely difficult for a number of reasons which I will get into during this discussion.

The U.S. Central Command, or USCENTCOM as it is called, has as its mission the protection of our nation's interests in the Persian Gulf, Horn of Africa, and southwest Africa; a mission which the recent October 1984 issue of *The Armed Forces Journal* article simply identified as "Oil, Influence and an Israeli Arab Peace." Although a catchy way of putting it, from a military planner's standpoint we might better explain CENTCOM's part in this as having the mission of deterring threats to the flow of oil from the area to our allies, while countering the Soviet's historical interest in obtaining a proprietary interest in the area. We feel this can best be done by fostering our own relationships with the nations of the AOR. Key to our aims in the area is a policy to do what we can to cause our friends in the area to be able to defend themselves, particularly since U.S. military forces will be at a premium and might be in demand elsewhere in the event of a conflict. Thus, key to our mission is the objective, in light of our global strategic needs, of having a peaceful area, as free from stress and strain as possible.

Prior to 1983 the protection of U.S. interests in the area was split, in terms of U.S. military responsibility, between the European and Pacific Commands—both of which had primary interests elsewhere; the European Command concentrating on its NATO relationships, and the Pacific Command concerned with the Pacific Basin. While certainly not implying that our attention was turned in other directions until recently, our interest in the area was forcefully focused in 1979 as a result of the wide-ranging effects of the Iranian revolution and the Soviet invasion of Afghanistan. Our inability to react to the threats to U.S. interests was graphically portrayed in November with the hostage seizure at our embassy in Tehran.

A presidential decision memorandum in late 1979 established the requirement for a force capable of rapid deployments in defense of U.S. interests. Since World War II we have maintained two rapidly deployable, forced-entry capable forces. The first, U.S. Army airborne troops, could be delivered worldwide by the Air Force. Marines are the second such force with their amphibious assault capability able to be moved to trouble spots by the Navy.

In early 1980 the Rapid Deployment Joint Task Force (RDJTF) was established in response to the President's decision memorandum. The RDJTF became our military's first four-service rapid reaction force headquarters to be formed in peacetime. Additionally, the RDJTF integrated the capabilities of a joint unconventional warfare task force into the organizational structure.

The present Central Command evolved from the Rapid Deployment Joint Task Force in just under three years and was established on 1 January 1983. The command is charged to continue to provide the capabilities of the Rapid Deployment Joint Task Force and its formal creation has added a sense of permanence to our (U.S.) commitment to regional security. It further served to signal the Soviets that we do not intend to tolerate their military adventurism. Beyond that, it signaled to our friends and allies that we are prepared to uphold our obligations in the area and reminded all Americans that the United States will defend its interests.

Our mission at the U.S. Central Command is the deterrence of direct conflict. Specifically, as I've already indicated, we seek to deter activities threatening the mideastern sea lanes and hence the flow of oil which is vital to the western economies. We also must prevent Soviet domination of the land bridge to Africa's mineral resources. Should this mission of deterrence fail, the command has the capability to commit forces when directed to do so by the national command authority (NCA). Our intent would then be to dissuade an aggressor from further aggression and provide an opportunity for him to reconsider the risks of direct confrontation with the United States.

In sum, USCENTCOM military planning is aimed at limiting the scope of conflict and attaining objectives which will lead to prompt termination of hostilities on terms favorable to the U.S.

With some few exceptions (which I will identify) USCENT-COM does not have combat forces assigned, except for planning, during peacetime. However, the command does have component headquarters assigned to do planning under which, in the event of a problem in the central region, all four military services would provide forces to the U.S. Central Command. Commander, U.S. Army Central Command (COMUSARCENT), in peacetime the deputy commander of the U.S. Army's Forces Command, is under CINCCENT, commander of the newly formed Third Army at Fort McPherson, Georgia. Commander, U.S. Central Command Air Forces (COMUSCENTAF), in peacetime also the 9th Air Force Commander under the Tactical Air Command as COMUSCEN-TAF, currently controls the U.S. air assets at Riyadh supporting Saudi Arabian air defense, and would command additional air assets assigned to the Central Command as necessary. Commander, U.S. Naval Forces Central Command, or COMUSNAVCENT, at Pearl Harbor, Hawaii, is currently responsible for the activities of the five surface combatants of the Mideast Force presently in the Persian Gulf (a force which has been operating in the region since 1949) and is charged with planning for possible use of additional naval forces should the situation dictate. In addition, Marine forces would also be available to CINCCENT during wartime. Our fourth component headquarters, the Special Operations Command, Central (SOC-CENT), plans for the missions of specialized ground, air, and sea units having the ability to conduct low visibility operations.

The difficulty in planning for activity in the AOR that I spoke of earlier in passing needs further amplification. Perhaps the simplest way of showing this difficulty might be to contrast the planning challenges in the central region with those of the U.S. European Command with its headquarters in Stuttgart, Germany.

In the European Command (EUCOM), there is a set of parameters that makes the complex task of planning at least understandable. There is a well-defined enemy threat: the Warsaw Pact nations. There are sophisticated fighting forces in place in NATO and alliances among the NATO nations that define the problems to be faced. In the event of tension in the area, there are in place well-trained allied fighting forces (to include U.S. forces) with U.S. component commands on-scene. In addition, on the logistic side the U.S. has a great deal of equipment pre-positioned and available for almost instant issue when necessity arises. A communications network, vulnerable though it is, is in place, and finally there is a massive, sophisticated intelligence network available to the planners and operators.

In the central region by contrast, we have the Soviet threat to the area less well understood by the region's nations—particularly those not sharing a border with the Soviet Union. There are relatively unsophisticated and ill-equipped indigenous fighting forces without interlocking alliances. In fact, the volatility of the area creates uncertainties in terms of support for U.S. plans/operations due to religious, ethnic, political, and economic frictions, not only among the nations of the areas but within each nation.

This lack of national/regional unity of purpose is currently being expressed vividly in its worst form: intra-regional war between Iraq and Iran. The Arab-Israeli confrontation, with its problems for the U.S. of our appearing to take sides, further complicates individual nation's responses to U.S. requests for access and/or host nation support, which is a given in the EUCOM area. This lack of access to the area is, of course, our greatest planning problem, exemplified by CENTCOM's not being able to position a permanent land-based headquarters in the central region and further exacerbated by being unable to have forces permanently stationed in the Middle East (except for the naval ships in the Middle East force in the Persian Gulf). Even host nation contingency support has been limited thus far with only Egypt, Sudan, and Oman providing significant help. The present planning efforts of our command, therefore, are dependent in very large measure on the uniqueness of the AOR and the capabilities of this nation to transport and sustain the forces the JCS would allocate to USCENTCOM to accomplish the mission, and less on the definition of specific host wartime support activities that access would have given us.

Lack of access accentuates the unique challenges that we face in any struggle that might occur in the area and gives our planners added heartburn in the traditional areas of strategic lift, sustainment of forces once deployed, communications infrastructure, and intelligence gathering.

The problem of strategic lift availability is not new; it has been a continuing challenge facing all deploying U.S. forces. However, the U.S. Central Command has a more glaring need for lift due to our limited access in the AOR, the extraordinary distances involved in reaching our area, and the time critical requirement for credible forces once the decision has been made to deploy. The air line of communication from our east coast to the Persian Gulf area is at least 7,000 miles, equating to a fourteen-plus-hour nonstop (air refueled) trip per aircraft.

To help relieve our nation's airlift availability problem, three current airlift enhancement programs have increased and will continue to improve our airlift capacity for the future: the conversions of the C–141 fleet to a stretched, air refuelable version; the C–5 service life extension program; and the introduction of the KC–10 aircraft which is both a refueling and cargo carrying aircraft. We would hope to double our cargo capable airlift capacity by 1989.

Another strategic lift challenge facing the U.S. Central Command is the area of sealift. Sea lines of communication are 8,100-miles long if the Suez Canal is open and 12,000 miles around the Cape of Good Hope—an average thirty-one-day transit for current cargo ships. More than ninety percent of the supplies and equipment during the Vietnam War were moved via the sea lanes and we expect this transportation mode to continue to play a primary role in future operations.

Sealift improvements will brighten this picture in the near future. The purchase of eight SL–7 containerships capable of thirty-three-knot speeds reduces our transit time to the central area by twenty-five percent compared to current shipping.

Without access, sustainment of deployed forces is made much more difficult, and neither forces nor supplies are pre-positioned in our AOR to a degree that is currently planned in Western Europe or the Pacific. Consequently, our command relies on a concept termed maritime pre-positioning. In order to reduce long-haul air and sealift requirements, supplies and equipment have been pre-positioned near our area of responsibility. The airlift savings associated with this pre-positioning are significant. For example, the total ammunition tonnage aboard the near term pre-positioning forces ships at Diego Garcia is as much as could be lifted by approximately 2,450 C–141 sorties from our east coast to the Middle East. In the next several years this program will pre-position the unit equipment of Marine amphibious brigades aboard fast, multipurpose ships.

In the area of intelligence, challenges exist in our war planning and war fighting abilities. A larger, more detailed data base of intelligence information is needed to effectively plan for combat operations in the central area. A significant redirection of resources would be required to provide sufficient collection and analysis of intelligence data. To support the war fighting needs in our area, our command needs the capability to rapidly collect, process, and distribute intelligence information.

The lack of an in-being modern communications system and our inability to have access to the area to build one is significant and only adds to the problems of deployment mentioned earlier. For example, one hundred percent of the first day's deployment cargo is devoted to communications gear and it isn't until day sixteen that the last of the initial communications gear is deployed.

USCENTCOM has produced over twenty-five plans to date. We are proud of our planning accomplishments and feel that the depth and detail of USCENTCOM planning is making a significant contribution to the security of the United States. While classification levels preclude my going into our plans in detail, suffice it to say that our plans consider all nineteen countries of the AOR and provide for graduated military responses and operational flexibility to support national security objectives.

We have concluded security assistance negotiations with fourteen of nineteen states and progress toward access is slow but security assistance will, I'm sure, be a positive door opener, albeit slowly but surely, for the U.S. in the region USCENTCOM initiatives and a vigorous exercise program give us hope that considerable assistance from friends and allies will be forthcoming inside as well as outside the region to support any contingency operations.

As a unified command we are not even two years old, but already we have been called on to deploy forces to deter intraregional aggression on four occasions. The deployment of U.S. forces beginning in early August to assist Egypt and Saudi Arabia in clearing the Red Sea of suspected mines has been the most recent demonstration of U.S. resolve to back the policy that created and sustains USCENTCOM.

Each year as USCENTCOM plans are reviewed by the staff, they are updated with latest force and deployment data which further reduce the risk associated with the current plans. The ultimate objective, through force modernization/upgrade and strategic list enhancements, is to have the capability to rapidly posture a force in the AOR which, in addition to deterring military attacks by the USSR, can defeat such attacks should deterrence fail.

Emerging Technologies and
National Security Strategy

Admiral Bobby R. Inman, USN, Retired

Recently I had the great privilege of working with a group of distinguished Americans under the sponsorship of the National Academy of Sciences, the National Academy of Engineering, and the Council on Foreign Relations, trying to assess emerging technologies. What are the technologies that are still emerging, full of life with great potential for the next ten to fifteen years, and what will be their impact on foreign policy? I was not one of those assessing the emerging technologies; I'm a liberal arts graduate, an avid user of technology. My role was to look at the potential impact on East-West relations. When asked to address this group on military planning in the twentieth century, I thought about the chore that's getting much closer, that is, military planning in the twenty-first century. I offered to alter my remarks for this evening, it was accepted, and so here we go.

The emerging technology part of my remarks comes from those gifted gentlemen who assessed for the national academies. The assertions and the suggestions on national security strategy are my own. The six fields of emerging technologies identified were: telecommunications, microelectronics, aerospace, materials, energy, and biotechnology.

In telecommunicatons, we are going to see a continued but very major gain in both capacity and reliability. We are going to see the introduction of networking in the commercial scene, on a scale that's going to fundamentally change the way we do business daily, not just in financial institutions, offices, factories, but also within buildings, within cities, within corporations spread over long distances, within countries. Interoperability on a scale not recognized today, is limited only by artificial constraints put in place by national telephone, telegraph instruments (the PPTs), limiting a market to a specific single domestic producer trying to protect a single domestic industry. That is the only constraint at work limiting the potential gains in interoperability. There are clearly going to be problems in managing access to the frequency spectrum, and that's going to be made even more complicated by direct broadcasting from satellites. Direct broadcasting was going to come early, but the major potential commercial users have been reluctant to fund the program. It's going to come, maybe a little further along into the early nineties. Teleconferencing is already here, and it will appear on a much larger scale in the years ahead of us.

In microelectronics, expansion in capacity will be by very many factors. Capability that now takes equipment at least the size of this head table will be done on a chip the size of your fingernail. Imbedded computers will become a standard commodity in weapons systems. Expert systems will not replace the human mind, but we will be able to store very large amounts of human knowledge, again on single chips, to do very diverse functions. And we will use those expert systems in software engineering to build a buffer between the would-be user or designer and the bright youngster who writes lines of code, and hopefully, to finally begin to impact on the enormously escalating cost both of producing software and of maintaining it. Every computer built to date, whether large or small, fast or slow, does every function sequentially. With reasonable luck, within the decade we'll go to parallel processing, just as your brain does parallel processing now, for enormous gains in speed and reliability. Packaging and integrated circuits will develop to a stage that can give you whatever form of packaging you want—plastic, ceramic, whatever the need is—to sustain those imbedded computer systems.

In aerospace, the gains in the air regime will be largely expansion of range, duration of flight, reliability, stand-off detection, and stand-off targeting at substantially greater ranges. Surveillance of very broad areas under all weather conditions will be a standard factor. The more exciting new gains will come from the use of space. For manned surveillance the critical question ahead of us will be the potential site for the use of weapons. It will be easier to get agreement on the great advantages that still lie out ahead of us in exploration of space. The space telescope is the early part of that. The prospect is bright for our understanding the very nature of matter for clearer ways and the use of space as a place to put platforms for production of materials where gravity is currently a constraint.

In the materials area, some wonderful things are going to be coming from chemistry: the ability to give you a material for the specific use you need at an affordable price, with great gains again in reliability and maintainability. There will be advances in shapes and surfaces to reduce detectability of platforms. There will be an ability to give you a material that is resistant to heat, cold, sand, wind, or rain, whatever your need is—and even to some degree to reduce dependence on imported minerals.

In energy, there will be gains in nuclear power generation, but the lead may well not be in this country. Of the six fields, this is the one area where the prospect looms that the United States will lose leadership for a variety of reasons—mismanagement, cost overruns, the Three Mile Island accident; we may well see the lead shift abroad. But in both fossil fuel discovery, particularly in the undersea regime, and in recovery of oil from aging fields, in conservation measures, in cogeneration, gasification, and solar power, the United States should retain leadership. If we invest, the potential is clearly there for gains in fuel cells and extended life batteries.

And finally in biotechnology—genetic engineering—the path will split in two directions. In the nearer term there will be major gains in health care. Over the longer term, great advances will occur in the way we care for animals and in the growth and preservation of food.

In thinking about those emerging areas and focusing on future strategies, there are clearly some early impacts on weapons systems themselves. The first is in accuracy—the ability to bring to bear the gains of pinpoint accuracy with conventional weapons at very long ranges. Other areas include range, fuel conservation, longer duration flights from batteries and/or fuel cells, the potential to stand off at great distance, reduction in exposed manpower, not a total elimination to exposure of manpower, but a substantial reduction in those who are immediately exposed to hostile fire, and autonomous vehicles. Clearly, when one thinks about the impact on weapons systems, there will be a major impact on detectability by existing sensors, as one brings to bear what can be offered particularly in the new materials.

In the impact on command, control, and communications, potential is clearly there for expanded surveillance, twenty-four-hour days, and under all weather conditions. I'm not sure yet how far into deep space continuous reliable surveillance will be possible, but certainly, several times current synchronous orbit positions. But it may still be feasible to store in very deep space without constant detectability. But from synchronous orbit below, through air, through surface, perhaps as far as 150 feet subsurface, the potential for continuous surveillance will exist. No technology is currently on the horizon that offers the prospect of continuous surveillance below the 150–foot depth. But there clearly will have to be major changes in the telecommunications arena to eliminate the hazards in the area from the surface down to 150 feet. Major changes achievable in correlation from multiple sensors discrimination, with the potential for targeting thousands of objects in seconds, will be made possible through gains in expert systems.

One of the potentials may not be greeted as a universal improvement, that is, the continuous exchange of information, in secure modes, at various command levels, in real time. And for teleconferencing, visual dialogue in the decisionmaking process is possible, if one elects to do it, even within alliance situations between national leaders on a secure basis. With all of these gains in command, control, and communications, there will be expanded opportunities for electronic warfare.

In our coming to grips with the opportunities that are offered by these emerging technologies, a very tough problem will be technology transfer: technology transfer in several different directions, transferring the technology from the laboratories to the production lines in reasonable time. Twelve to thirteen years is not reasonable time. We will need to transfer technology to allies to insure interoperability of systems and to prevent undesired transfer of technology to adversaries to improve their own military capabilities. We can't have it all, and we will ultimately have to make choices. I believe the ultimate decision will be to transfer, to take the risks, and to run faster rather than simply trying to lock up the technology to protect it against potential use by adversaries.

As you turn to develop the strategies to deal with these emerging technologies, there are some very real problems, some real threats, that you have to consider. Some are also opportunities. The reduction of the element of surprise for the large scale use of force outside territorial boundaries is clearly achievable. The potential will exist for removing ambiguity about deployments, and that is going to require steps beyond simply buying the surveillance and processing systems, and expert systems to correlate and discriminate targets. That probably says consider using manned space stations, jointly manned to remove ambiguity, a step one takes to reduce the possibility of escalating conflicts.

Clearly a premium will be placed on forward deployment and on the speed of response. Because one will in fact be able to detect the preparations for use, the speed with which deployment can be executed may be the critical difference in discouraging the execution of the plans. There is clearly a very major potential, expanded potential, for the use of conventional weapons. One deals effectively with the hiders-finders issue. The potential is there for using conventional weapons decisively, even in such distance problems as second echelon forces. But there will be the corollary of putting a premium on dispersed offensive capability, in not having all of one's capabilities massed and subject to attack, because these same abilities for surveillance are likely to be available to our principle adversaries. Stand-off tactics, use of a variety of sensors for penetration of defenses will pick up added benefits, particularly for the use of expanded potential in the conventional weapons area. Given the reality of exchanging additional information, we also have to deal with the reality of the human problem of assimilating those data. Expert systems will sort and correlate, but they will not deal alone with all the problems of assimilation.

One of the opportunities, but also one of the potential challenges for us, coming from the expanded use of materials, will be the potential for temporary or even extended use of inhospitable geography, whether deserts, arctic, or even undersea.

As one thinks about how one accelerates bringing these emerging technologies to bear in shaping future strategies, we have to look at the reality of the world in which this change will be taking place. Economic competition with our allies will be accelerating, with some major confrontations. The degree to which we create the technologies and transfer them to the commercial market place, and then are willing to export and license that technology, may turn out to be the critical ingredient in managing effectively that economic competition to hold alliances together. But that alone will not be enough. The perceptions of the threat will play a critical role.

In Western Europe, and indeed even to some extent in this country, we see a generation beginning to take up the reins of political power whose only memories of conflict are Northern Ireland, the Middle East, and Vietnam, without a clear understanding of the lessons of World War II or the real dimensions of Soviet capabilities, and our own diversion to other problems. The increasing likelihood of diversion of U.S. interest toward the Pacific basin for economic growth, and toward this hemisphere where the long-term problem of export of revolution exists, says that even greater strains will be placed on working relationships in our existing, and I think, vital alliances which will put a great premium on our finding ways to extend dialogue beyond currently defined geographic boundaries.

There are two additional larger, overarching problems. Terrorism and nuclear proliferation are going to give us great difficulties that these emerging technologies do not solve. Nor do they guide automatically toward strategies that deal with either problem. But state-supported terrorism used not only against embassies but against organized military units is a reality that is with us and is still growing.

My unhappy judgment is that by the early nineties another maybe five or six or maybe seven countries will have nuclear weapons. They will have different cultures, different hatreds, and regional feuds which raise an unhappy prospect of a decision to use a nuclear weapon in a conflict much earlier, at the outset, or if survival is viewed to be at stake. That will greatly increase the pressures not only on us, but also on the Soviets, to understand quickly and to try to prevent escalation.

Finally, you don't develop strategies in isolation. You take into account the status of major adversaries developing their own strategies. And here we have become accustomed to dealing with an adversary that in fact is increasingly beset with a rigidity in its decisionmaking process. That offers little prospect for substantive negotiation on major issues no matter who is President in this country.

But that situation is going to change quickly. For reasons of age and health, suddenly if not quickly—it may be a year, year and a half, it could be the end of the decade—but when it comes, a new generation of Soviet leaders are going to look at both their own potential, a dreary economic potential, and a burgeoning military potential, particularly in the conventional arena, and make judgments on how to employ all those assets. We may be lucky. They may be very cautious bureaucrats unwilling to risk their very privileged positions in that society. But we run a high risk that they will be much more arrogant about the use of conventional military capability to assert their great power status—without the same memories that the older Bolsheviks have of Germans on the banks of the Volga and around Leningrad. What is clear is that Soviet attitudes, Soviet doctrine for using those burgeoning mobile conventional forces, have very substantially trailed the actual capabilites that they are building. So in the time frame when they suddenly turn to adapt their own strategies, they will make judgments about our defense capabilities and those of our allies. They will make judgments about our will, and they will make judgments about the cohesion of alliances.

The degree to which we have accelerated the development of these emerging technologies, that we have employed them effectively, both in the defense sector and in modernizing our own basic industries, and the degree to which we have ultimately found the means to share those accomplishments with our allies and others in the non-Communist world, may be the largest single factor in persuading the Soviets not to take adventurous courses with their conventional military forces. The challenge of developing effective strategies will be every bit as exciting as it has been in the past, complicated by the reality that the pace of change will be far swifter in the ten years ahead, than in the three decades behind. Thank you very much for your kind time and attention.

Participants

JOHN C. CAIRNS. Professor Cairns received his Ph.D. from Cornell in 1951 and began teaching at the University of North Carolina, Greensboro. He joined the University of Toronto in 1952 where he is currently Professor of History. Professor Cairns has also served as Visiting Professor at Cornell, Stanford, and Rochester universities. His extensive study of France and work in the French archives mark him as an authority on French military planning and development before World War II. His publications on French history and international relations include *France, Soldiers as Statesmen*, and *Contemporary France*.

JACK CHILD. Dr. Child is Associate Professor of Spanish and Latin American Studies at The American University where he earned his Ph.D. in 1978. Born in Buenos Aires, his early years in South America guided his academic and military careers. Professor Child retired from the U.S. Army in 1980 after twenty years of service with primary duties as a foreign area specialist in Latin America. He also served as Assistant Professor of Spanish at West Point, on the faculty of the Inter-American Defense College, and as editor for the International Peace Academy. His publications include: *Unequal Alliance: The Inter-American Military System, 1938–1978*; *Latin America: International Relations—A Guide to Sources*; *Maintenance of Peace and Security in the Caribbean and Central America*; and *Quarrels Among Neighbors: Geopolitics and Conflict in South America*.

ALEXANDER S. COCHRAN. After graduating from Yale in 1961, Dr. Cochran served in the U.S. Army for ten years, including four years in Vietnam as senior advisor to a Vietnamese infantry battalion and a corps level operations officer. After leaving the Army, he became Assistant Professor of History at Notre Dame, and in 1977 he joined the faculty at Kansas University. Two years later the U.S. Army Center of Military History selected "Sandy" Cochran as a dissertation fellow, and he completed his Ph.D. from Kansas University in 1984. Currently working in the Southeast Asian Branch for the U.S. Army Center of Military History, he brings to the symposium firsthand experience in the Vietnam War and a deep interest in the impact of that conflict on American military planning. His publications include *The MAGIC Diplomatic Summaries,* articles in Ashley Brown's *War in Peace,* and Craig Symonds' *New Aspects of Naval History.*

ALVIN COOX. Professor Coox earned his Ph.D. from Harvard University in 1951 and began his career in Asian studies and Japanese military history in 1954 as Visiting Professor, Shiga National University. During the following ten years in Japan, Professor Coox lectured in history and government for the Far East divisions of the University of California and the University of Maryland and served as historian for the U.S. Army Japanese Research Division and military/political analyst for the Fifth Air Force. After returning to the United States in 1965, he became Professor of History at San Diego State University and Director of its Center of Asian Studies. Professor Coox comes to the Eleventh Military History Symposium after completing an eight-month Japan Foundation Fellowship study of Imperial Japanese armed forces. His publications include: *KOGUN: The Japanese Army in the Pacific War*; *The Japanese Image*; and *Nomohan, Japan Against Russia, 1939.*

HAROLD C. DEUTSCH. Professor Deutsch earned his Ph.D. from Harvard in 1929 and joined the faculty of the University of Minnesota where he taught until his retirement in 1972. During World War II Professor Deutsch served as a member of the Office of Strategic Services in London and Paris and interrogated high ranking German army and naval personnel while attached to the State Department. He became chairman of the History Department at the University of Minnesota in 1960 and for ten years chaired the university's Program for International Relations and Area Studies. He began teaching at the National War College in 1972 specializing in European studies and the Soviet Union. Since 1974 Professor Deutsch has served on the U.S. Army War College faculty as the Harold K. Johnson Visiting Professor on Military History and worked in three distinct assignments: the Strategic Studies Institute; the Department of Academic Affairs; and the Department of Strategy, Planning, and Operations. In addition to his position with the Strategic Studies Institute, Professor Deutsch holds the Brigadier General John McAuley Palmer Chair of Military History at the Army War College. His publications include: *Hitler and His Generals: The Hidden Crisis of January to June 1938*; *The Changing Structure of Europe*; and *America's Stake in Western Europe*.

THOMAS H. ETZOLD. In May 1984, President Reagan nominated Professor Etzold to be Assistant Director for the Multilateral Affairs Bureau of the Arms Control and Disarmament Agency, and the U.S. Senate confirmed his nomination. Before his appointment, he served as Assistant to the Director, Center for Naval Warfare Studies at the Naval War College. Professor Etzold earned his Ph.D. from Yale University in 1970 and joined the Yale history faculty. In 1971 he became an Assistant Professor of History at Miami University in Ohio. He went on to become Associate Professor and then Professor of Strategy at the Naval War College beginning in 1974. His Naval War College duties expanded as he became Director of Strategic Research at the Center for Naval Warfare Studies. He has been a consultant on strategic doctrine and war gaming to agencies of the U.S. Government, the North Atlantic Treaty Organization, and the Federal German Navy. His publications include: *Defense or Delusion? America's Military in the 1980s*; and *The Conduct of American Foreign Relations: The Other Side of Diplomacy*.

ROBERT F. FUTRELL. Dr. Futrell earned his Ph.D. from Vanderbilt University in 1950 after serving as a communications officer and historian for the Army Air Forces during World War II. He continued his association with air force history by becoming an Associate Professor of Military History at Air University in 1950 and Professor Emeritus in 1974. His most significant contribution to the study of airpower doctrine and planning is his monumental work, *Ideas, Concepts, Doctrine: A History of Basic Thinking in the United States Air Force, 1907–1964,* the single most comprehensive work on the subject. He is currently concluding a two-year tour as Visiting Professor, Airpower Research Institute, Center for Aerospace Doctrine, Research, and Education (CADRE), Air University. Other publications include co-authoring *The Army Air Forces in World War II,* and *The United States Air Force in Korea, 1950–1953.*

ADMIRAL NOEL A. M. GAYLER, USN. A 1935 Naval Academy graduate, Admiral Gayler's forty-one-year naval career included many assignments related to military planning. In 1946 he began ten years of participation in aircraft research and development concluding with his assignment as Chief of the Air Warfare Division of the Military Requirements Branch of the Office of Chief of Naval Operations from 1954 to 1956. Following duties as a naval attache from London and military assistant to the Secretary of the Navy, he returned to the military planning field in 1963 as Assistant Chief of Naval Operations for Development. His planning experience and responsibilities significantly expanded in 1967 when he became the Deputy Director of the Joint Strategic Target Planning Staff of the Joint Chiefs of Staff, and then he became the Director of the National Security Agency and Chief of the Central Security Agency. Admiral Gayler concluded his naval career in 1976 after four years as Commander, U.S. Forces, Pacific.

GENERAL ANDREW J. GOODPASTER, USA. A West Point graduate, General Goodpaster earned his Ph.D. at Princeton in 1950 and went on to serve on the White House Staff as a defense liaison officer and staff secretary to Presidents Eisenhower and Kennedy. As a presidential staff secretary, General Goodpaster developed a keen awareness of the importance of long-range military planning. Subsequent assignments as deputy commander for the U.S. Military Assistance Command, Vietnam, in 1968 and Commander in Chief U.S. European Command in 1969 gave him critical military planning experience. General Goodpaster retired in 1974 after completing a three-year tour as Supreme Allied Commander for Europe and the Middle East. After retiring, he became a senior fellow at the Smithsonian's Woodrow Wilson International Center for Scholars and Professor of Government and International Studies at The Citadel, Charleston, South Carolina. Formerly Vice President of the International Institute for Strategic Studies, General Goodpaster has also served in many public service organizations such as the Council on Foreign Relations. In October 1983 General Goodpaster became President of the Institute for Defense Analyses. His publications include *For the Common Defense.*

COLONEL ALAN L. GROPMAN. Colonel Gropman is Deputy Director of Air Force Plans for Planning Integration at HQ USAF and responsible for formulating Air Force doctrine, strategy, and war mobilization planning. After serving with the USAF Academy's Department of History, he earned his Ph.D. in history from Tufts University in 1975 and was a distinguished graduate of the Air War College in 1978. After three years in long-range and airlift planning duties at the Air Staff, Colonel Gropman became the Associate Dean of Faculty at the National War College where he served as the Director of Research, Elective Studies and Academic Budget. He also directed courses in the art of war and the Vietnam War. His publications include *The Air Force Integrates, 1945–1965*, and *Airpower and the Airlift Evacuation of Kham Duc.*

WALDO H. HEINRICHS. Professor Heinrichs earned his Ph.D. in history from Harvard in 1960, specializing in American foreign relations with special emphasis on East Asia, an interest growing out of his military service in the Asian theater during World War II. Following the war Professor Heinrichs joined the U.S. Foreign Service as a Vice Consul in Toronto, Canada. He has taught history at Johns Hopkins University, the Universities of Tennessee and Illinois, and is currently Professor of History at Temple University. His publications include *American Ambassador: Joseph C. Grew and the Development of the U.S. Diplomatic Tradition*, and *Uncertain Tradition: Chinese-American Relations, 1945–1950*.

I. B. HOLLEY. In 1947 Professor Holley earned his Ph.D. from Yale and began teaching at Duke University where he is currently Professor of History. Recognized as one of the foremost scholars on American military doctrine and planning, Professor Holley has been a Visiting Professor at West Point and the National Defense University. His research and writing on the relationship of airpower technology and doctrine earned him the position of Professor Emeritus at the Air War College in 1981. Professor Holley has served as Chairman of the U.S. Air Force Historical Advisory Committee and as trustee of the Air Force Historical Foundation. His publications include *Ideas and Weapons*, and *General John McAuley Palmer, Citizen Soldiers and the Army of a Democracy*.

ADMIRAL BOBBY R. INMAN, USN. Admiral Inman, President and Chief Executive Officer of Microelectronics and Computer Technology Corporation, directs a research conglomerate formed by twelve U.S. computer and microelectronics companies. Following graduation from the University of Texas in 1950, Admiral Inman's naval career featured varied assignments, including Assistant Naval Attache in Stockholm, senior aide to the Vice Chief of Naval Operations, Seventh Fleet Intelligence Officer, and Assistant Chief of Staff for Intelligence for the Pacific Fleet. Appointed Director of Naval Intelligence in 1974, he left the position in 1976 to become Vice Director of the Defense Intelligence Agency until 1977. Admiral Inman headed the National Security Agency from 1977 to 1981 and then became the Deputy Director of the Central Intelligence Agency at the request of President Reagan. Following his retirement from the Navy and departure from the CIA in 1982, Admiral Inman briefly served as a consultant to the House Permanent Select Committee on Intelligence before joining the Microelectronics and Computer Technology Corporation.

RICHARD H. KOHN. Dr. Kohn received his Ph.D. from the University of Wisconsin in 1968 and taught at Wisconsin, The City College of New York, and Rutgers University. Since 1981 Dr. Kohn has served as Chief of the Office of Air Force History, Washington, D.C. Widely known for his studies in civil-military relations, Dr. Kohn is the author of *Eagle and Sword: The Federalists and the Creation of the Military Establishment in America, 1783–1802*. As Chief of the Office of Air Force History, Dr. Kohn has directed the research and publication of books examining the development of airpower doctrine and its impact on operations and long-range military planning. IIis special interest and effort has resulted in a broadening of available material for use by Air Force commanders and planners, such as his most recent publication, *Air Superiority in World War II and Korea: An Interview with General James Ferguson, General Robert M. Lee, General William Momyer, and Lieutenant General Elwood R. Quesada.*

MELVYN P. LEFFLER. Professor Leffler earned his Ph.D. from the Ohio State University in 1972 and is Associate Professor of History specializing in American foreign relations at Vanderbilt. A recognized expert on the early years of the cold war, Professor Leffler has more recently focused on security decisionmaking while a fellow of the Woodrow Wilson International Center, the Council on Foreign Relations and the American Council of Learned Scholars. In 1980 he worked in the Office of the Secretary of Defense serving as a special assistant for policy planning with emphasis on arms control and contingency planning in the Persian Gulf. His work on arms control included assisting the Secretary of Defense representative to the Warsaw Pact-NATO negotiations on Mutual and Balanced Force Reductions in Central Europe. His publications include *The Elusive Quest: America's Pursuit of European Stability and French Security, 1919–1933.*

JAMES R. LEUTZE. Professor Leutze is currently Bowman and Gordon Gray Professor of History and Chairman, Curriculum in Peace, War and Defense at the University of North Carolina, Chapel Hill. He earned his Ph.D. from Duke University and began teaching at North Carolina in 1968. A recognized scholar in American naval policy and foreign relations, Professor Leutze won both the Bernath Prize for distinguished publication in the area of American foreign policy and the John Lyman Book Award in U.S. Naval History. His book, *Bargaining for Supremacy: Anglo-American Naval Collaboration, 1937–41,* established him as an authority on pre-World War II allied military planning. Other publications include *A Different Kind of Victory: The Biography of Admiral Thomas C. Hart.*

GENERAL BRYCE POE, II, USAF. General Poe, a combat veteran of three wars, spent thirty-eight years in the Air Force with a number of major command positions directly related to military planning and procurement. As a member of the Air Research and Development Command from 1956 to 1964, General Poe dealt with strategic missile research and development during the early stages of the American guided missile program. His duties involved researching and planning the development of strategic nuclear missiles during one of the most volatile eras of the cold war. While with the Air Research and Development Command he earned a M.A. in history from the University of Nebraska. He went on to command the Air Force Logistics Command from 1978 to 1981 guiding Air Force research and procurement of weapons and support systems capable of implementing Air Force policy. General Poe retired from the USAF in 1981 and has served both government and industry as a consultant in the areas of national security and defense planning. He is currently Vice President of the Air Force Historical Foundation.

FORREST C. POGUE. Dr. Pogue earned his Ph.D. at Clark University in 1939 after attending the University of Paris as an American Exchange Fellow in International Relations and Diplomacy. He served as a U.S. Army historian in Europe during World War II covering the Normandy invasion, liberation of Paris, and the meeting with the Soviet Army at Torgau. He has taught history at Western Kentucky and Murray State Colleges and lectured on international relations and diplomacy at George Washington University. Dr. Pogue is currently Director of the Dwight D. Eisenhower Institute for Historical Research and the Museum of American History, the Smithsonian. His publications include the three-volume definitive biography series on George C. Marshall, *Command Decisons*, and the highly acclaimed *Bicentennial History of the United States*. He is also a contributing editor to the *Guide to American Foreign Relations Since 1700*.

MAJOR GENERAL DAVID C. ROHR, USAF. General Rohr is Deputy Commander in Chief, United States Central Command, MacDill AFB, Florida. The U.S. Central Command provides political, economic, and military planning support to friendly nations in Southwest Asia, the Persian Gulf, and the Horn of Africa. A fighter pilot whose tours have included Korea, Japan, Germany, and Vietnam, General Rohr was most recently the Director of Plans and Policy in the U.S. European Command. His varied career includes an assignment with the Office of the Secretary of Defense, International Security Affairs, as Country Director for South America, and a tour as Chief, Office of Military Cooperation, Egypt. General Rohr also served in the USAF Academy Department of History from 1960 to 1964.

HERBERT Y. SCHANDLER. Professor Schandler earned his Ph.D. from Harvard in 1974 after twenty-three years in the military. His army career included a series of military, political, and economic planning assignments at progressively higher levels of command ranging from the Military Assistance Command, Vietnam, in 1965, the Policy Planning Staff of the Assistant Secretary of Defense in 1968, and finally the NATO Policy Branch of the Plans and Policy Directorate of the Joint Chiefs of Staff. Prior to his assignment with the Joint Chiefs of Staff, Professor Schandler served as Director, National Security Policy Studies, at the National War College. In 1983, he became Professor of International Relations at the Industrial College of the Armed Forces, National Defense University. His publications include *The Unmaking of a President: Lyndon Johnson and Vietnam* and *U.S. Foreign Policy: Options for the Future.*

JOHN W. SHY. Dr. Shy, Professor of History at the University of Michigan, earned his Ph.D. at Princeton University in 1962. Professor Shy was Visiting Professor of Military History at the U.S. Army War College in 1974, a Fulbright Professor at the University of London in 1975, and Harmsworth Professor of American History at Oxford University in 1983–84. A recognized scholar on the American Revolution, Professor Shy has developed a broad perspective of military history and the intricacies of strategic planning through his studies of both the colonial and British involvement in the Revolutionary War. His publications include: *A People Numerous and Armed: Reflections on the Military Struggle for American Independence*; *The American Revolution*; and *Toward Lexington: The Role of the British Army in the Coming of the American Revolution*.

PETER H. VIGOR. Mr. Vigor founded the Soviet Studies Research Centre at the Royal Military Academy, Sandhurst, England, in 1972 and served as its director until 1982. His keen interest in Soviet studies stems from his military experience in World War II. After suffering wounds at Tobruk, Libya, in 1942, Mr. Vigor joined the British Military Mission and worked to resettle Poles from Germany and Russia before the end of the war and after. This first-hand contact with war refugees in Eastern Europe sparked a life-long study of the Soviet war effort with special emphasis on planning and policy development. In 1948 he earned a B.A. in Russian, Polish, and French at Cambridge and went on to earn a M.A. in 1953. His publications include *The Soviet View of Disarmament and Arms Control* (forthcoming from MacMillan), *Soviet Blitzkrieg Theory*, *The Soviet View of War, Peace and Neutrality*, and *A Guide to Marxism and Its Effects on Soviet Development*.

Milton, Gen. Theodore R.: 266
Ministry of Finance (France):
45
Ministry of Foreign Affairs
(France): 43, 48
Minsk, USSR: 15
MINUTEMAN missile: 239
Mitchell, Gen. William
"Billy": 253–254
Momyer, Gen. W.W. "Spike":
254, 259
Mongolia: 69
Monroe Doctrine: 340
Morocco: 47
Moscow, USSR: 36, 51, 89, 90,
111
Munich, Germany: 46, 49
Munich agreement: 26
Mussolini, Benito: 48
Mustang aircraft: 232
Mutual Security Act: 349
Myer, Gen. Edwin C.: 378–379

Nagano, Adm. Osami: 71
Nagasaki, Japan: 207, 318
Nagumo, Adm. Chuichi: 79
National Advisory Committee
for Aeronautics
(NACA): 125, 126,
131, 138, 140, 144,
145, 237. *See also*
Army Air Corps,
planning betweeen
the wars.
National Command Authority
(NCA): 418
National Security Council
(NSC): 160, 180, 183,
261, 264, 277, 291,
295, 321, 410
National Socialism: 1
National Strategy Center: 414
National Strategy Council:
412–14

National War College: 414
Naval War College (Japan): 78,
79, 80
Navy, German: 16
Navy, Imperial Japanese (IJN):
68, 76, 78, 80–81, 108
Navy, U.S.: 70, 182
and Carter administration:
277–81, 282, 288
and insularity: 284–87
and internal debates:
289–91
and NATO: 281, 282
and naval theory: 283–89,
292–93, 318
and Nixon administration:
278
as peacetime bureaucracy:
275–77
and scenario-building: 290
and Soviet Union: 278,
280–81, 282–83, 290
Nazi-Soviet Pact: 37, 50
Netherlands: 9, 10, 70
New Look doctrine: 265, 267,
295. *See also* Deter-
rence.
Nicaragua: 350
Nivelle, Gen. Robert: 43
Nixon administration: 371, 374
Nixon Doctrine: 278
Nomonhan, Manchuria: 78, 80,
81
Normandy: 255
Norstad, Gen. Lauris: 174,
175, 257, 259
North Atlantic Treaty Organization (NATO): 94,
103, 262, 281, 282,
320, 336, 341, 344,
350, 377, 417, 419
and AirLand Battle con-
cept: 336, 377, 387
and Lisbon force goals:
262, 263, 264